T0330704

JEWISH IMMIGRANTS IN LONDON, 1880–1939

Perspectives in Economic and Social History

Series Editors: *Andrew August*
Jari Eloranta

Titles in this Series

30 Merchants and Profit in the Age of Commerce, 1680–1830
Pierre Gervais, Yannick Lemarchand and Dominique Margairaz (eds)

Forthcoming Titles

A Global Conceptual History of Asia, 1860–1940
Hagen Schulz-Forberg (ed.)

Mercantilism and Economic Underdevelopment in Scotland, 1600–1783
Philipp Robinson Rössner

Commercial Networks and European Cities, 1400–1800
Andrea Caracausi and Christof Jeggle (eds)

Consuls and the Institutions of Global Capitalism, 1783–1914
Ferry de Goey

Insanity and the Lunatic Asylum in the Nineteenth Century
Thomas Knowles and Serena Trowbridge (eds)

Philanthropy and the Funding of the Church of England, 1856–1914
Sarah Flew

Franco Modigliani and Keynesian Economics: Theory, Facts and Policy
Antonella Rancan

JEWISH IMMIGRANTS IN LONDON, 1880–1939

BY

Susan L. Tananbaum

Routledge
Taylor & Francis Group

LONDON AND NEW YORK

First published 2014 by Pickering & Chatto (Publishers) Limited

Published 2016 by Routledge
2 Park Square, Milton Park, Abingdon, Oxfordshire OX14 4RN
711 Third Avenue, New York, NY 10017, USA

First issued in paperback 2015

Routledge is an imprint of the Taylor & Francis Group, an informa business

© Taylor & Francis 2014
© Susan L. Tananbaum 2014

To the best of the Publisher's knowledge every effort has been made to contact
relevant copyright holders and to clear any relevant copyright issues.
Any omissions that come to their attention will be remedied in future editions.

All rights reserved, including those of translation into foreign languages. No part of this book
may be reprinted or reproduced or utilised in any form or by any electronic, mechanical, or
other means, now known or hereafter invented, including photocopying and recording, or in
any information storage or retrieval system, without permission in writing from the publishers.

Notice:
Product or corporate names may be trademarks or registered trademarks, and
are used only for identification and explanation without intent to infringe.

BRITISH LIBRARY CATALOGUING IN PUBLICATION DATA

Tananbaum, Susan L. author.
Jewish immigrants in London, 1880–1939. – (Perspectives in economic and
social history)
1. Immigrants – England – London – History – 19th century. 2. Immigrants –
England – London – History – 20th century. 3. Jews – Cultural assimilation –
England – London – History – 19th century – Sex differences. 4. Jews – Cultural
assimilation – England – London – History – 20th century – Sex differences.
5. Jewish women – England – London – Social conditions – 19th century.
6. Jewish women – England – London – Social conditions – 20th century.
7. Working class Jews – England – London – Social conditions – 19th century.
8. Working class Jews – England – London – Social conditions – 20th century.
I. Title II. Series
942.1'004924-dc23

ISBN-13: 978-1-138-66305-3 (pbk)
ISBN-13: 978-1-8489-3442-9 (hbk)

Typeset by Pickering & Chatto (Publishers) Limited

CONTENTS

ACKNOWLEDGEMENTS

It is a great pleasure to recognize the support and encouragement I have received over many years. Since my days at Brandeis, I have had the good fortune of the wisdom and friendship of a cohort of talented scholars, among them Liz Bussiere, Dan Cohen, Dan Dupre, Ruth Friedman, Matt Gallman, Wendy Gamber, Tammy Gaskell, Richard Godbeer, Dallett Hemphill, John Hill, Patty Ingram, Tom Pegram and David Sicilia. They became 'family' some thirty years ago and have enriched my life and scholarship in countless ways. During my student days, I worked with three gifted historians, the late Eugene Black, Jehuda Reinharz and Bernard Wasserstein, whose combined knowledge of European and Jewish history inspires me to this day.

Research depends on the vision of patrons of learning. I am very grateful for support I received from Bowdoin College, Brandeis University, the Indiana Center on Philanthropy (Indiana University/Lilly Foundation), the Lucius Littauer Foundation, the Memorial Foundation for Jewish Culture, the National Endowment for the Humanities and the University of Southampton. They supported countless hours in archives, the heart and soul of *Jewish Immigrants in London*.

Thanks to a number of fellowships I have received that most valued gift, time to think and write. I am happy to extend my warmest thanks to the Bunting Institute, Radcliffe College, the National Endowment for the Humanities Summer Seminar for College Teachers, directed by the gifted and generous Martha Vicinus, the Oxford Centre for Hebrew and Jewish Studies, and the Kaplan Centre at the University of Cape Town and its director, Milton Shain. In every instance, I had the benefit of wonderful mentors and colleagues, and the opportunity to share my work in engaging and nurturing environments.

Needless to say, no researcher can survive without support from those who can navigate the mysteries of archives and libraries. William Cutter and James Rosenbloom (Brandeis Judaica Library), Chris Woolgar and Karen Robson (University of Southampton), the Bowdoin College Library, especially Ginny Hopcroft, Guy Saldanha and Librarian Emerita, Sherrie Bergman, the staff at LSE, the London Metropolitan Archives, the Tower Hamlets Library, PRO, the British Library and the dedicated individuals at Jewish communal organizations, especially Betty Marks, have provided invaluable assistance. The late Trude Levy (Mocatta Library, UCL) not only shared her vast knowledge, she and her husband Franz welcomed me for delicious meals and valued companionship.

I am especially grateful to colleagues who offered ideas and provided valuable feedback over many years – Rickie Burman, David Cesarani, Bryan Cheyette, Todd Endelman, David Feldman, Bill Fishman, Sharman Kadish, Lara Marks, Kathleen Paul, Antony Polonsky, Elaine Smith, Meri-Jane Rochelson, Pat Starkey, Pamela Walker, Bill Williams, and Eileen Yeo. Dear friends Adam, Jackie and Sam Gold have hosted me more times than I can count and shared their love of fine food, travel and England – I am truly grateful to all of you.

Michael Berkowitz, Tony Kushner, Daniel Levine, Susan Pennybacker, Ellen Ross and Allen Wells, in particular, have generously offered commentary on chapters and articles, and written countless reference letters. Their support brought opportunities that made my work possible.

I would like to thank the two anonymous readers from Pickering & Chatto, who offered extremely helpful suggestions, and to their very helpful editorial staff, especially Stephina Clarke.

My sincerest thanks go to Molly McGrath for her superb editorial skills and especially for her faith in this project.

I have had the good fortune to work with amazing scholars and teachers at Bowdoin. I am indebted to them for their support and friendship. I could not imagine more collegial and supportive colleagues than I have had in the history department. Our now former academic coordinator, Josie Johnson, worked miracles on many occasions, as did Lynne Atkinson of the Government department.

Over many years, I have received the gifts of intellectual exchange and support from students, colleagues and friends. I especially want to recognize Beth Bordowitz, Sara Eddy, Tim Foster, Paul Franco, Marianne Jordan, Cynthia Goss, Margaret Hazlett, Karen Handmaker, Susan Kring, Craig McEwen, Mary Pat McMahon, Paul Nyhus, Carol O'Donnell, Anne Ostwald, Jill Pearlman, Jeff Ward, Bill VanderWolk and Tricia Welsch. I am very fortunate to be part of Bowdoin's vibrant research community, so enthusiastically supported by President Barry Mills and Dean Cristle Collins Judd. My family – my late parents, sister Amy, and the next generation, Becca and Noah, have been my greatest cheerleaders. It is hard to put in words my gratitude to my husband, Joe Frazer. Not only did he bring me a new family, his keen intellect has improved virtually every word of this project. I am blessed to have his encouragement and sense of adventure. His companionship on very welcome diversions on the sea and ski slopes has helped me keep perspective and balance.

It is with abiding love I dedicate this book to my parents and Joe.

LIST OF ABBREVIATIONS

AJY	Association for Jewish Youth
COS	Charity Organisation Society
JAA	Jewish Athletic Association
JADRK	Jewish Association for the Diffusion of Religious Knowledge
JAPGAW	Jewish Association for the Protection of Girls and Women
JBD	Jewish Board of Deputies
JBG / the Board	Jewish Board of Guardians for the Relief of the Jewish Poor
JC	*Jewish Chronicle*
JFS	Jews' Free School
JHO	Jewish Health Organisation
JHOA	Jews' Hospital and Orphan Asylum
JLB	Jewish Lads' Brigade
JMH	Jewish Maternity Home
JREB	Jewish Religious Education Board
JW	*Jewish World*
LCC	London County Council
LSPC	London Society for Promoting of Christianity amongst the Jews
MOH	Medical Officer of Health
PJTS	Poor Jews' Temporary Shelter
SPH	Sara Pyke House
SRHS	Sick Room Helps Society
UJW	Union of Jewish Women

LIST OF TABLES

INTRODUCTION

This book explores the lives of Jewish immigrants to Britain, with a particular focus on women and children who settled in London. As home to the majority of Britain's Jews, London functioned, often to the dismay of Jews outside the metropolis, as the religious and political centre of Anglo-Jewry. In the 1880s, when the pace of Eastern European Jewish immigration quickened, immigrants entered a country with a history of many fewer restrictions than continental Europe.[1] Britons, unlike continental Europeans, tended not 'to mobilize public opinion against Jews as the bearers of modernity' and overall, Victorians expressed more anti-Catholicism than anti-Semitism.[2] The pre-existing Anglo-Jewish community boasted a comprehensive range of philanthropic services, many of which served women and children. Cultural interaction and exchange between newcomers and natives shaped three generations of Eastern European Jews. These factors contributed to a very rapid process of acculturation – one that differed from virtually every other Western Jewish community.[3]

Definitions of acculturation and assimilation vary; for the purposes of this study, acculturation is the process of adopting '"the culture of another social group"' and does not imply fully casting off of one's culture of origin. Assimilation is more extreme and involves shedding attributes of one's '"former culture"'.[4] From early in the twentieth century commentators and historians have used the term 'anglicization', 'the act or process by which persons learn to conform to English modes or usages, in speech, in manner, in mental attitude and in principles', to describe Jewish immigrant acculturation.[5]

This book suggests how and the extent to which immigrant women and children, separated from old world institutions, facing a new environment, religious practices, culture and worldview, absorbed the language, behaviour and values of their new home. The study analyses the ways organizations, philanthropy, schooling and war eroded, but did not eliminate, Jewish distinctions and Eastern European culture.

Jewish Immigrants in London, 1880–1939 begins with a brief history of Jewish life in Britain and an overview of the history and historiography of British Jews, particularly in the East End, between 1880 and 1939. Through social services directed at women, and early intervention into the educational and recreational lives of children, middle- and upper-class Jews attempted – not always successfully – to mould a foreign and alien group into respectable and self-reliant Britons – values familiar in Victorian charitable and social discourse.

Early Jewish Population in Britain

The roots of modern British Jewry date from the mid-seventeenth century, when Menasseh ben Israel of Amsterdam tried to persuade Oliver Cromwell to legalize Jewish residence in Britain. Although ben Israel's effort failed, it triggered a slow process of largely Sephardic Jewish resettlement in England.[6] Anglo-Jewry experienced a twenty-five-fold increase during the eighteenth century.[7] By the mid-eighteenth century, roughly two-thirds of England's seven to eight thousand Jews were of Central, and secondarily, Eastern European, descent. During the remainder of the century, Ashkenazi migration vastly outstripped Sephardi. Many of the newcomers were very poor, took up traditional Jewish trades such as peddling and gained a negative reputation for their products, demeanour and criminal activity. The migrants also included artisans, many of whom created Anglo-Jewry's religious and social organizations, as well as small numbers of wealthy Ashkenazi Jews, who developed highly successful careers in international trade and finance.[8] In 1753, Jews won the right to be naturalized by a private Act of Parliament, but party politics, objections, especially in the City of London, and, some argue, xenophobia, resulted in repeal of the so-called 'Jew Bill' soon after its passage.[9]

During the nineteenth century, Jews arrived from Central and Eastern Europe. Travel from the Continent was inexpensive; those entering faced few restrictions and fellow Jews offered charitable assistance. Initially, most Jews lived in the City of London. After 1820, some began moving north and west and important Jewish centres developed in provincial towns and cities such as Manchester, Liverpool and Leeds. A number of prominent families emerged as leaders in business and philanthropic and cultural institutions.[10] During the last half of the nineteenth century, an influential middle and upper class emerged, though the majority of Jews made their livings as petty traders, shopkeepers and manual workers.[11]

Legal Status and Emancipation

By the mid-nineteenth century, Jews in Britain, and particularly in London, found far greater social acceptance than Jews on the Continent. While Jewish emancipation in Britain came later than in France, the 'Jewish Question' was less public and contested.[12] After Catholic emancipation in 1829, Jews remained the sole religious minority facing legal discrimination and a number of Jewish leaders began to promote the end of Jewish disabilities. Lack of the franchise tended to reinforce doubts about Jews' moral character and emphasized racial distinctiveness. Some anti-alienists believed Jews would always remain a race apart from Britons; others tempered this with sympathy, noting that many 'Jewish traits' resulted from living conditions forced upon Jews.[13] Few Jews met the financial qualifications necessary for voting. The small number seeking emancipation tended to be wealthier, more acculturated and desired greater political influence.[14] Frustrated with the quiescent gratitude of individuals willing to accept social equality, but legal inequality, promoters of Jewish emancipation created various rifts in the Jewish community and challenged a longstanding tradition of inconspicuous negotiation by communal representatives such as the Jewish Board of Deputies (JBD, founded in 1760 to represent Jews in political matters).[15] JBD leaders showed 'comparative reserve', with regard to emancipation, not wanting 'to outstrip public opinion', which was largely indifferent. Some Sephardi Elders on the Board wanted to avoid 'a high-pressure campaign [that] smacked of ingratitude'.[16] Historians Todd Endelman and Abraham Gilam argue that emancipation was unconditional and emerged from England's liberal tradition.[17] Others contend that Jews seeking to end legal disabilities accepted an 'emancipation contract'; in return for civic equality, they agreed to eliminate all national characteristics and to function solely as a religious community.[18]

The limited impact of inequality and a lack of interest 'in entering government service, studying at the ancient universities, or gaining admission to the Inns of Court' arguably reduced the incentive to seek legal equality, perhaps retarding the emancipation process.[19] Christian supporters of Jewish emancipation sought to eliminate restrictions in an effort to end Jewish clannishness, 'anti-social traits' and 'unsavoury vocations'. Jewish emancipationists greeted this support with ambivalence. Many long-time Jewish residents resented that their patriotism was suspect and denied charges that they constituted a distinct nation or were temporary sojourners waiting for the messianic return to the Holy Land. To prove their commitment – and worthiness – to England, emancipationists undertook 'public efforts to raise the social and occupational level of their fellow-Jews at and near the base of the Jewish social pyramid'.[20] Such endeavours reflected genuine charitable commitment, but also reveal concerns over public perceptions of Jews.

The test case for emancipation came in 1847 when the City of London elected Lionel de Rothschild to Parliament. He could not take his seat in the House of Commons because of the oath of abjuration, requiring that he swear 'on the true faith of a Christian'. In 1858, Rothschild, elected for the fifth time, finally entered Parliament after a compromise permitted each House to determine its own oath. The seating of Rothschild, the first Jewish Member of Parliament, meant England's Jews gained the opportunity, at least legally, to participate fully in civic affairs.[21]

Historiography: Existing Studies of the Acculturation of Jewish Immigrants to London

Scholars' approaches to the history of British Jews, which have shifted over time, tell us much about the community and the changing perceptions of those who have chronicled that experience. Anglo-Jewish history has received scant attention from British or Jewish historians; often scholars saw Jews as insignificant to British history and Britain as marginal to Jewish history.[22] While scholars now emphasize Britain's multi-cultural dimensions, traditionally, historians rarely focused on immigration and saw 'the study of associated minorities [as] belong[ing] on the outside track'.[23] The history of British Jews, argues Todd Endelman, 'marches to its own drummer'. The lack of drama and persecution typical of much of European Jewish history meant it did not fit into familiar paradigms.[24] These factors have had an important impact on the tone of early historical work – and the evolution of the field over the past thirty-five years.

Early Sanitized Accounts of Anglicization

The hierarchical structure of Britain's Jewish community, its religious, social welfare and defence organizations, its desire to present a success story, as well as the Anglo-Jewish press, contributed to early sanitized accounts of acculturation and reflected the insecurity of Jewish minority status in England. Middle-class Jews and community leaders felt the burden of responsibility very deeply – a sincere commitment to serve the needy and protect the good name of the Jewish community. The challenges of anti-Semitism and limited English tolerance for cultural plurality led to internal disagreements within the Jewish community. Insecurity generated compensatory actions and fostered a somewhat over-developed sense of gratitude among Jews for English hospitality. According to Endelman, before the 1970s, most 'Anglo-Jewish history was whiggish, apologetic and triumphalist, emphasizing the harmony between Jewishness and Englishness, while minimizing the discordant aspects of the assimilation process'.[25] Thus, a 1950's history claimed rather optimistically, that immigrant Jewish integration was rapid and 'fortunately, the long-established elements and the immigrants had not become separated groups'.[26]

During the first half of the nineteenth century, Anglo-Jewry received attention largely from Christian millennialists who believed that the Resettlement of Jews (1650s) and emancipation would hasten the Second Coming and increase conversions – and from amateur historians who located the first Jewish communities and synagogues.[27] Articles on crypto-Jews and converts figure prominently in the *Transactions of the Jewish Historical Society of England* from 1893 through to the First World War.[28]

Many early works were self-congratulatory, applauding the successes of angli-cization and the generosity of the Rothschilds, stressing that England's Jews were law-abiding and emphasizing the modernization of 'backward' Jews, and Jewish- and Christian-sponsored efforts at social control.[29] V. D. Lipman argued that in Britain, immigrant integration exceeded that of other communities. By 1914

> one could think of the immigrants and their predecessors as a single community, one which had maintained its Jewishness while acquiring English loyalties, one which could sincerely proclaim its united loyalty to England as the 1914–1918 war began – in the words of the placard outside the office of the *Jewish Chronicle*: 'England has been all to the Jews: Jews will be all they can be to England'.[30]

More Critical Analyses Emerge

Since the 1970s, Anglo-Jewish historians have re-evaluated the experiences of Britain's Jews. Geoffrey Alderman offered an antidote to the overly optimistic renditions, intending 'to tell the story warts and all'.[31] Trained in both Jewish and British history, recent studies recognize the particularities of Jewish experience, but analyse them in the context of British history. This work is part of a broader trend of interdisciplinary studies that have enriched our understanding of immi-grant acculturation and of Britain's diverse religious and ethnic communities.[32] New works offer sophisticated reassessments of modernization theory, anti-Semitism and Jewish political and economic behaviour. They have established a new standard of critical historical analysis and built on studies by Lloyd Gartner and V. D. Lipman, who laid the foundations of Anglo-Jewish history. Gartner's social history provides a general analysis of immigrant acculturation and stresses the modernizing impact of residence in Britain. Lipman's work concentrates on institutions and the politics of absorbing newcomers into the community, and downplays rifts caused by the wave of newcomers.[33]

Over the last thirty years, scholars have tended to move away from insti-tutional emphases and have complicated the benevolent image of society and linear acculturation put forward by their predecessors. Todd Endelman's focus on the eighteenth and nineteenth centuries considers the distinctive features of English culture and society and their impact on Anglo-Jewry.[34] Endelman makes two particularly important contributions. He opens a window on non-elites, contending they are as central to Jewish history as higher status co-religionists. He has also challenged the 'top-down' Germanocentric focus on the *Haskalah*, the Jewish Enlightenment, to explain patterns of Jewish modernization. Rather than an ideologically motivated shift as in Germany, social and political con-ditions in Britain account for Anglo-Jewry's pattern of modernization.[35] In his re-evaluation, Tony Kushner highlighted the tenacity of anti-Semitism in Brit-ish society and challenged older notions of the relatively innocuous and foreign nature of British anti-Semitism.[36] David Cesarani has revised our understanding of British policy and internal politics in a number of works.[37] His edited collection of essays focusing on 1870–1945 was an important forum for new scholarship on class, culture, politics and gender and offers insights into Jewish life in Manchester, Leeds and London.[38] Historians such as Bill Williams see anglicizing activities as middle-class efforts at social control.[39] Joe Buckman's Marxist analysis of the tailoring industry in Leeds, an important provincial city with a tradition of trade unionism, emphasizes its distinctiveness. His work, which challenges claims of limited class consciousness among Jewish workers, tends to underestimate the implications of culture and religion for immigrant–native relations.[40]

David Feldman is critical of modernization and social control theory, which cast Anglo-Jewry's motivations for its social policy too narrowly and minimize the complexity of power relations among Britons, native-born and immigrant Jews. Feldman also questions the view of assimilation as a retreat from Jewish identity and a privatization or movement of Judaism into the home and out of the public sphere. He points to the persistence of a minority with fundamentalist beliefs and sees the decline of religious observance as a matter of 'attenuated opportunities', not as the 'inevitable consequence of modernity'.[41] The more that British politics encroached on immigrants, contends Feldman, the more they participated in politics and the more they asserted their interests as Jews; anglicization was therefore not linear, but dynamic.[42] Feldman draws on extensive Yiddish sources and contextualizes Jewish workers' experiences within the British historical and economic context, while considering the impact of different notions of the nation and views of Jews as *homo economicus*. As David Englander and Bryan Cheyette have shown, racialized constructions of Jews, as 'programmed for profit' and highly individualistic, influenced the response to Jewish settlement in Britain.[43]

Emphasizing the Acculturation of Women and Children

While a number of studies have analysed the acculturation of immigrants, few have emphasized the experiences of women and children. The introduction of gender in Jewish studies, notes Paula Hyman has 'challenged the master narrative's presumption of the uniformity of the experience of Jews in modern Europe'.[44] Moving the focus from men in the public sphere to a wider range of actors – to women and children, husbands and wives – deepens our understanding of identity formation.[45]

Studies on Schooling, Middle-Upper-Class Women, Religiosity, Work and Home Spheres

Thanks to innovative approaches to British Jewish history, scholars are asking a broader range of questions. Ros Livshin, for example, analysed the messages children in Manchester received on the streets, in school and from within the Jewish community. Children learned English language and customs, manners, neatness and discipline, as well as a commitment to Judaism, albeit an anglicized version, through educational and social services.[46] In the first book-length study of the Jews' Free School (JFS), Britain's largest Jewish school, Gerry Black assessed the school's anglicizing and philanthropic mission. JFS provided not only education, but much needed food and clothing.[47] In a comparison of nineteenth-century Jewish and contemporary immigrant education, Geoffrey Short argued that Jewish children succeeded because of teachers' expectations, English language acquisition, positive views of parents, a willingness to meet needs of observant Jews and attendance at Jewish majority schools, which minimized daily experiences of anti-Semitism.[48] Among the histories of youth clubs, Sharman Kadish argues that leaders and activities of the Jewish Lads' Brigade (JLB) promoted anglicization through physical fitness.[49] These studies have shifted attention from areas dominated by men and enhanced our knowledge of British Jewry by focusing on the daily lives of children.

While studies of immigrants tend to dominate, the lives of middle-class and upper-class Jewish women have also received consideration. In a comparison of Jewish women's participation in British and American suffrage and feminist movements, Linda Kuzmack argues that Anglo-Jewish feminists created a 'distinctively Jewish' movement, sought equality in secular political, as well as in religious, life and participated more extensively in secular suffrage activities than generally acknowledged.[50] Women's changing role in religion takes centre stage in Ellen Umanksy's work on Lily Montagu, a founder of Liberal Judaism and warden of the West Central Girls' Club. Umansky examines the ways Montagu influenced the philosophical and institutional structure of Liberal Judaism and the key role women played in the development of Jewish clubs and settlement houses.[51]

Religious life is also central to Rickie Burman's work, which makes extensive use of oral history and highlights the interactions among women who settled in Manchester. Focusing on the different gendered and cultural expectations of Eastern European and Anglo-Jewish women, Burman found that immigration to Britain led to a gradual change in the status granted scholarly activity, women's work patterns and the significance accorded domestic religious observance.[52]

British Jews, however, tended to identify social status in the same ways as other Britons – the capacity of a man to support his family. Unlike Eastern Europe, where Jews had little hope for integration into mainstream society, England offered acceptance, but in a conditional manner. Thus, middle-class Jews eagerly sought to minimize Jewish distinctiveness and promoted behaviour acceptable in the host society. Typically, Victorians viewed women as innately spiritual – rather the opposite of the Jewish view.[53] In moving closer to the British ideal, 'women's traditional domestic practices acquired a new significance'. What was once merely daily routine took on special importance and now 'define[d] the Jewish identity of the household'.[54] Burman alerts us to the impact of the local society in defining women's roles.

Marks, the most prolific of those dealing with Anglo-Jewish women, explores Jewish prostitution, unwed motherhood and in a significant monograph, has analysed Jewish mothering in east London between 1870 and 1939.[55] Using extensive qualitative and quantitative sources, she explores the experience of childbirth, child-rearing and the connections between health and ethnicity. Britons viewed Jewish mothers as exemplary and credited them with infant mortality rates that were much lower than among other east London poor. This remarkable record, concluded Marks, resulted from a combination of 'certain ethnic and religious Jewish customs concerning the importance of hygiene, diet and breast-feeding as well [as] the types of communal provision available to Jewish mothers and their infants'.[56]

My own work builds on Marks's and extends the study of children beyond infancy to schooling, recreation and work, and of mothers beyond childbearing to child-rearing. It shows how mothers navigated poverty and slum living and took advantage of Jewish voluntary and state-sponsored services to nurture their children. This study also demonstrates that children exposed parents – but especially mothers – to English language and mores. Attention to the intersection of family, ethnicity and philanthropy exposes the tensions that emerged in this exchange and brings to light the ways immigrant Jews and their children responded to the challenges and opportunities of life in London during the three periods explored in this book.

The Advantages of a Nuanced Approach

Jewish Immigrants in London, 1880–1939 traces the anglicization of women and children through communal organizations and education. Focusing on gender, ethnicity and class, it considers a wider range of factors than previous studies, demonstrating the extent to which women and their children moved from arrival or birth in Britain to becoming Britons. Both the passage of time and changing circumstances meant that immigrants and especially their children could choose among increasing options for education, work and leisure. Britons, Jewish and Christian, orchestrated anglicization through various programmes. Ethnic and religious bonds led the Jewish community to provide an essential safety net – and directly linked the Jewish poor with their wealthier co-religionists. Most anglicizers directed their efforts at children or through their mothers; the campaign was comprehensive, conscious in nature and achieved rapid results.[57] If one accepts the growing anxiety at the turn of the century about declining Jewish observance and identity as reflective of reality, it may have been too successful.

In tracing the anglicization of Jewish women and children in the East End, several distinguishing features emerge, among them the higher standard of living despite poverty, extensive Jewish social services, limited domestic violence, substantial attention to children and lower mortality rates.[58] Typically, historians have emphasized the East End's high levels of poverty and crime, drawing extensively on the pioneering studies of Charles Booth.[59] Marc Brodie argues that historians have overstated the uniformity of the poverty and that the percentage of those '"in poverty"' (38 per cent) was only 7 per cent higher than the average rate for London.[60] Jewish women seemingly negotiated the pitfalls of poverty more successfully than others in the working class. Many Jewish children lived in more stable homes, received better care and were healthier – a reflection of differences in the allocation of income – arguably linked to values and priorities, but also thanks to extensive Jewish social services.

In her study of working-class women and mothers, Ellen Ross identified the many challenges and coping mechanisms employed by English working-class women.[61] While Jewish women drew on many of the same coping mechanisms, the immigrant community benefited from buffers against devastating poverty and was less likely to experience the adverse effects of alcohol use and violence. Jewish writer Ralph Finn claims that despite his family's poverty and experiences of hunger, he did not suffer as he did not know he 'ought to have been suffering' and assumed that 'poverty was a natural hazard of being alive'.[62] In the early 1930s, however, when Finn began teaching in West Ham, he learned of far greater depths of poverty. Some children of Irish dockers, recalled Finn, came to school without shoes. Rather than privileging food for the family, the pattern in most Jewish families, income in Dockside families belonged to the men, many of whom spent it on beer and gambling.[63]

Communal solidarity, while not unique to the Jewish community suggests ways that East End Jews assisted each other. Few homes came equipped with gas cookers and women spent part of Thursday at the bake house waiting for *challah*, bread for Sabbath, to bake. While this made preparations more difficult, it brought women together on a regular basis, gave them an opportunity to learn of one another's needs, aid each other in troubled times and reinforced neighbourhood sharing networks.[64] In the Rothschild Buildings where cookers were too small for the traditional Sabbath cholent, a casserole of meat and vegetables, children ferried the dish to local bakers such as Rinkoff's.[65]

While the vast majority of Jewish immigrants were poor, diet and accommodations varied widely, often related to the presence of a healthy male wage-earner. Kitty Collins described her family as 'very very poor'. Their first home was in Jubilee Street; it had three flights of stairs, two bedrooms, a front room with a piano, and was very cold. Yet, Collins recalled the flat as clean and comfortable, with adequate food. For Sabbath they had 'lovely old-fashioned food', tsimmes, schav, chopped liver and cholent and on weekdays, items such as eggs, onions, *freikochens* and cream cheese. Collins's mother prepared little meat; mainly they ate herring kippers, some smoked salmon, brown bread, butter, lemon and olives – items she remembers as relatively inexpensive.[66] This variety and quality contrasts starkly with typical working-class diets.[67] Bread was the chief component of many diets. Tenements had limited cooking facilities and fuel was very expensive.[68]

Jewish tradition influenced immigrants as well as those who offered philanthropy. Judaism's emphasis on charity and education, the dietary laws, the honoured position of the wife and mother and the limited resort to alcohol, affected expectations and behaviour. Caring for the family had many layers of significance. Hymie Fagan recalled his mother asking: "'What sort of a housewife was it ... who didn't cook a meal for her husband and family?'"[69] Such attitudes give us insight into women's sense of identity, competence and maintenance of culture. Because women tended to shape family life, they were crucial to the successful adaptation of most immigrants, especially children.

In Summary: What We Stand to Learn

By concentrating on areas of life more directly concerned with women and children, this book offers a more nuanced picture of Eastern European immigrant acculturation.[70] Literature on immigration, race relations, multiculturalism and political identity helps us compare the forces and responses at play among Jews and their environment at the turn of the century.[71] The focus on social services highlights the gendered views of Jewish and British providers and philanthropists and underscores aspects of acculturation less consciously considered in other works on Anglo-Jewry.

Rich or poor, Christian or Jewish, women and female children lived in a world that emphasized male superiority, a limited public role, marriage and childbearing. Working-class girls received an education that stressed domestic training, rarely continued after the age of fourteen and generally prepared them for work requiring limited skills. Daughters earned much less than their brothers and remained more dependent upon their parents longer than sons.[72] While girls and young women could help at home, they also represented a financial burden, originally owing to the requirement of a dowry.[73] Many parents took out loans to pay for weddings, which could include several meals (a large breakfast followed by pineapple, cream and cakes) and a band which generally played Russian and Jewish music, Yiddish tunes, or someone pretending to be Al Jolson.[74] Working-class boys received more intensive vocational training, messages of self-reliance and independence, often stayed in school longer and were more likely to enter apprenticeships. Most Jewish women did not expect to work after marrying or having children. Their adult lives centred on home and family, a full-time occupation in London's tenements. Jack Stein recalled the harshness of his mother's life. She was 'marvellous' and 'very orthodox'; she worked and scrubbed floors, did all the cooking and buying chickens, on just a few shillings a week.[75] Victorian philanthropists approved of this ideal of womanhood and their charitable endeavours tended to perpetuate a vision of women's natural position as keeper and protector of the home.[76]

Class, ethnicity and religion interacted with gender in very powerful ways in the Jewish East End. Most providers of education and philanthropy – upper- and middle-class men and women – absorbed the ethos of their class – to use leisure responsibly and to help others to help themselves, and took seriously traditions of Jewish charity. Neither gender nor ethnicity alone explains how immigrant women and their children stepped out of their insular Jewish world into the larger, indigenous culture. Religious or secular, Jewish culture with its gendered prescriptions influenced immigrants and native-born – as well as their interactions.

East End Jews lived in working-class neighbourhoods, laboured in factories and workshops and received many of the same lessons as their Gentile counterparts. Jewish communal workers responded to Jewish immigrants not only as co-religionists, but also as part of the labouring poor and the great unwashed. Prior to World War I, the Jewish East End was a world unto itself. To the native-born – Jew or Christian – 'a trip beyond the Aldgate Pump was often presented in the guise of an exotic, oriental adventure'.[77] Basil Henriques, social worker and warden of the Bernhard Baron Settlement, described an 'amusing' experience of mistaken identity during a walk with Robin Montefiore among newly arrived 'filthy looking Russian' immigrants. Henriques or Montefiore had recently purchased a soft furry black hat. A man approached them, asked if they were looking for the rest of their party and directed them to the immigrants.[78] These newcomers, who tended to cluster in particular neighbourhoods, represented an alien world for many middle- and upper-class Britons.

Patterns of acculturation, communal response, the differences in experience of, and expectations for, women and their children emerge from a wide range of sources.[79] However, one of the great difficulties of projects such as this is to hear the voices of immigrant women and children. This study often depends on information teased from materials written about, and not by immigrants. Voluminous contemporary journal literature examines women's labour issues, anti-alienism and philanthropic endeavours. A growing body of secondary literature analyses and compares immigrants to Britain, as well as Jews who settled throughout the world. Census data provide information on population, marriage and residential pattern of Jewish immigrants. Local, labour and Yiddish-language newspapers explore issues of importance within the East End. The *Jewish Chronicle* (hereafter, *JC*), the voice of Anglo-Jewry, reports on religion, education, health care, philanthropy and the activities of the officials of communal organizations. It generally presents the viewpoint of English-speaking Jews and helps identify areas of concern to England's established community. The controversies it follows offer hints at diverse, and sometimes opposing, views.

This study takes particular advantage of annual reports and extensive archival materials to explore the services British Jews established for co-religionists. Especially useful are the records of Jewish maternal and child welfare agencies, youth clubs and settlements and the Jewish Board of Guardians for the Relief of the Jewish Poor (the Board, JBG).[80] Reactions to the assistance and the providers suggest the ways immigrants experienced such interactions and offer a picture of the kinds of activities and the types of people with whom immigrant women and children came in contact.

Parliamentary papers offer not only official views on issues, but include witnesses from diverse backgrounds, with varying perspectives. Investigations on sweated industries and immigration inform us about the working lives of Jewish women. The Royal Commission on Alien Immigration and the Interdepartmental Committee on Physical Deterioration delve into the daily lives of immigrants, their health and criminality.

These rich sources offer a window on the lives of Jewish women and children. They suggest generational differences, the contrasts between Jewish and Christian working-class homes, the importance of gender, as well as the experience of being, and response to, a minority. Jewish women were more likely to be literate than other immigrant women, tended to raise fewer children and therefore could give more attention to each child, provide more food and may well have had comparatively more leisure time than other immigrant women. The Jewish community's impressive philanthropic network advanced anglicization and meant that offspring of Jewish immigrants experienced a qualitatively different childhood from many of their class.

While Jews found barriers to complete acceptance in Britain, acculturated Jews gained increasing access to most mainstream cultural, educational and political spheres. Through the period of this study, Jews remained highly self-conscious, and aware of the limits placed upon them; that anxiety certainly reflected the qualified acceptance all Jews faced in Britain. The sense of remaining an outsider motivated the provision of far-reaching social and educational programmes. Many Jews felt obligated to efface differences of language, occupations, mannerisms and backwardness that non-Jews, as well as anglicized Jews, recognized. Established Jewry believed such characteristics encouraged doubts about separatism, and ultimately raised questions about the ability of Jews to become English. Designed with both conscious and subtle assumptions of appropriate roles for women and men, Anglo-Jewry sought to mould roughly three generations of Jews and their offspring between 1880 and 1939. Anglicizing efforts evolved over time and indicate the changing perceptions of Anglo-Jewry with regard to immigrants and their children. The aim of this volume is to ask and explore questions about what it was like to be a Jewish immigrant woman or child in London's East End in 1880, at the turn of the century and on the eve of World War II. What did acculturation mean to them?

1 A BRIEF HISTORY OF THE ACCULTURATION OF A JEWISH COMMUNITY: LONDON, 1880–1939

Three Stages of Change, from 1880 to 1939

Three periods of change emerge during the years 1880 to 1939. Each features distinct reactions of Jewish immigrants and their hosts and signals evolving patterns of adjustment among London's Jewish immigrants. From 1880 to 1905, the period of most intensive immigration, migrants from Eastern Europe settled in Stepney and Aldgate, areas where Jews had lived for nearly two hundred years. Anglo-Jewry created and expanded social welfare services to meet immediate needs. The period 1905 to 1918 saw the passage of the Aliens Act, the rate of immigration decrease and Anglo-Jewry develop programmes with an interventionist emphasis. During 1918 to 1939, the period of most extensive change, concerns emerged that acculturation had gone too far.[1]

1880–1905: A Period of Intense Immigration

Poverty characterized the experiences of the majority of first generation immigrants.[2] Assessments of the nature of that poverty, such as Charles Booth's study, provide extensive information and insight into the attitudes of those gathering data.[3] East Enders shared subdivided housing, often came up short on rent day and faced the cold and damp English weather with inadequate food, clothing and shoes. Employment in seasonal trades deepened financial stress. Jews living in dwellings such as the Rothschild Buildings suffered disproportionately higher rates of consumption than Stepney as a whole.[4] Slum clearance in the East End, an effort to stem crime and prostitution, intensified pressure on housing.[5] These conditions created anxiety among established Jews which led to communal efforts at damage control and the provision of basic needs.

The generation who arrived as adults, especially grandparents, often remained the least anglicized. Writer Cyril Spector's mother settled in Bethnal Green in 1902 and some fifty years later spoke little English, and wrote none.[6] Raised in Eastern Europe, comfortable only in Yiddish, and unaccustomed to urban life, these women focused most of their attention on their families' survival. Generational changes developed quickly – anglicized children differed in language, appearance and self-perception from their elders.[7]

1905–18: Immigration Lessens, Acculturation Accelerates

While poverty remained pervasive, growing numbers received an English education, medical treatment, particularly prenatal care and perceived themselves as British. Acculturation resulted in fundamental changes. In 1910, the East End correspondent of the *JC* commented that 'the fact that the *sheital* [wig worn by religiously observant women after marriage], is going out of favour' served as one index of 'gradual Anglicisation'. Young immigrant women now rebelled against covering their heads. A wig maker too, noted the shift. Foreign 'Jewesses', except those with ultra-Orthodox husbands, now refused 'to submit to petty tyranny which decrees that her natural locks should be covered'.[8] While only impressionistic, this evidence suggests that women may have adopted modernized forms of observance before their husbands, or challenged structures of patriarchy thanks to influences of their new environment.[9]

During the years before World War I, many Jews began discovering a world beyond the East End. The children of first generation immigrants entered a wider array of occupations. Just before the First World War, the Girls' Apprenticing Sub-Committee noted difficulty placing all the girls seeking clerical positions.[10] Girls and boys young enough to attend school straddled two worlds. As the Chief Rabbi noted in 1914,

> The younger generation has tasted something of Western life, and to that extent has become alienated from the older generation ... The foreign speech, the old ideas – are a little strange to the children, and while they beget no sympathy may even attract derision. The young Jews and Jewesses, revelling in their English up-bringing look contemptuously upon their fathers.[11]

Intergenerational tensions intensified as children negotiated between anglicizing messages at school and in clubs and homes that remained suffused with Jewish culture, religious or secular, socialist or Zionist.

The advent of war bolstered doubts about immigrant Jews' commitment to the nation. East End Jews' lack of enthusiasm for enlisting deepened concerns in the Jewish community about behaviours that could arouse anti-Semitism. While many East End Jews enlisted, a significant proportion sought to avoid military service either in Britain or in Russia. Perceptions of Jews as a nation within a nation who took soldiers' jobs, reinforced notions of Jews' alienness.[12] The Russian Revolution, internal Jewish tensions over Zionism, as well as nationalistic fervour during World War I, left Jews feeling insecure about perceptions of their loyalty to Britain.[13] Jewish charities redoubled their efforts to aid poor Jews and to avoid charges that immigrants constituted a financial burden on the state.[14]

Communal priorities shifted from the absorption of unprecedented numbers of newcomers to the moulding of good British Jews. Schools emphasized English language skills, literature and culture, physical exercise, neatness and discipline. Club leaders wanted to keep Jewish youth out of the music halls and focused on appropriate use of leisure time. The established Jewish community still tried to remain inconspicuous – a longstanding Jewish approach to hostile surroundings – but also worked quietly to increase rights and minimize disabilities. The JBG reminded readers that Christian friends had gained many concessions for Jews and that it made sense for Jewish MPs to 'remain in the background'.[15] Slowly, the communal power structure shifted as children of immigrants moved into leadership roles and Anglo-Jewish elites lost exclusive control of communal institutions.[16]

Evidence of acculturation emerged alongside persistent old world traditions, apparent in the hiring of a Yiddish-speaking manager at Lloyds Bank. The bank 'cultivate[d] a "Yiddish" business"' by advertising in the Yiddish press. While many continued to think of 'the Ghetto' as 'a terribly dismal place – the abode of squalor, penury, and ignorance', a place for 'self-sacrificing charity' workers – a great bank had opened there. The time had come to sweep away 'many musty delusions about the East End Ghetto', to replace outdated 'popular notions ... with elementary fact'.[17] As change unfolded, some worried that rather than too foreign, many Jews became lax in their Jewish observance and the dangers of the street enticed impressionistic youth.

As services for immigrants developed, they generated a growing number of voluntary and paid opportunities for middle-class women. These women faced extensive scrutiny. The *JC*, for example, complained that women workers tended to 'apply to all a measure or rule which excluded a sufficient amount of sympathy and kindness'. The writer conceded that evidence already existed that women's work would become more effective as they gained experience.[18] Despite new freedoms, female community leaders expressed frustration with resistance to women's appointment to committees, arguing that membership on committees 'should be solely a matter of merit and should not be restricted by considerations of sex'. Many organizations successfully drew on women's talents, raising questions as to 'why archaic prejudices' continued to affect women's opportunities.[19]

1918–39: Emphasis on Full Acculturation, New Generation Leads the Way

East End services grew in size and sophistication during this last stage. Both denominational organizations and local governments increased the numbers of health visitors and infant welfare centres.[20] Immigrants became more independent and built their own institutions such as the London Jewish Hospital. Schooling, social organizations and the First World War facilitated some social and economic mobility. In this latest period, most East End Jewish schoolchildren were native-born, but many still had foreign-born parents. School leavers entered an ever-wider array of jobs and many became less religiously observant than their elders. The fear that anglicization had gone too far brought renewed attention to the leisure choices of Jewish youth, the content of programmes sponsored by the Jewish community and a focus on keeping young East Enders committed Jews.

The growth of the leisure industry in the 1920s and 1930s spurred development of settlement houses and girls' and boys' clubs. Although commercialization began before World War I, workers had more time and discretionary income after the war.[21] Boxer Jack Kid Berg noted that

> in the early twenties, the first British-born generation of Jewish boys was reaching adulthood. Since birth, Jewish children had been assailed on all sides by churches, youth clubs, schools and various other institutions that had, consciously or otherwise, aimed to rid them of their 'alien' heritage: vicars and youth leaders, scoutmasters and schoolmasters and school teachers had systematically chipped away at the Yiddish language and the culture it had carried, gradually loosening the hold of the Orthodox elders who had once held sway.[22]

Among the younger generations especially, clothing and cultural interests no longer identified them as 'aliens', as Jews' activities more closely resembled their English peers. Jewish youth responded to the new 'dance craze' and frequented clubs such as Mile End Old Boys' Club, where they made many *shidduchs*, or matches. Complaints increased about the looseness of women and their immodest dress and language.[23]

In 1935, *World Jewry* ran a series of articles on the East End, claiming: 'The East End is changing, rapidly – inexorably'. Many Londoners remained unfamiliar with the area or still associated it with 'crime, anarchy, and slums'. Just a few years before World War II, the East End combined narrow 'mediaeval-looking street markets [that] might be vivid reproductions of the ghettos of Eastern Europe' with wide boulevards and 'chromium-fitted shopfronts and Neon signs [that] are characteristic of an East End which has travelled a long way from the poverty, dirt and ignorance of fifty years ago'.[24] Nonetheless, Jews' 'race and tradition' created 'a more highly coloured character than the Gentile of his class'. Even Jewish writers believed the speech and clothing of Jews reflected this inner colour. 'There is a slight extravagance of cut, a tendency to vigour in the shade and pattern of the materials which, although classed by some as "flashiness", is probably a reflection of Oriental influence in the Jewish make-up'.[25] While Jews had become more modern in behaviour and outlook, the article's language identified Jews as foreigners.

During this period, Anglo-Jewry laid the foundations of modern Jewish life in Britain. Increasing numbers of East Enders emerged from the working class and moved to areas such as Stamford Hill and north London.[26] Many Jews remained distinct from Christians in their educational and occupational patterns and retained ties to their ethnic heritage, albeit a more British version than they brought from Eastern Europe. According to Jack Kid Berg, the younger generation, generally children of immigrants, demonstrated more confidence and less anxiety than immigrants. During the interwar years, young adults ventured beyond the East End with increasingly regularity. Berg, typical of his generation, found the lure of the West End very strong.[27] Others recalled that an evening out involved a trip to Lyons Corner House in the West End, where 'you would get an egg mayonnaise for eight pence, old pence, a baton and butter for two pence and a beautiful cup of coffee for four pence'.[28]

Men, Women and Children Face Different Challenges

Leave-Taking

For Jewish immigrants, even before their departure from Eastern Europe, men and women had vastly different experiences. In order to establish themselves in a trade and earn enough money to bring over their kin, many men, particularly between 1880 and 1910, emigrated ahead of the rest of their families. Some women, left on their own in Eastern Europe, faced insecurities of Jewish life such as pogroms and unemployment or underemployment, with little or no support from husbands and fathers. Others received small sums from those working abroad or depended on extended families for assistance.

Uprooting and moving to London, noted one woman, was hard; leaving family behind was especially painful, but a married woman had no choice.[29] Further, immigrants, particularly women, found travel precarious. Steerage was crowded, lacked ventilation and filth – and occasionally animal waste – contaminated passenger quarters.[30] Dishonest agents overcharged immigrants, promised them a marriage partner at the end of their journey, tricked them into the white slave trade or raped or harassed them en route.[31] When Roza Silverman and her four children boarded a Greek steamer bound for London, workers threw half of their clothing into the sea, sent Silverman's family 'into the coal bunks ... for three days without food' and attempted 'to outrage' Silverman and her fifteen-year-old daughter. An officer reportedly 'struck several of the children with an iron'.[32]

Once in Britain, assistance from the Jewish community regularly eased the way for newcomers, sometimes averting repatriation. In the spring of 1910, Zali Schwartz, a young Rumanian 'tailoress' who spoke no English, landed in Grimsby. The medical inspector, Dr Simpson, blocked her entry, claiming she was pregnant. L. H. Woolfe Jr, a solicitor provided by the Jewish community, appealed Schwartz's case and questioned Simpson, who pronounced Schwartz at least four-months pregnant. Following 'severe' cross-examination, the medical inspector acknowledged the 'cursory' nature of his examination and expressed doubt over his diagnosis when Woolfe produced evidence that Schwartz was still a virgin. Woolfe recommended that the independent examiner and Simpson 'make a thorough examination', after which the physician acknowledged his error. The appeal board next tried to disqualify Schwartz, claiming she might become 'chargeable to the rates, requiring the support of local government'. Woolfe objected to this tactic and eventually Schwartz received permission to land. Despite the success of her appeal, the young woman underwent three physical examinations by male doctors, making her experience with the immigration board most harrowing.[33] Such experiences underscore the gendered nature of migration and the crucial role of co-religionists in helping immigrants overcome isolation, callous officials and complicated bureaucracies.

Women Closer to Agents of Acculturation

Once in England, immigrant women encountered institutions and conditions similar to their male counterparts, but most remained at home caring for children. Mothers absorbed English culture both directly and through their children. Through philanthropy, education, associational networks and work, Jewish women and children learned the ideals of decorum and self-help, and a form of Judaism influenced by Jewish tradition, the Church of England and Victorian models of respectability and family. While philanthropists' motivations were not solely altruistic, their generosity clearly eased the difficulties immigrants faced in their new home. Women became both a target of and a conduit for acculturation. Jack Kid Berg claimed that although his mother spoke Yiddish in the house, she was more anglicized than his father.[34]

Children Deemed Most Promising

According to the *JC*, children proved the most promising candidates for anglicization. Anglo-Jewry could offer them 'a thoroughly English education'. Their parents, who came with 'fully formed' characters, were 'incapable of undergoing the radical change ... necessary to transform them into Englishmen'. A child's 'mind', noted the *JC*, 'is plastic; we can develop it in any direction we require'.[35] Domestic training and refinement for girls, cricket, marksmanship and boxing for boys and camping for all, introduced quintessentially English activities to children. This interaction of cultures and priorities – the lessons preached and the nature and level of acceptance – or resistance, all increased the complexity of acculturation.

Tensions in the Family

Arrival in a strange land left some traditional Yiddish-speaking wives feeling out of place in London and created tensions with some husbands. Frederick Mocatta, a community leader, pointed out, that 'in spite of strenuous efforts of the [Jewish] Board [of Guardians] to diminish the evil', increasing numbers of husbands abandoned families.[36] The JBG tried to assist such women. In one case, they arranged admission to the workhouse for four of twenty-three deserted wives, which entailed separation from their children. 'In vain, Mr Cohen [of the Board] explained to the women the arrangements which had been made [including kosher food], and the care which would be taken of their infant children'. Despite their desperate situation, the women refused to enter the workhouse. The JBG, in turn, denied them assistance.[37] Generally, Jews eschewed the workhouse. The *JC* covered the exceptional case of an elderly woman whose 'near relative' took her to the workhouse after receiving inadequate assistance from the JBG.[38]

Desertion remained a problem into the twentieth century. A number of women who appeared before the Alien Immigration Board had travelled to London in search of husbands. Dressmaker Leie Grunshaw hoped to find her husband who had travelled from Russia to London in 1912 and ended communication after a year. She wanted to locate him and get a divorce, but the Immigration Board barred her, concluding that divorce proceedings were too expensive. In another case, Broche Hirsch came to London to look for her husband who was supposedly headed for America. Although she had enough money to travel to America, her admission was doubtful, so the Immigration Board refused to admit her and her children.[39]

Husbands' reticence to portray the reality of life in England led some women to have unrealistic expectations. Mark Fineman's mother came expecting a comfortable life. His father

> had written glowing accounts of his job, what he was earning, the lovely house he'd found, um – what a goldene medina to use the vernacular, England was and the streets were paved with gold ... And you can imagine her horror when she found that um he had found two rooms in a rat-ridden alley-way slum in the East End where the entire family was supposed to live and in fact where I was born. I think her first instincts were to return to home – but that of course wasn't possible.[40]

Such circumstances resulted in some return migration, but most families simply had to cope.

Response of Established Jewry to the Newly Arrived

During the nineteenth century, Anglo-Jewry created numerous social and religious institutions to serve their small community, but the large-scale immigration of the 1880s found them unprepared. At its outset, Anglo-Jewry encouraged Eastern European Jews to remain in Russia and Poland, contending that foreign governments should protect their own nationals.[41] Community leaders such as Lionel L. Cohen, president of the JBG, favoured limits on alien immigration, a position initially supported by the *JC*.[42] Nonetheless, Britain's Jewish community accepted their co-religionists and offered a level of assistance remarkable for its breadth and depth. As the anti-alien movement intensified, the editorial position of the *JC* became more accepting of immigrants.[43]

Between 1880 and 1939, push factors – disabilities that encouraged Jews to leave Eastern Europe – and pull factors – those that drew them to England – resulted in England's Jewish population growing from about 60,000 to between 350,000 and 370,000.[44] America, with its extensive social services, attracted millions. In comparison, Irish migration to Britain increased from 1815 to 1845, reaching 806,000 in 1861.[45] Twenty-five-year military conscription and its attendant efforts at conversion, a demographic explosion, geographic restrictions and poverty all undermined Jewish survival in Russia and Russian Poland.[46] The 1881 assassination of Alexander II led to a new wave of anti-Jewish agitation. Alexander III introduced particularly restrictive geographic limitations on Jewish residence and occupations, exacerbating economic privation and forcing many Jews into the area known as the Pale of Settlement.[47] Nearly 96 per cent of Jews lived in the Pale according to the 1897 census.[48] Barred from agriculture, the professions and civil service, and facing university quotas, Jews turned to commerce and trade, including tailoring, shoemaking and joinery.[49] Life in the Pale led to changes in occupational structure, especially for women.[50] While pogroms, such as the one in Kishinev in 1903 and elsewhere, and the failure of the 1905 Revolution, provided additional impetus to leave, many scholars argue that population increases and poverty had the greatest impact.[51] For several million Jews, the opportunities of the industrializing West offered their best hope for the future.

Why Britain?

Only a minority of immigrants chose England.[52] Some paid for tickets to America, only to learn they had disembarked on the Thames.[53] Others believed that America could not sustain a Jewish life and the financial and physical demands of crossing the Atlantic inhibited still others. As the second largest country of reception for Jewish immigrants, Britain offered temporary refuge for thousands. England's tradition of asylum and the pre-existing Jewish community rendered it an attractive destination; immigrants could draw on existing philanthropic services and utilize family networks for assistance with housing and work.[54]

'England for the English'

Despite generous assistance from Britain's Jews, increasing concentrations of immigrants in neighbourhoods of London, Manchester and Leeds further aggravated anti-alien sentiment. Comments about the impact of immigration on England and Englishness reveal a great deal about how and why established Anglo-Jewry responded to the new arrivals the way it did. Negative assessments of immigrants increased in the popular press and journals. One writer associated Jews' appearance and habits with their 'narrow Oriental ideas'.[55] Jews competed unfairly, undercut rates, toiled through the night and put wives and children to work.[56] A 1903 article from *Blackwood's Magazine* reminded its readers, 'if the argument of "England for the English" carries any weight at all, the intrusion of a compact alien element into the heart of London cannot be considered, at the same time, other than a calamity'. 'Hebrew tenacity' accounted for Jewish unwillingness to play fair, for Italians and Jews did not 'recognise the sanctity of the "pitch", but will rise before dawn to oust an old occupant who has worked up a connection'. Despite the natural resentment such actions generated, the author proudly proclaimed that native wage earners never responded with Continental-style anti-Semitism. While a colonizing country could not take claims such as 'England for the English' too far, 'the inexorable law of racial rivalry enjoins that London shall be for Londoners, not for alien hordes debilitated by social and legislative persecution'.[57]

Government officials shared this pervasive attitude. A 1904 article from the rather reactionary *Daily Mail*, described by a Metropolitan Police report as 'fair and impartial', claimed that penniless 'uninvited guests' dislodged English citizens, participated in crime and had a detrimental impact on trade.[58] Competitors exported 'maimed' and 'criminal' elements to England who were, 'not citizens of the highest type, but beings to whom even the squalor of an overcrowded slum quarter in East London is paradise'. Immigrants worked 'for wages on which the Englishman would starve'.[59] Anti-alienists such as Arnold White felt it essential to eliminate aliens whose living and work habits undermined the health and welfare of the nation.[60]

Many reporters and charity workers who visited the East End also found it an exotic locale – intriguing, but foreign.[61] And the native-born Jewish community did not entirely deny these assessments. Indeed, the Visiting Committee of the JBG noted 'the deplorable conditions of homes in which the poor have to live'. Visitors used every opportunity to improve both the image and the reality of tenement life, to teach cleanliness, thrift and self-help, an approach that historian Frank Prochaska has described 'as social gospel to Victorian philanthropists'.[62] While anti-alienists tended to assume a Jewish indifference or even inherent tolerance for dirt, many established Jews considered the conditions the unfortunate by-product of overcrowding, low-paying jobs and Russian origins.

They were unsurprised that poor immigrants cared so little about the unsanitary nature of their dwellings:

> when we remember that so large a proportion of them come from Russia, and naturally bring Russian habits with them ... Of the Jewish poor in the Metropolis it is probable that ninety per cent are Russians. They have the Russian habit of living in dirt, and of not being offended at unsavoury smells and a general appearance of squalor.[63]

Poor English Jews differed from immigrants and lived in unsanitary conditions out of necessity.[64] Jews did have their defenders and immigrants recall valiant efforts to maintain cleanliness and the embarrassment associated with infestations of vermin.[65]

De-emphasizing Foreignness

Throughout the entire period under consideration, new immigrants spawned a complex set of issues for their more established co-religionists. Anglo-Jewry's social and economic standing, along with a certain apprehension over their own residual outsider status, fundamentally shaped their reaction to the wave of migrants. Many anglicized Jews regarded Eastern European Jewish men as 'bearded and observant out of habit' and their wives as 'be-shaiteled'.[66] Established Jews endeavoured to make immigrants less conspicuous because 'the habits of the foreign Jews in the East End, if not a menace, give rise to serious reflections on the community as a whole'. Noah Davis, an overseer of the poor, acknowledged, 'our motives are not wholly philanthropic; our own personal interests are involved, for we will have to take care of ourselves in looking after them'.[67] Recurrent references to foreign Jews and the potential backlash they might unleash dot the literature. According to the *JC*, outsiders did not distinguish among Jews , instead forming their 'opinion of Jews in general as much, if not more, from them [immigrant Jews] than from the Anglicised portion of the community'.[68] Furthermore, a number of contemporaneous writers argued that Britons, even those with extensive experience among Jewish immigrants, often misunderstood them.[69]

In the 1880s, established Jews worried that Britons might read retention of foreign ways as a lack of appreciation and saw 'the transformation of Polish into English Jews' as crucial to the community's future. While native-born Jews might not be able to make immigrants rich, they sought 'to render them English in feeling and conduct'. The *JC* complained that immigrants still behaved as they did in Poland and showed 'no desire to assimilate ... They appear altogether to forget that in accepting the hospitality of England they owe a reciprocal duty of becoming Englishmen'.[70] By the 1930s, anglicization, education and social mobility meant many children and grandchildren of immigrants moved to areas with larger numbers of native-born Jews, leading to increased contacts and greater integration within Britain's Jewish community.[71]

Approaches to Anglicization

Jewish charities, settlement workers and educators adopted a multifaceted approach: they focused on sanitation and mothering practices to lower illness and mortality rates; through educational and recreational programmes, they sought to develop character; and to diversify the occupational structure, they steered workers away from traditional immigrant trades.[72] Anglo-Jewry encouraged a wider geographic distribution of Jews and patterns of recreation and attitudes that more closely resembled the culture at large. Many of the lessons reflected both the gender and class divisions common at the end of the Victorian era.[73] Immigrants accepted many of these efforts with limited resistance, but they did reject some attempts to modernize religious practice, education and child-rearing.[74]

Battling Anti-Alien Sentiment

As the anti-alien campaign increased in potency, the Jewish community developed a defence strategy: they bestowed credit on immigrants when their behaviour met with approval, and exposed anti-alienist exaggeration and bias. Stuart Samuel, MP, pointed out that in 1903 only 1,753 aliens depended on government assistance and while some drew on the rates, a much greater number paid in.[75] Immigrants arrived poverty-stricken and harried from a long trip – and their appearance provided grist for the anti-alienist mill. Most, however, found housing and work very quickly. In a report on Poor Jews' Temporary Shelter (PJTS), the *JC* informed readers that the Shelter had a clean bill of health for 1901. 'There could be no clearer proof of the unjustifiability of calling the alien immigrants physically unfit, than this total absence of all reports of sickness among them, even after a long and wearisome journey'.[76] Nonetheless, the 1903 Royal Commission on Alien Immigration led to demands for more stringent control and the Aliens Act passed in 1905. Although numerous officials denied that the Act sought to restrict Jewish immigration specifically, most scholars challenge that contention.[77]

The East End

London's East End, where Jewish immigrants tended to settle, had developed as a working-class area in the early nineteenth century with the building of the docks. The demand for labourers spawned housing and the area expanded rapidly in both its residential and industrial sectors. From the mid-nineteenth century on, East Enders lived in overcrowded, dilapidated housing, accepting jobs characterized by long hours and very low wages, all of which could take a toll on their health. 'Perhaps the most noticeable feature of the entire district' announced the *Tribune* in 1907 'is to be found in the innumerable ragged children in every street, in every alley, in every courtway, in every yard. They swarm here like ants on a giant heap'.[78] From 1861 to 1901, Stepney's population consistently increased at a faster pace than its housing and the number of persons per house increased.[79]

Jewish Population Growth

In 1901, nearly half of all Britain's foreigners lived in London, and most of these in Stepney.[80] Jewish demographic patterns in London and elsewhere differed from those of other ethnic groups and had some important implications for socio-economic status.[81] One can estimate numbers of immigrants who arrived in London and the percentage of women and children among them from the census, reports from the Board of Trade and newspapers. Immigration officials did not have a specific category with which to enumerate Jews. However, English and American-Jewish scholars utilize data for those emigrating from Russia and Russian Poland and assume that nearly all were Jews. Jewish immigrants settled almost exclusively in urban areas, increasing the likelihood that Russians and Russian-Poles in London, Manchester, Liverpool and Leeds, or New York City, were Jewish.[82] While several factors make enumeration problematic, an early statistician of Anglo-Jewry noted that 'the Jews as a community are far more sharply distinguished from the rest of the population than any other religious body'.[83] As the data in Table 1.1 indicate, the Jewish population of England began a steady increase from the 1870s.[84] In 1887, Charles Booth estimated the Jewish population of the East End to be 45,000.[85] By 1914, estimates of the Jewish population of London ranged from 150,000 to 180,000.[86] Of those, about 100,000 lived in the East End.

Table 1.1: Immigration figures of Russians and Russian-Poles in England and Wales, 1871–1911.

	Russians				Russian-Poles			
	M	F	M	F	M	F	M	F
	Total	Total	%	%	Total	Total	%	%
	number	number			number	number		
1871	1,724	789	68.6	31.4	4,385	2,671	62.1	37.9
1881	2,639	1,150	69.6	30.4	6,097	4,582	57.0	43.0
1891	13,732	9,894	58.1	41.9	11,817	9,631	55.0	45.0
1901	34,013	27,776	55.0	45.0	11,562	9,493	54.9	45.1
1911	33,312	29,550	53	47.1	17,289	15,390	53.3	46.7

Source: Census Returns of Aliens in England and Wales, 1870–1911, cited in L. Gartner, *The Jewish Immigrant in England, 1870–1914* (London: George Allen & Unwin, 1960), p. 283.

From 1881 to 1901, the percentage of Jewish immigrants among all aliens continued to grow, constituting about 29 per cent of all aliens who settled in England between 1881 and 1911.[87] The East End suffered from very high population density, despite out-migration.[88] Although immigrants constituted a small percentage of the population, Jews clustered in particular East End neighbourhoods.[89] In 1881, approximately three-quarters of Russians and Russian-Poles lived in the parishes of Whitechapel, St George's in the East and Mile End Old Town, rising to 82 per cent in 1891.[90] Yet, foreign-born Russians and Russian-Poles constituted only 18 per cent of Whitechapel, approximately 11 per cent of St George's in the East and only a fraction of a per cent of Stepney and Poplar during the same period.[91] The movement across Commercial Street to the east began in the mid-1880s and towards St George's between 1881 and 1901. And by the late 1870s, Jewish communities developed in north-west London.[92]

Distinctive Demographics: Women and Children among Jews

The Jewish community's distinctive demographic patterns underscore the importance of gender and ethnicity in an analysis of immigration. Between 1871 and 1911, women made up a larger portion of Jewish migrants than other groups and that percentage increased over time. This trend likely indicates not only greater family migration, but suggests that women and children joined husbands, brothers and fathers. Significantly, many other groups travelled back and forth between Britain and their country of origin.[93] According to 1881 census data, women accounted for just over 40 per cent of Russians, Russian-Poles and Rumanians.[94] In 1911, the percentage increased to 47 per cent. In comparison, females made up 31 to 45 per cent of Italian, Austrian, German and Swiss immigrants.[95] By 1921, women accounted for almost half of Britain's foreign-born Jewish population, which probably reflected the deportation of some Russian men during the First World War.[96]

Jewish marriage patterns, age distribution and birth rates also distinguished Jewish immigrants. The 1911 census recorded twice the number of Russian and Russian-Polish Jewish women over the age of fifteen as married than non-Jewish women. Jewish men over the age of twenty also married in much greater numbers than non-Jewish men.[97] As Tables 1.2a and 1.2b show, Russians and Russian-Poles' marriage rates exceeded those of other immigrants. The migration included more children than among other immigrants and the percentage of young adults was higher than the population generally.[98] Stepney's demographic curve remained skewed through the first decade of the twentieth century; in 1902, the unusually high proportion of married immigrants temporarily inflated birth rates.[99] Five years later the Medical Officer of Health (MOH) predicted that over time 'families will get beyond the childbearing age and the birth rate will have a tendency year by year to decline, and approximate more to the normal rate'.[100]

Table 1.2a: Marital status figures among immigrant males and females of different age groups, Russians and Russian-Poles.

Age	Unmarried		%	Married		%	Widowed		%
	M	F		M	F		M	F	
All	18,247	13,113	33	31,257	27,895	62	1,097	3,932	5
Under 10	2,050	2,015	100						
10–15	2,699	2,580	100						
15–20	3,450	3,527	99	11	68	1			
20–25	4,898	3,520	70	1,184	2,488	30	4	16	0
25–35	3,917	1,144	19	10,028	10,816	80	51	258	1
35–45	788	181	5	10,108	8,193	91	167	665	4
45–55	283	72	3	5,463	4,187	86	248	934	11
55–65	105	37	3	2,396	1,635	72	279	1141	25
65–75	34	20	2	878	439	57	226	700	40
75–85	20	14	6	174	64	43	102	184	51
85+	3	3	8	15	5	25	20	34	68

Table 1.2b: Marital status figures among immigrant males and females of different age groups, non-Russians and Poles.

Age	Unmarried		%	Married		%	Widowed		%
	M	F		M	F		M	F	
All	61,305	37,734	52	51,997	26,579	42	3,859	7,815	6
Under 10	2,681	2,559	100						
10–15	2,733	2,791	100						
15–20	11,293	6,842	98	25	149	1	2	1	0
20–25	17,387	7,960	88	1,360	2,072	12	13	29	0
25–35	16,451	8,679	50	15,510	9,134	49	158	440	1
35–45	5,332	4,100	27	16,181	7,607	69	406	990	4
45–55	2,477	2,502	22	10,962	4,631	68	753	1,716	11
55–65	1,197	1,340	19	5,890	2,109	60	934	1,933	21
65–75	573	722	17	2,462	739	43	1,126	1,795	39
75–85	164	214	16	563	130	29	515	795	55
85+	17	25	15	44	8	16	76	116	69

Source: Census of England and Wales, 1911, *Birthplaces* IX, Cd. 7017, table 4, 'Country of Birth, Condition as to Marriage and Age of Males and Females of Foreign Nationality in England and Wales', pp. 176–7.

Between 1901 and 1908, the birth rate for the parish of St George's in the East fell from 43.1 to 37.6 per thousand.[101] This likely reflected the shift of the Jewish demographic pattern towards England's and suggests that couples practised some kind of family planning.[102] The Jewish birth rate continued to decline during the twentieth century. According to Lara Marks, between 1870 and 1885, 'completed family size for birth cohorts of ever-married women was estimated to be 3 children among the old Anglo-Jews, while among the East European Jews settling in London it was 7.3'.[103] By the 1920s, leading researchers concluded that the Jewish birth rate had declined even faster than that of non-Jews.[104]

Mortality rates provide another perspective on immigrant Jewish life. In the Borough of Stepney, infant mortality declined significantly between 1899 and 1909.[105] In 1915, the infant mortality rate in Limehouse, a largely non-Jewish area, was 26.5 per cent higher than in Whitechapel, an area heavily populated by Jews. Experts believed many infants still died unnecessarily.[106] In 1904, the same year the Interdepartmental Committee on Physical Degeneration published its results, the Stepney MOH determined the death rate for the borough was 19.5 per 1,000.[107] Eleven years later, areas with the largest Jewish population had the lowest death rates.[108] Comparable patterns characterized Manchester. The central district of the city had a death rate of 26.74, while Jews, who lived in some of the poorest houses, had a death rate of 16.99. Mr Horsfall, of the Manchester and Salford Sanitary Association, who seemingly viewed Jewish immigrants as outsiders, found the Jewish rates especially striking.[109] Despite a comparatively better record than non-Jewish communities, the Jewish community remained anxious to improve sanitation and health.

Literacy rates also highlight differences among ethnic groups. Because a significant percentage of Jewish immigrants could read, they likely absorbed information from a range of sources – newspapers and pamphlets. Instructional materials, some of them with anglicizing messages, reached Jewish immigrants. Numbers are unavailable for Jews in Britain, but corresponding figures for the United States (1899–1910) suggest that about 75 per cent of Jewish immigrants to America were literate.[110] Traditional demands on men to learn to read and write Hebrew resulted in higher literacy rates among men than among women. Yet, while Jews have a reputation for near universal literacy among men, there is evidence to the contrary.[111] However, even if limited, access to information via the written word likely contributed to acculturation.

The demographics outlined above have a range of implications and suggest that Jews saw their departure from Eastern Europe as permanent.[112] Arriving immigrants regularly sought and received support from family members, who often aided close, as well as distant, relatives with travel fares to England, housing, food, work, childcare and local customs. Much of Eastern European Jewish life revolved around family and home; the continuity of this pattern in London, albeit with significant disruptions, provided a familiar and supportive environment that eased the adaptation of immigrants in Britain. The unusual demographic structure, combined with Judaism's emphasis on family and education influenced not only the size, structure and nature of family life in the immigrant community, but its educational, occupational and recreational aspirations as well. It may be that Jewish women, though perhaps more dependent, had greater economic security than women of other ethnic backgrounds.

Sanitation Woes Weaken Status and Damage Reputation

If the Jewish community's demographic structure differentiated it, so too did its residential patterns. Before 1900, most descriptions of immigrants, by Jews and Gentiles, emphasized their industriousness, sobriety and preference for private homes, rather than common lodging houses. In this early era of immigration, the main criticism against immigrants related to their lack of cleanliness. According to the *Lancet*,

> the large quantity of refuse from the fish, which forms a staple of the Jewish diet, mixing with the cloth dust coming from the workrooms, may contribute to create this unpleasantness, and under these circumstances, we would strongly urge the extensive use of disinfectants.[113]

Towards the end of the century, the rhetoric shifted, particularizing and racializing Jewish dirtiness.[114]

Because of the density of Jewish settlement in London, and related sanitation problems, immigrants received disproportionate attention. In 1904, Lord Rothschild conceded, 'it is unfortunately true that a large number of them [Jews] live in the Borough of Stepney ... that the rooms are insanitary, that more people live in a room than ought to be'.[115] Overcrowding, noted the *JC*, constituted an evil that led to 'the contamination of mind and body'.[116] Whenever possible, established Jews contested Jewish responsibility for the problems. As early as 1902, the *JC* blamed 'the constant demolition of living-houses to make room for factories, depots, board schools, etc.' and not Jewish immigration for aggravating 'the Housing Question'.[117]

Many investigators, including Beatrice Potter, highlighted Jewish distinctiveness. While she acknowledged that the men were sober, the women chaste and that both sacrificed comfort for their children, the Jewish 'race' could withstand 'an indefinitely low standard of life'. Their working lives were characterized by 'long and irregular hours, periods of strain, and periods of idleness, scanty nourishment, dirt and overcrowding, casual charity – all conditions which ruin the Anglo-Saxon and Irish inhabitant of the East End [yet] seem to leave unhurt the moral and physical fibre of the Jew'.[118] Many descriptions of East End Jews emphasized racially unique characteristics, and connected it to Jews' clannishness, commercial skills and disturbing competitive nature.[119]

Negative Impact of Overcrowding on Family Life

In 1901, one third of the residents of Stepney, London's second most densely populated borough, lived in overcrowded conditions.[120] That same year the MOH for the Borough of Stepney identified Jews as responsible for nearly 87 per cent of 434 cases of overcrowding.[121] High rents exacerbated bad conditions and forced whole families, and often boarders, to squeeze into one- and two-room flats. Many living quarters doubled as workshops, with hundreds of contractors working out of their homes. By day, food, garments and refuse collected in the kitchen. At night, members of the household used the room to sleep. Lily Montagu, the famed warden of the West Central Settlement, contended that overcrowded homes 'limited the outward realisation of the joys of family life. In tenement dwellings ... every corner of the *home* is utilised for some domestic or industrial purpose ... Excepting during the hours of sleeping and feeding, most scenes of family life are enacted in the streets'. Dwellings lacked privacy, so highly valued among those who visited and wrote about poor Jews. Children grew up as a crowd and not 'as members of a family bound together to devote of their best to the service of the State'.[122] The critical shortage of housing and congestion created tensions in many households, and social reformers believed that the stabilizing effects of family life broke down when children and husbands sought refuge in the streets or pubs.

Migration from the East End

By the interwar years, overcrowding in Stepney began to decrease.[123] Despite this improvement, in the years before World War II, Stepney had the 'the largest number of overcrowded families, the biggest areas needing clearing' in London. Fewer than 10 per cent of families had bathrooms; many lacked 'modern conveniences for washing and cooking, and the supply of water'.[124] Even with out-migration, new immigrants and slum clearances meant a slow rate of improvement.[125]

According to Mark Fineman, who worked for the JBG, the First World War marked the beginning of the East End's 'demise'. Jews left because of bombs and anglicized children opted to live elsewhere.[126] By 1929, the Jewish population in the East End declined to about 85,000.[127] Yet, the 1932 annual report of the Bernhard Baron St George's Jewish Settlement noted that except for unemployment, housing remained the most important social problem in St George's in the East.[128] Moreover, while much had changed, in 1938 the Jewish Health Organisation (JHO) announced plans to hold three lectures in Yiddish on air-raid precautions.[129] Between 1941 and 1951, the East End had experienced an 'accelerated' reduction of the Jewish population. The number of children declined 'by about three times as much as the aggregate Jewish population'; while older people remained, young couples chose to raise families outside the East End.[130] The community remained vibrant, however, until the Second World War, when rising standards and wartime destruction of East End property discouraged many Jews from returning to the area.

2 PUBLIC HEALTH IN LONDON'S JEWISH EAST END, 1880–1939

From Cradle to Grave: Cleanliness, Sanitizing Jews and their Neighbourhood and Public Perception

When large numbers of Jewish immigrants began pouring into London's East End in the 1880s, poverty, health and other social problems had been matters of national concern for some fifty years. Widespread belief in Jews' 'racial' distinctiveness and the theory that certain common diseases rarely affected Jews stimulated medical research.[1] Jewish scientists mirrored the typical range of views of their era. Some denied the concept of race altogether; others accepted it, but denied Jews' inferiority. Still others pointed to Jewish 'racial adaptability'.[2] Leaders favouring both open and restricted immigration used such results to promote their views on the impact of aliens on British society.

The influx of poor, seemingly unhealthy immigrants fuelled apprehension over degeneration, infant mortality and infectious diseases. Native Jewry, inspired by genuine concern, charitable obligation and anxiety, undertook to improve the health and reputation of immigrants and developed services that offered medicine with a conscious programme of anglicization. They developed services to address the health and living conditions of Jewish mothers and their infants and children. Records from the JBG, Jewish maternal and infant welfare agencies, and the annual reports of the MOH for Stepney demonstrate that Jewish services contributed to a decline in infant mortality and enhanced overall well-being while shaping the immigrant community.

The sanitary movement and its pattern of intervention, initiated in mid-nineteenth-century England, associated public health and sanitation with communal order and morality.[3] In 1894, life expectancy at birth was 39.1 years for Londoners, but only 30.9 for those born in Whitechapel.[4] Anti-alienists exploited the stereotype of weak, sickly looking Jews. Some emphasized inherent biological or racial features; others focused on the environmental impact of poverty in Eastern Europe and Britain. Fear of Jews' innate frailty raised concerns about their impact on British health.[5] Concern over 'national efficiency', raised in the wake of the Boer War, encouraged eugenicists to guard Britain from influences that would further reduce its citizens' vigour and influenced Jewish welfare efforts.[6]

Sanitation and Overcrowding

Negative press reports, such as the 1884 exposé published in the *Lancet*, described East End buildings as extremely overcrowded, inadequately ventilated and dirty. According to the *Lancet*,

> the presence in our midst of this numerous colony of foreign Jews gives rise to a sanitary problem of a most complicated nature. Their uncleanly habits and ignorance of English ways of living render it difficult to maintain in a wholesome condition even those more modern dwellings where the system of drainage is well organised.[7]

The efforts to improve sanitation provided justification for governments and volunteers to intervene in the lives of the working poor. Early on in the wave of immigration, the press directed criticism at landlords, forcing many to undertake improvements. Such condemnation also implicated women, implying that their domestic skills were substandard, or worse – that they were satisfied to live amidst filth.

Anglo-Jewry reacted rapidly, seeking to remedy real and perceived problems associated with Jewish immigrants. Their responses reflected established Jewry's evolving perspectives over public health.[8] In the 1880s, the JBG adopted sanitation of homes and workshops as one of its earliest battles. Even schools joined the efforts; eighty parents from the Jews' Infant School received 'useful domestic articles' for keeping their homes 'in a clean and tidy manner'.[9] Like their contemporaries Jewish philanthropists viewed such efforts as a 'form of a moral crusade'.[10]

Rose Henriques, of the Oxford and St George's Jewish (later Bernhard Baron) Settlement, described the housing as 'dreadful ... [with] staircases that stank'. 'The tragedy was that the smells didn't necessarily mean that the tenants were dirty people, although often they were'. Even with 'incessant cleaning', buildings 'stank of generations of overcrowded bodies and of outer clothing that become odorous from long use'.[11] Accounts from immigrants suggest women struggled against enormous odds to clean their homes and took great pride in their scrubbed steps, children and clothing.[12] In his memoir, Charles Poulsen described his mother's annual and only partially effective ritual of 'bugicide'.[13] In 1902, the Metropolitan Water Board took control of London's water and provided Stepney with a reliable water supply.[14] As late as 1939, 90 per cent of Stepney's homes lacked baths.[15]

Government and medical officials alike assumed that death rates in Jewish areas would be high. Much to their surprise, the extreme overcrowding and unsanitary conditions did not elevate death rates above local averages. A 1901 letter to the Housing Committee of the London County Council (LCC) from the MOH noted that in the Backchurch Lane area of St George's in the East there was a greater death rate from certain chest-related diseases, but overall, a lower death rate than in St George's in the East. The results surprised the MOH since the population was almost entirely Jewish.[16]

Overcrowding and Disease

Extensive overcrowding raised concerns over smallpox and phthisis and its transmission via clothing produced in East End workshops. In response, the JBG appointed a sanitary inspector in 1884. In its first six months, the Sanitary Committee visited 1,747 houses and 'sought to inculcate habits of cleanliness amongst the poor, and to promote improvement in the condition of their homes'.[17] The inspectors found more than 1,600 water closets lacked water for flushing.[18] The Board's Sanitary Committee discussed a wide range of other concerns, including contingency plans for an outbreak of cholera and the appropriate response to the inspectors' reports of sanitary defects.[19] The Board's Special Committee on Consumption recommended against consumptive mothers breast-feeding, suggested publishing a leaflet 'in a language which the poor understand', and registering households engaged in home work, so inspectors would know the location of such workshops.[20] By 1900, the JBG reported success in 'arresting the spread' of tuberculosis.[21]

Despite increased attention, tuberculosis remained problematic. In cooperation with the MOH, the JBG asked their health visitors to keep records of families.[22] Tuberculosis left countless immigrants permanently disabled and had a disruptive impact on family life. More men than women contracted tuberculosis, compelling many women to become the sole supporters of their families and forcing some mothers to place their children at Norwood, the Jewish orphanage.[23]

In the years before World War I, the MOH for Stepney found more phthisis in the borough than the whole of London, and two Jewish districts, St George's in the East and Whitechapel, had more cases than in Mile End and Limehouse.[24] By 1913, the Health Committee of the JBG added over 1,200 new cases and discovered a proportionally greater rate of infected women and children than in previous years.[25] Typical of this period, the staff at Stepney's tuberculosis dispensaries became increasingly activist in their response; doctors began examining whole families, bringing previously undetected cases to light.[26] The JBG now concentrated on the health of the working-class poor to a greater degree than previously and professionals gradually replaced some of the volunteers.[27]

Smallpox too presented a major problem for London's poor and debates raged over vaccination. Public health workers endeavoured to remove the very ill to hospital and to vaccinate the healthy.[28] In one example, upon discovery of smallpox, the MOH prohibited the family from removing garments from a home workshop and fined them for ignoring his warnings.[29] Despite their overcrowding, immigrant Jews had proportionally less smallpox than their neighbours, and fewer cases than among native-born Jews. The MOH commented on this unexpected finding:

> Considering that within two or three years of their [Jewish immigrants'] arrival in Stepney from the Continent, they are almost totally ignorant of the rudiments of sanitation and that overcrowding is more prevalent among them, than among any other class of the community, the immunity of aliens from small-pox can only be explained by the fact that they are exceptionally well vaccinated.[30]

Youth clubs too had to contend with the implications of the disease. In February 1902, in a contentious decision, the Stepney Jewish Lads' Club barred members from the club 'unless they were re-vaccinated'.[31]

Causes of Infant Mortality

Pregnancy and childbirth, in particular, constituted a central formative experience for women – one with medical, educational and social implications. High mortality and low birth rates became a matter of national attention and figured prominently in medical circles at the turn of the century. Efforts to eliminate 'physical degeneration' and to increase 'national efficiency' informed the policy of many social service programmes.[32] Some municipalities began publishing pamphlets on childcare as early as the 1890s.[33] In Europe and America, the field of paediatric medicine developed and mothers' education, associated with her character, became a central element in the attack on infant mortality.[34] Debate continues whether better nutrition, decreasing virulence of infections, improved hygiene or the increase in health visitors had the most impact on infant mortality rates.[35]

One of the most common causes of death among infants was diarrhoea. To help combat this, the MOH distributed leaflets in English and Yiddish to nearly 8,000 homes with newborns stressing that breastfeeding minimized diarrhoea. To improve the health of infants, the MOH believed it necessary to understand the motivations for bottle-feeding when human milk provided superior nutrition, was less expensive and boosted immunity.[36] Some scholarship challenges the claim that breastfeeding declined between 1905 and 1919.[37]

By 1900, in an effort to lower infant mortality rates, local officials promoted motherhood classes and the creation of milk depots where mothers could purchase sterilized milk. The Milk Act of 1914 and the Milk and Dairies (Consolidation) Act of 1915 regulated the milk supply, but effective enforcement occurred only after the First World War.[38] Until then, many babies received milk that was spoiled, infected with the tuberculosis virus or adulterated. Inaccurate scientific knowledge and poor home facilities meant many babies received improperly sterilized milk.[39]

While health officials encouraged nursing, they were also anxious to improve 'artificial' feeding.[40] Depot organizers often failed to consider the realities of women's lives. Work, childcare, travel time and expense often made milk depots less convenient and more expensive than local sources. Focusing on supposed ignorance rather than real challenges meant reformers and government officials avoided consideration of deeper structural and economic causes.[41] While incorrect assessments provided contemporary justifications for new services, increased education for young mothers, early detection and food supplements probably aided the health of mothers and babies.

According to the Stepney MOH, mothers knew appallingly little about caring for their infants, clothed them improperly and provided them with diets that included tea, bread soaked in grease, meat, fish and vegetables.[42] Proponents of scientific motherhood advised women that they needed expert medical and scientific advice to raise healthy children. Social theorist Helen Bosanquet blamed mothers' ignorance for a great deal of physical degeneration.[43] In 1907, with the passage of the Notification of Births Act, the government and local authorities gradually systematized contact with new mothers. By the twentieth century, women increasingly received the message that they were responsible for their family's well-being, but incapable of that task.

Staff working in London's hospitals and health centres tended to view Jewish mothers as more skilled than their neighbours. They believed that Jewish mothers generally breastfed their babies, and because nursing required the mother's presence, most concluded that Jewish mothers stayed home with children. Dr Salaman claimed that Jewish mothers of all classes, but particularly among the working classes, breastfed to a much greater extent than non-Jewish mothers. Nursing, which resulted in 'temporary barrenness', gave mothers' 'vital organs' time for 'anatomical restoration and physical rest' and reduced 'summer diarrhoea', which lowered mortality rates.[44]

Infant Mortality and Labour

In addition to maternal and infant care, the relationship between female employment and infant mortality led to widespread public debate. The National Anti-Sweating League, for example, argued that employment in sweated industry diverted mothers from their 'proper occupation as the manager of the family ... and the maker of the home'.[45] Many argued that employment of women caused high infant mortality rates and pointed to districts such as Limehouse to substantiate their claims. According to the MOH, Limehouse women engaged in factory work more than in other boroughs. They returned to work soon after giving birth and left infants with an older child – and it was this hand-feeding that caused the district's high infant mortality rate. In contrast, Whitechapel, with a large Jewish population, had a low infant mortality rate, because 'the Jewish mother suckles her baby, and if she assists her husband at all in his employment, it is done by the means of home work'.[46] Public health workers assumed that women who stayed at home were more likely to breastfeed babies and provided superior care to siblings or paid baby-watchers.

Various studies contested the view that mothers' employment caused infant deaths. By 1906, the *Lancet* concluded that maternal employment did not decisively influence infant mortality.[47] The MOH also challenged assumptions about the dangers of female employment.[48] Stepney's MOH determined that most forms of female employment did not harm mothers or babies when compared to unemployed women 'in equally poor circumstances'. The three causes of death most affected by prenatal conditions did not occur more often among children of industrially employed women as long as other factors were comparable. Importantly, the report addressed the real causes of infant mortality: poverty, insufficient food and rest. The MOH doubted that moderate labour injured pregnant women and the improved diet that work supported probably 'counteract[ed] its disadvantages'.[49] Yet, the predominant causes of infant death, wasting, diarrhoea and respiratory disease, 'were actually more lethal' by 1900 than they had been in 1875.[50] In a continuing effort to upgrade maternal and child welfare, health visitors promoted 'mothercraft' and attendance at infant welfare centres.[51]

Jewish Communal Care

Infant mortality rates, as shown in Table 2.1, remained high throughout London's East End and convinced Jewish community leaders to concentrate on maternal and child welfare. Further, maternal responsibilities, which brought women into regular contact with organizations established and staffed by native-born Jewish middle-class women, provided an opportunity to influence women and their children. Compared to its neighbours, the Jewish community's maternal care and education was quite sophisticated.[52]

Table 2.1: Infant mortality in Stepney, 1899–1933, deaths per 1,000 births.

Year	Limehouse	St George's	Mile End	Whitechapel	Borough	London
1899	216	199	161	147	174	
1900	227	141	166	140	166	
1901	211	185	150	140	165	
1902	197	160	163	117	155	
1903	165	170	122	138	141	
1904	208	161	146	143	159	
1905	163	157	141	119	143	
1906	168	141	126	123	136	

Year	Limehouse	St George's	Mile End	Whitechapel	Borough	London
1907	131	130	112	110	119	
1908	171	141	117	108	130	
1909	133	145	106	104	118	
1910	137	120	100	110	113	103
1911	189	170	138	106	149	129
1912	126	128	100	96	110	91
1913	130	117	104	102	112	105
1914	134	152	119	101	125	104
1915	128	136	107	94	114	111
1916	101	100	90	74	92	89
1917	118	139	85	90	103	103
1918	120	148	97	120	115	107
1919	70	95	72	91	79	85
1920	86	98	84	98	90	75
1921	98	77	89	83	89	80
1922	76	82	75	90	79	74
1923	59	83	57	60	62	60
1924	69	75	72	87	74	69
1925	74	85	70	70	73	67
1926	70	68	53	83	65	64
1927	70	78	59	78	68	59
1928	68	70	69	79	71	67
1929	119	80	115	60	88	70
1930	90	72	102	58	76	59
1933	46	58	67	46		65

Source: MOH, *Annual Report*, 1899–1933. Limehouse was a predominantly working-class area, and tended to attract Irish dwellers.

Prior to 1905, significant numbers of women of childbearing age emigrated from Eastern Europe and did not attend English schools. Given the sheltered environment of East End neighbourhoods, these women were initially less anglicized and thus less at home with English culture, than women who were born and educated in London. Jewish women preferred to deliver their babies in a familiar setting among staff who could offer advice and support in their *mame loshen* (mother tongue), Yiddish, and provide essential services such as circumcision. The first immigrant women lacked extended family in London, having left female support networks in Eastern Europe. Some pregnant women applied to the London Hospital. As a last resort, immigrants could enter the workhouse, but most rejected such foreign institutions.[53] The lack of Yiddish-speaking doctors and nurses in hospitals, and the additional problems of obtaining kosher food and of observing Sabbath in the workhouses, made such alternatives unappealing. Further, Jews faced occasional anti-Semitism when applying for Poor Law relief.[54]

A crusader for women and babies, Alice Model devoted much of her life to voluntary causes in the East End. Considered 'the pioneer of many social services for women and children', she began doing social work in the East End after her marriage in 1880.[55] Like a growing number of women of her time, Model, born in 1856, extended the acceptable horizons for middle-class women through her involvement in charitable activities, many of which represented an extension of the nurturing roles traditionally assigned to women.[56] Beginning in 1895, Model actively promoted health care among the poor by establishing the Sick Room Helps Society (SRHS).[57] A unique Jewish contribution, the involvement of women in public health had roots in the mid-nineteenth century.[58]

Initially, the society had limited functions, generally helping in the homes of the poor, soon after babies were born. Before the establishment of the SRHS, poor mothers rested no more than two or three days before they returned 'to their domestic duties to the detriment of their own health and that of the infant'. SRHS helped with the baby and cleaning and 'perform[ed] the many tasks which belong to the wife when in health'. The Society's twenty helpers and three trained nurses quickly gained approval in the community.[59] 'This experiment', noted the JBG in its 1896 annual report, 'has proved a blessing to many poor families'. The committee believed their services meant 'the most distressing incidents attending sickness in poor homes have been removed'.[60]

Model's tireless efforts helped systematize maternal care among the poor. In 1895, the SRHS established a Mothers' and Babies' Welcome.[61] Four years later they hired trained maternity nurses and by 1906 added district nursing. While the JBG had a tradition of providing grants for maternity cases, they did not provide medical care or education. Model worked with the Board and together, in 1900, they agreed that the Board would, at a cost of ten shillings per case, refer maternity cases to the SRHS.[62] A year later, the Board reported that 'the arrangement with that Society works admirably'. They were especially satisfied that the SRHS had distributed relief in the form of nourishment and that there had been 'no diversion of the grant from its legitimate object'.[63] The SRHS served as an important referral service, informing the Board of cases that required their attention and provided a model for many similar services.

To assure good care during and after pregnancy, Model also founded the first maternity home for Jewish women. Many an East End baby came into this world at the Jewish Maternity Home, known as Mrs Levy's Lying-In Home (named after its first matron), which served immigrant women who could not afford doctors.[64] The home, with room for six women, opened in Underwood Street, Whitechapel, in 1911 and trained midwives. It was so popular that it required expansion by 1916, a project that ultimately waited until the end of the war.[65] Like their contemporaries, leaders of the SRHS wanted to help raise the quality of infant life. In 1915, they described their work as:

a eugenic work, inaugurated years before Eugenics attained its present vogue. But in the best sense it has been a national work, for what is more valuable to a State than healthy human life? At a time when the plains of Europe have become a vast shambles ... [the] object [of the SRHS] is to maintain rather than destroy existence.[66]

Convinced that maternal education would drive down mortality, schools for mothers and infant and child welfare centres became particularly important just before World War I. Ruth Eichholz supported the establishment of a school in the East End, even though the Jewish community had the lowest infant death rate of any group in Britain.[67]

Mothers' meetings began in 1896 and attracted ten to fifteen workers and about fourteen mothers. By 1902, just four workers and eighty-five mothers attended, forcing organizers to turn many mothers away. During meetings, mothers learned to sew and heard 'short practical lectures ... on the care and feeding of babies'.[68] Reformers sought to influence not only what people ate, but encouraged regular family meal times.[69] Volunteer and social welfare agencies directed attention at those who would have the most influence on children. In the years before the First World War, there were three Jewish schools for mothers, one connected with the SRHS, one in Leman Street and one in Stepney.[70]

The *JC* reported that non-denominational schools for mothers in Stepney and St George's in the East did not attract Jewish women because they could not understand the centres' doctors. They were, however, interested in education and wanted 'to do the best for their children'.[71] In 1914, Model and Eichholz considered the establishment of additional centres as 'a matter of the very greatest importance'. They wanted to bring the most progressive methods to the East End, and to enhance the already impressive record of Jewish mothers. Reformers found it easier to influence young mothers than older women, who had 'successfully reared part of their large families in the old-fashioned manner'.[72]

The impact of disease, the decline of Empire and increasing international tensions fuelled concerns over public health. World War I added a sense of urgency to the interest in mothercraft. Schools for mothers doubled in number during the First World War, most taking the name Infant Welfare Centre. The change reflected the declining emphasis on maternal ignorance among maternal and child welfare workers.[73] It was 'imperative', according to one physician, 'that we should save every saveable baby from any preventable maiming, since so much of life and health is being poured on the battlefield'. The doctor wanted to convert the Mother's Arms pub into a milk house, crèche and clinic and likened the saving of babies to a form of war service.[74]

By the interwar years, the SRHS had improved their facilities and acquired the 'accessories desirable in a modern maternity hospital'.[75] The Jewish Maternity Home (JMH) had kosher food and a Jewish atmosphere, offered prenatal advice and evolved 'into a complete maternity centre'.[76] The JMH undertook fundraising to extend the home and ultimately to rebuild it, through public appeals as well as by seeking grants from the King Edward Hospital Fund.[77] In 1925, the beneficence of Lord Bearsted (Marcus Samuel) enabled the maternity hospital to purchase the adjoining house. The new home had a reputation of rivalling the West End's best facilities, and in 1933 it gained the status of a hospital.[78] By 1926 the SRHS's Mothers' and Babies' Welcome had a medical practitioner and two health visitors. They held consultations three days per week and saw "'minor ailments'" every day, an important preventive measure. They also had a prenatal clinic and monthly social gatherings for mothers and members of the committee.[79] Well into the 1920s, the clinic emphasized teaching mothers about the 'feeding and rearing of their children'.[80]

Despite the impressive expansion of facilities and medical care, the needs of the Jewish community in and out of Stepney increased at an even faster rate. By 1920, the JMH received at least 1,000 applications for admission and the hospital had to turn away some women.[81] The hospital emphasized its low maternal death rate of 1.02 per thousand – one-fourth of England's rate – in its fundraising literature.[82] In 1935, the hospital made a special appeal and in 1937, they again sought funds to build a new maternity hospital with fifty-one beds, including twelve private rooms, an isolation block, a nurses' home, an antenatal department, an x-ray department, a pathology laboratory and lecture rooms.[83] By 1938, the hospital had relocated to Stoke Newington in north-east London, as more than half of the patients now came from Stoke Newington, Hackney and Stamford Hill.[84] Despite the acculturation indicated by movement out of the East End, the JMH had a continuing demand for Yiddish literature.[85] Not everyone agreed with the JMH's methods, such as its use of midwives. In a letter to the *East London Observer* (hereafter, *ELO*), one reader complained that the maternity home was becoming a school of midwifery. He expressed dissatisfaction that women received treatment from probationers.[86]

High Jewish birth rates, however, meant that both the extent and the quality of maternal and child welfare received ongoing attention during the years prior to World War II. Stepney boasted excellent services and received recognition beyond the borough. The 1930 report of the MOH referred to the recent decision of the Carnegie Trust not to build a maternity and child centre in Stepney because plentiful provision existed in the borough.[87] During the years before World War II, Stepney's private (voluntary) and municipal (non-sectarian) centres offered courses in home nursing, cooking, domestic economy and sewing. Of Stepney's ten voluntary centres, four were Jewish. Ten days after a baby's birth, a health visitor called on the mother and told her which centre she should attend.[88] Centres offered medical consultations, weighed babies, sold medicines at low prices, offered lectures in 'simple language' and conducted needlework classes to teach the making of proper baby clothes.[89]

In the mid-1930s, the Jewish Infant Welfare Centre experienced steady development in reaching its goals. Mothers attended with greater regularity and now brought children for several years, thus eliminating many of the health problems that arose when children only attended for a few months. Furthermore, the general level of health, clothing and cleanliness had all improved.[90] Various infant welfare centres still had to convince some mothers of their value and this may well indicate resistance to middle-class interference and English methods such centres sought to introduce.

The decreased mortality rate notwithstanding, many babies from St George's in the East were still born into great poverty. In 1933, Ruth Eichholz joined a controversy over the impact of conditions versus maternal competency. She had been active at the Infant Welfare Centre in St George's in the East for fifteen years. She described the obstacles mothers faced in trying to provide 'the primary needs' for their infants. 'In squalid courts devoid of light, with primitive ... sanitation, with walls with vermin, it is not possible to rear babies to a robust childhood'. While East End women gave birth to many babies who grew up to be healthy,

> there are too many who ... show a constant record of ill-health and debility – more marked latterly on account of the general economic depression. These young mothers make every effort to carry out the advice of doctors and health visitors, and they are broken hearted when they see their endeavours frustrated.[91]

Lady Sassoon served as president of the Jewish Infant Welfare Centre, which helped alleviate need during the economic depression of the 1930s. The centre provided mothers with forms enabling them to obtain free milk and gave them information about sources of relief.[92] Sassoon noted that some areas of London were less affected, but 'the dark cloud of unemployment and underemployment still broods heavily on the majority of our mothers, with the repercussions of ill-health, fatigue, frayed nerves, and domestic anxiety'.[93] The centre accepted the siblings of infants who attended, giving the staff additional opportunities to influence mothers and children.[94] Aware of the limited resources available to East End mothers, the Infant Welfare Centre ran a holiday home in Broadstairs, on the coast of Kent, for mothers and babies.[95] These holidays helped mothers recuperate from the privations they faced in their daily lives. Despite the overall tone of satisfaction, inadequate funds prompted appeals for donations. The authors of the 1938–9 annual report reiterated that the centre served as one of the few ways to overcome the difficulties of raising children in the congested East End.[96]

Caring for Children

Children too benefited from devoted parenting and communal programmes. Feelings of kinship, the desire to reduce cost through prevention and to promote behaviours that improved health and public perceptions – influenced the development of medical and social services.[97] In 1904, Dr Alfred Eichholz, the medical inspector for Lambeth schools, testified that the height of children, many of whom were foreign-born or the children of immigrants, at the East End's Gravel Lane School compared very favourably with children from schools in the best neighbourhoods. Rickets, which usually affected 50 per cent of children in poor schools, and 8 per cent in good schools, occurred in only 7 per cent of poor Jews.[98]

Jews and Christians alike praised Jewish mothers. According to the *Jewish World* (hereafter *JW*) squalor and poverty, conditions that excused 'the grossest dereliction of maternal duty' among other people, were 'simply non-existent even amongst the worst placed and poorest of Jewesses'.[99] Dr Smith, a witness to the 1904 Interdepartmental Committee on Physical Deterioration, contended that unlike Christian mothers who neglected their children, Jewish mothers provided better care 'because there is so much less drunkenness amongst [Jewish adults]'. Overlaying, a significant problem among the poor, rarely occurred among Jews.[100] Jewish children were 'much fatter and sturdier' than Christian children; it was rare to find an emaciated child.[101] Another witness, J. Prag, active in Jewish communal organizations and a merchant in the City of London, refuted charges that Jews lowered the standards of life in East London, claiming Jewish parents would starve themselves to enable their children to attend school. Immigrants had a 'fine physique' and Jewish mothers, maintained Prag, 'are a pattern to their Gentile neighbours in the East End'.[102] According to the Vice-Chairman of the Mile End Guardians, Jewish children received better quality lunches, 'which often consists of a meat sandwich and a banana', and during inclement weather, mothers met their children at school with coats and umbrellas.[103]

Many Londoners believed Jews were more respectable than their neighbours. Descriptions of working-class life in London often mention domestic violence and heavy drinking.[104] While not totally absent in the Jewish community, Jewish immigrant women rarely complained about such problems. Because poor Jews were 'always temperate', they 'usually [had] more to spend on food than a less temperate neighbour of equal poverty – no mean advantage in the struggle for life'.[105] Such perceptions of the different quality of family life continued into the years before the First World War. Although commentators claimed that English Christian children got more air, their inadequate diets consisted of condensed milk, tea, dry bread, drippings, jam and lacked fat. In contrast, Jewish children received wholemeal bread, eggs, oil, butter, fish, pudding and potatoes.[106] There were exceptions to the high standard of care. Basil Henriques described a member arriving at the St George's Jewish Club 'in a filthy & verminous condition', who 'howled like an animal' during a forcible washing.[107]

While Alice Model and others praised the care that Jewish mothers provided, they believed Jewish mothers would benefit from 'mothers' consultations'.[108] Rose Henriques, who moved to Stepney shortly before World War I, found a lot of superstition and desperation. One mother refused Henriques's offer of medicated shampoo, explaining "'Oh, but I wouldn't get rid of 'em – nits is 'ealthy, and some says they're lucky for the baby'". Another told Henriques that she wished she had gotten rid of her baby early in her pregnancy; her husband was unemployed, one child had already died and they had set nothing aside for the baby's arrival.[109]

Despite better health, as late as 1937 the JBG noted that many East End children still suffered from malnutrition and families of 'under-nourished children and pre-tubercular' children had 'crying needs' for milk, butter and eggs.[110]

The Jewish community and its agencies tried to meet a growing range of needs. The JBG's Health Committee turned to the best of science and hygiene 'to save the children of our poor brethren from the baleful inheritance of phthisis'.[111] They extolled the benefits of fresh air and country life in rehabilitating boys and girls 'with a tendency to disease'.[112] Describing this work as one of their most useful, they referred to the advantages of prolonged periods away from London. The Board had sent two hundred 'ailing children' to homes by the sea 'for periods varying from six months to a year'.[113] The children's 'ruddy cheeks and increased weights' proved its efficacy.[114] By 1924, the Board expected to begin construction on a second convalescent home near the shore that would offer medical care and provide a Jewish atmosphere and education 'during an impressionable year of their lives'.[115] The Jewish community also pioneered mental health services for children. The war years particularly accentuated problems owing to limited 'paternal influence' and mothers' war work.[116] The JHO responded to increased numbers of children with 'nervous disorders'.[117] Always conscious of the reputation of the immigrant community, the JBG allocated both time and money to improving the health of the children of immigrants.

In many instances medical care lapsed after children left school. Club leaders lamented the fact that school-leavers' families neglected treatment programmes prescribed in school. Settlements and clubs helped to fill this gap by instituting medical, and later dental, examinations for their members. In 1935, the Brady Club proudly announced the inclusion of a doctor's room in their new club facilities where girls would receive periodic examinations before heading off on club holidays.[118]

Eugenics and Children

The health of Jewish immigrants drew attention from many quarters and especially among those with a eugenic bent. In the mid-1920s, Karl Pearson and Margaret Moul studied approximately 1,200 Jewish children and used their findings to argue for immigration restriction.[119] They claimed that Jewish girls were inferior in intelligence to all Gentile children, and Jewish boys inferior to all but the very poorest of native-born British children. According to Pearson and Moul, one-third of the Jewish children they studied 'were in rather delicate, delicate or very delicate health' and the mothers of the Jewish children studied exhibited more ill health than among London's other working-class mothers and fathers.[120] Given Pearson and Moul's claims, it is inconsistent that they also found Jewish children in poor neighbourhoods to be taller and heavier than Christian children of similar circumstances.[121] They concluded that environment did not influence height and weight, but were 'racial' characteristics. Their research implied that Jews were biologically distinct and incapable of becoming thoroughly British.[122]

Eugenic theory, while more respectable in its time, indicates the kinds of attitudes accepted and fostered within influential circles and accounts in part for the pressures Jews felt to assist Jewish immigrants. Pearson and Moul's findings of Jewish inferiority led them to argue that 'any wise immigration law would admit into a crowded country only those who are physically as well as mentally *well above* the average natives'.[123] Over time, attitudes shifted and later studies, with biases of their own, concluded that compared to Christian children, Jewish children had superior intellectual abilities.[124]

The Jewish Health Organisation

Alongside the development of philanthropic services, health reformers founded the JHO. Established in 1923, it had a scientific and eugenic bent and employed three approaches to meet its objectives: investigations of health and sanitary conditions in schools and workshops; publication and distribution of literature; and free popular lectures on health. They promoted 'public health work and the teaching of hygiene' among Britain's Jews' and preventive medicine among East End Jews.[125] The JHO viewed the collection of data for statistical analysis as essential to enhancing public health. While some of the early anthropometric studies undertaken by the JHO reflected the racial theories of their time, the organization tried to debunk many longstanding racial myths.[126]

The JHO targeted highly visible projects and responded to complaints and allegations directed at the Jewish community. In the mid-1920s, the County Medical Officer found twice as many visual defects among Jewish as non-Jewish children and concluded that Jewish evening religious education classes aggravated short-sightedness. The JHO responded by forming a committee of ophthalmic surgeons. Following their investigation, the committee planned to publish a booklet 'addressed to parents and teachers' in both English and Yiddish on eye care that would emphasize 'proper requirements as to lighting, posture and rest intervals for children studying at home or in the evening schools'.[127]

JHO efforts suggest concern for children and discomfort with negative perceptions of Jews. While the JHO did not oppose health legislation, they believed that good health depended more on personal enlightenment than on official regulation.[128] In 1924, JHO medical professionals began an investigation of the condition of Talmud Torahs. They identified physical defects and recommended a plan to provide a medical officer to each school. Along with specialists, they would suggest physical changes, examine 'the weaker children' and arrange for their treatment.[129] Participating doctors received recognition for 'their zeal' in helping children receive Jewish education 'under healthy conditions'.[130] The JHO sought the assistance of the teachers, as their cooperation was essential in 'preventing physical and mental ill-health, and in raising the standard of racial physique'.[131] To this end, the JHO arranged lectures on 'school hygiene' for Hebrew school teachers.

Although the 1928 JHO report acknowledged progress in six Talmud Torahs, many remained unsatisfactory. Lack of money explained some, but not all failure to implement recommendations.

> A greater sense of responsibility for the physical well-being of the children would long ago have resulted in the removal of at least some of those elementary defects which would not involve any appreciable outlay, but willingness to take action and appreciation of its need are unfortunately not always present.[132]

JHO leaders expressed concern that poor conditions and 'overwork' might have a 'warping effect' on child development.[133] To encourage students to practise better personal hygiene, the JHO gave 'talks on cleanliness, and care of the eyes and teeth'. They made posters available to evening schools and asked headmasters to award them as prizes for 'personal cleanliness'.[134]

The JHO, however, remained dissatisfied with the rate of amelioration. Supplementary Jewish evening schools, whose students had already spent a full day in school, had a particular responsibility for their students' health.[135] The JHO felt obliged to step in if parents willingly exposed their children to risks. These conditions had a far greater impact on boys, who enrolled in Talmud Torahs in the thousands, than on the several hundred girls who attended this type of religious school. The organization justified their intervention, noting that 'the interests of the child, the community and the state are here identical'.[136]

Five years into its existence the JHO was more assertive, not only did they identify problem areas; they suggested that all patrons of Jewish schools make their assistance dependent upon the provision of satisfactory sanitary conditions.[137] Further, they called for the closing of those premises that could not be renovated and asked that the community force Jewish school managers to seek accommodations in day schools. The JHO regularly targeted immigrant-sponsored education, as they believed it compromised Jewish health.

Conditions among east London's Orthodox community continued to frustrate the JHO's efforts. The 1929 report on 'Supervision of Evening Schools' noted faulty lavatories and the absence of cloakrooms. 'Towel and soap are rarely seen; with this the schools should certainly deal'. The investigators tried appealing to the immigrants' commitment to religious observance. 'Apart from their being hygienic necessities, surely the religious rites demand the enforcement of cleanliness'.[138] Attention to the deficiencies led to upgraded heating and sanitation in several Talmud Torahs.[139] Children attended schools with conditions 'frequently associated, although only incidentally, with a type of religious instruction which is favoured by a considerable section of the Jewish population'.[140] Both the efforts and the rhetoric of the JHO revealed anxiety with the remnants of Eastern European life and the desire to modernize people as well as buildings. Consciously scientific in approach, the JHO used their studies to provide better conditions for East End Jews, but some of their assumptions mirrored some of those in the anti-alienist camp.

Immigrant Initiatives

For many years, the London Hospital had served Jewish patients by maintaining separate 'Hebrew Wards', and providing kosher food. In 1880, they cared for an average of 246 Jewish in-patients and approximately 2,500 outpatients, the cost of which exceeded contributions from the Jewish community. Sensitive to charges of Jews as a drain on public or private funds, Joseph Sebag pressed the community to demonstrate its gratitude by increasing donations.[141] Nonetheless, these services failed to satisfy some East End Jews.[142] In 1907, despite the availability of excellent medical institutions, East End Jews established the London Jewish Hospital Association and began raising money for a local hospital staffed by Yiddish-speaking doctors and nurses.[143] Hospital supporters believed patients' inability to describe their illnesses fully slowed recovery, especially from a psychological perspective. Opponents of the Jewish Hospital noted interpreters were available at local hospitals and denied that 'refugees' resorted to conversionist missions' dispensaries.[144]

Rev. Lionel Geffen, a vocal opponent of the hospital, argued that staff understood Jewish patients perfectly well, that there was an eminent Jewish doctor on the staff of the Metropolitan Hospital, and that a variety of people were 'always ready and willing to act as interpreters'. Frederic Franklin contended that Jewish wards in London hospitals already catered to the needs of Jewish patients. He feared that support for a Jewish hospital would divert charitable support for existing wards. Both Geffen and Franklin challenged the claim that the London Jewish Hospital's fifty beds would alleviate demands on other hospitals, since there were 500–600 Jews in hospitals at any one time.[145] Additionally, centralizing Jewish medical care contradicted the 'accepted' dispersion policy.[146] Some of the staff, however, of the London Hospital did indeed find it difficult to communicate with Jewish patients, many of whom spoke no English.[147]

Grassroots support for a Jewish hospital grew quickly. In its first eighteen months, the London Jewish Hospital Association reported that it had 'over 10,000 members ... paying a weekly contribution from a penny upwards'. The association's secretary referred to the opposition of 'our English Jews' and hoped they could be persuaded to assist the 'noble undertaking' which the Jewish working class had supported so generously.[148] 'The project has, of course, been consistently opposed by the richer and more influential members of the community, but this was quite expected, for these elements invariably oppose the establishment of new institutions, but accept control of them when they are firmly established'.[149] 'Mentor' offered a somewhat sarcastic analysis of Rothschild's opposition, noting the perception among philanthropists that better lights provide the best of everything, yet the poor still ask for more.[150] Those working to establish the Hospital noted that its doors would be open to Jew and Christian alike. They assumed that many Jewish patients would continue to utilize various London hospitals and expressed their gratitude, but maintained that those who did not speak English or who, because of 'religious scruples', were 'a source of trouble' to the staff, would have an alternative.[151] Supporters also maintained that it was 'only natural' that the very sick wanted to be among their 'own people'. In a letter to the editor of the *Daily Telegraph*, one writer argued poor Jews wanted 'Jewish surroundings' so they could 'follow their religious ritual away from the sometimes unsympathetic gaze of members of other creeds'. Italians, French and Germans in London, as well as the English in foreign cities, had built hospitals of their own. The Jewish Hospital would welcome all patients, but 'be adapted to the special requirements of the Jewish people'.[152]

By 1913, the Hospital had purchased a site and established a building fund. They placed a large advertisement in the *JC* emphasizing the need for more beds for Jews, the importance of environment 'in dealing efficiently with the Jewish poor' and stressed the value of the hospital in combating medical missions.[153] The outbreak of the war forced the Jewish Hospital to delay the opening of its outpatient department, but failed to end the debates over its necessity.[154] Lord Knutsford, Chairman of the London Hospital, defended his institution's care of Jewish patients and noted that Jews would be unlikely to choose a hospital unless it had the best staff. A hospital 'restricted to Yiddish-speaking doctors and surgeons, and Yiddish-speaking nurses', contended Knutsford, could not provide 'anything like the best skill or nursing', especially since so few Jewish women trained as nurses.[155]

The London Jewish Hospital, built in sections, opened in 1919. Several times in the mid-1930s they applied to the King Edward's fund to add facilities. The hospital had 108 beds by 1935 and wanted to double its capacity. In their public appeal, they stressed that the hospital had proven indispensable and 25 per cent of its patients were not Jewish.[156] While concerns about overlapping services and diverting Jewish support from general hospitals motivated some of the opponents, West End Jews exhibited insensitivity with regard to East End preferences for a Jewish atmosphere and frustration with the defiance the hospital symbolized.[157]

Missionary Medicine

Not every East Ender received medical care from the Jewish community. Christian missionaries responded to medical needs of some Jews, sponsored mothers' meetings and children's clubs. The 'exodus from Russia', noted the London Society for Promoting of Christianity amongst the Jews (LSPC), increased the number of Jews visiting the missionaries. 'Most of these came for the money, bread or clothing; but all heard something of the story of Redemption'.[158] Conversionist attempts, while widespread in the East End, had limited success, suggesting that immigrants had a utilitarian, rather than theological, interest in Christian-sponsored relief.[159] Though the LSPC claimed to be gaining increasing admittance into better Jewish homes, one staff member conceded that most Jews attending the mission were poor; some had 'sincere motives, others for what they could get'.[160] Missions denied that they offered inducements, yet they acknowledged providing food, medicine, reading materials and entertainment.

The Jewish community resented the missionaries' interference between children and parents, and masters and apprentices. According to the *JC*, missions attracted 'weak, unfortunate women, and especially helpless children', and provided services in areas where many do not 'even know that there is a God'.[161] Well-known Jewish physician Redcliffe Salaman, who trained at the London Hospital in the East End, also noted missionary activity. 'With enormous funds at their disposal', they used their money to 'corrupt a handful of weak-kneed Jews ready to adopt any creed at a price'. Yiddish-speaking officials gave a thirty-minute 'harangue' to Jewish immigrant women, who spoke no English, but sat with their screaming children, so they could receive medical treatment.[162]

Christian societies established their missions near the Jewish quarter and used various methods to reach Jews.[163] In bible classes, teachers used familiar Hebrew melodies that 'generally touch[ed] the Jewish emotions, and the words of the Christian message [brought the] consoling comfort of the Christ to the Jewish heart'.[164] Further, missionaries were quite open about the goals of their medical programme. They focused on women because 'medical work' provided an opportunity for influence.

> Hardly by any other means can Jewish women be brought into association with the Missionary; but when applying for aid, they not only experience something of what Christian love and kindness mean, but they are taught at least something of Christian doctrine, and not a few, chiefly of the unmarried, are induced to attend the classes specially held for them.[165]

The LSPC recognized that better off Jews 'seek medical aid elsewhere'.[166] By 1897, the London Society remarked that the Jewish community increased their attempts to counteract missionary work. Missionaries, however, understood the emotional as well as the medical needs of their patients. The Society offered 'sympathy, respect and careful treatment'. They communicated in Yiddish and the patients 'hear[d] words respecting their highest interests, which if they do not always understand and do not readily believe, yet are words that they find pleasure in listening to'.[167] Missionaries noted the speed with which immigrants learned of their existence. Despite the resentment they provoked, the East London Fund for Jews encouraged clergy and others to learn Yiddish to facilitate communication on East End streets where few spoke English.[168]

Missionaries continued proselytizing well into the twentieth century. In their 1927 report, the East London Fund for the Jews noted that Jews had 'great gifts to bring to the Church'. The Mission expressed optimism because Judaism was 'losing its hold upon the Jewish people'.[169] Children of immigrants tended to avoid such services as they became more familiar with Jewish and state-sponsored assistance and their level of acculturation made them less vulnerable.

While Jewish-sponsored services improved in scope by the twentieth century, significant gaps remained and missionaries capitalized on the situation. Some in the Jewish community saw the missionaries' presence as evidence of inadequate Jewish services. An investigation by a Jewish-sponsored Mission Committee concluded that immigrants did not need interpreters.[170] Yet, one section of the Report described many long-time East Enders who did not speak English and remained 'practically "Greeners" all their lives'.[171] Hannah Hyam, an active worker in the East End appended a note to the Report. Based on her experience, communication difficulties were 'the chief cause of the attendance of the better class of foreign Jew at the Medical Mission, and is thus the means of introducing large numbers, especially women and children, to the Missionaries'.[172]

Despite missionary efforts, the number of converts remained relatively small. According to Redcliffe Salaman, eleven societies and church missionary centres expended £88,426 in 1911, a figure that understated the amount, as many socie-ties did not publish accounts. The British Society for the Propagation of the Gospel took credit for sixty-two conversions that year, a negligible result consid-ering the nearly £6,000 they spent. Judaism lost far more adherents, according to Salaman, from 'indirect' methods such as non-observance – 'slid[ing]' from Judaism – than from conversion to Christianity.[173]

On the eve of World War II, when many had left the East End, the missions remained and attracted Jewish patients. In its monthly record, the Barbican Mis-sion to the Jews found that 'it was very encouraging to learn that patients come from long distances and preferred the treatment at our dispensary to anything they might obtain locally'.[174] Visiting Jewish homes continued to occupy a sig-nificant portion of missionaries' time. They remained focused on women. Men's suffering had 'embittered' them and they were 'the worst to deal with', 'the main obstacles in the way of talk about Christ'.[175] The editor of the *Jewish Graphic* reminded those Jews attending Missions that there was 'no need to accept such tainted gifts', and congratulated Rev. T. W. Manson, the superintendent of the Whitechapel Branch of the Presbyterian Mission to the Jews, for closing down his medical clinic. Rev. Manson concluded that raising 'even the faintest sus-picion that we are trading on the poverty and ignorance or youth of people in order to make converts, is to place ourselves in a hopelessly false position'.[176]

Undeterred, the LSPC encouraged Jews to utilize their medical dispensary for long-term treatment, enabling the Mission to provide regular Christian education. The Barbican Mission encouraged patients 'to come for dressings several times in the week, and in these genial surroundings a heart to heart talk is more readily possible, with the result that often the treatment is finished, but they still like to come regularly for a talk'.[177] Few Jewish communal organiza-tions responded with similar personal attention. As the JBG and settlements learned more about the missionary activity, they improved their own services and encouraged East Enders to utilize Jewish-sponsored services.

Conclusion

The range of sanitation and medical issues, and the expansion of maternal and child welfare services, suggest that prevailing, as well as particularistic Jewish concerns were integral to Jewish communal efforts. The experiences of the early years of the mass immigration taught the established community that anti-alienists gained many supporters from the attention they drew to immigrants' sickly appearance. Anglo-Jewry established public health services out of sincere motives and a conviction that English methods were superior to those from the old country. Prominent Jews participated in reform activities that typified

Victorian philanthropy. They viewed medical and sanitary improvements as an important route to integrating Jewish immigrants into the larger society.

By 1905, sanitation no longer occupied the singular position it had when Jewish immigrants first arrived; health and sanitation services became increasingly preventive over time. Despite the negative perceptions of them, Jewish East Enders had an impressive array of medical options from which to choose. And, Jewish health was surprisingly good given the circumstances – evidence of the high quality of Jewish mothering and comprehensive communal services. Immigrant women and children received assistance that healed not only body and soul, but also tried to change behaviour by instilling new values. This pattern reached its greatest level of sophistication in the years between the two wars.

By the outbreak of World War II, the East End's Jewish community had met their two primary goals: Jewish health improved dramatically and the community received accolades for its many services. Female volunteers saw themselves as part of a specifically Jewish contribution to the future. Native Jewry directed their efforts at immigrant women and their children and expected those whom they assisted to leave behind their traditional lifestyles, to adopt the English language, to feed and clothe their children according to English standards. While immigrants regularly took advantage of services, they did not accept all the advice they received. Some, especially those who arrived as adults, never learned English, continued eating Eastern European-style food and remained steeped in Yiddish culture.[178] As the controversy over the Jewish hospital demonstrates, some immigrants felt resentment towards their more affluent co-religionists. Even with the extensive change of the interwar years, one could still hear Yiddish on the streets and traditional Jewish foods – Dutch Herring, *beigels* and calf's foot jelly – filled market stalls.[179]

In the years after World War II, the welfare state would take responsibility for many services pioneered by private and denominational organizations.[180] While justly proud of their efforts, their didactic approach must have felt patronizing to East End beneficiaries. Medical and sanitation experts declared the improvement of immigrant health as their primary goal, yet the emphasis on hygiene and the improvement of dwellings and schools – areas that were visible and had been subjected to criticism – also indicate that communal leaders remained equally dedicated to eliminating vestiges of foreign culture, characteristic of some Jews.

3 COMMUNAL NETWORKS: TAKING CARE OF THEIR OWN AND EFFORTS TO SECURE THE COMMUNITY'S REPUTATION

'The reputation of the community', noted the JBG in 1893,

> is obviously a subject which touches vitally and directly all classes, and it is certain that the fair fame of the Jews in England is intimately bound up with, if indeed it does not directly depend on, the manner in which they apply themselves to grapple with this question of the care of their poor, aggravated as it has become in recent years by the immigration consequent on the cruel Russian persecutions.[1]

From birth to death, England's Jewish community provided an impressive range of assistance for a small community, including food, clothing, dowries, scholarships and industrial loans.[2] Whether consciously philanthropic or not, these efforts improved immigrants' quality of life and reinforced English cultural standards, values and contemporary gender roles.

As recipients of charity or as participants in social and recreational programmes, many immigrant women encountered more established Jews, large numbers of whom gave time and money to support such services. The resulting interactions played a role in anglicizing immigrants and developing a cadre of female leaders in Britain's Jewish community. While the Jewish community always accepted women's participation in charity, Jewish women's involvement followed much of the trajectory unfolding in Britain. Even as domestic duties remained paramount, new opportunities arose in education, employment and volunteerism, especially in the years leading up to and following World War I.[3] Often, and quite strikingly, self-consciously Jewish men and women explained their philanthropic motivations in language that mirrored the attitudes and gendered assumptions of non-Jews immersed in Victorian charitable work. Jewish volunteers and professionals absorbed the dominant discourse of their day, yet viewed their actions as quintessentially Jewish.[4]

Organizations such as the JBG, the Jews' Temporary Shelter and the Norwood Orphanage offered social welfare services. Others were more social, educational or political. The Jewish community developed 'an extensive support network for the socialisation of those who were determined to stay' in Britain. Generally, recipients accepted assistance with little complaint and rarely resorted to protest and violence. Jews, according to David Englander, did not garner the stereotype associated with 'the fighting Irish'.[5]

Several factors motivated Jewish philanthropists. *Tzedakah*, literally righteousness in Hebrew, and the term used for charity, is a Jewish obligation. Within Jewish communities, all are responsible for one another, with orphans and widows deemed especially worthy. A second influence derived from the British environment in which native-born Jews functioned.[6] As Todd Endelman has noted, Anglo-Jewish elites, while not traditionally observant, had a 'positive attitude' towards religious tradition. Among upper- and middle-class Christians, respectability included some level of religious practice, 'matters of "good taste" and "correct behaviour" as much as anything else'. Jewish elites looked to upper-middle-class Anglicans for guidance on domestic arrangements, fashion, recreation and religion.[7] Several scholars have suggested that acculturated Jewish women, unlike their husbands, responded to the social expectations of their day with regard to Jewish observance. In so doing, they created what historian Paula Hyman described as 'a Jewish version of the bourgeois Protestant wife and mother'.[8]

A myriad of Victorian charities, secular and religious, aided the 'deserving poor', promoted independence, 'the strengthening of character', self-help and morality. While Jews lacked the obsession that many Victorians had with sin, they feared that foreign-looking immigrants might endanger their own status if they became a burden on the rates.[9] Anti-alien, and arguably anti-Semitic, rhetoric described Jewish immigrants as 'birds of prey', implying they were parasitic. Rather than spreading out, which would make the 'evil' more 'manageable', Jews congregated in a small number of areas.[10]

Anxious to counter such views, established Jews sought to dissuade poor co-religionists from accepting non-Jewish charity.[11] By taking care of 'their own', Anglo-Jewry hoped to minimize the impact of large numbers of Eastern European Jews and meet the needs of their co-religionists.[12] Poor Law records from 1902 to 1904, suggest that the Jewish community had mixed success in keeping aliens out of the public relief system. During those years, Russians and Poles accounted for 56 to 62 per cent of non-vagrant aliens who received relief from the Poor Law. Those seeking assistance from the Poor Law, were however, a tiny fraction of Jewish poor assisted by Jewish communal charities.[13]

The Extent of Jewish Charity

Evidence abounds that Anglo-Jewry accepted their responsibility for aiding the poor. The JBG, a wide-ranging social service organization established in 1859, undertook activities that raised living standards, while attempting to improve the popular image of East End Jewry.[14] The JBG and the Russo-Jewish and JBG Conjoint Committee assisted approximately ten times as many Jews (not all of whom were aliens) as the Poor Law.[15] Table 3.1 summarizes the numbers of cases and individuals the JBG and the Conjoint Committee assisted. The JBG claimed not only to preserve, but to restore the independence and self-respect of those forced to apply for charity.[16] While many of these programmes drew on British models, Jews pioneered services in childcare, mental health, job training and provision of small loans for those starting a business venture.[17]

Table 3.1: Charitable relief from the Jewish Board of Guardians and the Russo-Jewish Committee.

| | Jewish Board of Guardians | | | | Russo-Jewish and JBG Conjoint Committee | | | |
| | Number of cases relieved | | | | Number of cases relieved | | | |
Year	Number of applications	Total number	Number of new cases only	Number of individuals	Number of applications	Total number	Number of new cases only	Number of individuals
1885	3,586	3,408	1,586	11,014	106	106	70	184
1886	4,497	4,139	1,944	14,357	151	151	109	174
1887	3,415	3,313	1,205	11,298	121	121		91
1888	3,719	3,513	1,318	12,921	379	307	278	316
1889	3,131	2,980	932	11,066	526	329	286	330
1890	3,569	3,351	1,319	12,047	391	252	205	472
1891	4,722	4,474	2,092	15,409	618	438	366	952
1892	4,552	4,313	1,527	16,801	1,697	1,387	1,155	1,654
1893	5,178	4,881	1,826	18,852	1,409	1,202	1,043	3,468
1894	5,421	5,157	1,757	20,434	727	612	469	1,919
1895	5,080	4,794	1,565	19,363	518	406	264	1,510
1896	4,686	4,366	1,529	16,744	502	429	305	1,334
1897	4,694	4,286	1,495		258	469	332	1,610
1898	4,907	4,462	1,837	16,241	767	657	459	2,074
1899	4,702	4,319	1,784	15,236	635	558	368	1,959
1900	6,069	5,439	2,903	17,614	713	640	471	1,921
1901	5,624	5,061	2,322	18,371	515	439	247	1,308
1902	5,330	4,806	2,082	17,790	434	366	229	1,084
1903	5,822	5,113	2,644	18,250	555	439	298	1,286
1904	6,602	6,018	2,807	22,859	620	397	241	1,111

Source: PRO, MH/19/237/97416, Papers Relating to Emigration and Immigration, Appendix, 70, 1904.

Although ambivalent, middle- and upper-class British Jews assisted succeeding waves of immigrants who settled in Britain.[18] N. S. Joseph, a long-time leader of the JBG, compared Anglo-Jewry's ability to absorb immigrants to a nearly full lifeboat. 'If we admit any more passengers', insisted Joseph, 'they must be such as can lend a hand to the oars, and keep the craft afloat ... to admit an unlimited number of helpless souls, who are mere dead weight, would not be mercy, but homicide'. By 1900, the JBG stressed its inability to aid new immigrants. They announced they would assist those 'arriving here [in England] in a helpless condition' by repatriating them to the countries which 'they had left with such deplorable absence of foresight'.[19] The Board resorted to the futile policy of trying to discourage Jews from settling in England. They sent messages to rabbis in Eastern Europe explaining that England could accept no more immigrants and that the Board would withhold relief for immigrants' first six months of residence. The JBG also earmarked funds to send immigrants on to the United States.[20] Severin Hochberg argues that the JBG hoped to prevent the passage of aliens' legislation by administering a restrictive policy internally. While a failure on that front, voluntary action may have reduced anti-Semitism between 1900 and 1905.[21]

Sheltering Newcomers

To make clear they did not want to attract new immigrants, the Board refused to support a shelter for the newcomers. Despite the Board's position, Hermann Landau, Ellis Franklin and Samuel Montagu agreed to finance the PJTS. The JBG hoped 'that the evils which they feared will not arise', but hoped the promoters would achieve their goals.[22] The *JC* defended the JBG's position, arguing that the 'benevolent but shortsighted men' who wanted to found 'a quasi-religious Refuge' would entice the wrong kind of Jews to England who would live a life of 'degradation and beggary'. Furthermore, their actions would encourage others to follow. Even more worrisome to the detractors, they believed the shelter would encourage a return to separatism that created tensions with non-Jews. English Jews had 'risen above both the separatism and its consequences' but the *JC* feared newcomers 'will not follow our example, and will create, if they have not already created, a little Poland in the East End of London'.[23]

Supporters of the shelter parried such criticisms by pointing to the 'preventive' nature of their work. They protected newcomers from those ready to 'despoil' them.[24] In 1901, the shelter admitted 2,350 individuals, 359 of whom were women and children and 1,632 had a regular trade. Only six remained the full two weeks and fewer than 700 stayed longer than a week.[25] For many, including the father of boxer Jack Kid Berg, the shelter at Leman Street, served as a first home and base from which to find employment.[26]

In 1927, during a fundraising dinner for the PJTS, Home Secretary Sir William Joynson-Hicks explained that owing to unemployment, Britain could not open its doors to refugees. In his response, Lionel de Rothschild recognized the difficulty facing the government, but reiterated the familiar themes of pride in English traditions of fair play and civility, and expressed gratitude that England took in refugees. According to Rothschild, 'there had always been fairness in this country in all things and ways ... If only British rule was in Eastern Europe, there would be no need for the Shelter'.[27] During the years prior to the Second World War, the shelter catered to significant numbers of trans-migrants, but aided local cases in need of a meal or a night's shelter, the majority of whom were healthy and under the age of thirty.[28] Persecution of Jews in Germany, Austria and Czechoslovakia increased demand on the Shelter.[29]

Additional controversies surfaced over the nature and control of Jewish philanthropy. In 1914, the JBG withheld assistance from twenty-five families, arousing criticism from 'decent generally self-supporting people' who had fallen on hard times. They accused the Board of a 'callous attitude', and suggested the unacceptable treatment of those receiving charity justified 'a public condemnation'. Some critics of the Board suggested the poor go on a hunger strike to bring publicity to 'the suffering of those dependent on the assistance of the Board'. One plan called for men with sandwich boards to display them on West End streets. Others cautioned against such action, fearing 'it would play into the hands of anti-semites'.[30] While the *JC* supported the JBG, they averred that the difficult situation of the poor called for 'a double degree of kindliness and sympathy'; the Board needed to temper discretion with mercy.[31]

The Board had its defenders. At an East End Society meeting, Rev. J. F. Stern acknowledged the need for accountability on the part of the Board, but considered the attacks scandalous. A 'tender hearted body of men' served on the Board; none had any interest in adding to the difficulties of the poor. Stern decried the critics' 'rash and random statements', and the unfortunate lack of gratitude of those, who 'on the slightest provocation, threatened to write letters to the JEWISH CHRONICLE condemning all and sundry, or as an alternative to go to the missionaries'. The JBG had 'the ability and genius to carry out the work required of it'.[32] The perceived insubordination of the poor disturbed Jewish leaders at least as much as the complaints themselves.

Scientific Philanthropy

The Jewish community took great pride in both the amount and method of their philanthropy. Articles on charity regularly appeared in the Jewish press, suggesting that, as a science, charity required the same careful study as other endeavours.[33] Many Anglo-Jewish organizations rejected relief based on sympathy in favour of investigation and 'scientific method' even before the Charity Organisation Society (COS), an organization well known for this approach. Jewish charities accepted much of the ideology of the COS, which saw character as essential to the reduction of poverty. Basil Henriques, however, found COS meetings exasperating. He described one 'very dull' committee meeting, where an 'old lady' kept asking questions about cases they were no longer discussing. While appreciative of COS accomplishments, Henriques complained that they 'only help the most respectable & spotless & the amount of time & trouble spent in discussing whether they are respectable and spotless seems to be rather wasted. The idea is good, but the system annoys me'.[34] Most Jewish leaders favoured eliminating overlapping relief and promoted services that did not pauperize.[35]

Eagerness to aid the poor, however, did not qualify one to work among them. Helen Bosanquet, a leader of the COS believed, as did many of her Jewish compatriots that lay people often contributed to the problem of poverty. 'The frivolous public', claimed Bosanquet, 'which, whether moved by fear, or pity or sheer carelessness, supported the great army of beggars, and made laziness and imposture more profitable than work'.[36] Loans, according to Bosanquet, were an appropriate form of aid, and she praised the model utilized by the JBG.[37]

The emphasis on science, however, led to additional layers of bureaucracy. Helen Lucas, with fifty-five years of experience in relief work, complained that unnecessary hardship resulted from delayed assistance. She held 'that a district visitor should see and help a case immediately'; discussion could follow. Critical of modern methodology, Lucas argued that relief workers needed 'common sense and sympathy' and to 'give less attention to statistics and clerical duties'. Her own experience taught her that 'the exercise of sympathy had a wonderful influence' over the girls in the JBG's workrooms.[38]

Such notions typified nineteenth-century rationales for women's involvement in charitable work. According to Frank Prochaska, the use of women visitors reflected society's view of the protection of the family as 'the cornerstone of nineteenth-century social policy'. Women, who were familiar with 'domestic management' and understood the problems of wives and mothers, best improved society by starting with individuals in their domestic settings. Further, parish work of this sort – which Jewish women also undertook – enhanced their status. Attending meetings and fundraising events provided middle- and upper-class women with a respectable activity outside their homes and reinforced a set of gendered ideals for providers and receivers.[39]

Women saw philanthropic activity as particularly suited to female nature. Middle- and upper-class women could undertake unpaid labour that drew on perceived female skills. Prompted to see the poor as friends, philanthropists promoted cross-class interactions.[40] Numerous historians have noted that for women, participating in voluntary organizations 'represented one of the very few bridges to the world beyond home and family' and combined adventure and duty.[41] During the early years of the twentieth century, middle-class women gained increasing opportunities for leadership roles. Generally, men and women alike saw these new women workers as having particular skills associated with their sex. Jewish women were 'rapidly showing that for certain departments of activity they are even better fitted than men. With greater leisure and freedom from anxiety that they can command, they excel in attention to detail'.[42] Rev. G. J. Emanuel thought women exhibited more skill as philanthropists than men. Unlike men, they could 'visit the houses of the poor. They can help their poor sisters to make the best of their surroundings, teach them something of sanitation, and the proper feeding of children'. Emanuel encouraged Jewish women to approach such work with religious feelings, similar to those they practised at home.[43]

Women's volunteer activity improved the reputation of the Jewish community. In its capacity as a coordinating agency, the Union of Jewish Women (UJW) could respond to 'gaps in the network of communal effort'. Their successes highlighted the benefits that accrued to the community when Jewish women took up philanthropic work.[44] Leaders such as Alice Model believed, 'it was only the leisured who could give voluntary work, but leisure in itself was a great responsibility'.[45] The *JC* dedicated their 2 January 1914 edition to women. Like other publications, they were 'appealing more and more to the intelligence, the sympathy, and the power for good of their women readers'. What, asked the *JC*, would happen to social work without 'strenuous [female] toilers' and how had they fared without women workers in the past?[46] At a November 1921 meeting, Rev. Green claimed that the Jewish community gained more from one woman serving on the Committee of the Hampstead Hospital than from her husband giving £1,000.[47] Interacting with immigrant women enabled social workers and volunteers to offer aid and encouraged anglicization.[48]

Women's Work

A number of the East End's most active women workers volunteered beyond the Jewish community. Alice Model sat on the Maternity and Child Welfare Committee for Stepney and represented Stepney on the London Federation of Infant Welfare Centres. Eichholz, Irwell and Model served on the Stepney Council for Infant Welfare. Miriam Moses, a social worker, active in the Labour Party and Warden of the Butler Street Settlement, sat on the Public Health Committee. The involvement of these women improved the networks of communication and coordination within the Borough of Stepney and between the Jewish community and other service providers.[49] Further, it demonstrates how philanthropy, an arena deeply embedded with gendered expectations, enabled women to integrate Jewish and secular interests and cultivate attitudes and behaviour among recipients.

The challenge of survival did not end with birth. Provision of childcare surfaced as a major issue and another arena for contact with immigrant women.[50] Poverty, illness and underemployment meant some mothers had to work; childcare became a personal and a communal responsibility. Towards the end of the nineteenth century, municipal and private maternal and child welfare agencies emerged. Decrying the use of baby-minders, members of these societies promoted the establishment of crèches and schools for mothers, and identified the working class in particular as ignorant about childcare.[51] Social workers used their contact with mothers to encourage adoption of English child-rearing.

In 1896, thanks to the efforts of Alice Model, a nursery for Jewish infants opened. A year later, it moved to Shepherd Street in Spitalfields, and offered places to twenty-five children.[52] Social reformers and health officials approved of the nursery's careful supervision of the children and credited the staff with adopting the 'best hygienic principles'.[53] Some feared pauperizing mothers, but the managers charged a small fee and noted that the crèche enabled mothers to work, and thus encouraged independence.[54] The LCC also favoured day nurseries, as they reinforced acceptable habits and influenced practices at home.[55]

The nursery prevented neglect and enabled staff to play a role in child-rearing and to exert control over the environment of a small number of youngsters whose mothers entered the work force. Rachel Adler, wife of the Chief Rabbi, involved in charitable work since the age of sixteen, said even when she was a young woman, there had been a need for a crèche. She once found 'a poor mother forced by circumstances to be the bread winner for her family – hawking, sewing, or "dealing" in the Lane'. She left her children 'with some old and decrepit woman, whose only qualifications for the task were that she was capable of doing nothing except sit at home'. 'Imagine' she continued, 'babies under such care! Left to crawl about in squalid rooms, fed on anything that might be at hand from cucumbers and strong tea to Dutch herrings and cheese, never washed, never bathed, never fondled, never caressed'. Adler credited Model with recognizing the difficulties facing working mothers. The nursery provided good care and brought 'cheer to poor mothers' who were 'lifted above the life of the pauper, away from the dole of charity'.[56]

The nursery took credit for eliminating many illnesses that had been 'rife in the East End' during the summer. Children remained at the nursery for twelve hours a day; the nursery bathed the children, disinfected their clothing and provided breakfast, dinner, tea, milk and clothing. They accepted children from five weeks to four years of age, but made occasional exceptions for older children who once attended the nursery.[57] While Jewish welfare agencies generally discouraged married women from working, Anglo-Jewry supported limited childcare institutions.

The facilities quickly proved too small, so they leased new accommodations from the London Hospital in May 1900. Admission required a medical exam.[58] Daily visits from a doctor helped prevent illnesses from reaching epidemic proportions, and 'rickets, that common trouble for weakly and underfed children, are nipped in the bud'.[59] By 1904, the nursery had an average daily attendance of fifty children, about 8,400 attendances per year, reaching a peak of 11,342 in 1914. By the interwar years medical personnel contended the nursery functioned as 'an antidote' to excessive parental affection.[60]

The day nursery, like many forms of philanthropy, had its detractors. Critics claimed nurseries enabled mothers to abandon responsibility for their children. 'E.H.C.' visited the day nursery to assess that charge. She described Mrs X, an Austrian charwoman, born with only one arm, whose husband deserted her after the birth of their daughter. Mrs X earned enough to support herself and her child until unprecedented poverty affected the East End. The SRHS then located work for her, but she lost her job because clients 'objected to seeing a one armed woman scrubbing and cleaning'. Mrs X's child attended the day nursery for 2*d.* per day. 'E.H.C.' concluded that abandoning responsibility was a distant thought for mothers such as Mrs X and the day nursery assisted mothers who worked hard to provide for their children.[61] Lady Rothschild served as president of the day nursery; most committee members lived in north or north-west London and included Rachel Adler, Alice Model, Mrs Nathan and Gertrude Spielman. These women played leading roles in nearly every woman's organization in the Jewish community and, in particular, in the UJW.

Philanthropists also provided meals, clothing and holidays to improve the quality of life for thousands of Jewish children each year. Table 3.2 shows some of the types and amount of assistance children received during the first decade of the twentieth century. The Jewish Children's Penny Dinners, for example, supplemented the diets of many children. By 1906, the twenty-one-year-old Boot Fund had distributed nearly 2,200 pairs of boots. Like many charities, they avoided pauperization by investigating the recipients, generally providing boots to children of sick or unemployed parents.[62] Rachel Adler, an active member of the Schools' Boot Fund sought the aid of Anglo-Jewry, to 'save' Jewish children 'from the ills arising from broken boots and wet feet which too often undermine their health and strength'. Ill-clad children were so anxious to attend school that a ten-year-old girl would arrive in her mother's 'discarded boots'. Despite her sympathy for these children, Adler did not want them or their parents to lose their 'feeling of independence', and always induced the parents to contribute towards the boots.[63]

Table 3.2: Types of charitable assistance for children.

Organization	Number per year					
	1900–1	1902–3	1903–4	1905–6	1907–8	1909–10
Country Holidays Fund (Jewish Branch) (children sent to country	1,800	1,711		2,332	2,795	2,943
Jewish Children's Penny Dinners (Dinners given)	48,741	47,118	55,348	70,015	87,750	146,609
Jewish Schools' Boot Fund (pairs given)		2,000	1,906	2,137	2,088	2,135

Source: *The Jewish Yearbook* (London), 1900–1; 1902–3; 1903–4; 1905–6; 1907–8; 1909–10.

The Union of Jewish Women

Membership in the UJW provided one of many ways to engage in charity work. The UJW, founded in 1902, described itself as 'essentially a Guild of Service for women, centralising and distributing the work, the experience, the energy and the sympathy of an all-embracing sisterhood'.[64] The UJW's Ruth Eichholz, daughter of the chief Rabbi, believed 'Jewish ladies' had to do 'Jewish work'. In her address to the 1908 Annual Meeting, Eichholz, spoke 'on the urgency of social service'. The Jewish community, could not, according to Eichholz, 'disguise the fact that with respect to the large influx of late of the foreign element, assimilation caused a loosening of the link which bound them to Judaism, and it was women's duty to counteract this'.[65] Combining sympathy with noblesse oblige, Julia Cohen, also of the UJW, encouraged women who had travelled or had talent to come to the East End to chat with 'their poorer sisters' and share 'the gift of music'. Women 'who had been enabled to cultivate their tastes – music, artistic ... should help the good work of the Union (of Jewish Women) by going among the poor, and giving freely of their own knowledge and experience, so sharing with them some glimpses of the good things of life'.[66]

UJW members regularly interacted with immigrant women and developed programmes that ameliorated hardships of East End life.[67] The Union functioned as a coordinating agency, matching trained women with philanthropic work and worked hard to spread word of their activities. Members befriended Jewish women, established a labour exchange and helped to coordinate services and programmes for women.[68] The *JC* noted that the type of work undertaken by the UJW justified the appointment of women to responsible positions in communal organizations. Yet, the *JC* felt obliged to remind the Jewish community to support the organization.[69] While focusing on the needs of Jewish women, the Union maintained a broader outlook.

> This Union [noted the *JC*] is, without doubt, the most important achievement of Jewish women, and, being in touch with every one of our communal institutions, as well as keeping itself closely informed of all the women movements of the day it represents a most progressive note amongst our womenfolk and is entitled to the hearty support of everyone of us.[70]

The UJW helped extend much-needed childcare, especially after school until parents returned from work at about eight o'clock in the evening. Volunteers established 'happy evenings' and recreation schools in several East End locations.[71] The school at the Old Montague-Street Council School served children of working or deceased mothers.

In 1903, twenty women helped at the school 'where these forlorn children can assemble from neighbouring schools, receive a half-penny tea and spend their time as they would in a well regulated home'.[72] *The Times* praised the UJW school, where children 'pass these hours as they would in an ideal working-class home'.[73] Most of the founders and the children were Jewish, but any child could attend. The organizers taught even very young children about independence by charging them for their dinners.[74] In 1906, Miss Halford, the Secretary of UJW, travelled to an International Congress of Women to learn more about the *Kindehorte*, a childcare centre and the inspiration for the Recreation School. In the *Kindehorte*, little boys were required to 'wash up the tea things' to prepare them for 'the domestic duties they have to perform when in military training'.[75] One former beneficiary recalled having learned housewifery at a play centre she attended as a young child.[76] Similarly, in 1905 the Jews' Free School sponsored 'happy evenings', serving nearly 5,000 children.[77] By teaching games, volunteers introduced structured play, rules, team work – all central Victorian priorities – and provided a time and place for children to play.

The Jewish community continued sponsoring after-school programmes during the years of the First World War, and reported progress among those attending. A visitor to the Berner Street Happy Evenings described Jewish children as more 'vivacious' and 'more keenly appreciative of the spirit of play' than those who attended other schools. Some years earlier, children 'did not know how to play' and volunteers needed a great deal of 'time and patience to infuse the necessary love for recreation, into these poor little denizens of slumland'.[78] One of many programmes that helped shape the experience of childhood, 'happy evenings' also reveal much about the sponsors.

Concerned about the impact of city life, the Jewish community arranged for immigrant children to venture beyond the East End through organizations such as the Jewish Branch of the Country Holidays Fund. Hannah Hyam, collected the pence 'of the little ones whose parents endeavour to aid their children to obtain that delightful holiday in the country or by the sea, which means so much for the little pale-faced dwellers in the crowded East End'.[79] Working girls, no longer eligible for the Children's Country Holiday Fund, could rarely afford a holiday for the first several years they worked, unless they went with their clubs.[80] In 1909, the Sub-Committee of the JBG Girls' Industrial Committee introduced summer holidays for apprentices. To the extent that the girls could afford it, they paid for their vacation.

The First World War placed strains on most communal services. An appeal for the Country Holiday Fund reminded readers that 'the war has not made the slum areas more sanitary, more comfortable for habitation, less disease-yielding; it has not brought health or strength to the little ones, nor equipped them the better for facing the rigour of the winter months that are to come'. Children needed time away from the city and while the war demanded sacrifice, the risk 'of little ones growing up sickly, ill, weak, emaciated' to save money, was 'not only false economy, but parsimony which is bound to yield a crop of evils in days to come'.[81] Sponsors of such holidays believed they had medical and emotional benefits, not just recreational. Mothers too benefited from time at a Holiday Home. After the founding of 'Roseneath' in 1911, mothers and babies enjoyed the opportunity for a holiday or much needed convalescence, when Jewish working girls' clubs were not making use of the home.[82]

During World War I, Jewish communal organizations had to re-evaluate priorities as increased demands strained communal coffers. The JBG took responsibility for aiding aliens and asked the Stepney Borough Central Committee of the National Relief Fund to refer all Jewish aliens seeking relief to them.[83] A week after the outbreak of war, the National Organisation of Girls' Clubs opened workrooms for unemployed girls. The demand was so great that the workrooms moved to Montagu's West Central Girls' Club.[84] During the first weeks of the war, the Jewish rescue society also created workrooms, which became so overcrowded, that they limited assistance to alien girls.[85] Efforts by patriotic middle-class women unintentionally worsened trade conditions as well-meaning ladies took up sewing and displaced poor girls and women who had to work for their survival.[86]

As Belgian refugees arrived in England, the Jewish community faced new demands. The work with Belgian refugees began with 'startling suddenness and in gigantic proportions'.[87] Placement of well-educated refugees proved difficult.[88] The greatest demands lasted until the spring of 1915, when unemployment decreased.[89] The PJTS accommodated many of the refugees and set up an information bureau to help with location of relatives, passports, permits, etc. Some Belgians objected to staying in hostels. Poor immigrant Jews in the neighbourhood generously hosted some of the new refugees. More affluent Belgians, those from classes who had given to charity, moved into the Manchester Hotel. Working men went to the Portland Street hostel and women and children remained at the Shelter.[90] The UJW also opened a hostel, provided clothing, arranged children's education and tried to locate employment for the refugees.

Rose Hertz, wife of the Chief Rabbi, who felt it was very important to find work for young women, suggested training some to be servants or children's nurses and others as dressmakers and milliners.[91] While she did not elaborate, it seems she wanted to prevent the girls from spending their leisure time in unacceptable ways. Thanks to voluntary classes, students made progress with English. Some Belgian students attended the London University, the School of Economics, University College and Hospitals.[92] Yet many adults found their exile more difficult. Rev. Morris Joseph recommended alleviating 'the terrible monotony' by establishing a workshop.[93]

While the receiving community assisted all refugees, they believed that individuals deserved treatment that accorded with their former status. 'A professor and a shoemaker are not ideal companions – though the shoemaker may be an excellent fellow in himself'. The *JC* argued that 'available accommodation should be carefully apportioned among our involuntary guests, more or less according to their past lives and standards of comfort'.[94] In a striking departure from the response to poor, uneducated Russians, leaders in the Jewish community saw many of the Belgians as their equals and acted out of their class biases.

Initially, the onset of war caused disruptions. Soon after, work became plentiful.[95] During the war, women entered a 'bewildering number' of new occupations. Organizations, the UJW, among them, helped women train for new jobs.[96] The number of those seeking apprenticeships declined because good paying jobs, which did not require a training period, attracted most young women. The JBG viewed many of these positions as offering no future. The post-war era economic depression forced many women out of the market as employers reserved jobs for ex-soldiers and 'breadwinners'. Despite these pressures, women had entered the widest range of employment in history, resulting in permanent changes in their occupational structure.

Sheltering Young Men

Young men, especially those who lacked parental supervision also came to the attention of the Jewish community. A small number of boys who were 'single' or 'double' orphans, for whom there was no space at Norwood, found a home and surrogate parenting at the Samuel and Myer home. Denzil Myer and Gerald Samuel originally purchased the house, located in Stepney, and intended to live there with a group of boys and young men. Tragically, like so many of their generation, the two men died in action in 1917. Friends and family established the home and an endowment in their memory.[97] The initial endowment enabled the JBG to fill five of twelve spots in the home.[98] The home made provisions for religious education for those with inadequate knowledge of Hebrew and religion.[99] Establishing a sound institution proved challenging. The committee had difficulty hiring qualified staff, faced discipline problems with the young men and struggled to find the proper balance, as the home was not an institution. The home permitted the resident member of the Committee to administer punishments, including 'fines, loss of recreation, or by the cane', but required documentation and reporting of caning to the Committee.[100]

Members of the prominent Sebag-Montefiore family, Ida and Muriel, served on the Ladies' Committee. In 1922, they expressed dissatisfaction with nearly every aspect of the home. Despite notifying the home three weeks prior to visiting, they found '"the premises were deplorably dirty"', leading them to question what the home was like during times between their visits. They found litter collected in the kitchen and most utensils '"unfit for use"'. Such conditions could not '"fulfil the intentions of its founders"', and they pressed the committee to consider ways to bring the home in line with its initial goals.[101]

The committee decided to search for a husband and wife who could also gain assistance from the Ladies' Committee and hired the Mendozas in the spring of 1923. Within six months, Mr Mendoza's guidance led to improvements in the residents' personal cleanliness and behaviour. There was limited bullying, the boys showed a desire to do things for the home and each other and had begun inviting friends over.[102] Over time, Mendoza built a programme that drew on the same kinds of values and resources the community promoted for all its youth.

Concerned 'to counteract any evil tendencies which might arise in boys of 14–18 years of age', Mendoza and his wife encouraged the young men to participate in indoor and outdoor games and sports. They competed against other clubs and promoted 'a feeling of good fellowship among the boys by a series of friendly chats chiefly about health and morality'. The boys all joined a lads' club and several attended evening institutes. Many 'old boys' returned for Sabbath, when they experienced difficulties or earned inadequate wages.[103] The Mendozas appear to have been sensitive and loving influences in the lives of the boys from the home. In 1927, Mendoza reported on the sixteen boys who had left the home over the past four years. They were 'justly proud' of ten and had lost track of two. Mendoza took responsibility for four young men about whom they were 'sorry' and while he expected some challenges among adolescents, he acknowledged that 'we do not want failures, yet we must own that we do have them'.[104]

The early 1930s brought even greater problems owing to unemployment, especially for former residents who had completed their apprenticeships. One young man, out of work more than two years, was reluctant to meet with Mendoza. In a second case, a boy who had just completed his apprenticeship did not receive a permanent offer from his master and was out 'tramping the streets trying to find work'. Clearly anxious for the welfare of those he helped raise, Mendoza worried that after leaving the safety of the home, a tragedy would ensue if the young men found themselves lacking work and 'security'. He hoped that the JBG might help find employment for the young men.[105] Mendoza sought to remain in touch with Old Boys, appreciated their visits, the men's camaraderie and the opportunity of meeting their wives. Like many clubs and services, after care was a significant priority and distinguished the Jewish community from a number of Christian organizations such as Barnardos. The leadership of the home reminded the public that demand for the home's services demonstrated the community's need for such a place.[106]

Over time, declining numbers within the Jewish community knew about the home, resulting in diminished donations and fewer gifts 'that cost the giver so little and give so much pleasure to the boys'. The Committee sought donations of books, old magazines, tennis balls and tickets to Jewish charitable entertainments, to help the Warden create a home, rather than an institution. While aware that orphans often came from difficult living circumstances and had many physical and emotional needs, they tried not to lower the 'tone' of the home by accepting 'boys of lower mentality'.[107] Leaders of philanthropy regularly found it a challenge to serve the wide range of children and young adults who came to their attention.

Conclusion

Immigrants did not receive all their assistance from communal organizations. Numerous sources note the generosity of the poor to one another – whether housing an evicted neighbour, providing meals when a parent was sick or babysitting services. Indeed, some families could count on the kindness of a shopkeeper. Kitty Collins's mother often gave away food. Customers 'only had to say I've got to make for *shabbas* and *shabbas* you don't take money so she gave them the goods'.[108] East End families also responded generously to those fleeing Nazism. Businessman turned writer, Morris Beckman's family regularly hosted refugees for Sabbath.[109] While these acts of *tzedakah* provided indispensable aid, the established community had far greater resources and a more deliberate agenda.

By the interwar years, Jewish services became increasingly preventive. In 1926, the Jewish Association for the Protection of Girls and Women (JAP-GAW) claimed the housing shortage caused 'misery' and 'many of the family ruptures'. Growing families could not move into larger accommodation. They provided advice to women in an 'overwrought state' who came to their office to complain about husbands who spent time in billiard halls and saloons to escape crowded homes. The JAPGAW was concerned that girls would spend time on the streets or cheap eating-houses rather than homes 'where the meal had been taken, where the washing would be hanging up and where some of the children would or should be sleeping'.[110]

The economic stresses of the 1930s led the Jewish community to reassess its services. The JBG pronounced 1931 the worst year 'in the history of man'.[111] In 1932, for the first time, they decided they could not assist young able-bodied unemployed Jews and referred them to the Public Assistance Department of the LCC. They were however, quite defensive in their justification of this decision, indicating continued anxiety over their status. With the slowing of immigration, the JBG concluded that Jews were equally deserving of 'the statutory assistance afforded by the State and the Municipality'. Conscious of potential resentment, the Board cautioned that 'it is perhaps politic to avoid sending to the Public Assistance Committee those of foreign birth and pronouncedly foreign appearance, but even this is a matter of opinion'.[112] Despite these challenges, Jewish communal services alleviated much need, established a clear set of expectations and over time more openly asserted the rights of Jews.

4 THE IMPACT OF EDUCATION: ANGLICIZATION OF JEWISH EAST ENDERS BEGINS WITH SCHOOLING

The Reach of Education

By the time of the mass migration, Britain had established universal and compulsory education, a crucial component in the rapid transformation of immigrant culture.[1] Schooling tells us a great deal about the cultural and social expectations Britons had for Jews – as immigrants and as members of the working class.[2] By virtue of their course of study, educators socialized girls for roles that differed from that of their parents and their male contemporaries. Victorian ideals, such as decorum, modesty and domesticity for girls and manliness, athleticism and character-formation for boys, suffused educational and vocational programmes.[3] Drawing on school inspectors' reports, records from the UJW and contemporary press, this chapter demonstrates how diverse educational opportunities – formal and informal, secular and religious – moulded generations of Jewish youth – and to some extent, their parents.[4]

School officials, teachers and care committee members used every means at their disposal – curricular, philanthropic and recreational – to eliminate foreign culture and create 'good Britons'. 'I think' suggested Nettie Adler, daughter of the Chief Rabbi, 'that no one will deny that the school is the most potent factor for good among our East End population'.[5] Educators and philanthropists hoped that as East End Jews entered the larger world through schooling and the English language, they would gain access to additional occupations, which would reinforce the adoption of an English lifestyle.

First generation, adult immigrant women rarely benefited directly from formal education; some attended adult education classes sponsored by the Russo-Jewish Committee. While many never gained English fluency, their children's facility with the language led to a 'breakdown of cultural solidarity' in the immigrant community. Immigrant mothers thus often found themselves in conflicting roles. Many functioned as the link to Eastern European religious and cultural life and to the values that their children's educational institutions tended to disdain. In turn, mothers absorbed a great deal from their children, reading, and from encounters with various school officials and volunteers.

The high rates of school attendance among the East End's Jewish children meant that decreasing numbers spoke or even understood Yiddish. Efforts by schools to substitute English for Yiddish, the language of most immigrant homes, advanced a process of 'de-judaization', one aspect of anglicization.[6] By the early twentieth century, few East Enders needed interpreters to complete census forms. Despite the presence of Yiddish posters, Rev. S. Levy's personal experience indicated 'that the influence of the Anglicisation has penetrated most peacefully far beyond all imagination'.[7] For some, the extent of change caused consternation. Many in the community believed mothers, as guardians of the home, had to promote the value of Judaism and Jewish observance.[8]

The expansion of non-sectarian elementary education in England had a significant impact on London's Jewish immigrant children. Between 1894 and 1903 the Jewish student population in London's schools increased dramatically (see Tables 4.1 and 4.2). In 1894, 15,964 Jewish children (4,799 foreign born) attended elementary schools.[9] By 1905, this number reached 31,543 (5,789 foreign born).[10] From 1903 to 1911, more than twenty thousand Jewish children attended London board schools each year.[11]

Table 4.1: Jewish children in voluntary schools, Metropolitan London.

| | | | | | | | Born in England to | |
| | | | | | | Born | Foreign | Native |
Year	Boys	Girls	Infants classes	Mixed	Total	abroad	parents	parents
1894	3,218	2,293	2,625	–	8,126	2,498	3,984	1,644
1896	2,875	1,941	2,262	–	6,180	2,003	4,009	1,046
1897	3,758	2,351	2,291	–	8,400	2,402	4,226	1,672
1899	3,451	2,228	2,521	–	7,304	1,718	5,101	1,788
1900	4,039	2,274	2,495	–	8,808	1,853	5,510	1,445
1901	3,450	2,290	2,506	–	8,246	1,760	5,159	1,327
1902	3,480	2,315	2,410	–	8,250	1,847	5,138	1,220
1903	3,486	2,371	2,243	–	8,100	1,649	5,409	1,042
1904	3,517	2,226	2,302	–	8,045	1,614	5,295	1,136
1905	3,281	2,261	2,350	–	7,892	1,610	5,372	910
1906	3,254	2,210	2,208	–	7,672	1,623	5,235	814
1907	3,221	2,182	2,066	–	7,469	1,623	4,964	882
1908	3,228	2,247	2,048	–	7,523	1,546	5,100	877
1909	3,190	2,278	1,938	–	7,406	1,543	4,970	893
1911	3,242	2,339	1,604	–	7,184	–	–	–
1912	3,025	2,238	1,735	–	6,998	–	–	–
1913	3,137	2,412	1,788	–	7,337	–	–	–
1914	3,153	2,425	1,739	–	7,317	–	–	–
1915	3,153	2,427	1,659	–	7,239	–	–	–
1916	3,073	2,434	1,662	–	7,169	–	–	–

Year	Boys	Girls	Infants classes	Mixed	Total	Born abroad	Born in England to Foreign parents	Native parents
1917	2,792	2,181	1,675	546	7,194	–	–	–
1918	2,795	2,183	1,581	546	7,105	–	–	–
1919	2,811	2,191	1,584	546	7,132	–	–	–
1922	2,304	1,791	1,449	546	6,225	–	–	–

Source: *The Jewish Yearbook*, 1894–1924.

Table 4.2: Jewish children in board schools, Metropolitan London.

Year	Boys	Girl	Infants	Mixed	Total	Born abroad	Born in England to Foreign parents	Native parents
1894	2,264	2,467	3,107	–	7,838	2,301	3,875	1,662
1896	2,711	3,141	4,170	–	9,982	3,200	5,118	1,694
1897	2,904	3,080	4,046	–	10,038	2,817	4,991	2,230
1898	3,202	3,287	4,789	–	11,278	3,525	5,391	2,362
1899	3,264	3,285	4,475	–	11,224	3,329	5,553	2,035
1900	4,061	3,906	4,728	–	12,695	3,496	6,859	2,340
1901	4,079	4,006	4,967	–	13,052	3,756	7,090	2,206
1902	5,574	5,641	7,465	–	18,680			
1903	6,189	6,416	8,741	–	21,346			
1904	6,306	6,669	8,332	–	21,307			
1905	6,364	6,658	8,421	–	21,443			
1906	6,731	7,047	8,187	–	21,965			
1907	6,463	6,316	8,584	–	21,563			
1908	6,779	6,740	9,389	–	22,908			
1909	8,109	8,315	10,142	–	26,566			
1911	8,509	8,332	9,631	1,752	28,224			

Source: *The Jewish Yearbook*, 1894–1924.

Like non-conformists, many Jewish families objected to the influence of schools' Anglican religious education classes. Catholics approached the teaching of scripture differently from Anglicans and non-conformists; while willing to attend non-Catholic schools, they wanted control over their children's religious instruction.[12] The 1870 Education Act gave power to locally elected school boards to create elementary (board) schools and to levy rates to finance them. Although these schools offered religious education, the new Act required that the instruction be non-sectarian.

Compulsory Education

With the institution of compulsory elementary education, the government gave privately funded voluntary schools one year to reach government standards. Schools had to institute the 'conscience clause', permitting parents to remove their children during religious instruction. Satisfying these guidelines made schools eligible for government grants. The implementation of separate religion classes aroused some resentment, but legal guarantees remained secure.[13] By the early twentieth century, working-class girls, though usually less educated than boys, were, according to Julia Cohen, president of the UJW, 'no longer left in the appalling state of ignorance and drudgery, amounting almost to slavery'.[14] Nonetheless, most East End immigrants left school at age fourteen.

Jewish children attended Jewish voluntary schools (similar to Jewish day schools) or board schools. Between 1896 and 1920, there were approximately ten to twelve Jewish voluntary schools in metropolitan London, about one third of which were in the East End.[15] Table 4.1 shows the numbers of children attending voluntary schools and Table 4.2, the numbers attending Board schools. Voluntary schools offered a fairly intensive Jewish education, though some argued this religious education was ineffective – trapped in its Victorian origins. The Jewish community generally provided religious education in board schools.

Voluntary and Board Schools

The JFS, originally the 'Confraternity for the Study of the Law', first opened in the 1770 'as a small religious school in the vicinity of the Great Synagogue'.[16] In its early years the school provided clothing, but did not allow children to keep the best set of clothes at home, fearing parents would sell or pawn the items.[17] The community added an elementary school in 1817[18] and changed its name to Jews' Free School in 1819.[19] In 1821, the school moved to Bell Lane, Spitalfields. Leading citizens, Jewish and Christian, supported the institution.[20] Twenty-six hundred boys and girls attended the JFS in 1870.[21] By the early twentieth century, the JFS was the largest elementary school in the kingdom.[22] In 1898 the school built a wing for technical education, hoping to direct their students into more promising trades and erected a 'magnificent building' in 1906.[23] Some voluntary schools, such as the Stepney Jewish School had a more technical bent than JFS.[24]

The JFS student population fell by nearly 25 per cent between 1899 and 1913, as the population around Houndsditch and Commercial streets declined. The area surrounding JFS had increasing motor traffic and many parents opted to send children to neighbourhood schools that seemed safer. Moreover, the appeal of board schools increased as they added Jewish staff and closed for Jewish holidays.[25] In 1880, 300–400 children attended the Stepney Jewish school, which doubled in size by 1902. Girls studied cooking, laundry-work and dress-making; all students had drill, gymnastics and swimming.[26]

School managers at the JFS viewed education in the broadest possible terms and committed themselves to 'the mental and moral development of the humbler classes'.[27] The school received recognition for helping children who entered as 'Russians and Poles', leave the institution 'almost indistinguishable from English children'.[28] Celebrations such as Empire Day promoted anglicization. The *East London Observer* claimed the JFS celebration 'reached heights of fervour unparalleled by the less insecure sections of the community'.[29]

Despite charges that immigrants disregarded sanitation, the JFS never closed because of an epidemic. Daily attendance averaged 89 to 95 per cent, as compared to 79 per cent for London board schools overall.[30] Alfred Eichholz, a physician and prominent member of the Jewish community, attributed Jewish attendance and academic success to parental regard for education.[31] Similarly, the 1907 inspector's report praised Jewish parents.[32] In contrast, some non-Jewish working-class parents resisted compulsory education; they saw it as an example of government interference.[33] Jewish parents seemed largely exempt from the common criticism of parents' inadequacies.[34]

In addition to support from families, the JFS had good physical facilities, excellent teachers and a favourable student teacher ratio.[35] Class size at JFS ranged from forty to seventy students. Photographs from early in the century show fairly spacious, but poorly lit, classrooms with wooden benches, girls neatly dressed in pinafores and boys in simple suits. Girls' lessons included laundry, needlework and brushwork. Boys appear in their Chemical and Physical Laboratory, studying Hebrew and using the newly opened miniature rifle range.[36] The students had a heavy workload, and many, boys in particular, also attended *cheder* (religion classes) in addition to Jewish studies classes at the JFS.[37] The school regularly achieved London's highest scores in mathematics.[38] Even in the nineteenth century, the JFS organized outings; children visited such places as the Crystal Palace where they enjoyed tea, bread and fruitcake. For some, it was the first time they had treats such as lettuce and butter.

Many JFS teachers believed that system of secular studies plus *cheder*, injured the health of young students, particularly boys. Community leaders argued that *cheder* and some Talmud Torah classes, taught in Yiddish for long hours in primitive conditions, hindered anglicization.[39] JFS managers who did not want parents to send their children to *cheder* had Dr Maurice Davis study the children's health. The study had unexpected results; JFS students, despite attendance at *cheder*, had better health, school attendance and achieved a higher standard of work than pupils their age who did not attend *cheder*.[40]

Moses Angel, an ardent anglicizer, served as headmaster of the JFS from 1842 to 1897 and made the most of the resources at his disposal. As students' examination scores determined government grants, the JFS changed its curriculum after the passage of the 1870 Education Act. Benefactors did not raise any objections when English instruction increased from eighteen to twenty-two hours and Hebrew slipped from twelve to seven and one half hours.[41] In 1880, Angel received an additional grant of ninety pounds, which showcased 'the high state of efficiency which the JFS still maintains under the direction of its zealous and talented headmaster'.[42] To increase test scores, Angel assigned the best teachers to the worst students.[43] Such methods led to 90 to 98 per cent of the JFS's students passing the school exams for their level – a rate that was twenty points higher than the national average.[44]

At the 1884 JFS Festival Dinner, A. J. Mundella, MP and education reformer, praised the school's success, which was all the more remarkable considering the impact of poverty and persecution, the inability of many entering students to speak English and the fact that students devoted one-and-a-half hours a day to Hebrew and sacred writings. Mundella noted that 'every good teacher' working in 'Jewish schools throughout the length and breadth of this land', had studied at JFS.[45] The government inspector praised 'the high degree of excellence' and noted there was 'little evidence of a foreign element among the children'.[46]

By the turn of the century, however, Jewish students increasingly attended state-sponsored board schools.[47] Jewish leaders approved of the new, religiously neutral schools. Despite significant growth, the Jewish community did not add voluntary schools after 1881. In contrast, Christian voluntary schools increased with the passage of the 1870 Education Act.[48] The immigration of poor Eastern European Jews created other philanthropic demands and support of voluntary schools became an unnecessary expense with the establishment of a national system of free education.

Board schools, however, did not gain immediate acceptance from immigrant parents. The Old Castle Street School, built in the 1870s, became the focal point of controversy over religious influences. Designed to serve one thousand children, immigrant parents refused to send their children there, for fear of missionary activity. The school board sought Moses Angel's advice. He recommended removing Christian influences and closing early for Sabbath and other Jewish holidays.[49] The board appointed Abraham Levy, a JFS staff member as headmaster. Though non-denominational, Old Castle offered Hebrew as a special subject and Levy persuaded the school board to permit after-school Jewish religion classes to meet at the school.[50] The model proved very popular and by 1880, nearly 9,000 children attended London board schools.[51] The post-1890s generation of parents expressed less concern about their children's religious education and sent them to board schools more willingly.[52]

Fourteen East End schools had an almost exclusively Jewish enrolment. By 1891, Old Castle Street School educated about 1,500 Jewish children and Settles Street about 800, but neither school had any Jewish staff, except for two young pupil teachers.[53] Most board schools offered non-sectarian Christian education from which Jewish parents could withdraw their children upon request. In many board schools, Jewish children received two to three hours of religious education a week, either as a substitute for the government-mandated classes or after school. The Jewish Association for the Diffusion of Religious Knowledge (JADRK), founded in 1876, and its successor, the Jewish Religious Education Board (JREB), established in 1894, accepted responsibility for almost all Jewish education of elementary-age children in non-Jewish schools.[54] The JADRK praised the London School Board's 'religious liberality' – their practice of hiring Jewish teachers in schools with a substantial Jewish population. They urged the community to acknowledge 'its share of the burden, and cheerfully provide for the religious education of these children'.[55]

Other schools with large numbers of Jewish students also secured impressive government grants. Both the Jews' Infant Schools and the Old Castle Street Board School earned increased grants in 1880.[56] Table 4.3 shows the amounts of grants earned by Jewish board schools and Table 4.4 compares grants per pupil for a variety of voluntary schools. The *JC* reported that the average grant for 1879–80 for Jewish schools was higher than for all schools in England and Wales.[57]

Table 4.3: School grants, 1878–80.

Official name of school	# of scholars for whom accommodation is provided	Average attendance	Amount of Grant 1878–9	Amount of Grant 1879–80	Certificated	Assistant	Pupil	Total
Birmingham Hebrews School	389	274	212 5. 0.	255 2. 0.	5	1	5	11
Liverpool Hebrews Education	512	285	242 1. 0.	251 12. 0.	7	2	6	15
Bayswater Jewish	267	73	*517 9.	68 13. 0.	2	0	0	2
Jews' Infant, Tenter St	287	205	149 8. 0.	145 16. 0.	3	1	6	10
Jews' Free Spitalfields	2,790	2,220	1987 12. 0.	2073 6. 0.	16	15	42	73
Jews' Infants Commercial St	605	591	443 0. 0.	465. 8. 0.	2	4	14	20
Borough Jews'	230	113	87 19. 0.	86. 5. 0.	3	1	1	5
Westminster Jews' Free	366	282	244 4. 0.	249. 10. 0.	4	1	3	8
Whitechapel Old Castle St Board	1,264	1,002	723. 5. 6.	855. 7. 0	16	4	10	30
Manchester Jews'	1,276	705	659 6. 0.	722 16. 0.	8	13	16	37
Total	7,986	5,750	4754 18. 3.	5173 15. 0	66	42	103	211

*the grant for 1878–9 is for three months

Source: *JC*, 1 October 1880.

Table 4.4: Grants per scholar in average attendance, 1878–9.

Voluntary Schools	s. d.
Church of England	15. 2 ¾.
Wesleyan	15. 8 ¼.
Roman Catholic	15. 0 ¼.
British and Undenominational	15. 5 ¾.
London	15. 7 ½.
England and Wales	15. 3 ½.
England and Wales Jewish School	16. 6 ½.
Estimated Grant for all Schools in England and Wales for current year	15. 8.

Source: *JC*, 1 October 1880.

Wide-ranging challenges faced educators in London's poor neighbourhoods, where schools too felt the impact of Jewish immigration. In January 1896, the Managers' Yearly School Report for the Commercial Street School in Whitechapel made no mention of Jewish children. Just three years later they reported they would be closing on Jewish holidays.[58] Recruitment of teachers proved arduous in the East End.[59] There was little incentive for teachers to seek employment there, as the area lacked amenities and meant higher expenses for travel and meals. The best teachers sought positions in 'happier surroundings, and the earnest ones who remain at their posts are unfairly burdened', a source of anxiety for head teachers.[60]

Despite numerous difficulties finding and keeping teachers, East End schools benefited from the traditional Jewish commitment to education.[61] The relatively small proportion of Jewish child labour disproportionately benefited Jewish boys, whose parents often permitted them to remain in school longer than girls. While Jewish parents kept their children out of school for religious holidays, many Christian children worked through hop picking season rather than attend school.[62]

In the early years of the twentieth century, important changes in education affected denominational control of voluntary schools. The 1903 Education Act permitted local government intervention in voluntary schools and local authorities gained the power to appoint some of the managers. In addition, the LCC became responsible for secular instruction and its financing; in 1904, they took over the supervision of secular studies at the JFS.[63] The LCC tended to appoint Christians to the managing committees of voluntary schools.[64]

By 1911, about 37,000 Jewish children attended elementary schools in London. The local press frequently, and approvingly, noted the positive impact of East End schools on Jewish children, and complimented hardworking staff. School inspections offer a lens on the curriculum, facilities and progress of Jewish pupils, and inspectors' assumptions about students' foreignness and poverty. The Davenant Foundation School, with its large population of Jewish boys, had a particularly strong academic emphasis. Many of its students studied Latin and planned to become teachers. Ironically, at a school with large numbers of Yiddish speakers, German was available at the elementary level only.[65]

Schools' curriculum reflected academic and social goals. At schools populated almost entirely with children of foreign birth or with parents of foreign birth, observed a LCC inspector, 'the teaching of English becomes the central feature of the curriculum demanding all the knowledge, experience and information which the teacher can command'.[66] In the years before the First World War, the JFS continued to receive large numbers of recent immigrants whose foreignness remained salient. The inspector who assessed the JFS in 1913 reported that the school's greatest academic challenge 'lies in the teaching of written and spoken English'.[67] Many of the boys who entered the JFS were older and knew only Yiddish. The inspector praised the methods of teaching oral English and noted that the teachers 'show the boys by mouth and lip movements the exact pronunciation of vowel and consonant sounds'. He suggested changes in the choice of literature as many 'boys are unacquainted with English scenes and English family life and much more explanation of the subject matter than is usual in schools is necessary if the lesson is to be really successful'.[68]

Many of the same issues surfaced in board schools. In 1915, the Stepney Central Foundation School received praise for 'performing a national service' owing to its 'civilising influence' on the girls, and for instilling patriotism among pupils of different races and religions.[69] The inspector emphasized that the school's social work required 'much tact, patience, and individual attention to such simple elementary matters as cleanliness and manners'. In addition to the typical problems facing secondary schools, Stepney Central also had to meld 'heterogeneous' students and 'turn alien children into self-respecting English citizens'.[70] Such attitudes highlight the combination of sympathy and condescension common among school officials.

Schools helped reinforce cultural expectations through academic and co-curricular programmes. Teachers, headmasters and headmistresses de-emphasized Hebrew, made Yiddish unwelcome and encouraged physical education, Shakespeare and membership in the Brownies and other youth clubs.[71] Special educational opportunities were also available beyond the classroom, such as music lessons.[72] Girls' education prepared them to be wives and mothers, rather than significant economic contributors, and boys learned they should be the sole supporters of their families. Gendered attitudes about the appropriate training of the working class ran very deep. Throughout the late Victorian and early Edwardian periods, British schools sought to develop girls' intellectual capacities, but especially emphasized skills that would make working-class girls better wives and mothers and discouraged 'over-exertion' in girls nearing puberty.[73] At the beginning of the century, classes in home economics and childcare had become a sizeable component of girls' education in Britain and America.[74]

Especially in the years before the First World War, poverty and 'a considerable foreign element' remained challenges.[75] In 1910, 60 per cent of the parents of girls and 47 per cent of the boys at Raine's School worked in retail trades, as contractors or artisans.[76] In addition to English, girls at Raine's studied needlework, and beginning in the third form, took four hours of science a week in two different areas. Their science curriculum included courses on hygiene and botany, and the inspector recommended 'that the general Elementary Science lessons should draw their illustrations from the Domestic Arts, so as to add to the intelligence of the girls when they do the Domestic work in the Upper Forms'.[77] Girls prepared meals that utilized only those items one could expect to find in working-class homes.[78] Typical for its era, maternalist priorities, in part a legacy of the Boer War and eugenic concerns, remained influential. Having pioneered technical training for boys, Stepney Jewish 'hoped it might also become the pioneer of advanced domestic training among the girls' schools of London' and started a special class that split its time between academic and domestic subjects.[79]

The need of schools to incorporate domestic training implied the inability of mothers to teach proper housewifery skills to their daughters, a bit ironic given the praise that Jewish women received. Apparently, some women doubted the value of these lessons. One writer explained that the typical Jewish mother viewed 'the teachings of domestic economy centres' with 'condescension'.

> She has no faith in cookery books ... She knows without the assistance of thermometers, heat recorders and the dozen and one adjuncts of scientific cookery, just when her meal is prepared 'to a turn', and regards with feelings akin to amusement the dicta of those wiseacres who are so fond of discussing the 'wastefulness' of the poor.[80]

Indeed, many children fondly recall excellent meals. For Chaim Lewis, "'the act of feeding answered [his mother's] every maternal instinct'".[81]

Over time, East End schools prepared students for jobs beyond the borough. Stepney Central School reports for 1915 and 1926 referred to the large Jewish population and the desire of the girls to leave school early in order to enter commercial life.[82] The established Jewish community, who sought to alter the Jewish occupational structure, supported this contribution to anglicization.[83] Despite the high priority placed on vocational training, the East End also boasted an impressive number of academically successful children. Relative to their numbers, more Jewish students received scholarships, attended Central or became fee-paying students at secondary schools than Christian children.[84] While girls had far fewer opportunities than boys to attend university, working-class Jewish students were comparatively successful in entering advanced academic programmes. Jewish-sponsored and government scholarship programmes enabled many students to continue their schooling in non-technical subjects and beyond the legal school leaving age.

Differences in curriculum persisted. In 1926, Stepney Foundation Girls' School limited their mathematics' study to arithmetic, algebra and geometry, but offered a chemistry course for girls, available their last two years – an indication of the increasingly academic nature of girls' education.[85] Boys generally had access to a wider range of science courses, including chemistry and physics. At the Davenant Foundation School, some boys in the sixth form studied botany and zoology. In 1927, the inspector noted that the boys' school used nearly all class time for science and recommended spending more time on mathematics to enable boys to gain 'a working knowledge of the calculus'.[86]

The Raine's School included an academic track, as well as a commercial one for girls. Capable girls studied French and German; girls and boys who wanted to qualify for an arts degree could take Latin. By 1935, the oldest boys at Raine's could study advanced mathematics and science.[87] The girls' chemistry, however, had 'a domestic bias'.[88] All girls at Raine's studied art until at least the fifth form. They learned to make puppet theatres, costumes and scenery, as well as linoleum cutting, weaving and lettering. Unlike similar schools, boys at Raine's took art only in the second and third forms, and the teacher had no training in art, which led the inspector to recommend additional art instruction.[89]

Girls' programmes increased in rigor during the years just before World War II. The JFS girls' school received higher praise than the boys' school for their English classes and girls studied principles of heating, ventilation and water, and its purification. Despite those incremental changes, the JFS set up a model flat in 1936 to teach housewifery 'where social entertainment by the girls is undertaken as part of the regular training'.[90] They hoped that the young girls would practice this new knowledge in their homes. And, the teacher who ran the school's domestic centre taught science classes 'on general topics closely connected with the home'.[91] By 1938, fewer than 1,000 students attended the JFS, yet some 100,000 Jewish youth had received their education at the school, many of whom 'gained distinction in many walks of life'.[92] The East End no longer received waves of new Jewish immigrant and residential areas continued losing ground to the forces of industrialization. Despite decreasing destitution, many East End children had not escaped poverty.

Anecdotal evidence indicates the ongoing impact of class on children's educational opportunities. Ena Abrahams, who grew up in the East End, passed the entry exam for the City of London schools. 'The headmistress', however,

> spoke to my mother about our circumstances, what my father did, and my father was unemployed at the time, and she said to my mother that she didn't think I could benefit from that type of school, because my background would be so different from the other girls, that it would be impossible for me actually to integrate into the school.

Abrahams described her mother taking her by the hand, crossing the Thames, and 'crying all the way across the bridge'.[93]

In addition to supporting board and voluntary schools, British Jewry also developed educational and social services for the sizeable number of Jewish children who lacked one or both parents. Many single and double orphans, attended the school attached to the Jews' Hospital and Orphan Asylum (JHOA), known as Norwood. As a residential home that provided physical, social and educational services, the orphanage faced significant financial challenges and expenses that often exceeded income.[94] Like other charitable institutions, Norwood required communal support and took advantage of its annual prize day. The boys performed a 'display of military drill' and the girls, 'performed a Maypole dance and old English dances, to the delight of the audience' to promote interest in the school.[95]

Norwood education emphasized character development and had high standards for discipline.[96] As school records demonstrate, girls reprimanded in the dining hall, who came into line late or sulked after being corrected, lost privileges. The school punished older girls by sending them to bed at the same time as the younger girls. After three infractions in six weeks, which included sulking, displaying temper, shuffling her feet and muttering, one child lost the right to join school clubs.[97] Such behaviours, carefully noted in the records, give us insight into the attitudes and expectations of those running institutions such as the Norwood Orphanage.

Over time, the orphanage and its school increasingly attempted to create a home-like environment. The school curriculum included singing and dancing to bring 'some brightness' to the children's lives.[98] Ordinarily the children spent part of their summer holiday at the seaside town of Margate, but economizing during World War I forced the school to suspend such excursions. Such efforts, a conscious part of the curriculum, provided a break from institutional life.[99]

School Philanthropy

Looking beyond the academic needs to children's physical and mental well-being demanded more than teachers alone could provide. The Jewish community, and in particular Lord Rothschild, offered generous assistance.[100] Volunteers visited children's homes, met with school staff, oversaw the distribution of boots, clothing, penny dinners and organized services for delicate or invalid children. Such efforts required Jews to mediate between ethnic/religious obligations and their commitment to Victorian ideals of self-help. Jewish social welfare provision occurred well ahead of the state and provided a model for state services. It was not until the first decade of the twentieth century that the Education Act of 1906 introduced feeding programmes, which some historians see as a first step towards the welfare state.[101] Victorian assumptions about the 'fecklessness of the poor' meant such programmes remained controversial.[102]

Widespread poverty, however, meant children really needed the dresses and corduroy suits supplied by the JFS.[103] In 1902 and 1903, needy children at Lower Chapman Street School received meals.[104] The numbers of 'underfed children' led to 'great anxiety'. Children benefited from donations from the Berner-Street School Jewish Association and the Rothschilds.[105] Because school managers feared that regular reliance on charity might lead to pauperization, schools charged the children small amounts for their lunch. At Lower Chapman Street School, a manager supplied clothing and shoes to needy 'Hebrew children' and the London Needlework Guild aided Christian students.[106] Similarly, the Jewish Ladies' Clothing and Schools' Boot Societies assisted pupils at the Commercial Street School.[107] At the outbreak of World War I, Claude Montefiore, president of the Jews' Infant Schools, reported that unemployment meant three times as many children as usual required meals.[108]

Volunteer managers had a particularly influential role in East End schools. Thus, in 1907, the Julia Cohen expressed dismay that in over 123 schools she found 'barely a dozen Jewish managers'. Jewish school managers had responsibility for 'seeing that the regulations as to Bible instruction were carried out', acted as confidantes for teachers, counselled parents about post-school opportunities for their children and served both the state and the Jewish community. Cohen strongly urged UJW members to volunteer.[109] Two years later, Nettie Adler repeated the call at a meeting of the UJW.[110] Hannah Hyam claimed one could count the number of workers on a single hand. Schools needed additional care committee workers to arrange for meals and clothing, visit parents, deal with physical defects that doctors discovered, find work for school leavers and to stay in touch with new workers during the two critical years after they finished school.[111] Organizations such as the UJW helped explain the work of care committees and apprenticing programmes by offering lectures in Yiddish to parents.[112]

Board schools, while extremely successful, could not offer the comprehensive care typical of Jewish voluntary schools. Jewish philanthropic organizations worked to fill some of the gaps. Nonetheless, children who did not feel deep attachment to Commercial Street took advantage of openings at a nearby Jewish school that rewarded good attendance with clothing.[113] Disruption occurred throughout the year because Jewish schools tended to draw away 'the brightest boys and girls' after they had learned English.[114] In a tone of frustration, the Commercial Street managers' report recounted that 'the "leakage" of children, however is still exceedingly great, and militates seriously against the success of the teaching, besides acting as a continual discouragement to the staff'.[115] In just six months during 1901, the Commercial Street School lost over 150 students.[116]

Early in the twentieth century, schools began to provide medical services. Starting in 1909, the Stepney Central Foundation School offered medical treatment, regardless of students' ability to pay. The increase of such services reflected a growth in government intervention.[117] The 1912 report of the Buckle Street Infants' School in Whitechapel stressed its attention to 'the bodily health and comfort of the children' in addition to its academic mission. The headmistress demonstrated 'great capabilities of experiment', and was keenly aware of the health 'of the weakly and backward children'. She had arranged 'simple talks with the parents' to encourage them to improve their standards of domestic cleanliness.[118] A school with a very large Jewish population, Buckle Street's headmistress trained the children through their parents and parents through their children.

Schools also incorporated facilities considered progressive for the time. The Jews' Infant Schools for example, added an open-air classroom, popular during this period and provided glasses for many of the children.[119] The JFS planned to build baths to 'further assist in the cultivation of pride in appearance and personal self-respect'.[120] Contemporary views about gender and lingering concerns about race deterioration reinforced assumptions that girls who were bookish or who failed to demonstrate maternal instincts were abnormal.[121] Efforts to shape future mothers reinforced women's dependence on men, and offered girls – even more than for working-class boys – a vision of adulthood that was severely circumscribed.

During the 1930s, the JFS continued its tradition of extensive charitable assistance. In 1933, the school's care committee distributed clothing, boots and shoes, and sent more than 150 children on country holidays.[122] Though most of the students were healthy, Commercial Street School noted that there were 'a few of poor physique'. The students benefited from 'an exceptionally good care committee' that provided assistance in the years prior to the Second World War.[123]

Scholarship Assistance

Many East End children had the ability but lacked the funds to continue their education after the age of fourteen. Most families could not afford to lose even the small income a child could contribute to the household. The JBG objected to the placement of children in overcrowded dead-end jobs. Over time, apprenticeships, technical education and advanced study increased choice and offered a passport out of the East End. Private donations to individuals enabled some children to remain in school, though communal leaders criticized this type of indiscriminate philanthropy, preferring a 'scientific' approach to financial assistance.

One such organization, the Education Aid Committee (EAC, later EAS), explained its 'true function is to assist the embryo genius to mount the top of the ladder, not to drag mediocrity laboriously up a few rungs'.[124] Unfortunately, observed the EAC, many benefactors spent money unwisely. The EAC recommended that a single committee 'be constituted the trustee and administrator of all funds raised in the Community for the assistance of budding talents in distress'.[125] Eventually, the organization modified its goals and decided to assist all students, not just exceptional ones, and added women to the committee. They cooperated with the UJW, which reviewed all female applicants and funded cases the UJW recommended for university or higher art education.[126]

Difficult financial circumstances and social upheaval during the years of the First World War led the EAS to review their policies and to suspend their scholarship programme 'until more settled times'. The war had particularly adverse effects on artists and musicians at the early stages of their careers. Some changed professions and the Society found it 'gratifying' that some students opted to leave work and enlist.[127] Although the Society limited its activity during the war, the national demand for doctors, chemists and engineers kept the science section busy.[128]

The First World War disrupted many other educational programmes and brought about increased anti-alienism. In particular, the immigrant status of many East End parents and some children raised questions as to their eligibility for government scholarships. The LCC barred foreign-born students from the London Day Training College unless they could prove they did not have to serve in the military of their country of origin. This affected a small number of Russian Jews who could neither return home, nor serve in the British military and generated debate as to whether such regulations were anti-Semitic. Established Jews discouraged intervention, fearing 'it would create very great prejudice'.[129]

During the war and after, the issue of scholarships for alien students created tensions between the Jewish community and the LCC. In 1917, Sir Stuart Samuel (the newly installed president of the Board) and Charles H. L. Emanuel (secretary of the Board) met with Cyril Cobb (chairman of the LCC Education Committee) and Sir Robert Blair (education officer of the LCC) to discuss confidential information that Samuel had received from Nettie Adler. The LCC Education Committee was about to receive a recommendation limiting scholarships to British-born children of either British-born parents, or parents who had been naturalized by before January 1914.[130]

Cobb explained LCC scholarships supported the training of teachers and civil servants. Alien Jews were not, according to Cobb, 'the best material for these appointments'. Samuel and Emanuel noted that such a policy meant that, for the first time, the LCC was drawing distinctions 'between classes of British subjects', on the arbitrary basis of whether or not a child's parents had been naturalized, a process, which until recently had been quite problematic. Samuel suggested that the LCC require both parents and their child to have been residents for five years and would encourage the JBD to support this compromise, which Cobb and Blair seemed to support.[131]

In March 1918 the LCC reached a decision: scholarship candidates had to be British when applying for assistance, or must have been born in Britain or have fathers who were born in Britain or the Dominions.[132] As a result, the JBD received letters from a number of students seeking assistance with scholarships.[133]

While this policy had a decreasing impact over the course of the interwar years, it did effectively bar Jewish children from receiving financial assistance, and kept some out of civil service jobs. Table 4.5 indicates the types of scholarships and the number of persons who were ineligible for LCC scholarships.

Table 4.5: Successful applicants who were denied LCC scholarships.

Years				
	1924	1925	1926	1927
Senior County	–	–	1	2
Intermediate County	3	1	2	2
Supplementary Junior County	2	2	3	-
Junior County	4	2	2	1
Total	9	*5	8	5

*   Excluding three students who were accepted for special reasons.

Source: London Committee of the Deputies of British Jews, Woburn House, Education Committee, file E3/42 2/2, extract from the Report presented to the Education Committee of the LCC, 'Eligibility of Alien Children for the Council's Scholarships and Exhibitions', 11 July 1928.

It was not until March 1920 that the LCC changed its policy. They required candidates to 'be British subjects at the time of application and during the tenure of the award'. In 1928, the education committee of the LCC concluded they should ease restrictions. Children of foreign parents would now be eligible for scholarships if their parents had made 'a *bona fide* endeavour ... at a reasonable time before the gaining of the scholarship to secure naturalisation'.[134] As opportunities increased, Jewish students benefited from advanced education.

Anti-alienism did not disappear with the end of the war. In 1925, for example, Karl Pearson and Margaret Moul published their study of Jewish immigrants. In it they asserted that approximately one-third of immigrant mothers and one-quarter of the fathers spoke little or no English (see Table 4.6).[135] The researchers' eugenicist program undoubtedly influenced both their data collection and analysis. They found it 'remarkable' that after many years in England parents had not learned to speak English and concluded that nearly two-thirds of the fathers and over three-quarters of the mothers had inadequate English to make them 'effective citizens'. According to Pearson and Moul, it was 'a very serious matter' that there was 'no educational standard' for immigration and they questioned if illiteracy was a matter of education or intelligence and what it said about children's intelligence.[136]

Table 4.6: Literacy of immigrant parents.

Type of literacy	% of mothers	% of fathers
Do not speak English at all	22.0	16.3
Speak a little English	11.5	9.7
Speak, but cannot read English	48.5	38.3
Speak and read English	28.0	35.7

Source: K. Pearson and M. Moul, 'The Problem of Alien Immigration into Great Britain', *Annals of Eugenics*, 1:1 (1925), p. 10.

A variety of sources mention the abilities of Jewish children. Certainly, there were school officials who believed that Jewish children were unintelligent. Some teachers equated the inability to speak English with lack of ability. Traditional prejudice against aliens generally and Jews in particular, biased the attitudes of others. In 1925, many Jewish children still attended schools located in slums. Researchers asserted that few of these children, 'show[ed] the usual characteristics of the slum child'. They were 'well-grown' and 'age for age, are in intellectual advance of Christian children of the same social class'.[137] Given the challenges, it appears that many East End children had an impressive record of achievement.

Adult Education

Acquisition of the English language was a priority for many immigrants, regardless of their age. From their arrival, communal leaders created programmes to teach adult immigrants to read and write English.[138] 'The object of these adult education classes', noted the *JC*, 'speaks for itself. They are intended to Anglicise the foreign Jews of the East End'.[139] A combination of reading, some evening classes and membership in clubs, provided older women with the basics of the language. Jewish students could also attend the Tower Hamlets Evening Schools, where drama and literature classes were particularly popular with girls.[140] Some studied English only after an unfortunate experience. One immigrant explained that her mother decided to learn English after she accidentally signed a liability release.[141]

Generally, Jewish women were more likely to learn 'foreign' languages – Polish, Russian, German or English – than men were. While many women did not learn to read English, they often spoke English better than their husbands did.[142] Secular study was more acceptable for women and activities in the marketplace brought them into regular contact with the vernacular.[143] While statistics do not cover the rate of language acquisition for immigrants, anecdotal material suggests that women learned to speak English faster than men. Perhaps men's employment experience enabled them to retain use of Yiddish in their daily lives, and their long work hours resulted in less exposure to English-speakers. Further, mothers spent more time among children who learned English at school and used it among their friends.

The Jewish community supported adult education language classes. The Russo-Jewish Committee held classes at board schools and clubs. The PJTS paid the fees of resident aliens at London School Board classes. Facility with English meant immigrants could work for Jews or Christians, in any part of London or the provinces, and thus promoted the dispersion of foreign Jews.[144] The Russo-Jewish Committee classes opened in 1892 to 'impart a knowledge of English language, habits and usages to adult Russian Jews and Jewesses'.[145] Satisfied with attendance, the English evening classes committee reported that their classes regularly provided enough English 'for at least ordinary purposes'.[146] Of the 500–600 immigrants attending the twice weekly evening classes, most were under thirty and half were female.[147] Classes for men and women also met at the Old Castle Street and Settles Street board schools, and a men's class met at Buck's Row and Chicksand Street schools. Students usually attended forty classes.[148]

East End women also benefited from a large number of informal language and education programmes. For many adults, such programmes constituted the only opportunities they had to further their learning. Many women were too old or destitute to attend school when they arrived in England; others had to remain at home to care for ailing parents or younger siblings. Many immigrants, however, women in particular, were too tired after a long day of work and household chores to attend English classes. Among the men, there is some evidence for a preference towards Talmudic study.[149] During the late 1930s, like their Christian counterparts, growing numbers of Jewish women continued their education at institutions such as the Barrett Street and Bloomsbury Trade Schools and the City Day Continuation School.[150] There were significant numbers of cultural events, concerts and art openings at the Whitechapel Gallery that made the East End a culturally rich district.

Ironically, one did not have to learn English to feel the impact of anglicization efforts. The Yiddish press also played an important role in educating immigrants.[151] This press, according to Ronald Cohen, 'forged an intimate relationship with the masses while seeking to raise their social and cultural awareness'.[152] In the spring of 1918, a Yiddish advertisement from the Smith Street Evening Institute asked rhetorically: 'Do you want to learn to be able to do work of national importance? Then it is absolutely necessary for you to learn to write and speak English'. Certainly, the Evening Institute's interest was partially financial, but they also promoted patriotism.[153]

In addition to primary and secondary education, women could take LCC classes, some of which took place at settlement houses. In the 1930s Edith Ramsay organized the 'Women's Evening Institute', which drew some East End women. Other LCC Evening Institute classes took place at the Robert Montefiore School, whose English classes for adults were the largest in London and many housewives attended 'Make and Mend' classes.[154] Women studied dressmaking, millinery and physical training at Evening Institute classes held at the JFS.[155] Many of these courses, regardless of their subject matter, tried to inculcate middle-class standards of cleanliness, child-rearing techniques and citizenship.

Conclusion

Undoubtedly, elementary schools, followed by clubs, were the most successful of all anglicizing efforts in the East End. Until the years before the Second World War, education included extensive domestic instruction for girls and manual and vocational training for boys. Schools garnered enthusiastic support from native-born and immigrant Jews alike.[156] The school curriculum prepared boys and girls for London's many industrial jobs, but rarely gave the first generation of young men and women the tools they needed to leave the working class. Over time, boys, and growing numbers of girls, received a more academic education and could aspire to higher levels of education and more skilled work. For immigrant women with limited opportunities for education, clubs, settlements and evening classes met some needs. Women certainly absorbed some of the anglicizing messages, but those same institutions completely transformed their children.[157]

Given the cataclysm of World War I, the curriculum in most working-class schools remained remarkably similar to the pre-war era. Thanks to changes in LCC scholarship rules, increasing numbers of Jewish youth remained in school past the age of fourteen, enabling many Jewish 'lads' from homes of poor tradesmen to attend Oxford and Cambridge.[158] However, LCC scholarships alone were often inadequate and most children did finish their schooling at fourteen and even fewer girls than boys continued on to secondary school.[159]

While immigrants helped to develop some of the programmes, the state or the established native community organized and sponsored the vast majority, and nearly all promoted anglicization. Schools consciously collaborated with parents. In 1932, the JFS formed a mothers and teachers union and hosted both an 'Open Evening' and an 'Open Day'.[160] Educational services for immigrants and their children were impressive in scale and scope. Even on the verge of World War II, JFS children still received free dinners and milk and other charitable assistance thanks to 'the school's care committee and the private effort of the staff'.[161] JFS continued to play an important role in the extra-curricular lives of its students by supporting an evening play centre, a brownie pack and girl guides, as well as boys and girls clubs.[162] While immigrant parents may have doubted the practicality of keeping children in school past the age of fourteen, especially daughters, they understood the benefits an education could bring. Such change meant that by the early 1930s, East End schools had little or no students to anglicize, having so successfully accomplished their task during the previous generations.

5 RELIGIOUS EDUCATION: CONFLICTING EDUCATIONAL VIEWS WITHIN THE JEWISH COMMUNITY

Jewish education was an arena of conflict – a conflict between orthodox Jewish immigrants and the host community, but also among anglicized Jews of differing levels of observance. Drawing on organizational reports and the press, this chapter considers the evolution of religious practice and explores the ways established Jews used religious education to promote anglicized Judaism. Initially committed to minimizing religious distinctiveness, by the first decade of the twentieth century concerns about inadequate knowledge and observance brought a new urgency to Jewish education.

Styles of Jewish Education

Jewish children could learn about their religion in three types of schools.[1] Imported from Eastern Europe, *cheder* (plural, *chedarim*) offered very traditional, intensive after-school study, usually in small, crowded spaces, taught in Yiddish. Talmud Torahs provided a relatively traditional course of study, often taught in English and in modernized buildings. Least intensive, the Jewish Association for the Diffusion of Religious Knowledge (JADRK, founded in 1860) and its successor the Jewish Religious Education Board (JREB, founded in 1894), provided classes at some board schools and supplementary Sabbath classes. Early in the twentieth century, JREB leaders sought to improve instruction by introducing more effective teaching methods.[2]

Two major umbrella groups of synagogues, representing two approaches to Orthodox Judaism emerged during the late nineteenth century. The more dominant United Synagogue, founded in 1870 as a union of five Ashkenazi synagogues in London (the Great, the Hambro', the New, Central and Bayswater), developed under the leadership of the Chief Rabbi and represented anglicized, Orthodox Jews.[3] More sensitive to immigrant priorities, Samuel Montagu, the Orthodox bullion broker and Liberal MP for Whitechapel, organized the Federation of Synagogues in 1887 to bring order to the small *chevrot* (small religious congregations).[4] Members of these small communities of worshipers had refused to join United Synagogue.[5] Anglicized Jews in particular found *chevrot* objectionable and suggested a variety of schemes to eliminate or improve them. Few women attended *chevrot*. In contrast, the large, 'sometimes predominant' number of female worshippers at non-Orthodox, anglicized Reform synagogues indicated the extent to which Reform congregations adopted 'Christian patterns of behavior'.[6] Attendance patterns likely reflected the adoption of English cultural patterns, but perhaps also the luxury of having more leisure time at women's disposal.

United Synagogue and Federation leaders both considered the provision of religious education a primary responsibility, albeit one that presented a range of problems. Anglo-Jewry – those who were only nominally Orthodox, as well as more traditional Jews, shared overlapping concerns about immigrants' places of worship and education, but offered different of solutions. Between 1896 and 1898, the United Synagogue proposed several East End Schemes to improve the social, intellectual and spiritual conditions of the East End's poorest Jews, including a building with a hall to seat 1,000, a gymnasium and other meeting rooms.[7]

When mass migration began, the unsatisfactory conditions of the *chedarim* – their excessive hours, substandard facilities and poor educational techniques – led to calls for change. Ardent anglicizers argued that the conditions of traditional schools hurt the health of young students.[8] In response, they created the JADRK and many immigrants received their Hebrew and Jewish education in JADRK or JREB classes. Many JADRK founders did not practice strict Orthodox Judaism and critics believed their classes lacked substance. Samuel Montagu, in particular (who appears in more detail below), objected to their approach and the JADRK's influence.

Creating British Jews

Increased immigration drew attention to places of worship and education. Notorious for their sanitary faults, one Whitechapel Board of Works inspector found a building where the ground floor was 'occupied as a school by a foreigner'. The room was nine-feet- square with six-feet-high ceilings, its floor eighteen inches below the level of the yard. The inspector described it as filthy and 'the children of the school, whose ages ranged from five to seven years, "looked very pale and sickly"'.[9] The children in such schools 'huddled together, in violation of the most obvious laws of decency and hygiene, in a small ... room, which is generally the sole living apartment of the poor teacher and his family'.[10] Detractors regarded the schools as substandard spaces that tended to escape the attention of the sanitary inspectors.

The established community often claimed they did not understand immigrants' preference for traditional education and places of worship. In reality, Anglo-Jewry realized that the *chevrot,* like the 'chedarim' ... originate partially in the aversion felt by our foreign poor to the religious manners and customs of English Jews. This prejudice is almost natural and may excite our pity, but we cannot encourage it ... The sooner immigrants to our shores learn to reconcile themselves to their new conditions of living, the better for themselves.[11]

British Jews encouraged the integration of immigrants and saw their isolation as a liability.

Established Jewry redoubled their efforts to reform the religious education immigrants brought with them. In 1891, Lord Rothschild responded to a request from Rev. Dr Adler for free use of the JFS for evening Talmud Torah classes. Rothschild noted that the JFS Committee fully agreed with the Rabbi that children needed to learn in more sanitary spaces than available in the *chedarim* and would work out a plan with Dr Adler.[12] Jewish leaders believed that ultimately the Board of Works would eliminate *chedarim*, but emphasized the community's obligation 'to use all the indirect moral means at its command to remove what is nothing less, literally and figuratively, than a plague-spot in its midst'.[13]

Spreading Jewish Education

In addition to concerns about facilities and the style of education, many leaders saw immigrants as ripe targets for conversionist activity. In 1888, for example, the JADRK learned of Jewish children receiving Christian religious education in board schools. They asked Jewish clergy to visit schools in their area and to make sure parents were aware of the Conscience Clause.[14] Concern about the provision of Jewish education increased with time. Because fewer children received a comprehensive religious education and increasing numbers grew up in less observant homes, the JREB argued for the urgency of extending their work.[15] In 1902, the organization provided instruction for about 8,000 of the 20,000 Jewish children who attended East London's non-Jewish schools. The rest, they maintained, even those in schools with large Jewish populations, received barely any Jewish education.[16] They argued that students who did not receive their instruction were 'growing up innocent of all Jewish training, sadly deficient in moral instruction, and, in consequence likely to cause grave scandal to the community in later years'.[17] It is unclear whether the Board considered the possibility of instruction in the children's homes. They considered girls, with their superficial knowledge of Jewish traditions, particularly susceptible to outside influences.

Many in the anglicized community viewed traditional education as ineffective and inappropriate to the modern world in which the immigrants now lived. Somewhat disingenuously, the *JC* suggested 'it may be worth enquiring into the reasons that induce our poor to uphold these schools', and asked why immigrants held English schools in contempt. After all, schools such as the JFS, 'with its vast and almost perfect organisation, and its commodious premises, and many other advantages', Castle Street Board School, with its Jewish headmaster, and Stepney Jewish Schools, convenient to those living further east, all boasted better facilities and English methods. Why, asked native-born Jews, did immigrants pay to send their children to bad schools, when good, free ones existed? 'We fear', remarked the *JC*, 'that some are impressed by the mistaken notion that the Hebrew and religious instruction imparted by intelligent Englishmen is not as efficient as that given by foreign *melamedim*'.[18] Although the established community commonly applauded self-reliance, they discouraged this instance; they could not indulge independence that compromised the welfare of children. The *JC* rejected the justification that some parents preferred the *chedarim*, which were traditional in approach, under immigrant control, and closer to home. Convenience, chided the paper, was no excuse and donations to the JREB would enable them to remove these 'nuisances' as quickly as possible.[19]

Immigrant Resistance

The establishment of *chedarim* demonstrates Jewish immigrants' commitment to traditional Jewish education and observance, and reveals opposition to anglicization. It also speaks to the ability of immigrants to create alternatives when those available from the established Jewish community were unacceptable. Typically, immigrant families did not object to their daughters' attendance at the JADRK or the JREB's classes. Most sons, however, attended *cheder* or Talmud Torah to supplement their studies. Barely able to make ends meet, working-class Jews suffered 'great self-denial' to pay for education.[20] Viewed as an act of resistance or rebellion by anglicized Jews, these institutions 'reflect[ed] with more or less accuracy the ideas and desires of the parents as to the religious education of their sons'.[21] And in spite of efforts to eliminate them, *chedarim* and Talmud Torahs, organized by immigrants, proliferated in the East End.

Clearly exasperated, native Jewry found these holdovers of Eastern Europe both archaic and embarrassing. A number of contentious issues, including the continued use of Yiddish and a level of independence, divided immigrants and anglicized Jews. Rev. A. L. Green found parents sent children to 'these so-called schools' despite his exertions to the contrary. 'Beyond their knowledge of Hebrew', the men had 'few qualifications ... to act as teachers of Jewish children in England'.[22] The JADRK and JREB, on the other hand provided competent teachers in an appropriate setting.

The JADRK opened its first classes for over 1,000 students at the Old Castle Street School; Abraham Levy, Old Castle's headmaster, served as honorary superintendent.[23] Girls learned the Hebrew alphabet, enabling them to read Hebrew prayers.[24] The JADRK committee assured the readers of their 1890 *Annual Report* that they will spare no effort to train the children who are instructed in their schools to habits of honesty, truthfulness, and loyalty; that they will seek so to develop their moral faculties as to produce a community of English Jews, who while not surrendering one principle dear to Judaism, while being reverently attached to the religion of their fathers, shall be bound with equal fetters of love to their country, their race, and their God.[25]

The JADRK questioned parents' ability to provide lessons deriving from Judaism's moral teachings. Quite intentionally, the organization did not limit itself to the study of Torah and stressed their role in forming good citizens.[26]

Anglo-Jewry used the JADRK classes in part to eliminate the foreignness of immigrant Jews. Six to seven hundred children 'all faultlessly tidy and neat in appearance, and all wonderfully well behaved and seemingly happy' attended the 1880 Prize Day, held at the JFS.[27] The Jewish Association claimed hundreds of children 'flocked' to the Sabbath classes rather than 'to the recreation which they might almost pardonably regard as their right after the schooling of the week'.[28] They emphasized the quality of their classes, but particularly their value in drawing children away from 'the unpleasant atmosphere of their confined homes to the brightness and cheerfulness and kindliness which greet them at the Sabbath School'.[29] Yet, as Table 5.1 shows, the organization had mixed success attracting children to supplementary classes.

Table 5.1: Jewish Religious Education Board Classes, attendance figures.

Year	1905	1906	1907	1908	1909	1912	1914	1916	1918	1922
JREB classes	8,314	8,295	9,321	9,229	8,393	6,366	7,007	6,251	4,673	4,402
JREB Sabbath classes	1,268	1,360	1,297	7,523	1,337	1,032	664	622	600	600
Jewish voluntary	7,892	7,672	7,469	1,450	7,406	6,988	7,317	7,169	7,105	6,225
Congregational classes	1,657	2,313	2,500	2,872	1,788	3,405	3,739	3,426	3,477	3,830
Talmud Torahs	2,660	2,454	2,500	2,500	2,500	3,044	3,746	3,512	3,654	3,942
Other	300									334
Chedarim	3,000	3,000	3,000	3,000	3,000	3,000	3,000			
Total	**25,091**	**25,428**	**26,087**	**26,574**	**24,424**	**22,813**	**24,809**	**20,385**	**18,909**	**18,999**

Source: *The Jewish Yearbook*, 1894–1924.

Samuel Montagu and the Federation

Samuel Montagu opposed the JADRK's religious philosophy and refused to permit the Federation of Synagogues to support the organization; its members did not gain JADRK representation until the 1890s. The Federation also wanted to eliminate many of the *chedarim* and *chevrot*, but endeavoured to provide a more comprehensive option than that of the JADRK or the JREB. In 1891, a Federation of Synagogues investigation located more than 200 *chedarim* that provided lessons to 2,000 East End boys aged between five and fourteen. Classes met from five p.m. until nine p.m. and fees ranged from 6*d*. to 1*s*. 6*d*. Some classes met in spaces set up 'as school rooms'. Most used a bedroom or kitchen, 'sometimes with a sick wife or child in the bed room, with cooking or washing being done in the kitchen'. In 90 per cent of the schools, the teachers spoke in 'Judisch', which many students, born in London, did not understand.[30]

Montagu led the effort to support traditional Jewish education while eliminating substandard teaching and facilities. A committee of the Federation that visited schools learned that 2,000 of 7,000 students attended *cheder*, 'their parents being dissatisfied with the progress made, and the short time devoted in the schools to Hebrew and religion'. The Federation supported the right of immigrant parents to provide their children with a sound Jewish education. 'It is urged', recorded the committee, 'that this desire of our working classes for further instruction in these subjects for their children, should be respected and granted'. They particularly expected this from the JFS, whose existence 'as a separate establishment, can only be justified because it is the *Jews'* Free School'.[31] Like other anglicizers, Montagu believed that aspects of traditional education adversely affected health and secular studies. Under Montagu's leadership, the Federation supported the formation of committees that would assess classrooms and recommend improvements or relocation. The Federation wanted to see more Jewish masters and pupil teachers appointed in schools with large Jewish student populations.[32] Anglo-Jewish leaders differed on the content and method of Jewish education, but overwhelmingly regarded religious instruction as essential to Jewish persistence and part of a proper English education.

Samuel Montagu further organized East End education by forming the Talmud Torah Trust in 1905 and offered funds to schools that agreed to eliminate Yiddish as the language of instruction.[33] Talmud Torahs tended to be larger and better organized than the *chedarim* and in many respects had more power within the community. Many owned their own buildings and most had a parents' committee. Leaders of the Federation wanted the Trust to become part of the Federation, but the Trust contended they were a 'representative body of vital importance' and did not want to 'become sectionalised'.[34] Most schools joined the Trust, which reached a combined enrolment of about 4,000 students.

The Jewish Religious Education Board

The JREB used all the moral suasion it could muster to encourage support for their efforts. They publicized gaps in Jewish education, in one case reporting on a letter they received from a teacher at Commercial Street Board School. The teacher claimed only ninety of 738 Jewish students received religious education, and those were at a *cheder* and that many children attended missionary services. If the community refused to finance additional voluntary schools, argued the *JC*, at the very least they ought to support the JREB.[35] By 1905, the JREB taught approximately 10,000 of 25,000 children attending board or church (voluntary) schools, but insufficient funding kept them from expanding. Children received three hours of instruction weekly at a cost of 3*d.* a child per week, amounting to about £5,000 a year.

From the mid-1890s until 1907, the JREB added classes at London board schools and created a teacher-training programme.[36] Appeals for money appeared regularly in the JREB reports, indicating their difficulty raising funds. In 1907, the JREB Board refrained from opening any new schools and anxiously awaited the returns of the 1908 Triennial Festival Dinner.[37] Financial difficulties from 1908 onwards forced the organization to exclude children under the age of seven, those attending Jewish voluntary schools and Talmud Torahs, and to increase class size and decrease the number of teachers. The Board felt these necessary actions impeded their goals. Children willingly attended religion classes at their own schools; attracting them to other schools was very difficult.[38]

The JADRK and the JREB catered overwhelmingly to girls, who typically made up 60 to 80 per cent of the students. Unlike their brothers, few girls attended privately sponsored classes. Table 5.1 above shows the numbers and types of schools where Jewish children received religious education and indicates that between 1905 and 1922 most children received their Jewish education in JREB classes and voluntary schools. The Jewish Association felt they did not receive the gratitude their organization deserved. Annual reports rarely discussed the curriculum, but habitually expressed frustration that many children received no Jewish education and increasingly mentioned attendance problems.[39]

Not only did the JREB supply the only Jewish education that many children received, they occupied children in a useful and safe manner. The Board's objective, according to Claude Montefiore, was 'not so much the imparting of facts as the training of character'.[40] As the Board noted in 1905,

> apart from the religious aspect of the matter, we must have some regard for the terrible moral dangers that abound in this 'modern Babylon' and against which the Board, by withdrawing the children from the streets, and imparting to them religious instruction, wages a useful war.[41]

In emphasizing the educational needs of immigrants, the *JC* implied that such parents failed to raise their children properly, and that East End children, those mostly likely to inhabit the streets, lacked the character necessary to resist temptations. Ironically, it was anglicized Jews who tended to reject very traditional forms of Orthodox Judaism.

During the years before World War I, the established community continued its efforts to eliminate traditional Jewish education. This lack of sensitivity, or as Norman Bentwich pronounced it, 'perversity or indifference of the anglicised Jews', prevented them from seeing any positive aspects in the traditional forms of learning and teaching.[42] Only a few years later, community leaders expressed concern at diminished Jewish practice and knowledge, wary that the masses of uneducated Jews pointed to a bleak future for Anglo-Jewry.[43] In 1912–13, only 20,000 of 35,000 Jewish children in London received some form of formal Jewish education. Approximately 2,000 received private instruction at home, but 13,000 youngsters learned only that which their parents imparted to them.[44] Reportedly, only 50,000 of New York's 200,000 Jewish children received a Jewish education.[45]

Modernizing Talmud Torahs

On the eve of World War I, poor conditions still characterized some Talmud Torahs. At the 1914 prize distribution at the Talmud Torah for Girls, Arthur Franklin expressed satisfaction 'that the classes were conducted in such well ventilated and comfortable rooms ... a good example to some other places where Hebrew and religion were taught in independent rooms and buildings where the pupils were cramped'. In a not too subtle attack on Yiddish, Franklin acknowledged that while occasionally it was necessary 'to make use of another language ... he was glad to see that that language was English'. In his experience, people who used Yiddish and other Jewish languages lived in countries 'in which they were not citizens or took no part in public affairs, either because they did not wish to or were not allowed to'. He thought it would be calamitous if England's Jewish children considered any language other English 'as their language'.[46]

During this same period, Talmud Torahs for girls numbered only two – and only a handful of schools still taught in Hebrew or Yiddish. Although it had to contend with a deficit in 1916, the Talmud Torah for Girls argued that girls' education was essential to 'keeping Judaism together'.[47] Members of the Jewish community who favoured in-depth education for girls did so largely to prepare them in their role of bearing and rearing the next generation.

Despite the financial challenge, the Commercial Road Talmud Torah, established in 1898, extended classes three times over by 1915.[48] According to the *JC*, the Talmud Torah movement, which had grown during the previous twenty-five years, had the 'respect and confidence of the parents', and received the pennies and shillings of self-sacrificing members of the industrial classes. Their 'energetic ladies society' provided 'material requirements' for large numbers of needy students. They stressed their use of modern teaching methods, challenging critics who mistakenly believed that they used methods common long ago in *chedarim*.[49] In 1915, the Great Garden Street Talmud Torah reported they had 480 students taking classes 'under modern hygienic conditions' in which the school 'trained its pupils to be not only good Jews but also good Englishmen'. They expressed pride in the past scholars who had joined the military. Yet Talmud

Torahs still felt the disapproval of established Jewry, who 'sometimes appeared to think that attendance at the Talmud Torah tended to retard the external Anglicisation of their pupils'.[50] Despite extensive modernization, the defensive tone indicates that tensions persisted between supporters of the schools and those committed to even greater levels of anglicization.

Fighting Indifference

Just before the War, the number of children taught by the JREB dropped to about 8,000 per week.[51] By 1916 they were exploring ways to guarantee that all Jewish youth had a minimum level of Jewish education and wrote notes to parents of children who did not attend religious school.[52] Recruitment remained challenging during the interwar years and the JREB's leaders decried both the lack of support they received from the Jewish community and irregular attendance of children registered for their classes.[53] Girls remained the majority of the JREB's students, contributing to a disproportionately greater anglicizing effect on Jewish women than on men. Indeed, many boys attending JREB classes still received a traditional Jewish education that likely minimized JREB's impact.

JREB reports and the Anglo-Jewish press enable one to follow the development of community-sponsored education and to track changes in religious observance. While the *JC* expressed disapproval of the approach to education offered in the *chedarim*, they did encourage religious observance. Certain styles of religious practice might be 'foreign', but minimal religious observance was equally problematic. A correspondent of the *JC* claimed that

> there must be something radically wrong with a religious organisation such as ours, which is able to countenance with equanimity the sight of a score of Jewish children – mostly girls of twelve or thirteen waiting on Sabbath afternoon outside the doors ... of an East End theatre.[54]

The 'stirring melodrama' was inappropriate for young girls who should have been 'attending their Sabbath classes'. 'What', inquired the writer, 'are the parents thinking about? Have they no sense of shame; of duty to the community of to-morrow?'[55] On the eve of World War I, a correspondent to the *JC* noted a teacher friend of hers had inquired of a young Jewish girl if she liked '*Shabbos*' to which the 'future mother in Israel replied' '"Never tasted them, auntie!"' The writer appreciated the candour, but felt certain the child would have answered a question on the Battle of Hastings without hesitation.[56]

The JREB's leaders attributed low levels of observance to economic causes rather than a by-product of the anglicization campaign and viewed the Sabbath classes as all the more significant. Their classes and short services kept children from 'undesirable influences' and instilled 'a proper sense of the Day of Rest'.[57]

During this same period, the JREB also experienced increasing problems recruiting staff members. Teachers were moving out of the Spitalfields area.[58] As Sabbath School teachers volunteered their services and time, travel and effort depended on goodwill and not the inducement of a salary. The decision to provide subventions to schools outside the East End underscores the growing awareness of the shifting population and the new demands these changes entailed.[59]

Economic challenges continued to plague the JREB, leading the *JC* to ask if the community was ready 'for the wholesale creation of little Jewish heathens' and suggested that the 'starvation' of the JREB would be of great advantage to the missionaries or would create 'a godless Jewish community'.[60] Missionary societies too, noticed the abundance of poorly or uneducated Jewish children; they claimed some success in educating Jewish boys and girls, who enjoyed the lessons. The LSPC took credit for saving such youth from the plague of irreligion since so many Jewish children grew up with no religion.[61]

Concern over religious laxity and ignorance mounted. Denzil Myer, an active volunteer in the East End, believed that many 'would be astounded if they knew that in the East End of London, which they have looked upon as the home of Jewish orthodoxy in this country, there is perhaps less religious feeling than in any other district where Jews are to be found'. Myer encouraged young Jews to attend special Sabbath services. The services stimulated discussion about the serious problems facing Anglo-Jewry.[62] According to 'A Young Israelite', Jewish youth were becoming apathetic with regard to spiritual matters and 'courted' pleasure on Sabbath. 'Gaily dressed young men and women' had only 'a hazy recollection' of synagogues and no sympathy for their pious elders.[63]

As the JREB battled a preference among immigrants for traditional education, British Jews recognized that indifference and decreased Jewish learning were taking their toll. The *JC* reminded its readers that Britons saw religious education as 'the one rock on which character could be built' and that citizenship without religion 'was to the true Englishman abhorrent and alien'.[64] The lack of substantive Jewish education and growing consternation over the pace of assimilation became a central theme in the years before World War I. In reference to Rev. Levy's estimate that 10,000 Jewish children received no Jewish training and equal numbers received only a few hours a week of 'altogether inadequate' education in JREB classes, writer D. B. Steinberg asked:

> What can be sadder than the thought that the greater number of these mothers-in-Israel-to-be are growing to womanhood ignorant of our prayers and Scriptures as well as the meaning, and very often the practice also, of all those observances that have made for the preservation of Israel and Judaism to this day?

Steinberg was especially concerned that Jewish education ended during the 'dangerous period of transition' between childhood and maturity.[65]

Just before the war, the JREB noted declining numbers of children in parts of the East End.[66] Wartime dispersal of the Jewish community created new demands and air raids forced many out of the district, large numbers of whom never returned.[67] As they encountered the success of anglicization, and movement out of the East End, the JREB concluded that the quality of their classes had to reach that of secular schools 'so that the children will learn to regard the religious teaching with proper respect as forming part of their ordinary education'.[68] Despite these convictions, the JREB's difficulties persisted.

In 1915, the JREB announced that it would 'confine itself to the education of such boys only as do not attend Talmud Torah classes'.[69] Soon after, the organization faced a new challenge with the arrival of war refugees from Belgium. The JREB's leaders believed that the war would further increase their responsibilities.[70] Yet, the JREB classes consistently attracted a diminishing number of students. In 1916, the Attendance Committee reported that attendance averaged about 75 per cent. The darkened streets and Zeppelin raids further reduced enrolments,[71] and finding teachers became even more problematic as many of the Board's teachers left to serve in the military.[72] During the winter, darkness forced the JREB to cancel evening classes in many schools.

Interwar Years and the Jewish Memorial

After World War I, Jews and Christians alike endeavoured to renew interest in organized religion.[73] The war years left the system of Jewish education severely compromised and in need of rebuilding. A sense of gratitude, but also a deeper sense of belonging, emerged within the post-war Jewish community. One expression of this gratitude was the establishment of the Jewish War Memorial. In 1919, Robert Waley-Cohen, F. C. Stern and Lord Swaythling (Samuel Montagu's son), wrote to Major Rothschild, 'leader of the Jews of the British Empire', about the need for new measures. It was time to erect a War Memorial 'as a monument to the Jews of the British Empire who have fallen in the War, as a thank-offering for those who have been spared'. As British Jews, 'prouder than ever of our British citizenship, loyal to the Faith which has sustained us, we wish to retain both our British citizenship and our inherited Faith'. They favoured creating an organization to support 'traditional Judaism'.[74]

Supporters of the War Memorial promoted the establishment of a British college of Jewish learning. By training native-born men to serve as religious leaders, Anglo-Jewry could eliminate dependence on foreign-trained scholars. The community had many challenges, including insufficient numbers of teachers and ministers. Jewish leaders had a clear image of the community's needs: they wanted clergy steeped in Jewish learning, with 'broad sympathies' patriotic and able to exercise spiritual influence on the 'present day Community made up of educated working men and women of the world'. They believed such training required the atmosphere of the ancient universities and recommended that Jews' College move to Oxford or Cambridge.[75]

By the end of the First World War, the dispersal of Jews demanded changes in the Jewish education system. The JREB felt the ongoing impact of war as military service left many potential teachers untrained and others had left the East End and taken 'more favourable openings in other quarters'.[76] Throughout the 1920s, the JREB commented on the out-migration of families in the East End, the end of migration to England and falling birth rates.[77] Jews no longer congregated in Stepney alone; decentralization increased the burdens on the JREB's meagre resources. The new conditions necessitated more schools with smaller numbers of students in areas of north-east and north London.[78]

Even with movement out of the East End, and declining observance, reformers still found unacceptable conditions in some Talmud Torahs. Critics looked to medical professionals to provide scientific evidence to support their calls for change. Dr Sourasky, a leading member of the JHO, found many classes in spaces 'that ought never to be used as school rooms'.[79] As late as 1930, the JHO still promoted proper sanitation and comfort of evening schools.[80] Native-born Jews remained convinced that immigrant-sponsored classes reinforced habits and attitudes of the old country. In turn, the established community became even more certain of the importance of modern religion classes and JREB classes that taught children about personal hygiene, alongside Hebrew and religion.[81]

Despite all the changes brought by time and World War I, JREB's modern approach continued to receive criticism. The Chief Rabbi, an anglicized Jew, designed the curriculum for these classes, but very observant immigrants did not trust the Chief Rabbi. His curriculum, taught in English, included Hebrew and Jewish practices, but also stressed 'the moral and ethical foundations of Judaism, truthfulness, honesty, loving and obeying God, cleanliness, and decency'.[82] Such lessons were certainly not at odds with traditional Judaism, but did not emphasize the text-based learning typical of a *cheder* or a Talmud Torah.

Leaders who just a decade before expressed concern over Eastern European *chevrot*, now feared that the rising generation had too little connection with Judaism. 'It is but blinding one's eyes', reported the *Jewish Graphic*, not to acknowledge that young East End Jews did not practice Orthodox Judaism as the 'founders of the United Synagogue would have wished'. Similar laxity characterized other London neighbourhoods.[83]

The JREB's organizers expressed growing frustration as student enrolment decreased. In 1927, the JREB suggested organizing a meeting with local parents to stimulate interest in Jewish education. While the declining population hindered communal efforts, the JREB regarded the 'lamentable lack of interest on the part of many of the parents in the religious education of their children' as a major cause of poor enrolments.[84] The JREB's leaders feared that the apathy that characterized parents' efforts for their daughters might soon affect their sons' education. 'The mother who has not herself come under the influence of Jewish religious teaching is not likely to make a great effort to secure such influence for her sons'.[85] As the Second World War approached, attendance challenges increased.

New Initiatives

Beginning in the mid-1920s, some synagogues instituted innovations with regard to girls' education, apparently in response to a call from the Chief Rabbi. In 1924, the Committee of the Council of the Jewish War Memorial referred to the increasing number of schools and Synagogues that offered 'special courses for girls, leading up to the Consecration Service established in accordance with the Chief Rabbi's scheme'.[86] As with the JREB curriculum, consecration services lacked a foundation in traditional Judaism. The Stepney Jewish School and the Jews' Free School were among those sponsoring such classes. Teachers 'testified to the great value' of the classes, noting the 'somewhat curious result' that only girls were being tested. Indeed, ministers and laypeople now asked why boys were 'immune from tests girls had to pass'.[87] The UJW also expressed support for girls' confirmation classes.[88] Much like the early days of immigration, community leaders turned to mothers to gain support for community initiatives. In 1930, the *JFS School Magazine* included a special note to mothers urging them to read the report of the girls' confirmation ceremony. As a home's 'Jewishness' often depended more upon mothers than fathers, JFS training of girls 'should gratify those mothers who regard Jewish observances as an important factor in life'.[89]

During the same years, the organizers of the War Memorial suggested that the opening of classes to girls in two Talmud Torahs was symptomatic of what would become a general movement.[90] In 1938, the *ELO* referred to a Talmud Torah at which more than two hundred girls attended free classes three times a week.[91] A sense of the urgency of providing and improving girls' religious education emerges from a wide range of sources and suggests that established Jewry, while committed to modernization, now concentrated upon sowing the seeds of Jewish continuity.

Curricular changes depended upon acceptance of new approaches by more traditional Jews. The slow adoption of such changes again indicates resistance to anglicization. Physical renovation also required money and the Talmud Torahs were in a perpetual state of financial crisis. To compound the situation, the established community, who disapproved of them, refused them financial support, increasing the difficulty. The JHO report from 1929 to 1930 noted sanitary improvements in Brick Lane and Bethnal Green Talmud Torahs, but the 1934 report made a pejorative reference to traditional methods, indicating the tenacity of Eastern European culture and ongoing efforts to eliminate this form of Jewish education and its dilapidated meeting spaces.[92]

The JREB remained committed to providing every child with a Jewish education, but they acknowledged that their efforts alone would be in vain. In 1930, they announced 'that the time has come when a concerted campaign should be undertaken by the whole community to deal with the grave problem of Jewish illiteracy, which is a growing menace to the future of Judaism in this country'.[93] Attendance increased somewhat in 1930, and in 1931, despite a 5 per cent decrease in the East End school population, the Board experienced an 11 per cent increase in its class sizes.[94] Growing numbers of boys now received their Jewish education in board schools – a victory for anglicizers and a defeat for the more traditional and intensive education of the Talmud Torahs and *chedarim*.

Long term, many observers predicted a mixed outlook at best. The challenges of attracting students remained a theme during the 1930s.[95] As one East Ender recalled, parents sent boys to *cheder*, but 'no girls went to Hebrew, or anything like that'.[96] While a significant number of East End children continued to attend traditional schools, Anglo-Jewish leaders helped hasten the demise of the Eastern European style education. Talmud Torahs managed to retain nearly 4,000 students as late as 1922. By the late 1920s, the Talmud Torah Trust recommended amalgamating schools in some districts – which would save money, improve standards of accommodation and, most importantly, raise the standard of education.[97] This trend revealed both a move away from traditional Jewish education and reflected the movement out of the East End.

Despite communal efforts, religious education classes for Jewish students at board schools had their challenges. Further, they led to conflicts among government education officers, the JREB and the schools. From October 1936 to July 1937, a sizeable correspondence discussed procedures for Jewish religious education at the Robert Montefiore Senior Girls' School and Christian Street Junior Girls' School. Nathan Morris, education officer and secretary of the JREB, approached the LCC about organizing twice-weekly religious education classes. The JREB would get parental consent and qualified teachers would offer classes in a local building.[98] The LCC reviewed the request and the school managers and the head teacher agreed to allow the 'educational experiment'.[99] The issue resurfaced when a JREB representative sought approval for a similar plan at the Christian Street School. The headmistress's reluctance prompted the representative to refer to the scheme at the Montefiore School. Although such classes did exist at the Montefiore School, the LCC claimed they were still waiting for paperwork from the JREB. The LCC believed it had 'been double crossed'; moreover, 'the Robert Montefiore children show little inclination to go'.[100] The JREB had indeed gathered the required parental permissions, but had failed to deposit the forms at the school.

Such incidents point to the very delicate balance facing Anglo-Jewry. They were anxious to provide religious education in board schools, yet these programmes underscore the anomalous position of a religious minority in a country that perceived itself as culturally homogenous. Taking advantage of the right to receive a non-Christian education had potential costs – the annoyance and disruption it might cause – and risks of public discussion that focused attention on Jews' distinctive identity.

Nonetheless, the JREB classes began at Christian Street. Three months later, much to the surprise of the JREB, the headmistress called for 'drastic modifications'.[101] 'It is impossible', she contended, 'to get my secular instruction in'.[102] Correspondence continued among the headmistress, the LCC and the JREB which expressed a willingness to work out the difficulties associated with their classes. Committed to the provision of Jewish education for East End youth, Jewish leaders were now willing to risk the consequences of the strains that arose over the implementation of their programme both within and beyond the Jewish community.

Missionaries and Education

Since the influx of Jews meant potential converts, missionaries undertook language and religious education. In 1906, the LSPC started a women's class, though some women had already been attending mothers' meetings for many years. One potential member of the women's class, who was unable to read or write, explained that the leaders would have to speak or read to her. The mission concentrated their work in the Goulston Street Hall in the East End and reached out to women and children with lantern lectures and mothers' meetings.[103] They held several worship services each week and calculated 1910's cumulative attendance at 3,000. The organization sponsored evening language classes for Jews in Whitechapel. Approximately twenty-five Poles and Russians attended. The mission 'instilled the principle of Christian love, which has led in many cases to earnest and sincere enquiry'.[104] A minute fraction of Jews, including small numbers of local children, attended such missionary meetings and even fewer converted.[105] Undoubtedly, English lessons, music and personal attention attracted some participants, but others likely took advantage of material inducements.[106] By World War I, attendance dropped because of pressure from the Jewish community and the difficulty of attracting more anglicized, and presumably less vulnerable, Jews. Yet, in 1925, despite continuing efforts of institutions such as the JFS to counter missionary activity, the LSPC reported a slight growth in attendance and the need to hire an extra teacher.[107] Given the geographic scope of the mission, and the population of Jews in the East End in this period, the LSPC attracted insignificant numbers.[108] The concerns they provoked within the Jewish community were far more substantial.

The Jewish community especially resented efforts to draw young children from Judaism.[109] The LSPC was clearly aware of the contempt with which many Jews held missionaries, observing that children attended special meetings and lantern services despite 'the gauntlet' through which they had to run, which included 'threats of other children to tell their parents or their Jewish teachers'. Missions justified their efforts, claiming Jewish children suffered through lack of religious education.[110] In a conversation with a Jewish social worker about the situation, a Protestant minister recommended that rather than complain, the Jewish community ought to provide 'for their own religious welfare and distribute ... literature appertaining to the tenets of their Faith'. In response, a group of women founded the Society for the Distribution of Jewish Literature in 1916.[111]

Responding to Missionaries

The Society's Jewish Free Reading Room (JFRR) opened in 1917 and during its first nine months attracted 156,509 adults and 13,610 children. Apparently, women demonstrated some reluctance to attend, assuming it was 'for men only'. The Reading Room set up a separate table with special papers for women.[112] Large numbers of women and girls stopped in 'to find relaxation from their daily toil and enjoy the opportunity of the perusal of good literature in restful surroundings'.[113] The JFRR expanded its reach by establishing a Friday night lecture series that attracted both young people and adults. According to their reports, the glowing Sabbath candles, white tablecloth and flowers brought feelings of Sabbath joy to all who attended.

Children were a high priority and the JFRR committee sponsored worship services, holiday celebrations and hearth talks. 'Jewish children' reported a committee member, 'are generally keen readers, and from the first they forced an entry; a corner of the room was fitted up for them, the only stipulation being that they should come with clean hands'.[114] In its appeals, the organization stressed the important role it played in maintaining contact with adolescents. While most charities supported the sick and hungry, 'hunger and thirst of the soul' also needed attention.[115] The JFFR served a key educational role and did so within a religiously and ethnically conscious framework.

Conclusion

In the years before the Second World War, disagreements over appropriate education remained. Many immigrant parents still favoured intensive orthodox-style education for boys as they had little respect for the anglicized Judaism of their social betters. Yet, growing numbers of children received little or no Jewish education. Parents who traditionally provided limited religious training for girls continued that pattern, but offered limited resistance to JREB classes. Those who attended the Board's classes or refurbished Talmud Torahs did so under much healthier conditions than their predecessors.[116] Boys, in many cases still attended *cheder* or Talmud Torah and, much to the disappointment of native Jewry, large numbers of classes still met in unregulated private homes amidst terrible sanitary conditions. The JHO and communal leaders exerted both moral and financial pressure on Jewish schools to anglicize their curriculum and meet in appropriate locations.[117]

The interplay within the Jewish community and between government and voluntary associations suggests some areas of tension over anglicization. Many Jewish educators acknowledged the need to reform Jewish education. British Jewry 'ahead of the rest of the world in our charitable provision', lagged 'behind them in our organisation of religious education'.[118] Significantly, in the area of religious education, established Jews felt comfortable enough to press for the needs of the community. Victorians supported religious education, making it respectable for Jews to arrange for this kind of education among their poor. This liberal policy was not, however, a one-way street; anglicized Jews cherished, and expected, immigrants to support England's institutions. As early as the 1880s, Jewish parents received the message that they 'ought to be thankful for the advantages they possessed'. It was argued that other countries with much larger Jewish populations denied Jews the freedoms granted in England. Anglo-Jewry encouraged parents to demonstrate their gratitude by 'avail[ing] themselves of the education offered their children, so as to give them a sure foundation on which to build in after life'.[119]

During the late 1930s, the East End remained home to large numbers of traditional Jews, including Chassidim. Communal leaders recognized with some anxiety that 'with increasing anglicisation this last citadel of orthodoxy is being gradually undermined by the indifference of the young masses'.[120] Yiddish largely met its demise when immigration slowed; the declining number of speakers could no longer support multiple newspapers or theatres. The movement of Jews out of the East End pointed both to the damages the war brought to the East End, as well as to the success of immigrant Jews. As immigrants, but especially their children, moved into the upper reaches of the working class and into the middle class, they settled in areas free of Yiddish and 'Jewish trades', and left behind their alien culture, *chevrot*, missionaries, overcrowded tenements and the programmes that contributed to their acculturation.

6 JEWISH CLUBS AND SETTLEMENT HOUSES: THE IMPACT OF RECREATIONAL PROGRAMMES ON THE ANGLICIZATION OF EAST ENDERS

In addition to material assistance, Anglo-Jewry combined science, sympathy and *tzedakah* to sustain the spirit and occupy the body of Jewish immigrants. Reformers and philanthropists developed cultural, athletic, educational and recreational activities to redress the disadvantages of slum life. Youth organizations – Scouts, Guides and Lads' Brigades – Christian, secular and Jewish – reveal contemporary apprehension over the weak physical condition of Britons, declining birth rates, inadequate military readiness and imperial decline.[1] As club records and the Jewish press indicate, Jews felt additional pressure to demonstrate the health and vigour of its immigrant community.[2] Club programmes and membership peaked during the interwar years, many developing into multi-service settlement houses.

Jewish Clubs and Settlement Houses

Typically, clubs functioned as stand-alone organizations for boys or girls of a particular age group or one of many groups within a settlement house. Jewish clubs varied in size, but most capped membership at 100 and catered to boys and girls ages thirteen to sixteen. Generally limited to Jews, a few, such as the Victoria Boys' Club included several non-Jews, hoping that the mixing of Jews and Christians would benefit the members.[3] Settlements served East Enders from cradle to grave. The 1927–8 Oxford and St George's Jewish Settlement *Annual Report* explained that settlement work 'is more comprehensive and goes deeper than "Club" work'. Settlements operate 'behind the scenes', assist with domestic problems and aid 'the physically weak and mentally infirm'.[4] Undoubtedly, Settlement activities closed many gaps between young East Enders and native-born Britons, but may have unintentionally widened the cultural and generational differences between parents and children.

During this era, many social reformers concluded that children of working parents lacked proper supervision and needed training and appropriate places to play. 'We shall all agree', claimed the *JC*, 'that the aim of all education is the formation of character'. Parents were responsible for the 'dos and don'ts', but clubs took on 'the equally urgent side of character training; the prompting to "be this", to "think of that"'. The first aim of clubs was not a creative one, but to keep boys and girls off the streets and give them some culture.[5]

The Model of Toynbee Hall

Among the earliest leaders of the settlement movement, Samuel Barnett, Vicar of Saint Jude's Church, moved to the East End in 1872. Discouraged by his inability to implement change through his church, Barnett founded Toynbee Hall, the first university settlement, in 1884. He encouraged university graduates to move into the settlement, to live and work among residents of the East End. Part of Christian social service, many settlers felt motivated by Christ's example.[6] Barnett spearheaded efforts to improve local housing, libraries and playgrounds; he ran a boys' club, a working men's club, supported local cooperative societies and the work of social reformers and researchers.[7] He promoted a notion of 'disinterested service' and recruited residents who accepted this philosophy, whose background and education meant they could look at society objectively and offer impartial recommendations.[8] Toynbee Hall's residents hoped to bridge class divisions by recreating community.[9]

Barnett established a positive relationship with arriving Jewish immigrants and the Jewish communal workers who followed. Toynbee Hall, proud of its tradition of religious pluralism, served 'Churchmen, Nonconformists, Roman Catholics, Jew and unsectarians'.[10] Thousands of Jewish residents benefited from free legal advice offered at Toynbee and from the support it offered during strikes such as that of the Amalgamated Society of Tailors in 1889. The needs of the community, however, soon exceeded the services of a single settlement.

The Founding Jewish Settlements

Native-born Jewish women played central roles in clubs and settlements, reaching out to, and influencing, East End women and children from early childhood to adulthood. A wide range of recreational programmes took place at London's four Jewish settlements, West Central, Brady, St George's Jewish and Stepney, all of which developed from clubs that met on their premises.[11] Leaders responded to 'the awakening social conscience of the time' and arranged activities that helped 'more recent immigrants rapidly to adjust themselves to life in their new country'.[12] Many of their ideas derived from the work of reformers such as Samuel Barnett.

Jewish settlement houses and youth clubs would become the most comprehensive, and, after the schools, the most significant anglicizers.[13] They developed in part, because Jews could not, or would not, join Christian organizations. Clubs enabled the community to provide supplemental education and most importantly, maintain contact with young adults once they left school. Julia Cohen, like her Christian counterparts, explained that 'the club seeks to lure girls from the streets, the penny-gaffs and the music halls'.[14] These organizations introduced immigrants and their children to British leisure activities, middle- and upper-class managers and the values of self-help. Large numbers of Jewish youth participated in organized sport, an innovative aspect of the new leisure industry.[15] As historian David Dee argues, British Jews saw sport as 'encapsulate[ing] key notions of Englishness'; participation would lead to a natural transformation of Britain's most recent residents.[16] Concern over images of weak, unmasculine Jewish men, played a role in shaping the response of Jewish communities throughout Europe.[17]

Jewish volunteer leaders' enthusiasm for proper leisure tended to reinforce traditional gender roles. Boys' clubs, consciously athletic from the start, endorsed a sort of muscular Judaism.[18] They advocated self-restraint, encouraged patriotism and opposed gambling, which Jews and Gentiles perceived as a particular Jewish vice. Beatrice Potter apparently learned more about gambling than tailoring during a visit to the Amalgamated Tailors' club.[19] Initially, girls' clubs emphasized good mothering, needlework and music and drama to refine girls' taste. They added athletics over time. Similarly, Girl Guides initially highlighted the maternal training they offered – a reflection of contemporary attitudes and the need to parry charges that the movement was 'unfeminine and dangerously public'.[20]

Clubs did not, however, meet with universal approval. Helen Lucas, a lay leader, whose activities included serving as president of the JBG's workrooms, thought clubs encouraged girls to shirk responsibilities at home.[21] Unlike most of her contemporaries, Lucas believed that after work 'girls do best to spend their evenings at home. Clubs she distrusts, as encouraging a habit of gadding about'.[22] Another critic, 'Recluse', found clubs 'extremely rough and noisy' and suggested that money needed for serious philanthropic work 'is diverted into a dozen different channels and frittered away for their [club members'] amusement'. It was enough to assist the poor and the ill and to allow others to 'amuse themselves'.[23]

Most East End workers, however, credited clubs with countering attractions of the street.[24] In her response to 'Recluse', Lily Montagu, warden of the West Central Girls' Club, assured readers that in her nine year association with clubs, she had received as much sympathy from working girls as she had given. She was confident that the hundreds of girls' clubs in London had a positive impact and were inculcating 'a high ideal of home life'.[25] Most discussion of clubs emphasized leaders' opportunities to 'direct lagging feet to really profitable paths ... in short, to civilize and spiritualize ... keen-witted boys and girls'.[26]

In the 1880s, many districts in London had no boys' or girls' clubs. By 1902, the Girls' Club Directory listed over 300 clubs and guilds for girls, and many more for boys, but only three 'well organised and managed' Jewish girls' clubs.[27] Since British concerns about morality focused on girls more than boys, it is not surprising that girls' clubs predated boys' clubs and lads' brigades, even though the latter grew at a faster rate. Possibly, the slow development of girls' activities reflected ambivalence about girls spending time outside their homes. By the early years of the twentieth century, boys' club membership soared. As many as 40 per cent of men born between 1901 and 1920 claim to have belonged to either a Boys' Brigade or the Boy Scouts.[28]

The tradition of Jewish settlement houses in England began with Lily Montagu.[29] The West Central Jewish Club and Settlement opened in 1896 and became the model for many clubs and services available to immigrants. Montagu believed that if middle-class leaders approached 'working-class members in a spirit of friendship', clubs could improve class relations. Befriending a member involved knowing about 'her life and circumstances' and working on her behalf.[30] Jean Spence suggests that Montagu's commitment to 'rights-based education' was distinctive. Montagu strove to understand her members' working conditions, which created 'a moral obligation' to promote girls' character.[31] Arguably, though, like many of her colleagues, Montagu combined sympathy with elements of paternalism.

Religion in Clubs

From the outset, the role of religion and the 'Jewishness' of clubs generated debate. According to a member of the Stepney Jewish Club (established in 1901), religion was popular in few Jewish clubs, though Stepney held religious services, 'attendance at these being optional'. Most Christian clubs included prayer meetings and Bible study.[32] Stepney's Wednesday evening Jewish Study Circle remained small and Saturday Sabbath services, held in English, attracted few worshipers.[33] Up to nine members attended the Jewish Study Section, which one member described as 'not at all bad considering that most Stepney lads are thoughtless, happy-go-lucky boys'.[34] Even clubs that did not promote religious observance claimed they valued a positive Jewish identity. While the Brady Street Boys' Club chose not to introduce religion, they were 'particularly anxious to do all in their power to encourage Pride of Race in their members'. They tried to enhance such feelings through weekly lectures on Jewish History.[35]

Organizers of the West Central Lads' Club believed that clubs that lacked a religious foundation had no reason to be denominational, but the voluntary basis of club life meant they could not force religion on members. They acknowledged that Bible classes, prayer, and services 'appear to flourish better in girls' clubs' because 'women are less shy than men of talking to one another about religion'.[36] At Lady Magnus's (Leman Street) Club, religion, along with refinement and recreation, was one of the three R's they cultivated. When it opened, Leman Street attracted 'city working girls, who assembled to be told Scripture and other stories' while sewing – 'a delightful combination of the practical and the ideal'.[37]

Moulding Jewish Boys and Girls

During the early days of club life, physical space mattered less than it would over time. Very quickly managers saw that programmes benefited from spacious, well-equipped and attractive facilities. The founders of the Brady Street Club for Working Boys, noted that organizations for working men and women existed, but nothing met 'the equally, if not more, urgent wants of young working lads'.[38] At the point a young man was 'most readily susceptible to external influences, good or bad, he was left to shift for himself ... proper facilities for passing his spare time in a healthy and rational manner, being virtually non-existent'. Brady Street provided working boys with opportunities 'to improve their stunted physique, raise their general tone and bearing, [and] inculcate into them habits of manliness, straightforwardness and self-respect'.[39]

Clubs set high standards for members. The Stepney Jewish Club magazine commended the new Anti-Gambling Association, reflecting a concern over Jewish behaviours and reputation.[40] The Brady Club had successfully formed a similar association. Stepney Club managers promoted the signing of a pledge form, which would offer moral support when boys faced the challenges of 'undesirable companions'.[41] By September, half of Stepney's members had signed the pledge.[42]

Brady's facilities were open five nights a week; a club superintendent and minimally two members of the committee attended, along with some forty-five members on week nights and approximately seventy on Saturday and Sunday. Total membership fluctuated between ninety and 160. Despite efforts to foster a level of commitment, the club acknowledged the difficulty of 'checking the nomadic tendencies of the average East End boy'. The managers generally voiced satisfaction with the boys' conduct; indeed 'maintaining order ... proved unexpectedly light'. The club had a well-stocked library, papers, magazines, games, bagatelle, chess, draughts, dominoes and boxing equipment.[43]

Brady was especially committed to physical fitness and felt that immigrant boys lacked proper enthusiasm for exercise. Reflective of late Victorian values, they sponsored gymnastics, musical drills and swimming, which, like general attendance, suffered decline after a promising start. Work and the club's distance from homes accounted for some of the losses, but the managers saw a deeper character flaw: 'It must be admitted, however reluctantly, that a considerable proportion of the boys have an undoubted aversion to physical exercises in any form'. Only twelve of one hundred members attended the athletics class, which the committee saw as a liability to their future health.[44]

Social reformers believed clubs could change the geographic and moral landscape. The opening of the West Central Working Lads' Club brought about a transformation. The house, once 'a night club of the very worst class', was a 'veritable hell on earth; one of those dens where men gamble away their health and manhood, and girls their womanhood'. A 'good fairy', Emma Montefiore, used a pen and a conveyancing lawyer to open the club in 1897. The facilities enabled members to 'cultivate the upright frame of the athlete and its almost universal corollary, upright bearing in their daily dealings with their fellows'.[45] Claude Montefiore continued his family's financial support of the club.[46]

Also committed to fitness, lads' brigades emerged at the end of the nineteenth century. In 1895, the Jewish community founded the JLB as the Christian foundation of the Boys' Brigade meant they could not accommodate Jewish companies.[47] Organizers hoped members would 'become a source of legitimate pride' and sought Jewish communal support 'in establishing healthy minds in healthy bodies in our rising generation'.[48] They promoted 'drill, discipline, and manly sports, such as cricket, football, and athletic exercises', as a replacement for 'loafing' and 'gambling'. The Brigade's principle medical officer emphasized that vast differences of 'cleanliness, erectness of carriage, and muscular tone' distinguished a recruit from an 'efficient member'.[49] Similar to clubs, the leadership of the JLB believed that contact with cultured middle-class Brigade officers was of immense benefit to East End lads.[50] Unlike the Boys' Brigade, founded to keep working-class boys involved in church activities, the JLB emphasized drill and physical activity over religious life.[51]

The Butler Street girls' club, which opened in Spitalfields in 1903, drew Jewish girls from north of Whitechapel Road and sponsored activities until 1943. Initially, Butler Street served approximately one hundred girls and included two large rooms, one with a kitchen, two conversation rooms and a large hall for drilling, concerts and social gatherings. In addition to a social programme, Butler helped develop the girls' political knowledge by sponsoring debates which became so popular that they partially replaced Saturday night dances.[52] Clubs tried not to compete with other activities and the Butler and Leman Street clubs specifically encouraged girls enrolled in evening continuation schools to attend their club on nights when they did not have classes. Club leaders also hoped to sponsor their own classes under a Board of Education scheme and to secure grants for them.[53]

Club managers also helped school leavers by serving as guardians to apprentices. The Stepney Jewish Lads' Club arranged with the JBG to collect premium repayments, simplifying the process for apprentices, and enabling club staff to monitor the working lives of their members.[54] The JBG believed such relationships were effective because young people had an opportunity to get to know their guardians in a congenial atmosphere.[55]

Over time, clubs became more democratic. The Stepney Jewish Club had a lads' committee, and club members expressed satisfaction that the managers had granted more power to the boys.[56] The boys took up their leadership roles with a combination of purpose and humour. The *Stepney Jewish Club Chronicle* editors noted that with the coming of winter, the club would see increased attendance. They suggested that the boys find a 'more useful occupation than that of exerting their lungs to their greatest capacity to the discomfort and annoyance of the Managers and other quieter fellow members'.[57]

Clubs and Masculinity

Significantly, from the outset, boys' clubs defined and promoted Jewishness via a set of contemporary standards of Englishness and were grateful to 'the many institutions in our midst for the fact that what has been styled "the Ghetto bend" is fast being ironed out of our youth'. The *JC* expressed pleasure at the change and were proud that Jews of all classes had 'rallied to the country's call to arms'.[58] The *Jewish World* reminded its readers that 'every Jew who becomes a proficient in manly sports' served as a response to critics who claimed 'we train our minds to get the better of our neighbour'. Rather than denying such charges, showing interest in sport would prove Jews were ready to 'to take their places as citizens, physically and mentally equipped for the battle of life'.[59] Patriotic duty and gratitude to England created a self-conscious Jewish leadership who took seriously their commitment to moulding respectable working-class boys.

Many English-born volunteers spoke openly about the public image of Jews. According to Claude Montefiore, good acts 'would help to raise the name of Jews as a body', but 'every bad act' would bring 'harm to Jews all over the world'. Montefiore urged the boys to remember this in the club and beyond.[60] A similar tone prevailed at the Stepney Jewish Lads' Club. At their Second Annual Meeting, Rev. Stern introduced Mr Micholls, who congratulated members for their unselfish work for the club. The club helped 'make the Jews worthy of England, the country that was the first to extend a welcoming hand to them'. According to Micholls, more than 1,000 British Jews had volunteered to fight against the Boers, the highest percentage of any denomination. Micholls thought there would be no 'alien question' 'if all Jews behaved outside these walls as well as the lads did inside'.[61]

Members too championed clubs. PMV, for example, recommended that to become the 'Ideal boy', members' 'chief hobby should be physical and moral self-development'. 'The Ideal Boy' need not 'be a cherub' as that was 'the mission of the Ideal Girl', but he 'must be true to his religion, and to his country of either birth or adoption'.[62] It is difficult to measure the extent to which boys identified with club goals. The contest to replace the Stepney Jewish Lads Club's motto 'Our true intent is for your delight', suggests some members believed the club had a serious side.[63] When the club paper announced the winning motto, 'The Club for all and all for the Club', it encouraged members to carry out its teachings.[64]

Proper Jewish Womanhood

Girls' clubs developed activities designed to create ideal British 'Jewesses'. The Leman Street girls' club had the typical range of classes, with a particular emphasis on Jewish history, and Sunday teas for the cultivation of manners. In 1910, the club had 240 girls on its list, 180 of whom attended regularly.[65] The Beatrice Club for Working Girls, established in 1901 also, had a full schedule of classes, including singing, English, German, Hebrew, plain and fancy needlework, drill, swimming and bible. The club held Sabbath services and described them as 'a valuable means of stimulating the love of their religion among the members'.[66] They organized cultural events and rambles to the countryside. They too sought to give the girls a greater say in the management of the club.[67] The Beatrice Club emphasized sports less than other clubs, which probably reflected the nature of their membership, girls who worked nearly a twelve-hour day – and had little time for the negative influences so feared by middle-class Jews.

Clubs often attracted single women from North London who engaged in 'practical social work' between their own departure from school and marriage.[68] They could teach 'the disinherited in our midst ... how first to regain and then to retain, that sanctuary of home which is the ideal of womanhood and the foundation of a prosperous state'.[69] Social convention deemed club work an appropriate extension of middle- and upper-class education and a useful way for the leisured to spend their time, while mentoring immigrant girls.

The Expansion of Jewish Clubs and Settlements

The early years of the twentieth century saw a significant growth of clubs and settlement houses.[70] With the slowing of immigration, the community turned from immigrants' immediate needs to programmes that shaped youth for British Jewish adulthood. In December 1913, Basil Henriques, who began his career through an association with Toynbee Hall, sought support from the West London and Liberal Jewish Synagogues for a Jewish boys' club. He stressed that the boys in the club would receive as little assistance as possible and would do as much as they could for themselves. The club was to have a Jewish religious influence. The leaders

> would lay before the boys an ethical code of morals recognised by most of the civilised world and help them to live up to that code, not only for the honour of their club, not only for the honour of the Jewish religion, but above all for the sake of their God.[71]

The club needed men to help as managers; likewise, Henriques also appealed to women whom he felt would have 'a most refining influence on the lads' and would 'awaken in them, much good which at present might lie dormant'.[72] Henriques was staunchly anti-Communist and had a reputation for dissolving committees whose actions deviated from his goals.[73]

On 3 March 1914, the Oxford and St George's Jewish Lads' Club opened on Cannon Street Road in part of the old Raine's Foundation School. Henriques moved into a room upstairs and the club activities took place in a single room. Fifty boys waited to enter the club the first evening.

> In spite of their foreign parentage, these youngsters were English born, and at once it became the object of the Club, to make them worthy citizens of England, through the very same methods as were used to achieve that end in the public schools – tradition, the team spirit, athletics and sports on the one hand, educational activities on the other.[74]

In a diary entry of May 1915, Henriques described his realization of the need for a club for girls. 'It was', he argued, 'little use to educate the boys to a certain way of life if girls were not being trained to strive for the same ideals and one day to share their lives with them'.[75] Henriques persuaded Rose Loewe to work with him and start a girls' club. It opened in July, based on the same principles as the boys' club.[76] The clubs functioned separately, with the exception of an occasional dance.[77]

Soon after the club opened, Loewe, while hesitant to seek assistance in the midst of the war, sought gifts in kind. The new organization intended 'to teach its members to be good Jewesses, showing them both the spiritual and practical sides of Jewish home life' and providing a 'substitute for all the powerful fascination of evenings spent in the streets or in picture palaces'.[78] At the end of 1916 Basil Henriques and Rose Loewe married; she moved into the club and took over Henriques's responsibilities when he went off to the front.

Despite many successes and supporters, critics continued to voice their disapproval of clubs, especially regarding their lack of a specifically Jewish ethos. No clubs, according to Samuel Solomons, offered 'any real Jewish educational work'. 'It is a distorted sense of proportion', he contended, 'that instils the spirit of the sportsman in Jewish lads, and feeds pride of race with Jewish Imperialism'. Providing 'wholesome amusement', noted Solomons, was a poor *raison d'être* for any Jewish institution.

> To some, Judaism in all its connotation, can only survive when neutralised by British traditions. When members and managers of Jewish clubs sum up their Jewish work with such naive serenity, one can only feel that the policy of being more loyalist than the king himself is responsible for more than one sore that afflicts Anglo-Jewry.[79]

Rev. Stern's son Leonard, who served as a manager at the St George's Jewish Lads' Club, also condemned the absence of religion in clubs. He chastised H. L. Nathan of the Brady Club, who sympathized with 'the more athletic form of Sabbatarianism', and claimed that 'the whole question of religion in Jewish Clubs stinks in his nostrils'. Home life, according to Stern was decaying and 'East London is not exactly a nursery of religion'. Clubs should not usurp the functions of the home and synagogue, but should encourage members to practice the type of Judaism that reflected the preferences of members' parents.[80]

Rev. Stern, minister of the East London Synagogue, believed club managers were the key to creating a Jewish tone in clubs.[81] Stern wanted managers, who had deservedly won their members' trust, to foster a religious milieu. Since boys would respect those interests their leaders valued, religious 'indifference' by leaders had a negative impact. For Stern, the minimal religious influence managers introduced into clubs encouraged 'the evolution of the Yom Kippur Jew who is so ugly a feature of the community'. In contrast, Stern claimed there was Christian influence at church-sponsored clubs.[82]

Girls' clubs, too, faced this criticism on the eve of the World War I. The Myrdle Club played hockey on Sabbath, which garnered sympathy for its hard-working members. The *JC* hoped 'that something may be done to obviate the collision between Sabbath observance and the admitted needs of industrial life in a great modern city'.[83] One member, Nellie Virsof, thought it reasonable for girls to spend their few hours of leisure playing sport, especially since 'the health of a nation is of the greatest importance'. Further, sport was preferable to the way most East End Jews spent Saturday, 'parading Whitechapel Road in the latest fantastic fashions'.[84]

This viewpoint aroused a strong response from Miss Lilian Victor who believed that hockey, and the travelling it required, violated the Sabbath and asked how Virsof and her friends justified playing hockey on Saturday. 'It is mistaken nobility' to compromise 'religious principles' in order to contribute to the nation's health. Victor asked Virsof to consider 'whether the nation requires – or welcomes – physical fitness at such a cost' and recommended spiritual and mental welfare, contending they too would add to the nation's well-being.[85] Evidence of shifting needs and perceptions emerge in these disputes. When the community first established clubs, they fostered acculturation. Over time, concern surfaced that young people had moved too far away from Judaism.[86] Some supporters argued that rambunctious boys who attended clubs did not want religion and managers had no influence unless children learned about religion at home.[87]

Alongside detractors, many championed clubs and their potential for 'improvement of the race'. Sensitive to negative images of Jews, the Jewish Athletic Association's (JAA, founded 1890) Prize Day epitomized Jewish attitudes about the need to eliminate ghetto characteristics. They emphasized their contribution as the only organization providing outdoor sports for Jews. By 1914, JAA had fifty-one affiliated schools and eighteen lads' clubs.[88] In referring to Jews' 'physical improvement', the 1914 Prize Day speaker asserted that the 'reproach formerly hurled at them of being a stunted race' was vanishing. In its appeal for funds, the JAA referred to games on Friday afternoons and Sundays, spoke of the value of fresh air and made oblique reference to 'serious evils ... arising from the want of some healthy interest in life'. The JAA's 'preventive' policy saved twenty pounds 'that might be begged later on to alleviate consumption and other ills' for every pound they spent.[89] Some girls, whose behaviour did not meet the standards of clubs, received attention from the Jewish Association for the Protection of Girls and Women. Primarily a 'rescue' organization, the agency branched out into preventive care. During the First World War and after, the JAPGAW worked with other agencies dedicated to discouraging young girls from loitering in the streets of London.[90]

The Impact of War

The many clubs established at the end of the nineteenth century served as the foundation of anglicizing and recreational programmes in the decades to come. The outbreak of the First World War, the increased freedoms accompanying it and especially competition from other forms of recreation, all forced changes in clubs and led to a commitment to improve facilities. The aims of clubs still caused significant debate in the Jewish community. And there is the occasional indication that some parents lacked enthusiasm for the clubs. On the twelfth anniversary of the Butler Street Club, Chief Rabbi Hertz reminded parents that their children deserved recreational options unavailable at home and urged girls to try to understand their parents' attitudes. He believed clubs could foster mutual understanding. Hardly revolutionary in their offerings, the 1916 annual exhibition indicated that Butler girls received excellent instruction in a variety of domestic skills, including dressmaking and cooking.[91]

During the war, publicizing club members' military contributions gave the Jewish community the opportunity to demonstrate that youth organizations helped create patriotic English Jews. The Stepney Jewish Lads' Club had representatives in seventy-three regiments and on nineteen ships; those too young to join or unable to enlist started a fund to send parcels to members fighting abroad.[92] About four hundred managers and boys from the Stepney Jewish Lads' Club entered the military, 'many ... making the supreme sacrifice'.[93] Despite the absence of many managers during wartime, the leaders of the Stepney Jewish Lads' and Oxford and St George's Club decided to continue operating. Often St George's members would stay at the club during leaves, providing a sense of continuity and evidence of members' devotion.

Through the 1920s, settlement and clubs leaders often played the role of social worker. When club leaders recognized a young woman, her face 'painted and powdered' and 'dressed in a manner to draw your notice quickly to her', it felt 'like a dagger thrust'. Two years earlier, that same 'modest and charming' girl had refused to join the club.[94] The Settlement now dealt with young people who considered themselves more English than the English and shared the nation's craze for American dances such as the Charleston and Blackbottom. Henriques hoped to influence those who 'made money faster than they have made knowledge of the things that are worth while', and to 'Anglicise those who are becoming Americanised, and to Judaise those who have become Anglicised'.[95] For Henriques, one role of the settlement was to 'bridge' generational differences.[96] Success would improve relations with parents, restore the sanctity of the home, and importantly for Henriques, undermine the appeal of Zionism.[97]

Youth unemployment rose after demobilization and clubs competed with new forms of commercial entertainment. Rose Henriques noted that unsavoury men 'lurked round the cinemas and billiards saloons, on the look-out for bored young people'.[98] The Stepney Lads' Chairman expressed concern that several members had 'attended undesirable Clubs which encouraged gambling'. The Chairman and Hon. Secretary felt strongly enough that they raised the issue with the police, who explained that current law prevented them from taking any action.[99] Unquestionably, World War I transformed the expectations of East Enders, yet nostalgia for the pre-war world emerges in the mix of attitudes and the blend of 'modern activities and nineteenth-century values' common in youth organizations, including those in the Jewish community.[100]

By the interwar period anglicization altered the needs of the community, especially for second- and third-generation residents. The Jewish community, led by a dedicated cadre of established Jews, continued to support co-religionists. Clubs increasingly groomed managers from within, but settlements found it necessary to make regular appeals for workers. Although air raids no longer served as an excuse, St George's had received few offers from women willing to serve as managers. The paucity of workers impeded efforts to expand.[101] The St George's 1923 annual report expressed disappointment that more members of the community and sponsoring synagogues had not become involved.[102] Club managers responded by hiring professional teachers and purchasing better equipment. At St George's, girls could take classical music classes and performed a yearly opera, beginning with the *Meistersinger*. Rose Henriques introduced ballet classes, and, with great ingenuity, arranged for teachers from Sadler's Wells to teach at the club.[103]

Post-War Building

Significant upgrading of facilities occurred after the First World War, in part to redress war-time neglect, but also to provide attractive recreational facilities that counteracted other forms of leisure. As life began to resume its normal contours, the Stepney Jewish Lads' Club re-established a full programme, refurbished their building and revived the annual camping trips.[104] As Oxford and St George's Club's original members were now sixteen and seventeen years old, Basil and Rose Henriques formed Old Boys' and Old Girls' clubs. And it was only limitations of space that hampered further growth. In 1919, after a successful appeal, and donation from Lord Bearsted, St George's Clubs purchased larger facilities and opened the Oxford and St George's Jewish Settlement.[105] Of all the settlement's groups, the girls' club benefited most from the new building. The club now had a dancing hall and rooms for a diverse range of activities.

During the 1919–20 season more than sixty St George's Jewish Settlement girls camped at Leigh-on-Sea, where 'dressed in drill shorts', they spent the week shouting, laughing and hiking through the countryside.[106] The trip became an annual tradition, which the club lauded as successful, despite inadequate food, water and sanitary arrangements. Settlement leaders claimed the time spent at camp proved more valuable than any other programme.[107] The rejuvenating qualities of nature and fresh air – the respite from crowded neighbourhoods – aided girls' development and the establishment of corporate feeling.

Club expansion continued during the 1920s. Early in the decade, St George's renovated the girls' facilities next door to the settlement. Improvements included a shower, quite a change from the days when the girls had to line up in the yard with one girl behind a canvas curtain and another, pouring water from a watering can. By 1923, the St George's Jewish Settlement claimed to have direct dealings with 1,000 children, and indirectly with 2,000 more.[108] Basil Henriques increased his work as a neighbourhood trouble-shooter, dealing with financial, marital, housing, clothing and health problems. He believed settlement programmes served as counter-examples to the charge that Jews had been a negative influence in the East End.[109] Athletics and recreational activities continued to occupy girls in communally sanctioned leisure. A play centre for children up to age eleven and facilities for residential social workers opened, and various clubs settled into Cannon and Betts Streets. The Settlement added girl guides and a junior girls' club for eleven to fourteen year olds, run by members of the old girls' club.[110]

Clubs evolved with the times; as more girls and boys entered the work-force, clubs had to find a way to accommodate both old boys and old girls during the August Bank Holiday Week. In 1927, the St George's took both boys and girls away, to different sections of the same field. Objections, emanating mostly from the boys' clubs' managers, did not foil the plan.[111] Although commercialization of leisure began before World War I, many workers had more time and discretionary income after the war, leading to increased family tensions.[112] On one occasion Kitty Rappaport Collins recalled that her mother

> was horrified when I wanted to go to a dance – it was either (the Jewish holiday of) *Succos* or *Simchas Torah* – she she [*sic*] – it really broke her heart. My father said 'well why shouldn't she go? Everybody's dancing at *Simchas Torah*'. She gave in, but she didn't really care for it.[113]

Many young women considered themselves quite innocent and worried much less about the temptations of the street than did Jewish leaders and parents. According to Collins, girls considered gum-chewing boys as crass. As East Enders earned more, they ventured out to the Locarno Ball Room, to the Astoria on Tottenham Court Road and the theatre at the Old Vic. Collins's parents had no objections to her participation, but did not share her enthusiasm for such activities. Typically, her parents asked where she was going, but they trusted her. She had to be in at ten – 'and wipe your lipstick off', hinting at an area of potential conflict. Collin's first dance clothes were long evening dresses; her ordinary clothes, beautiful suits made by her father. Generational differences come into relief when one compares her parents' evening leisure. Occasionally, they went to the Pavilion Theatre in Whitechapel, to a nearby cinema, to the Grand Palais for Yiddish theatre, but more typically visited family or played cards, calling it 'an evening in'.[114]

Challenges of the day continued to occupy youth leaders. In 1928, the Association for Jewish Youth (AJY, established in 1927 as an umbrella organization) sponsored a conference to consider 'knotty problems' such as 'The Adolescent Girl Problem'. One speaker argued that because a girl was 'a mother in the making', she had to live by a different 'standard of values'. When accompanied by understanding and sympathy, girls responded to clubs that provided leadership and guidance. The conference discussed mixed clubs and concluded they were 'impracticable and undesirable' and 'also agreed that greater efforts should be made to get in touch with mothers, and, if possible, reintroduce the girl into her own home on a better footing'.[115] Efforts to influence girls – and to reach them through their mothers, continued whenever possible.

Given the perceived dangers, young men and women who did not join clubs were a source of particular anxiety. Ida Samuel, a very active volunteer leader, noted that despite the work of the Jewish apprenticing committee and other similar groups, 'many children, through ignorance, mistrust, or laziness, were still left to their own devices and allowed to drift, without education, employment or the benefit of a club membership'. The chair of the 'Aftercare Committee' session described some of these non-members as 'derelict boys and girls', and portrayed them as a 'potential source of danger to themselves and to the whole community, being one of the chief causes of anti-Semitism'.[116] No doubt that clubs influenced their members, yet the image of troublesome young men and women giving a bad name to the Jewish community, once again points to undercurrents of insecurity within Anglo-Jewry.

During World War I and beyond, as concern over assimilation increased, the role of religion in clubs became even more contested.[117] Basil Henriques reasserted his commitment to 'bring God into the clubs', which aroused vigorous opposition. One correspondent to the *Jewish Graphic* argued that 'a religious onslaught in the clubs ... would not only split the workers, but stop their growth in strength and numbers through quarrels over formulas and precepts'. The writer thought it more important to attract new members before promoting religion. Others maintained that managers were not 'fitted to preach or conduct prayers'.[118] Nonetheless, Henriques, who was associated with the Liberal branch of Judaism, organized regular services at the Whitechapel Gallery. Numerous leaders of Anglo-Jewry, along with 800 to 900 men and women attended the first New Year's services in 1922, including Rev. Morris Joseph, Lily Montagu and Ben Mocatta.[119] The 'decorous' *Erev Rosh Hashana* service combined a 'reverence for tradition' and 'modern needs'.[120] Henriques's attachment to the Liberal Jewish movement created concern in some traditional quarters of the East End, though he regularly reminded parents that he had no intention of drawing children away from traditional Judaism and encouraged his members to attend services with their families.

Supporters far outweighed detractors. Regardless of an individual's 'outlook on Jewish affairs', everyone, claimed the *Jewish Graphic*, admired the work of the settlement and the 'unstinted devotion of the warden, Mr Basil L. Q. Henriques, and his charming wife'.[121] According to the editor of the *Jewish Graphic* the criticism reflected 'extreme narrow-mindedness'. Ultra-orthodox Jews' fears 'that the children brought up under the fostering care of Mr and Mrs Henriques would ... eventually become in later life attached to the Liberal Synagogue' were absurd.[122] Butler Club too, taught their members to be 'Jewesses of the right sort, who knew and understood, and were therefore, proud of their religion'.[123] In keeping with the mission of clubs, most club leaders promoted a respectable form of religious identity and observance.

The ongoing expansion of membership of East End clubs during the 1920s points to the unmet demand for recreational and educational programmes. Managers believed that clubs' formative and preventive influences were a sound investment for the Jewish community. The Stepney Jewish Lads' Club took credit for achievements of many former members, who were grateful to the club 'for the beneficial guidance and help they received during their early years'.[124] During the 1920s the Stepney Lads' Club was open every evening except Friday and had a wide-ranging programme that included athletics, games, a library, a savings bank, concerts, debates, dramatics and annual camps. Evening activities ended with a short religious service.[125] Athletics remained a central focus of most clubs. Leaders, a number of whom were themselves products of public schools, believed that East End children benefited from knowledge of British sports and notions of fair play. Boxing and physical drill were extremely popular in Britain; many saw them as very valuable for training Jewish youth.[126] According to Lady Janner, a mainstay of the Brady Club, club leaders passed on their ardent enthusiasm for sports to the youth in their clubs.[127]

Settlement leaders continued to secure services for their young members by sitting on the care committees of elementary schools in the area. The poor remained under scrutiny. Social investigators increasingly believed deficient home conditions produced wayward children. Settlements such as St George's believed they could contribute in this area and improve the prospects of children becoming productive citizens.[128] Such attitudes also tended to perpetuate the view that immigrants and workers required guidance, and that such intervention was legitimate.

By the mid-1920s the St George's Settlement once again outgrew their space. An unannounced visit by Bernhard Baron, in 1925, initiated his relationship with Oxford and St George's and Rose Henriques bought a used piano with the donation from the visit. In 1927, the Henriqueses travelled to Brighton to visit with Baron, who offered them 15,000 pounds. The figure, while generous, was inadequate for a building that could house the settlement's activities under one roof. The Henriqueses declined the offer, adding they would raise the money elsewhere. Rose Henriques's response to Baron reminded him of the frustrations of own his youth, when investors refused to finance his new cigarette machine.[129] Apparently, Baron had decided to offer a larger sum, but not to inform Basil and Rose during the meeting. A short time later, Baron returned to Oxford and St George's, offering to donate 50,000 pounds and provided an additional 15,000 pounds for a roof-top playground. Baron laid the foundation stone for the Bernhard Baron St George's Jewish Settlement in April 1929, and encouraged a speedy completion of the building, lest he die before its opening.[130]

The new facility on Berner Street opened in March 1930, with an official opening by the Duke of Gloucester in June; unfortunately, Baron had died the previous August. Henriques described the goals of the enlarged settlement, many of which resonated from the past, thus:

> We aim here to provide for all those contingencies which take place between those two events [of birth and death]. A Club is not merely a place to which boys and girls go in order that they may be away from the temptations of street lounging, but it is an institution with a very positive policy. We aim here at the glorious ideal of fitness – of physical fitness, mental fitness, and moral fitness, and we set out to make our members worthy of this great empire.[131]

The settlement, which now had a membership of 1,700, still concentrated most of its energy on children and adolescents.[132] Settlements could prevent girls and boys from 'deteriorating in mind, body and soul, and of becoming little less than a caricature of what they are really capable of doing'.[133]

The 1930s brought a combination of new opportunities and social, economic and political challenges. The Bernhard Baron Settlement decided to build new model flats to house some of the most overcrowded families in the neighbourhood. While overcrowding had diminished since the settlement's founding, 'dwellings unfit for human habitation' filled the neighbourhood.[134] St George's in the East remained London's most overcrowded district, a major social problem itself.[135]

The Bernhard Baron Settlement continued its focus on women. In 1932, they started a mothers' club, but instead of emphasizing anglicization, they offered recreational facilities. The club's sixty members were 'firmly cemented together' during their camping trip at Goring-by-Sea. The advantages of working with parents did not escape the notice of the settlement's organizers. Not only did the club bring 'joy' to members, 'the close co-operation between parents and those who look after their children in the Settlement is of inestimable value'.[136] The mothers' club, a fairly late development, points to continued efforts to reach children through mothers.

During this period, clubs ceded increasing responsibility to members of the senior groups. The Bernhard Baron Settlement took pride in the fact that its clubs had no written rules; tradition set the accepted boundaries.[137] The Settlement's diverse activities suggest their popularity among a number of different constituencies. Alongside new programmes, they still offered cookery, laundry and dressmaking – skills for girls' futures as homemakers.[138] The Settlement proudly reported that a glance at the homes of the old boys and girls who had been club members showed they were raising 'their children in accordance with the ideals of the Club'.[139]

The settlement took credit for the virtual disappearance of 'rampant' juvenile delinquency.[140] In contrast, the JAPGAW reported some increased criminal activity.[141] Club leaders implied that clubs, rather than twenty years of education and upward social mobility of immigrants, explained the improved ability of East Enders to offer their children a cleaner and safer environment. By the mid-1930s, the Bernhard Baron St George's Settlement was moving away from prevention, but still argued that their 'activities are positive in purpose. Relaxation and re-creation are made a means for teaching the right use of leisure. The educational activities are cultural rather vocational; they aim at self-expression and self development rather than direct inculcation of knowledge'.[142]

However, the needs of the East End were shifting and new challenges lay on the horizon. With the depression years, Stepney's unemployment level rose. Those affected could stay out of trouble by spending their free time at the Settlement. The economy made it difficult for girls entering the work force to escape 'blind-alley' employment. The Bernhard Baron Settlement assisted boys in finding suitable employment because they, unlike most girls, did not 'retire at marriage'.[143]

In 1935, the settlement's annual report noted that there had been no time when it was more important for Jews to demonstrate their loyalty to their country and their religion. Despite the unsettled times, High Holiday services attracted numbers beyond capacity, club membership continued to rise and organizers formalized medical and dental schemes. By 1936, a new concern permeated the Bernhard Baron annual report; the rise of Hitler, increased anti-Semitism and the prospect of another war placed new burdens on the Jewish community. Again, the settlement stressed the value of Judaism. In keeping with a history of Jewish self-consciousness in Britain, the settlement reaffirmed the value of a positive Jewish image – the importance of members proving that 'to be a Jew means to be a good neighbour and a good citizen'.[144] Troubled times also generated acts of solidarity. After one of Oswald Mosley's marches, the local Presbyterian church sent a note of support to the Bernhard Baron Settlement and a Jewish Christian Fellowship brought Stepney boys and girls together for a talk and informal prayers.[145]

Throughout the 1930s, most clubs retained single-sex membership. In 1933, Basil Henriques wrote that 'mixed clubs are almost certainly to be a failure for both sexes'.[146] By 1948, he had modified his view. By then he supported mixed 'recreational education' as long 'each sex can keep apart when they want to ... and where ample chance is afforded for the full development of all that is virile in the boy, and all that is graceful and delicate and feminine in the girl'.[147] He maintained that boys from fourteen to sixteen should remain separated from girls, who tended to be more developed than the boys.

Though he acknowledged that modern influences encouraged a swift movement from early puberty into early manhood, Henriques seemed to fear budding sexuality among his boys. He tried to limit mixed activities to times and places where leaders could maintain a high level of control and favoured a full programme for boys – and an equally attractive one for girls 'so that the girls are not hanging about luring the boys away from their classes'.[148]

According to historian Sally Smith, by the interwar years, many young Jewish men were sexually active. Thanks to the double standard, such behaviour was far riskier for young women.[149] Indeed, Morris Beckman described the guilt young men felt if they slept with a Jewish girl – and the challenges associated with purchasing condoms, owing to limited availability and embarrassment.[150] Clearly, club leaders such as Lily Montagu hoped to control their members' behaviour. Girls' 'sensitiveness' allowed for the 'highest potentialities', but meant girls, more than boys, 'surrender[ed] their best selves to the degrading influences of their environment'. Working girls who were 'individualistic' and 'pleasure-loving' often had a negative influence on boys.[151]

Lily Montagu also preferred single-sex activities. She approved of the occasional carefully prepared 'mixed evening' whose 'tone' compared 'favourably with that of many West End drawing-rooms'.[152] Specially arranged mixed events as a privilege and not a right, meant boys and girls would demonstrate more self-control when they did 'seek closer contact'.[153] Some activities, such as theatre, benefited from the inclusion of boys – as Montagu held they could only produce good plays when men and boys took male roles.[154]

Montagu believed girls required a wide range of classes, religious influence and understanding adult role models to promote self-respect and channel their energies. She approved of 'sex instruction' in clubs and 'unrestricted questions after each lecture', but thought lessons from mothers should begin well before adolescence. They 'saved' children 'from associating with the beginning of life anything sordid or unclean'.[155] Only recently, contended Montagu, had there been a 'conscious effort ... to teach girls that they do not exist as the mere supplements to men'.[156] Nonetheless, Montagu accepted and promoted traditional gender roles; girls required 'separate training' since, 'by nature' they differed.[157] She favoured the presence of refined women in boys' clubs, so boys would 'begin to reverence womanhood'.[158] Managers of boys' clubs could teach young men a sense of responsibility, which would discourage early marriage and would keep young men from becoming prey to girls who 'wanted a lark'.[159] Such attitudes and anxieties help to explain the sense of urgency with which the Jewish community promoted recreational programmes.

Youth programmes continued to develop into the 1930s, when leaders read-dressed educational needs for all ages. Descriptions of the Brady play centre capture something of this philosophy. Organizers saw 'no reason why play should not be directed into definite channels of educational and physical value'.[160] During winter, they served cocoa and biscuits to children who came to the centre after school, where they learned 'the excellent lessons of deportment and self-discipline' at tables set 'with clean and attractive cloths'.[161] Even the Brady's youngest members received lessons in the good use of leisure and respectability.

Rising membership throughout the early years of the 1930s meant Brady activities soon outstripped the available space. During 1933, Brady's Council located a building site and hoped to add a small settlement to the new facilities. Ida Sebag-Montefiore provided substantial financial support for this development. The new building, opened by the Duchess of York in Hanbury Street in 1935, included areas for activities and had a room for giving out clothes, which serves as evidence of continuing poverty in the East End. The settlement had a cookery and laundry centre, living accommodations for the warden, a managers' sitting-room; a roof-top playground and a garden with flood lighting topped the new facility. Brady managers expected 150 girls to attend on week nights and between 200 and 300 on weekends.[162] Although some individuals had questioned the need for girls' clubs, the club pointed to the quality of the 1938 Display and Prize Giving ceremony, as proof of their benefit.[163]

Stepney Girls' Club, which opened a settlement in 1938, was most fortunate in having two remarkable women at its helm. Anna Schwab, chairman of the club, and Phyllis Gerson, the Warden, both devoted long careers of service to the club, its members and the East End. One hundred girls utilized the club's facilities every night before World War II.[164] The club closed temporarily when the war forced the evacuation of much of the membership from London. Gerson retired in 1973, at the age of seventy, after forty-five years working to mould the Settlement into a multi-service community centre.[165]

Gerson recalled the first time she became aware of the East End and its immigrant population. She accompanied her father to his office in Bevis Marks and he suggested she go for a walk around the neighbourhood. Upon her return, she mentioned to her father that she had had some difficulty understanding a 'funny German' and found it surprising that all the women in Stepney had the same colour brown hair with a part in the middle. Such was her introduction to *sheitals*, Jewish immigrants and their mother tongue. Gerson learned about poverty from Basil Henriques. Rose and Basil Henriques encouraged Gerson to take an interest in the children. She began volunteering in the East End, and unlike many, she attended the London School of Economics where she trained as a professional social worker.[166]

While reports of dire poverty had diminished by the 1930s, hardship still affected East End families.[167] The Jewish Working Girls' Club maintained a 'Comforts Fund' which assisted girls who were ill at home or in the hospital, and they provided holidays for needy girls.[168] Concern about girls extended to their families. The committee from the Beatrice Club willingly offered advice to families in response to problems they discussed with the leadership. The club reported on the developing comradeship between managers and members as they worked and played together.[169] Club leaders engaged in home visits and tried to befriend whole families. While need continued into the 1930s, the *New Survey of London* recognized the Jewish community's high quality social work, particularly commending the girls' clubs at the Oxford and St George's Jewish Settlement.[170]

Alongside impressive development, Jews were experiencing increased anti-Semitism. Many responded by reasserting their value to Britain, rather than refuting the charges. The feelings of insecurity were real and understandable, and the sense that Jews still did not fully belong consistently re-emerges in the literature. As the children of immigrants came of age, many expressed resentment towards fascists, but also towards the quiescent approach of many Jewish leaders, including the JBD.[171] Just prior to World War II, annual reports from the various clubs indicated that managers believed that greater fellowship and understanding could resolve many of the world's problems.

Anti-Semitism was not the only influence that led settlement leaders to reaffirm the importance of club activities. They continued to face competition from a number of directions. The need for greater technical and commercial education meant club members spent time at evening institutes that they once spent at settlements. Clubs did meet some of the newer needs of the time. Increased motor traffic made the necessity for play centres all the greater. Many long-time members maintained club memberships after marriage and children. More than ever the Bernhard Baron Settlement claimed its religious life and the synagogue served 'as a harbour of peace from the turmoil of the outside world' in which 'materialism, agnosticism and even atheism are rife'.[172]

Clubs increased their use of professional teachers and took advantage of LCC classes. Unlike its pre-war days, the Beatrice club created opportunities for the girls to 'associate freely and without self consciousness with the Christian neighbours from other clubs'.[173] Clubs continued to stress their ability to promote their members' self-improvement.[174]

War on the Horizon

Club records provide a window on the rapid pattern of acculturation and reveal shifts in opportunities for immigrants and their children, including significantly improved recreational facilities and classes, as well as increasingly diverse occupational choices. On the eve of World War II, many Jews in the East End experienced a rise in their occupational status. While large numbers still entered factories, retail sales, teaching and secretarial work grew in popularity.[175] In 1937, Freddie Cohen, one of Stepney Jewish Girls' Club's original members reflected on changes during the club's first decade. Initially, only the best behaved girls could attend events outside the club. In the early days, it was a 'novelty' to be a member of a girls' club and 'they enjoyed every minute spent in the hall where we met every night'. Old members remembered a time when there were no quiet rooms and the only LCC classes were Gym and Dramatics.[176]

However, significant change loomed and preparation for war occupied club leaders. As the Bernhard Baron Settlement began planning for potential air raids and the girls formed a Girls' Training Corps.[177] In 1938, the JLB and the Girls' Divisional Committee of the AJY organized courses on air-raid precautions.[178] On 25 August 1939, a few days ahead of schedule, and just days before the war started, the girls' annual camping trip ended. For leaders feared that should the war begin, the girls would be unable to return to London.[179] The East End would suffer extensive damage during the war, forcing many people and institutions to build their post-war lives beyond the East End.

Conclusion

Clubs and settlements worked hand in hand with other communal services, identifying need, providing assistance when appropriate, and promoting self-help. Organizations for girls and boys probably involved no more than one-third of the East End's youth, but were attractive to many East Enders. East Enders welcomed recreational opportunities, built lasting friendships and Anglo-Jewish leaders believed that they trained future generations for Jewish and English life. Clubs and settlements successfully responded to many people and a wide range of needs. Perhaps their sense of achievement was overrated, but Basil Henriques for one believed that 'through the Settlement the Jewish slum child may become the glory of England'.[180]

While tensions and resentment do occasionally surface in the sources, the enthusiasm of members and leaders, the opportunity to participate in athletics, competitions, plays, camping trips and classes suggest the popularity and influence of the many East End clubs. Well into the 1930s, clubs reported excellent attendance, though they did not attract or serve all of the Jewish East End's adolescents.[181] Stripped of their alien ways, second and third generation Jews extended the movement of Jews north, north-west and south. They brought with them the lessons learned in clubs and from contact with native Anglo-Jewry. The 'children of the ghetto' had indeed become almost indistinguishable from those with much deeper roots in England.

7 WOMEN'S AND CHILDREN'S MORAL HEALTH IN LONDON'S EAST END, 1880–1939: THE MAKING AND UNMAKING OF JEWS AND 'JEWESSES'

As information emerged about the risks facing women travelling alone from Eastern Europe – unfulfilled marriage promises, problematic divorces and men seeking women for prostitution rings – women's groups in Britain, Germany and America developed services to aid women and children,[1] their 'natural clientele'.[2] By the mid-1880s, acting out of Jewish values and Victorian morality, prominent Jewish women began to combat the association of Jews with trafficking by founding a Jewish rescue association. Rescue work attracted a number of Christian and Jewish women who sought to 'purify' public and private spheres. Some of the reformers promoted restrictive legislation – a controversial approach for feminists. Religious faith motivated many rescue workers.[3] Jews wanted to challenge public associations of foreigner with 'Hebrew' and white slavery.[4] Because prostitution was, as Paul Knepper notes, 'profoundly embarrassing for Jews concerned with framing Jewish identity within British class, racial and gender sensibilities', it sparked an atypically visible response.[5]

Drawing on extensive records from the JAPGAW, the Montefiore House School and the Jewish press, this chapter demonstrates not only the perceived dangers facing Jewish girls and women, but the Jewish community's approach to assistance. Given the virtual absence of immigrant voices, gauging the motivations and perceptions of women who strayed from traditional respectability remains a significant challenge. Occasional glimmers of resistance to Jewish communal standards emerge through discussion of behaviours that communal leaders and volunteers deemed inappropriate. The Jewish communal fight against vice and juvenile delinquency combined sympathy with a commitment to sexual purity, concern for girls and women as well as disdain for the Jewish men who brought shame to the community.

Founding a Rescue Society

In 1885, a non-Jewish social worker, Mrs Cooper, approached Lady Battersea (née Constance Rothschild) to discuss the problem of homeless Jewish girls. Cooper explained that someone brought two young women involved in prostitution to the East End Mission. The girls, unwilling to renounce Judaism, refused to enter the shelter.[6] Spurred to action, Lady Battersea called a meeting and gave a 'stirring address' about rescue work. The meeting closed with the passage of a resolution to begin prevention and rescue work in the Jewish community, and led to the establishment of the Jewish Ladies Society for Prevention and Rescue Work.[7] According to the organization, the

> term 'trafficking' implies that the girls have been lured from their parents and natural protectors, to be taken for immoral purposes to lands strange to them where a language they cannot understand is spoken. They are then forced to lead lives of shame and misery, watched at every turn by taskmasters, treated with savage cruelty, and often sold from dealer to dealer.[8]

The founders soon learned that local prostitution was only a small part of a worldwide sex slave trade involving a number of Jews and extending from Eastern Europe to South America.

Under Lady Battersea's direction, the Jewish Ladies Society created services to assist unmarried mothers, girls and women facing neglect and at risk of prostitution. Battersea sought the assistance of Claude Montefiore, who became a central figure in the organization, and in 1896, the founders established the JAPGAW as successor to the Jewish Ladies Society for Prevention and Rescue Work.[9] They worked with other Jewish and secular organizations dedicated to ending white slavery; through international cooperation, they hoped to stem the traffic and frustrate the efforts of procurers. After the 1904 establishment of the German Jewish Jüdischer Frauenbund, the Jewish Women's League of Germany, JAPGAW worked with their founder, Bertha Pappenheim.[10] In addition to fighting white slavery, the Jüdischer Frauenbund pursued equality for women in Jewish communal affairs and promoted career training for women.

Anxious to parry charges of large-scale Jewish involvement in white slavery, the JAPGAW publicized their exertions to eradicate this blot on the reputation of England's Jews. In 1899, they cited Alex Coote of the National Vigilance Association. Jewish rescue efforts, explained Coote, 'gave full and public testimony to the fact, that if the Jews unfortunately supply their share of brothel keepers and bullies, they are equally ready to expend money, time, energy, and devotion upon combating to the death a gigantic evil'.[11] Unlike the women of the Jüdischer Frauenbund in Germany, JAPGAW women rarely, if ever, entered brothels themselves. Although women founded the organization, they concluded that men were best able to handle certain branches of the work.[12]

At the 1899 international conference on white slavery, feminist Millicent Garrett Fawcett reported that the 'miscreants who engage in this trade' chose poor girls who could not speak English and lacked influential relatives. 'The cruel persecution of the Jews in Russia, has I am informed, been the cause of a terrible increase in the number of Russian Jewesses who have been victims of the white slave trade'. Procurers lured young women from Odessa to Constantinople and sent them all over the world.[13] While small in total number, Jews made up a significant proportion of white slavers.[14]

In response, prominent Jewish women and men developed extensive services to prevent prostitution and rescue 'the fallen'. Jewish rescue workers' motivations did not overlap entirely with those of their Christian colleagues who, as guardians of the home, believed that prostitution broke 'marriage and baptismal vows and poisoned family relations'.[15] Jews tended to focus on the impact on individuals more than on families.

As part of their communal services, the JAPGAW opened the Domestic Training Home and Charcroft House for unmarried mothers. They hoped to combat high infant mortality rates among illegitimate babies, though illegitimacy rates among Jews appear to have been quite low.[16] These typical Victorian charitable endeavours had some anglicizing impact. As importantly, they demonstrated Jewish commitment to the protection of women and an intolerance of vice within the community and served as a productive response to anti-Semitism.[17] The organization opted for a visible campaign to restore those who had slipped into immorality and create good 'Jewesses' who were self-respecting and capable of earning a living.[18] While quite common among Victorian philanthropists, Anglo-Jewry generally preferred to remain inconspicuous.[19]

Within months of their first meeting, Lady Battersea and her cousin Emma Rothschild created the skeletal features of the rescue society. They opened a shelter in Stepney for single Jewish girls, developed a scheme for meeting foreign girls at the docks and had contacted London workhouses to determine how many Jewish girls passed through their hospital wards.[20] Few Jews resorted to such foreign environs; on average the Infirmary ward of Whitechapel workhouse served only 'twelve unmarried Jewesses' a year.[21]

Beginning about 1888, the Jewish Ladies Society sent agents to assist girls travelling alone who were 'unprotected', unfamiliar with English and 'ignorant of the dangers awaiting them at the port'.[22] Lloyd Gartner estimated that unaccompanied Jewish girls and women numbered less than 3 per cent of steerage passengers who travelled to London from the Continent.[23] The JAPGAW was quick, like other Jewish charities, to assure its readers that their assistance did not encourage immigration.[24] Staff and volunteers verified the respectability of travellers' London destinations before escorting young women to them, and then reported the addresses to the Association's Visiting Committee, which arranged follow-up visits.[25] Often, the addresses required rather creative deciphering: Buxton Street, Bricklane being rendered 'Bakster St. Breksaen', and Hunts Place, as 'horts plats'.[26] As Table 7.1 indicates, the numbers of girls and women met by the JAPGAW increased until 1905 (year of Aliens Act) and levelled off in the years up to the First World War.

Table 7.1: Boats met by the Jewish Association for the Protection of Girls and Women.

Year	1894	1897	1898	1899	1903	1904	1905	1906
Ships met	450	457	373		586	673	706	782
Number of passengers met in steerage		10607	11836					
Number of passengers among whom unprotected girls had to be sought out	3,380				29,252	38,794	35,817	37,982
Number unprotected girls	275	315	364	655	1,087	1,233	1,366	929
Girls left at the home in default of destinations or imperfect addresses	84	60	93	145	351	351	290	99
Girls conducted to other ships or London addresses	191	255	271	510	817	882	1,076	830
Non-Jewesses assisted	42	30	41	70	87	95	108	71
Girls under 14 travelling alone					45	39	38	33
Young married women travelling alone					61	34	61	52

Year	1907	1908	1909	1910	1911	1912	1913	1914
Ships met	712	698	721	689	660	661	724	506
Number of passengers among whom unprotected girls had to be sought out	28,856	17,656	19,715	22,935	18,924	22,979	27,406	21,235
Number of unprotected girls	712	621	676	698	541	517	739	409
Girls left at the Home in default of destinations or imperfect addresses	81	33	26	31	17	23	18	23
Girls conducted to other ships or London addresses	631	588	650	667	524	494	721	386
Non-Jewesses assisted	97	86	88	76	60	43	73	21
Girls under 14 travelling alone	29	28	38	21	15	11	14	13
Young married women travelling alone	72	114	90	68	72	61	85	35

Source: JAPGAW, *Annual Reports*, 1894, 1897, 1898, 1899, 1903, 1904, 1905, 1906.

The JAPGAW described their efforts as 'entirely directed towards the saving of girls and women'. While they had the 'zealous support' of men in the Jewish community, they also worked against corrupt men and women who plotted 'the ruin of countless girls and women'.[27] The organization described the many means men used to convince girls to leave home: they fostered 'discontent', promised 'easy and well-paid work, engagements in marriage, mock marriages, and even legal forms of marriage'. After girls left family and friends, procurers used the 'utmost cunning' as well as 'drugs and brute-force' to the get 'the isolated victim to stray from the paths of virtue'.[28] The JAPGAW insisted such descriptions involved no exaggeration.[29] Yet, as historian Susan Mumm reminds us, rescued women typically emphasized their innocence.[30]

Preventive Efforts

Demands on the JAPGAW led them to hire an assistant in 1898. They wanted to add a third officer in 1904, but lacked the funds. As the organization developed, leaders strategized about aiding young women and handling publicity about Jewish involvement and convened an international conference in 1910. In rather impassioned language, the JAPGAW argued that the community could not 'allow our maidens to be debased and bought and sold as merchandise. We *cannot* and *will* not let them go down to ruin, misery, degradation and suffering, without a determined effort to prevent it'.[31] One of the organization's male leaders contended that the community should discuss the matter 'openly and frankly' to avoid the charge that the Jewish community was concealing anything.[32] The rise of anti-alienism during the early years of the twentieth century and characterizations of Jews as over-sexualized and cunning heightened the community's sense of responsibility to attack any problem forcefully.

JAPGAW created a multi-prong approach. Their officers tried to distinguish themselves from con men by wearing badges with Hebrew and Yiddish inscriptions.[33] They distributed literature warning susceptible women and unsuspecting parents of the hazards of travelling alone and the risks associated with improperly registered marriages.[34] Physical rescue fell to the Gentlemen's Committee who identified cases calling for protective or punitive action.[35] After rescuing girls, the Association tried to place women in safe homes and find work for them. After helping to restore the health of a girl who had received a beating after trying to escape her captor, the JAPGAW found her a position as a servant, 'where her work and conduct are giving perfect satisfaction'.[36] Perhaps the mention of her good behaviour served to reassure both writers and readers of the report that they had indeed saved a deserving individual.

Most JAPGAW materials portrayed Jewish prostitutes as victims of poverty, ignorance and deception. In a case from 1898, the JAPGAW reported on a husband and wife who became separated en route from Russia to America because of a lack of money. The husband continued across the Atlantic and the wife ended up 'at a house of the lowest description in one of the worst streets in London'. She escaped 'attempts to cause her ruin', and contacted the JAPGAW. The

Association brought her to one of their homes, provided careful treatment, and sent her, with an escort, to re-join her husband in America.[37]

Cases came to the attention of the JAPGAW from relatives, Jewish charitable agencies, educational authorities and police court missionaries. The Association cooperated with other agencies, Jewish and governmental, such as the United Synagogue, the JBG, and the LCC Education Committee, in their attempts to eliminate Jewish involvement in vice. In 1904, they had 177 cases. They located sixty-one of the young women, seven of whom resided in unsatisfactory surroundings. They also discovered thirteen women leading immoral lives, and twenty-seven cases of robbery, alleged assault, wrongdoing or immorality.[38] Alice Model contended that immorality had increased since she began working in the East End in the mid-1890s. She blamed 'the Oriental love of pleasure and finery' and 'sweated trades'. The various lodging houses in the East End that housed 'crowds of unattached men' were evil, as were the penny gaffs.[39] Such comments suggest Model doubted that coercion accounted for all the cases of immoral behaviour.

Preventive and rescue work attracted support from key leaders in the Jewish community. Basil Henriques described a meeting he attended at which the organizers suggested starting a girls' club. They attracted more than two hundred girls, many of whom 'were obviously on the streets at the present' or were 'reformed prostitutes'. Large numbers who attended 'and these were the really interesting ones – were on the brink of that awful abyss'. Many could not speak English and a significant percentage had arrived recently from Eastern Europe. Henriques saw great potential in a club, but it needed assistance from 'west end ladies of character & sympathy'. He thought the girls were open to advice and was extremely discouraged that only two 'ladies', both from the JAPGAW, circulated among the girls. Further, he was 'inclined to strangle' Mrs Micholls, who 'sat on the platform as a duchess & patronised these poor creatures with nods & smiles'. The programme included music and recitations, some in Yiddish, which 'appealed to many of the girls, who broke down and sobbed'. With only two women to offer comfort, Henriques asked 'oh, Bridge players of the West End, where are you?'[40] Like many organizations, finding dedicated and sensitive volunteers was a constant challenge.

The JAPGAW aimed to befriend those who perceived themselves to be alone in the world, offering support and advice that again speak to the comprehensiveness of the Jewish safety net. When two sisters tried to commit suicide because of a business failure, a JAPGAW committee raised money and helped the girls open a drapery stall in a London market. Each week the girls stopped in at the JAPGAW office and the staff checked their account books.[41] The JAPGAW also counselled young married couples facing difficulties, because the break-up of marriages often meant that the young people drifted into bad company.[42]

The greatest problems arose among adolescent girls. The JAPGAW traced this to 'the lack of organised recreation and helpful supervision, which high-spirited girls living in unsatisfactory environments require'. The Association believed that 'promiscuous friendship with young men of whom they know nothing' resulted in moral lapses. They identified insufficient interest in the girls as the cause, evidence of the need for volunteers to offer 'some form of healthy diversion from the drab routine of their lives'.[43] The JAPGAW concluded that girls with unsatisfactory home lives and poor relations with parents turned to the streets for their amusement, but close supervision and 'respectable employment' restored seemingly hopeless cases to 'a decent mode of life'.[44]

The Sara Pyke House

Facilities such as the Sara Pyke House (SPH), a supervised Jewish hostel for 'respectable but friendless working girls', focused on prevention.[45] The shelter, one of the JAPGAW's earliest projects, also helped young women whose family life left them at risk. In 1898, soon after its establishment, SPH assisted a sixteen-year-old with an unfit mother, no father and a home 'frequented by the most undesirable visitors', who was also being pressured to earn her keep on the streets.[46] In fact, generally demand was so great that requests outnumbered spaces in the shelter.[47]

Some hint of immigrant attitudes emerges in the histories recorded by the JAPGAW's agents. One girl, for example, arrived with a young man and 'metamorphoses her relationship to the young man in four stages within a quarter of an hour, viz., brother, cousin, fiancée, friend'. The agent 'retained' the young woman and sent her companion to the Poor Jews' Temporary Shelter.[48] In another case, after arriving at SPH, the staff directed two girls to the bath, one of whom insisted that she had never had a bath and could not see what she had done to deserve one. After a verbal struggle, 'she is initiated' and emerged looking bright and happy enough.[49] After settling in, those in residence incorporated the 'greeny' girls into the shelter and community activities.[50]

The management of SPH appreciated the residents' positive attributes, but recorded weaknesses as well. Some questioned the girls' integrity, noting that 'they liberally lend each other wearing apparel and steal from each other even more liberally'.[51] The 1904 *Annual Report* offered mixed praise, observing that the girls 'all have a tendency towards respectability, and seek it in the flourishing feathers of their hats and the impossible shades and shapes of their garments'.[52] The JAPGAW took pride in the fact that former residents regularly returned to the hostel, especially on the Sabbath and believed the visits reflected the warm feelings the young women felt for the home and its matron.

New challenges materialized in the years after World War I. In 1919, when discipline problems emerged at the home, one volunteer wanted the committee to approve a plan giving the girls one more warning before requiring them to leave 'if they persisted in coming in very late', acted 'in a deceitful way' or failed to maintain 'the discipline of the Home'. The recently hired superintendent was unable to control the girls, some of whom 'were hanging out of the windows long after it was time for them to be in bed'.[53] In November 1919, the committee hired a new superintendent, Annie Landau, whom they believed had the qualifications to handle SPH inmates.[54] The house had a continuing problem finding domestic, particularly live-in, help. Its location meant employees tended to leave when they found 'more congenial employment' in better neighbourhoods.[55] The house, which lacked a sitting room, no longer met the standards of the day. The dormitories were inadequate and led to petty pilfering and disorder. The committee thus concluded they needed to move to a better neighbourhood to provide real advantages for residents in an economical and efficient manner.[56] The committee considered 'excellent schemes', but like many other philanthropies, lacked the money to carry them out.[57]

On a more positive note, Landau received high praise. The committee particularly appreciated that she created a nice atmosphere for Sabbath evenings and shared her love of music and literature with the residents. She was a particularly good influence on girls who had previously 'been unable to find happiness except in the gratification of personal desires, or in seeking excitement and pleasure not always of the most wholesome nature'.[58] Landau instituted concerts and amateur theatricals, no doubt a welcome diversion, and activities deemed refining by the middle-class supporters of the JAPGAW.

After the war, some challenges diminished, including a significant decrease of 'very young girls' led astray by 'the glamour of the men in uniform'.[59] Nonetheless, the leadership believed much work remained. The long waiting list for space in convalescent homes caused anxiety.[60] They had more than 400 names on the visiting list in 1919. JAPGAW visitors judged many cases as satisfactory, though six entered the hostel for unmarried mothers, one entered an asylum, one died, and eight were living immorally. Their new visitor spoke Yiddish, evidence that the JAPGAW still dealt with foreign-born women and their families.[61] Five years later, the SPH moved out of the East End to Highbury.[62] The girls would now live in a nicer neighbourhood, surrounded by a higher class of people.

The Charcroft Home

From its earliest days, the JAPGAW became involved in several other communally sanctioned activities. They sponsored Charcroft House, a home for unmarried pregnant women and single mothers. The leaders had clear expectations regarding the behaviour of girls and women, but tempered their moralizing with genuine sympathy. In keeping with their goals, the JAPGAW did not accept women who were near the end of their pregnancies because many came for shelter alone, 'without wishing to work their way back to an honest and respectable livelihood'.[63] They expected healthy girls and young women to train for 'a useful, domestic life' and required them to share responsibility for cooking, washing and sewing.

At the home, girls learned to read and write, and 'are also taught what they find more difficult – to speak the truth; to curb their fierce and sullen tempers, and to obey'.[64] Many of the girls and women were foreign-born, 'untutored, uncultured', and spoke no English. They were 'ignorant of most things that they should know, knowing perhaps others that they should ignore'. Even some of the English-born had the same 'faults' as the foreign-born. The JAPGAW speculated that they had been rebellious or hard to discipline.[65] Miss Levi, the superintendent, provided 'motherly care'.[66] Organizers tried to give the institution 'a home-like character'. Charcroft reports reminded readers that their doors were 'open to those who have sinned and been sinned against, to those who are anxious to hide their shame, and to face life under new and better auspices'.[67] Ideally, they sought to restore women to a respectable life within the Jewish community.

Charcroft policy evolved over time, and its ideology combined traditional and progressive elements. The JAPGAW's leaders focused a great deal of energy towards shaping the character and temperament of 'imperfect specimens of womanhood', encouraging pleasant dispositions and fostering industriousness.[68] Religious education was highly instrumental, emphasizing that religious belief should lead to good conduct. The home stressed maternal and domestic duties as well as morality. Initially, mothers and babies lived apart, so Charcroft promoted 'maternal instincts' by allowing mothers to visit their babies. The organization expected that, in the future, the girls would care for their children.[69] Over time, the JAPGAW changed its approach and housed mothers and babies together, more closely replicating child-rearing practices among children of married parents.[70]

The home assisted girls and women of different ages and origins. From 1880 to 1905, most residents were foreign-born. Of eighteen inmates in 1904, four were native-born and four had arrived in England as infants, indicating that, as one might expect in a large industrial city, girls and young women went astray for reasons unrelated to immigration and trickery. The two youngest Charcroft residents were eleven and fourteen. The report described the younger child as intelligent, with a surprising 'knowledge of evil' for someone so young. Although the matrons had expressed concern that older girls would corrupt her, their young charge was the resident most in need of discipline.[71] In 1910, Charcroft admitted fifteen women. One of them, a young 'tailoress', had 'been ruined by her employer, a married man'. The JAPGAW was apparently unable to bring charges against him.[72] They blamed feeble-mindedness for a few cases, but since the house did not admit 'avowedly feeble-minded' mothers, such an explanation does not account for most girls and women who came under their care.[73]

The association did not see all young women as unwilling victims, however; some were 'devoid of moral fibre'. They suffered from a 'faulty up-bringing', as well as a poor education and limited religious training.[74] As Phillipa Levine notes, prostitution was problematic not only because it defined women 'by their sexual nature' but more threateningly, because women benefited from using their sexuality.[75] The choice to sell their bodies implied a rejection of Jewish and middle-class expectations for women. The JAPGAW granted that the promise of 'ease and luxury' tempted some girls who longed for an escape from terrible poverty. They viewed these girls and women too, as victims who had no sense of 'the misery, debasement and slavery' in their futures.[76] Sympathy, tinged with condescension, characterized the language of JAPGAW publications, as well as other nineteenth-century commentary on prostitutes' motivations.

The organization acknowledged their mixed success. As the women with whom they worked lacked self-reliance or self-control, moulding their characters was challenging. Not only did the organization create high expectations for those they 'saved', but often directed them towards unpopular occupations such as domestic service, and not surprisingly, some resisted. They reminded supporters that training capable workers or good wives and mothers could take months, if not years 'of anxious, steady, constant toil'.[77] While that 'transformation seems at times to be impossible ... steady constant work is the magic wand that is employed, and it is certain that the wand possesses untold power. Sheer stupidity and hopeless ignorance have again and again yielded to its influence'.[78] Persistence was the JAPGAW's by-word; recalcitrant inmates did not seem to frustrate the JAPGAW's efforts. This same tenacity characterized Christian women philanthropists, who refused to accept anyone as 'lost'.[79]

The organization capitalized on success stories and regularly published letters from former residents and those whom they assisted. One girl assured the organization that 'I think I am what you can call a good girl, for I don't go anywhere by myself, for I am afraid of seeing the bad company I once used to mix with'.[80] These letters expressed gratitude for the maternal care the girls received, the structure and discipline the organization expected them to adopt, and declared a commitment to remaining good girls.

The JAPGAW's leaders urged British Jews to acknowledge moral lapses more readily. Reformers regretted that over the past thirty years Jews had acted like 'ostriches'. Recently, the community had awakened 'to the existence of the moral canker which was eating at the heart of Jewish domestic life' and supported efforts to stem problems.[81] Asked in 1915 how things had changed since 1904, Mr Cohen, Secretary to the Gentleman's Committee, explained that earlier they had done their work 'privately, in fact, almost secretly', and at rail stations and ports. More recently, there were fewer 'foreign Jewish women of ill fame', but growing numbers on the verge of immorality. Cohen noted that girls fell prey to white slavers and quickly accepted offers of employment and marriage, in response to low wages, employment as 'household drudges', and a lack of education. Neglecting girls' education caused problems and focusing Jewish education on boys alone meant that girls grew up 'not only in a state of general ignorance, but in complete ignorance of the ways of the world'.[82]

By World War I, the JAPGAW found it very difficult to convince young women to enter Charcroft House, 'and when there to retain and influence them'. Previous mention of such resistance was rare in JAPGAW's records. "'It is to be feared'", professed the Annual Report, "'that immorality is rather increasing than diminishing'". Lax parental control made it easy for men to influence young women.[83] Yet, only a few months earlier, Cohen had reported that 85 per cent of their 'inmates' turned out satisfactorily, returned home, married or got respectable work.[84]

Among the challenges of the interwar years, the JAPGAW, much like Christian rescue organizations, found it increasingly difficult to find suitable foster parents.[85] JAPGAW's staff and members wanted to prevent young mothers from returning to the streets to prostitution and promiscuity. They were optimistic about the potential superiority of the new hostel and the policy that placed infants with foster families.[86] Babies in the day nursery received care and attention from a new nurse-matron, who was an excellent 'disciplinarian and organiser'.[87] The organization hoped to increase opportunities for the residents to run some of the home's affairs by introducing some level of 'self-government'.[88] In a plan that encouraged independence and more closely approximated life outside the institution, the JAPGAW allowed the mothers to keep some pocket money and encouraged the women to save some of their earnings.[89] In the 1920s, Charcroft's committee stressed their desire to help infants begin life on the 'right footing'. To achieve this, Charcroft residents spent the first year of their babies' lives learning domestic duties and infant care, after which they gained a bit more freedom and could leave the house for work. The mothers would return to care for their babies each evening.[90] Residents, who generally found work as domestics and in the garment trade, paid for their own and their baby's maintenance.

Like most charities, JAPGAW advanced moral and behavioural expectations, but represented a relatively progressive policy towards single mothers. It helped to place girls and women in employment with wages that would enable them to support themselves and their children. The youthful ages of some of the mothers made such placements difficult.[91] The house rules allowed unmarried mothers to enter only on their first pregnancy; but, occasionally the committee bent this rule. The work of the Charcroft House though expensive, aimed to rehabilitate girls who might have become a 'disgrace and burden' without such support.[92] In 1930, the JAPGAW reported little fluctuation in illegitimacy rates;

between one-quarter and one-third of the mothers went to Charcroft House. The association hoped to establish a programme of pairing guardians with young women who did not enter Charcroft and ran an after-care programme to remain in touch with those they had assisted.[93] Through visitors and monthly recreational meetings, the JAPGAW hoped to keep their reformed charges moving along respectable paths. Jewish values of charity, coloured by Victorian attitudes towards morality, suffused this and other JAPGAW schemes.

The JAPGAW also intervened on behalf of children living in unsuitable domestic situations, by opening Highbury House, 'a commodious, bright house with a large garden' and a Jewish atmosphere.[94] Many children living at Highbury were motherless or had mothers who were unhealthy, leading distressed fathers and guardians to 'clamour for their [children's] admission'. The home provided physical and emotional care, as well as recreational activities and occupational counselling.[95] In 1919, fifty children resided at the house, which received approximately thirty applications for admission for the year. The committee considering applicants urged support for these 'poor bairns, starting life with such a handicap'.[96]

Training and Support

After completing their schooling, many in the community favoured the placement of girls as domestics. To this end, the community supported the Jewish Domestic Training Home, founded in 1893. The training home preferred young candidates, which maximized opportunities for influence.[97] The home offered protection to poor girls at risk from negative influences and prepared them for domestic service, described by established Jews as work offering 'good wages in respectable situations'.[98]

In addition to creating shelters for women, members of the Jewish community worked to improve moral health by visiting prisons. Jewish volunteers hoped to create relationships with Jewish prisoners so they could assist them on release. On visits to Wormwood Scrubbs, Hannah Hyam found few Jews, but noted the challenge of providing communal services for such women.[99] Volunteers also visited Jewish patients in workhouse infirmaries.[100] JAPGAW contacted Jewish women at the Holloway Prison and the Borstal Institution at Aylesbury to induce them 'to lead better lives' once 'they regain[ed] their liberty' and to publicize the association's willingness to assist them.[101]

Community volunteers intervened in an effort to stem the appearance of immorality. In one case, Basil Henriques called on a woman living in a particularly bad neighbourhood. Deserted by her husband, she became dependent on the charity of a married man whose family was due to arrive shortly. 'It is what she gives him in return that is the mystery!', mused Henriques. He concluded she was not 'living on "immoral" lines' because she spoke so openly about neighbours' accusations that she was the man's mistress. The woman could not work because her baby suffered from a skin disease, so was ineligible for a day nursery. His diary shows that Henriques believed the woman was respectable and wanted to find her a flat in a better neighbourhood away from her benefactor.[102]

Just after World War I, the JAPGAW had 105 cases involving courts or Holloway Prison; sixty-four charges were for offenses against public morality or order and forty-one for stealing. An additional thirty-one girls and young women were on probation; among seventy cases of 'ruined' girls or unmarried mothers, thirty-four were cases of promiscuous immorality.[103] The organization found they were dealing with an increased number of unmarried women and their children. They blamed the conditions of war and its aftermath. Most single mothers did not know the whereabouts of the fathers, making it impossible for the JAPGAW to induce the men to marry the women or support the children. The organization contended, however, that the white slave trade, the transport of girls from abroad, had practically ceased among Jews.[104]

Unlike the early years of Jewish settlement, the JAPGAW believed those involved in prostitution during the interwar years were less innocent and naive. They deplored 'the fact that there are still many young girls who are wilfully leading immoral lives and who cause our workers grave anxiety'.[105] The cases resulted from crowded homes and insufficient parental influence. 'Craving for pleasure, excitement, and distaste for regular work in workshops and factories are other reasons'.[106] The organization continued to use personal contacts to encourage acceptable behaviour.[107] Throughout the interwar period, parents found it increasingly difficult to control their children, more evidence of generational tensions and young women's increasing assertion of their independence.[108] JAPGAW received some referrals from parents whose daughters were on the border between 'respectability and immorality'. The agency provided 'constant supervision' to keep such girls from straying into 'degraded and unclean lives'.[109] They helped locate jobs and recreation, taught respect for parents and encouraged the avoidance of the many dangers around them. The years from 1918 to 1939 were pivotal for both the East End and established Jewry. The period began on a more difficult note than some predicted. According to the Jewish Board of Guardians, there was more suffering during the first year of peace than during the war.[110] Many had anticipated 'more abundance' and 'lower prices' and a rapid return to the *status quo ante*.[111]

During the interwar period, social service agencies found that East End girls still needed advice and services, and it appears that with acculturation, small, though increasing numbers of young women succumbed to criminal and immoral activities. Disreputable behaviour still aroused anxiety and helped sustain a commitment to seek out wayward girls and to assist low-paid working girls, unmarried mothers and children in unsatisfactory homes, most of whom were children of immigrants. The JAPGAW sued men who neglected their families, forcing them to provide financial support. They traced deserters and took responsibility for girls placed on probation by a magistrate.[112] They also cultivated a cooperative relationship with the Police Court Magistrates. To avoid imprisonment, the association supervised thirty-one young women and reported back to the court. Happily, their 'probation inspectress' had a positive influence.[113]

The slow economic growth of the post-war years contributed to the kinds of social problems voluntary societies sought to eradicate. In 1925, difficult economic conditions in Britain and Europe caused hardship for many of the women and girls JAPGAW assisted.[114] In 1928, Viscountess Bearsted (née Dorothy Montefiore Micholls), presided over a major fundraising dinner. Though 'not a great feminist, nor ... an upholder of what is known as Women's Rights', she thought it appropriate that a woman appeal to those gathered 'for that great unhappy sisterhood of ours, who, whether by grievous weakness or sin, or by force of circumstances which have proved too hard for them, are suffering in a condition which is a blot on modern civilisation'.[115] JAPGAW's mission justified the community's support.

The war and years following brought growing attention to venereal diseases. The JAPGAW responded by offering education and treatment. In the spring of 1917, the Borough of Stepney invited the JAPGAW to a conference on the treatment of sexually transmitted diseases.[116] The same year the association reported that the Royal Free Hospital had started a small hostel for girls with venereal disease who lacked other means of treatment and invited the JAPGAW to recommend cases.[117] Despite such efforts, sexually transmitted diseases remained a problem in the Jewish community. In 1921, Dr Salaman noted that the moral environment, Jewish family life and education had, until recently, kept incidences of syphilis very low. Recently, indisputable and 'disquieting reports' indicated that young Russian–Jewish women were less chaste than they had been just ten years earlier. Not long before, staff at the London Hospital ruled out venereal disease if a woman was Jewish.[118] In 1925 the JAPGAW expressed concern over the consequences of sexually transmitted diseases and had the organization's workers discuss its consequences and urge those infected to seek proper treatment.[119] While the organization could be quite moralistic, rather than chastise, they provided information and encouraged treatment.

Increased criminal activity, even if only petty crimes, reveal behavioural changes among the East End's Jewish women, as do emerging programmes of the JAPGAW in the 1920s and 1930s. Though the JAPGAW concerned itself with only a minority of girls and women, new initiatives sought to prevent those numbers from rising. In 1926 the JAPGAW opened their office on an experimental basis, from eight to ten, as a drop-in centre for 'wayward and unruly', but not immoral, girls who were ineligible for local clubs. The organizers happily reported that young girls chose to relax at their club-room rather than on the streets.[120] The club-room remained open the following year, but needed one or two additional volunteers to assure its further development. JAPGAW, under the auspices of London County Council, also established a gymnasium class for the girls who attended the weekly 'Social Evening', but found it a challenge to sustain.[121] Many girls did not take advantage of the JAPGAW's facilities and the 1927 annual report expressed concern over the growing 'number of girls who are wandering about certain streets in the evening, thus placing themselves in great danger of becoming involved in undesirable methods of obtaining their recreation'.[122]

The JAPGAW continued their international efforts to stem white slave traffic and participated in the first meeting of the Permanent Advisory Committee of the League of Nations in the Traffic in Women and Children. In 1927, they sponsored their own conference. Some of their work, beginning during World War I, involved cooperation with non-denominational groups. They joined the National Union of Women Workers (NUWW) and organized voluntary patrols of women looking for girls on the streets of various London neighbourhoods. The inspector of police in the Piccadilly district had reported on increased numbers of Jewish women in the neighbourhood for 'immoral' and 'frivolous' purposes. In response, the NUWW patrols recommended that the JAPGAW encourage the police commissioner to appoint a woman police officer.[123] The NUWW and the JAPGAW reached an agreement whereby the NUWW would report all cases of wayward Jewish girls to the JAPGAW. The association had difficultly securing volunteers and sought the UJW's assistance in advertising for women to join patrols.[124] The JAPGAW criticized the light punishments that girls received for prostitution. The fines were low enough that 'only the very poor and friendless' failed to 'borrow the money from the very people who thrive upon their immoral earnings'.[125] Young women quickly returned to prostitution in order to repay their loans. The numbers 'rescued' and trained by the JAPGAW remained relatively small, which serves as evidence that Jews were largely law-abiding. What is significant is that the level of JAPGAW concern underscores Jewish insecurity over a fragile reputation.

Industrial Schools

While most children did not have scrapes with the law nor require special schooling, both the British and American Jewish communities struggled over how to deal with very young criminals and those in precarious living situations. Prior to the early twentieth century, Jews experienced limited demand for reformatories and industrial schools. For, as Eugene Black noted, the numbers were just too small. As demand grew, the community faced the reality that there was no suitable facility for Jewish delinquents and neglected children. Often the court placed children of this type in industrial schools, institutions designed to reform their behaviour, but not part of the penal system, as their crimes were not serious enough to warrant Reformatories.[126]

Jews had a complicated problem in that such institutions, especially British ones, often had Christian sponsorship or – at the very least – Christian influence. While there was an increase of problem children over the period of this study, the numbers remained fairly small. In 1880, according the *JC*, 'the number of Jewish prisoners is below the average among the general population' and there were fewer than ten boys and no girls in any industrial school or reformatory in England.[127] The Jewish community however, had 'insurmountable difficulty' inducing industrial schools to take Jewish boys.[128]

St Paul's Industrial School accepted a few boys and permitted them to attend the East London Synagogue.[129] When St Paul's license was withdrawn the Jewish community had to request the discharge of their students. The school never served more than seven boys, inadequate numbers for a separate Jewish school.[130] In 1888, the JBD wrote to the Secretary of State for the Home Department, who was about to introduce a measure into Parliament, to remind him of his promise to consider the special privileges the Jewish community had requested.[131] In essence, they sought an arrangement that would enable Jewish boys to attend Christian industrial schools.

As the JBD pointed out, Jewish boys' religious needs were mostly of 'a negative character' – exemptions from chapel attendance, Christian religious education, and eating pork. They sought permission for the boys to attend Synagogue on Sabbath and Festivals and to receive instruction in Judaism, for which the Jewish community would provide a teacher to offer lessons during Christian Chapel. Industrial Schools generally refused to distinguish among boys and thus typically denied such requests. The Jewish community considered the practical consequences of this position to be unduly harsh, as it would likely lead to the children's conversion 'a penalty which the Legislature ... never contemplated for such trivial delinquencies as school truancy, and small mis-demeanours'.[132] The Jewish community required a school in London or another large city, because rabbis had to be within walking distance to avoid violation of the Jewish Sabbath.

In discussions with the government, the JBD referred to the reformatory at Netherton, near Newcastle, which willingly received Jewish boys.[133] The JBD produced a letter from Netherton that outlined their methods for accommodating Jewish and Catholic boys. The scheme caused no problems and the managers pointed to advantages of a school in which 'lads of different nationalities and persuasions ... live[d] together in forbearance and harmony'.[134] Nonetheless, the needs of the Jewish community eventually led them to sponsor two industrial schools: Hayes for boys and Montefiore House for girls.

Hayes opened in 1901 and had discharged 209 students by 1915. The managers reported that 'the lessons of discipline, duty and loyalty inculcated in and out of the schoolroom have not been in vain, and the promise given by every boy on leaving the school ... to uphold its honour and to live up to British traditions has been well and truly redeemed'.[135] By the spring of 1915, of the 132 young men eligible for the military, forty-six were serving. The school's leadership believed the institution no longer required justification and claimed great success. 'Lads who might have deteriorated into outcasts of humanity have been turned into honourable, self-respecting, and useful men'.[136]

Further evidence that Jewish community leaders saw industrial school boys as troubled, but not really criminal, comes from a discussion within the JBG's Apprenticeship Committee. They received a letter from the Secretary of the Visiting Committee of the United Synagogue and the Superintendent of the East London Industrial School, about apprenticing Jewish boys. In 1894 there was some question as to whether such boys deserved the assistance of the Apprenticeship Committee. The committee had placed one previous case, but noted that it was not to constitute a precedent. However, the committee decided to help where possible, even though the apprenticeships might require special terms and cost the Board of Guardians a bit more than other placements. The young men in question were not felons. The Board had played a role in placing the boys at the industrial school where they had received 'a good character'. As such, the committee concluded that 'it would not be right for the Committee to refuse to entertain such cases & to allow the lads to again go to the bad'.[137] Leaders of the Jewish community sought creative solutions to reform the boys, but as importantly, to ease their way back into respectable involvement in the Jewish community.

Montefiore House took girls under the age of fourteen who had committed offenses or whose parents could not control them, as well as children with neglectful or criminal parents. Located in Stamford Hill, the school had an excellent reputation. Poor Law Guardians committed some of the children, guardians and voluntary contributions covered the cost of others. The Montefiore House also received grants from state and local authorities, which depended upon the efficient running of the school.[138] The school provided a 'refuge' to keep children from 'a life of increasing misdemeanour and further degradation'. Montefiore provided 'careful, sympathetic guidance' helping their charges 'to grow into happy girls and women, a credit to their race, and useful citizens of the Empire'.[139]

The Courts placed many of Montefiore House's students at the institution, where the school's management had a good deal of influence over the future of the children, including their return to families. Often, parents realized that their lifestyle and behaviour determined whether they would regain control of their children. The JAPGAW noted that strong 'parental affection' typically functioned 'as a potent stimulus to reform'. Through the work of the superintendent, Mrs Falk, parents had come to understand that the school existed to aid students

– and was not a 'prison school'. The committee believed the school helped reform parents and children, making a two-fold contribution to the community.[140]

Between 1919 and 1935, approximately 120 Jewish girls and about ten boys, convicted in Police Court, ended up at Montefiore. Table 7.2 indicates the grounds for admitting students to Montefiore House, the largest of which were being beyond control, stealing, larceny or in danger of seduction. Among the children assigned to Montefiore House, approximately twenty per cent were illegitimate, a proportion that was much higher than the Jewish community as a whole.[141] Industrial schools tried to reform their charges, with the ultimate goal of reintroducing them into the larger society and preventing their being treated as criminals.

Table 7.2: Montefiore House School Admissions, 1919–35.

Children in danger of seduction	39
In need of care, or in moral danger	9
Residing in house used by prostitutes	5
Found wandering	24
Has parent who failed to provide efficient elementary education	4
Being beyond control, stealing, larceny	39
Having unfit parent	10

Source: Hartley Library, Special Collections, University of Southampton (hereafter, HL Southampton), MS173/ 2/8/11, Montefiore House School Admissions, 1919–35.

Conclusion

Jewish community leaders feared the consequences of an impoverished environment and asserted that preventive work was a direct denial of the charge of Jewish indifference to the degradation of women and children.[142] Their efforts also reflected the competing realities faced by established Jews – a genuine desire to aid their poorer co-religionists, to encourage their acculturation, influence immigrant behaviour, and challenge the negative images of Jews that immigrants might reinforce. The JAPGAW, which Basil Henriques described as 'the most important and the most essential charity in the whole of their Community' helped young women about to drift into prostitution and children who needed a stable home. The JAPGAW proudly asserted that Charcroft House stood for 'an amount and variety of work, which finds no parallel in any kindred Christian establishment'.[143] Such an organization aided those at risk, offered important and acceptable leadership roles to women and helped shape public response to Anglo-Jewry. While the numbers of delinquent children, or children suffering from neglect remained fairly small, volunteers responded to those in need, all the while defending the reputation of British Jews.

8 BECOMING ENGLISH IN THE WORKPLACE

Upon arrival in Britain, many Jews entered a relatively narrow range of jobs, including the garment trade or boot and shoe industries, in which nearly 40 per cent of Jewish immigrants had worked before emigrating.[1] Records from the JBG, the press and parliamentary investigations offer a picture of women's changing experience in the labour market. Over time, Jewish women experienced improved working conditions and entered a wider range of occupations. Especially as women found employment beyond the East End, work contributed to their acculturation through new friendships, increased access to the consumer market and greater self-sufficiency.

The Extent of Female Labour

In recent years, there has been a good deal of debate over the extent and nature of women's work and economic roles prior to emigration. Traditional images of Jewish women often place them at the centre of the family's economic survival. Zborowski and Herzog described work in Eastern Europe as sex-less and respected scholars claim women toiled while their men-folk prayed and studied the great works of Jewish law.[2] According to sociologist Arthur Ruppin, 'distinguishing features' of Jewish family life included chastity before marriage, matrimonial fidelity, respect of children for parents and 'boundless love and devotion' by parents. Women did not participate in public life, 'but attended to their domestic duties or assisted their husbands in their work'.[3] Certainly, the popular image of women supporting their families had a basis in reality, but did not characterize the majority of Eastern European Jewish families.[4]

Full-time study was always an elite pursuit, and only those of comfortable means – or exceptional talent – lived this idealized lifestyle. Many marriage contracts included several years of support from fathers-in-law, enabling young men to continue their studies. Some men pursued Torah-study after this initial period, supported in part or entirely by their wives or dowries. We have very little evidence as to wives' views about their economic role and the status their facilitation of religious study conferred upon them. Some wives lived on their own or with children, for many years, while husbands travelled to far-flung *yeshivot*, academies of higher Torah study, or to rabbinical posts.[5] The large number of men who arrived in London with industrial experience, however, evidences their pre-emigration involvement in the workforce.[6]

According to the Russian census of 1897, women made up 21 per cent of the Jewish labour force.[7] The nature of traditional society meant that women ran some businesses owned by husbands and enumerators probably underestimated part-time female employment. Unmarried female labour was likely more extensive in London than Eastern Europe, but women's contributions to the family economy were undoubtedly indispensable to the survival of many, and possibly most, Jewish families in the East and the West.

Works by Rickie Burman locate the roots of Jewish women's economic activities in immigrants' Eastern European experiences. Burman found that women who functioned as the sole breadwinner in the family typically supported husbands pursuing scholarly activities. In some households, both men and women worked, yet many observers considered a wife's contributions to her family as 'subsidiary' to her husband's.[8] Commentators did not necessarily perceive a woman as working if she assisted her husband or engaged in domestic labour. The predominance of small workshops in London's garment industry encouraged the use of female homeworkers. Small workshops with irregular business led contractors to hire virtually unskilled homeworkers who received particularly small compensation and work at the will of the owner.

Patterns of New York's Jewish immigrant community are also suggestive of women's labour patterns. Making use of folk songs, poems and memoirs, historian Susan Glenn builds a rich description of Jewish women's work in New York City, particularly the garment industry. She too finds a pattern of continuity; some 50,000 women, 70 per cent of the female artisans registered in the Pale of Settlement, had worked in the needle trades.[9] While exact figures are unobtainable, Jewish social convention accepted female employment and in some cases made it a route for her husband to honour God.

Late nineteenth-century sources offer contradictory assessments of the extent of Jewish women's labour in Britain. Among working-class families in the East End, many could not subsist on two incomes, let alone one, and women often took in boarders, cleaned houses or did odd jobs.[10] Social reformers such as Beatrice Potter (later Webb) noted the presence of some married Jewish women in sweatshops.[11] In 1890, the *JC* responded to a Potter article and reiterated that upon marriage, a Jewish girl 'restricts her attention to the management of her home'.[12] In a 'Jewish family', claimed one Jewish unionist, 'the husband is the sole bread-winner'.[13] Charles Booth concurred and partially attributed the taller heights of Jewish children to the presence of women at home.[14] Some commentators disapproved of female labour, suggesting it took work and wages from men who typically supported at least one woman, and often more.[15]

Upon arrival in Britain, most Jews entered England's already burgeoning industries. Early studies suggested that such work constituted a break from Eastern Europe, where Jews were peddlers, but not wage earners. David Feldman's review of records from the PJTS, however, demonstrates that the percentage of immigrants with manufacturing experience increased over time.[16] A number of historians now recognize that there was greater continuity between pre- and post-migration occupations than scholars previously assumed.

Most immigrants came from small towns, arrived exhausted and penniless, and flocked to the small workshops and sweatshops – to occupations that quickly became known as 'immigrant trades'.[17] Several factors influenced immigrant women's work options. Women left school with few skills and employers rarely provided women with opportunities to learn new ones. Jobs that taught useful domestic skills gained the support of established Jewry, but tended not to attract large numbers of immigrant girls. The sewing machine, mass produced by 1861, probably prolonged homework because individuals could purchase machines on instalment and did not need to enter factories.[18] In London, most Jewish women worked in small workshops, as opposed to factories; some found work in the tobacco trade or peddling wares. In 1882, for example, of girls leaving Norwood orphanage, one became a cook, six entered clothing and shoe industries, two became nursery maids and two obtained work as pupil teachers or assisted parents.[19] Young men had additional options. At the turn of the century, most entered the garment trades, but in positions that offered better pay than those available to women. Other considerations, such as geographic concentration, Sabbath observance, and the proximity of work to one's home – the cost of travel was prohibitive and time-consuming – influenced occupational choices.

Wages

Typically, men in immigrant trades earned barely enough for subsistence. The *Lancet* described a fully employed man's wages in Liverpool as insufficient for basic needs and noted that many secured fulltime employment no more than seven months per year.[20] Further, workers sometimes had to pay for trimmings, thread or needles.[21] Some bosses charged for hot water for tea or deducted for lateness at a higher rate per hour than they paid their employees. This practice, concluded Clementina Black, meant that employers acknowledged that their 'ordinary pay is below the value of the work done'.[22]

Working-class women, Jews among them, struggled to survive on their wages. Women received both piece and hourly wages. A number of investigations, such as the one Clara Collet conducted for the Board of Trade, include wage information, most of which came from employers. Collet verified seemingly high wages with workers, since employers may have inflated figures to avoid accusations of underpayment. Nonetheless, only one woman earned as much as 6s. to 7s. per day.[23] Table 8.1 provides wage data for men and women who made coats. Table 8.2 draws on wage data compiled in 1886 and 1887. Both tables demonstrate that women commonly earned considerably less than men – sometimes only half of men's wages – and received only the lowest paid types of work.[24] Work arrangements varied widely – from factories to homes, from large numbers of workers, to a husband and wife team.[25]

Table 8.1: Comparison of occupations against earnings for men and women.

Occupation	less than 2s.	2s. to 3s.	3s. to 4s.	4s. to 5s.	5s. to 6s.	6s. to 7s.	7s. to 8s.	8s. to 9s.	9s. to 10s.	10s.	total	avg earnings
Women and girls												
Fellers & Finishers	6	27	42	5	–	–	–	–	–	–	80	2s. 10d.
Button-holers	–	–	4	6	1	–	–	–	–	–	11	4s. 2d.
Machinist(s)	–	–	1	2	1	1	–	–	–	–	6	4s. 8d.
Men and Boys												
Machinist(s)	–	1	4	10	12	10	7	9	4	1	58	6s. 0d.
Pressers	–	–	–	1	8	–	11	10	1	–	31	6s. 11d.
Tailors	–	–	2	4	7	12	7	5	1	–	38	6s. 3d.

Source: Board of Trade (Alien Immigration), Reports on the Volume and Effects of the Recent Immigration from Eastern Europe into the United Kingdom, *PP* 1894, LXVIII, c. 7406, p. 108.

Table 8.2: Comparison of daily wages of men and women.

Type of Work	Time or Piece	Maximum Wage	Minimum Wage	Average Wage	Number of Cases
Women					
Machinist	time	6s.	1s. 8d.	4s.	17
Baster	Time	4s. 6d.	6d.	2s. 9d.	12
Feller	time	5s.	6d.	2s. 7d.	243
Buttonholing	Time	6s.	1s. 8d.	4s. 0d.	12
Buttonholing	Piece	6s. 6d.	1s. 6d.	3s. 9d.	94
Less deductions for gimp & materials		1s. 3d.	4½d.	9½d.	
Apprentices	time	1s. 6d.	3d.	10d.	14

Type of Work	Time or Piece	Maximum Wage	Minimum Wage	Average Wage	Number of Cases
Men					
Presser	time	9s.	2s. 6d.	6s. 5d.	108
Presser	Piece	7s.	4s. 6d.	5s. 6d.	4
Machinist	Time	10s.	2s. 6d.	6s. 0d.	188
Machinist	Piece	10s.	3s. 4d.	7s. 0d.	10
General tailor	Time	10s.	4s.	7s. 3d.	23
Baster	Time	9s.	3s.	6s. 2d.	89
Baster	Piece	7s.	3s.	5s. 5d.	5
Feller	Time	6s.	3s.	4s. 8d.	12
Apprentice	Time	1s. 2d.	4s.	8s.	4

Source: Compiled from House of Lord's Commission on the Sweating System, XXI, Second Report, *PP* 1888, Appendix, 584–8.

According to the *Anti-Sweater*, Abraham Solomons, a Whitechapel sweater, had a forty-foot-wide by fifty-foot-long workshop that employed eight men and eleven girls. The two good male machinists earned 7s. 7d. for seventeen hours of work, the plain machinists earned 1s. to 3s. 6d. per day and the women earned 1s. 6d. to 3s. for a thirteen-hour day. Like many workshops of the time, Solomons's had only one bathroom for the men and women, as well as a coke fire and fifteen gas lights.[26] In the 1880s, when social reformers began investigating the conditions of such labour, they found that a typical working week could be sixty to seventy hours and still not yield a living wage.[27] May, June and December tended to be very busy, but from Christmas to Easter, most shops were open only three to three-and-a-half days per week.[28] Considering slack time, Gartner estimated that annually, the average working week was as little as two to three days per week.[29] While many critics blamed Jewish immigration for declining wages, the Women's Liberal Federation noted that even if Jews brought down wages – they tended to compete in tailoring and boot trades only – and sweating occurred in many trades in which there was no Jewish competition.[30] Unskilled females found it very difficult to locate work that would enable them to be self-supporting. And these problems continued into the next century; the UJW suggested that single, often-called 'surplus women', might consider 'fitting themselves for Colonial life', to expand their opportunities for employment.[31]

Employment Patterns

A remarkable consistency existed in the pattern of employment for Jewish women at the turn of the century. Between 1891 and 1911, approximately 65 to 70 per cent of Russian and Russian-Polish women in east London and Hackney appeared in the census as 'unspecified' or 'unoccupied'. During the same period, the garment industry attracted between 16 and approximately 20 per cent and the tobacco industry employed between 1.2 and 2 per cent of Russian and Russian-Polish women.[32]

In addition to workshops and factories, some women worked as domestics. In 1898, the JAPGAW claimed increasing numbers of girls willingly entered domestic service, but tended to leave those positions. To encourage them to stay, the association provided prizes, such as excursions to Epping, for young women who remained at a post for at least one year.[33] In 1891, 3 per cent of Jewish women worked as domestics.[34] By 1901, the number had risen to only 9 per cent, quite atypical of immigrant women. In comparison, among employed Italian immigrant women, approximately 30 per cent entered domestic service.[35] In part, Jews shunned domestic service because they feared attempts at conversion, but in addition to this, most women considered such positions demeaning.[36] This attitude characterized immigrant women in America as well. Only Irish women, who made up the largest number of single women and tended to marry later, chose domestic service.[37]

Jewish dietary needs, Sabbath laws and strict sexual mores made it difficult for many Jewish women to work in Christian homes, domestics earned extremely low wages and high marriage rates meant many women had short working lives, especially outside the home.[38] Nettie Adler learned that friends of some young women removed them from domestic service shortly before marriage so the groom remained unaware that his fiancée had engaged in such labour.[39] In contrast, the *JC* supported domestic service, contending it was not onerous, offered reasonable pay, and 'lenient and kindly' supervision.[40] The established Jewish community, in keeping with their social and economic status, promoted domestic service and saw it as an effective form of socialization and exposure to middle-class habits.[41]

The Garment Trade

Of the approximately 8,000 Russian and Russian-Polish women enumerated in the 1901 census of England and Wales, nearly half worked as tailors and clothiers. Women's jobs included felling, finishing and button-hole making. About 12 per cent worked as milliners, dressmakers, shirt makers and stay makers, and another 6 per cent made hats and caps. In 1901, about 30 per cent of London's Jewish male immigrants worked as tailors, 10 per cent in the footwear industries and 9 per cent as cabinet makers – a pattern that differed from others in the working class.[42]

A minute subdivision of labour (the task system) characterized the garment trade.[43] Many workers, especially those trained in England, never learned to make an entire garment, thereby remaining unskilled their whole working lives. Those Jewish women who arrived in England with a high level of skill used their abilities to move up, possibly to a supervisory position. Economic circumstances and parental pressure often forced sisters to enter the labour market before their brothers. Many came to London hoping to continue their education only to learn that their families needed whatever income they could contribute. For other women, work was liberating; factories provided a social life, new friends, exposure to new fashions and recreation, as well as some freedom from parental supervision. Movement into the business world brought women into contact with people from different walks of life, out of the more traditional sphere of activities in the East End.

Investigations of Jewish immigrants' work habits began in the 1880s. Nearly all critical, some descriptions suggested that Jews possessed a unique ability to work harder than, and thus undersell, their Christian neighbours. Others pictured immigrants as middlemen, living off the labour of their sweated employees. The *Anti-Sweater*, for example, complained that Jewish philanthropists aided sweaters 'by opening a registry for Jewish unemployed' to the disadvantage of workers. Philanthropists, who claimed they would 'not interfere in a question of wages', told fellow Jews to take 'work at any price, but don't bother us'! The paper 'advised' philanthropists to end this 'trickery' as it was 'a dangerous thing to play with labour'; only workers had 'a right to govern the affairs of the workers'.[44]

The negative publicity surrounding sweated industries did not affect clothing sales; nearly all people bought clothing produced by the subdivision method. While some manufacturers completed entire garments in their workshops or factories, most used Jewish subcontractors at some stage of the process. Subcontractors worked long hours, but a sweater's income was often lower than his best worker, but 'he has the consolation, no small one to the average Jew, of being an employer and not a hired hand'.[45] Since newcomers generally could not find work in their exact field, they sought out a 'Jew "sweater", who alone knows his language, and will not ask him to work on the Sabbath'. Immigrants laboured in 'unwholesome and overcrowded houses'; some even helped their bosses 'to defy the Factory Act, the Sanitary Act, and other laws instituted to protect him'.[46]

Efforts at Unionizing Workers

Periodically, workers attempted to organize unions for Jewish women, to address both their low wages and squalid working conditions. Since many women worked out of their homes, their isolation hindered recruitment.[47] In December 1880, Samuel Barnett of Toynbee Hall presided over a meeting convened by the Women's Protection and Provident League. The League noted that women received 40 per cent less in wages than men for the same class of work. A number of people addressed the meeting; the last speaker, Mrs Levy,

> urg[ed] with much vigour upon the women present the desirability of agitating for better wages and less [*sic*] working hours. She could speak from her own knowledge, that many tailoresses were working as late as eleven o'clock at night, literally working their eyes out and damaging their health.[48]

A meeting held in the East End in 1884 addressed some of these issues, and promoted the establishment of a 'Protective and Provident League for Jewish tailoresses'. They believed that there was 'some prospect of women benefiting by the present movement as well as men'.[49] Women also gained some benefits from husbands' unions or *landsmanshaftn* (mutual aid society, often of individuals from the same town in Russia). Frederic Mocatta, a supporter of provident societies, addressed the meeting to promote the League, noting that among the many advantages of a society was the opportunity 'to put away a little money, as men had done for many years past ... which would instil habits of providence and give them the power of sustenance when out of work or when incapacitated by sickness'. Apparently, unlike many of his contemporaries, Mocatta believed 'God had ordained that work should be the foundation of human existence, and if wives and daughters could supplement the earnings of the head of the household, they would place their families in a far better condition'.[50] At a meeting a month later, the chairman explained that the society intended to help the working classes to help themselves.[51]

Some women found help through unions and in 1890, a group of fifty 'tailoresses' joined the International Tailors, Machinists and Pressers' Union. While there is no evidence as to the proportion of Jewish women among the group, two of the organizers, Miss Edith May Abraham and Mrs Lyons, may have been Jewish. Abraham told those gathered that the women of Dundee received a 20 per cent rise in their wages after organizing a union. The bringing about of substantial improvements to tailoring trade conditions required women to stand alongside men against their common enemy, the 'sweater'.[52]

Union efforts to redress substandard conditions had mixed results. Few women could afford to commit any of their meagre wages for future work benefits. Further, many unions did not recruit women, believing that they would displace male workers. In 1895 the *JC* reported that unions attracted no more than 1,700 of 10,000 workers, most of whom were men. Workers feared dismissal if they joined a union.[53] In 1910, when Lewis Lyons, a socialist trade unionist, spoke to a group of workers on the Trade Boards Act and Jewish Workers, he addressed them in Yiddish, an indication that they were foreign-born and perhaps felt vulnerable. He encouraged all men and women employed in the clothing industry to join one of the existing Jewish trade unions.[54]

Although established Jews made every effort to disperse workers to other occupations, immigrant women continued to find employment doing finishing work on garments. The growing demand for ready-made clothes fuelled industry expansion. Kinship or communal ties to bosses, the need of some to work for Yiddish-speaking employers, and the physical proximity of workshops to immigrant neighbourhoods, all attracted women to the garment industry.

That few Jewish women joined unions disappointed Lily Montagu.[55] She believed that 'trade unionism could be a force for industrial progress'.[56] Owing to persecution, Montagu surmised that parents were individualistic and had '"been inclined to teach their children to get on with their work, [and] mind their own business and let other people get on with theirs"'.[57] Because she acknowledged that Jewish immigrants faced many challenges and not all could afford membership in unions, Montagu looked to a range of means, including girls' clubs, to promote industrial organization.[58]

By the early twentieth century, Montagu expressed concern that girls once employed in home-based workshops, under close supervision, had moved into factories 'and become to a large extent independent of home control'.[59] The seasonal nature of the work was dangerous and a girl's 'natural tendency to loafing becomes more marked'.[60] Montagu contended that after work, girls went out in search of fun. 'She loves crudities, for she has not been initiated into refined joys'.[61] While some working girls already had 'perceptions of truth, beauty, and purity' and a 'capacity for self-restraint', others were 'individualistic, irresponsible, and pleasure-loving'.[62]

Little in the sources reveals the development of a powerful Jewish labour movement in London during the years before the First World War. Anne Kershen, however, disputes the notion that Jews joined unions less often than their Christian counterparts.[63] Female unionization increased after 1911, when the availability of health insurance made membership and dues more attractive.[64] Parliament passed legislation regulating factories, and commissions and exposés made the public aware of the nature of the sweating system, but collective action by Jewish workers brought slow improvement. During the same period, London's Jewish immigrant women, unlike New York's, had limited leadership roles in the union movement. The smaller immigrant population may not have constituted a critical mass and émigré socialists from Russia played a larger role in America than in England.[65] Several of Britain's labour leaders left London for the greener pastures of New York and Chicago.

Hazardous Working Environments

In addition to low wages, many reformers focused on the moral and physical dangers of working conditions. They criticized the close proximity of male and female workers and argued that women's nature made them ill-suited to heavy labour. Some reports note that workshops were overcrowded even during 'slack' periods, suggesting far worse conditions during peak periods.[66] According to the 1884 report by the *Lancet*'s Special Sanitary Commission, bosses 'always [have] a ready reply' when inspectors discovered violations. 'The one is a niece, the other is a daughter; and if they are working, it is only for the family, and not in the pursuit of their trade'.[67] The need for work meant few foreign-born workers risked complaining or reporting employers. And the pace of work added challenges. Often tailors had little to do at the beginning of the week, only to have employers 'rush' them at week's end. Homeworkers, who worked for almost nothing, finished their garments by drawing on help from wives and children and would '"sweat" profit out of them'.[68]

The hazards of female employment did not end with poor working conditions. Numerous women complained of sexual harassment by bosses. One writer noted that Jewish working women faced both economic and sexual exploitation, especially by workshop foremen.[69] And Lewis Lyons reported that girls turned to prostitution because of the starvation wages they received.[70] Complaints by workers found their way into the press. One such case was of a women who, after her husband lost his job, 'went to the sweater and asked [him] to take her husband back. The sweater, however, replied, "I will not take your husband back, but I will allow you so much per week". In consideration the sweater committed adultery with the woman'.[71] The *Anti-Sweater* encouraged women to unite against 'the despotic sweater' who tried to take advantage of them.

Workshop and factory conditions took a heavy toll on many women's health and left them susceptible to contagious diseases and difficult pregnancies. Few workshops had working toilets, proper ventilation or lighting. Many were overheated, the irons contributing to the stifling atmosphere. Further, workshops commonly became a breeding ground for consumption and other diseases. One woman, Fanny Eisenberger, who worked as a hand-sewer along with three other women and four men, described the small workshop where she toiled thirteen-and-one-half-hours per day. It had four gaslights which made her 'very ill'. No matter how hard Eisenberger worked, her boss demanded more 'and when they bring us tea or coffee he does not give us any time to drink it, but we must drink it immediately; and he shouts and holloas [*sic*] at the hands'.[72]

For many, the work day began early in the morning and often continued until ten o'clock at night; police observed women leaving workshops as late as one or two in the morning.

> When compared with the more prosperous English Jews and the English working classes, these foreign Jews seem weak in muscle, emaciated in frame, and stunted in growth. Their pale unwholesome complexions and dejected attitudes clearly indicate that the law has failed to protect them from the deteriorating effects of overwork and overcrowding.[73]

The *Lancet* often used charged language to describe the negative impact of sweating on Jewish immigrants.

Employment conditions left women weak and unable to provide themselves with healthy accommodation or diet. While Factory Acts throughout the nineteenth century and unions brought some improvement, their impact was more long term. More immediate assistance came in the form of free holidays and inexpensive camping trips organized by settlements. The leaders of the girls' clubs and fundraisers for country holidays asserted that restful days on the shore or in the country, good food and exercise contributed to both physical and mental well-being.

By the 1880s, interest in the 'sweating system' led to intensive investigations of home industries, alien immigration and factory conditions. Witnesses called by investigators from the 1887 Board of Trade on the Sweating System at the East End of London and the 1888 House of Lords' Select Committee on the Sweating System, provided data on hours, working conditions and the extent of female and child labour.[74] On visits to East End workshops, Beatrice Potter recorded the working conditions, age and religion of workers, and she concluded that sweating was not a system.[75] She testified that in many workshops bosses preferred to hire Jewish rather than Christian women. 'They are more skilful', could handle machines and missed work less often. During the winter of 1887, the Free [Labour] Registry for Jews found men out of work, but no unemployed Jewish 'tailoresses', because, according to Potter, there was demand for Jewish women even during slack periods.[76] Potter seems not to have considered the possibility that fewer Jewish women sought work, or supplied their labour at a lower cost.[77]

The LCC health inspector cited overcrowding as the most serious defect in workshops, leading to workers' 'unhealthy appearance' and the prevalence of anaemia.[78] Social reformers and factory inspectors contended that if the law limited the number of hours that workshops could be open, manufacturers would have to introduce more efficient systems that distributed production more evenly throughout the year.[79] While owners who created the system demonstrated limited concern for their workers, it was not necessarily economically irrational. The careful use of seasonal labourers, greeners, some out-workers and the task system, meant that, from the master's perspective, production was rather efficient. Factory owners and masters could hire and fire labourers when needed, and replace inefficient or uncooperative workers. Such manufacturing methods discouraged unionization, meant that owners of factories did not need additional space for peak periods and avoided paying for unused space during slack seasons.

Strikingly, the JBG claimed the findings of the investigations on workshops necessitated no action on their part. Reacting to a suggestion from the communal press, the Board declined to become involved in discussion of Jewish working conditions in the tailoring trade. As a 'dispensing charity', they did not feel they had a right to intervene 'between an employer and his workmen who are independent of charity'. Their position on sanitation differed and the Board reminded the community of their attempts to eliminate defects.[80]

The Trade Boards Act of 1909, which set wages in different industries, led to some improvement. During discussions over the terms of the Act, some employers claimed that girls did not need or want to earn more than their current wages. Since girls and women either lived at home with family members, or were married, or widowed, many contended they had other sources of income. As R. H. Tawney noted, such an argument assumed 'that women workers, because they are women, are satisfied with a low fixed standard', a perspective that some manufacturers challenged.[81] Others claimed that women preferred to work at an easy pace rather than to speed up in order to earn more.

Community-Sponsored Training

Leaders in the Jewish community believed changes in occupational structure would improve Jews' image. From the outset of immigration, the Industrial Committee of the JBG diverted 'Jewish labour into more remunerative and less precarious directions'.[82] The Board established workrooms 'founded for the purpose of training daughters of the humble classes in every kind of needlework' and during 1880 they taught nearly sixty girls 'habits of industry, regularity, and thrift'.[83] The workrooms employed an average of thirty-two to fifty-seven women between 1881 and 1901.[84] The organizers called on the ladies of the community to purchase items to enable the hiring of additional girls.[85] In 1881, twenty-one girls completed their apprenticeship, qualifying them 'to earn their own living'.[86] The Board added needlework in gold and silver and hoped many girls would select this more lucrative alternative to plain needlework and dressmaking.[87] This training gained support because it remained true to notions of self-help, directed workers from crowded trades, served the unemployed and influenced hundreds of young Jewish women.

At a sale of workroom products, Rev. Green, who spoke on behalf of Lady Rothschild, noted that she thought that 'any industrial movement' the Board suggested was far more helpful 'to the rising generation than any doles to supply immediate wants'. Moreover, unlike 'ordinary workrooms' where girls unlearned 'propriety and modesty', Helen Lucas's weekly 'religious instruction', furthered established Jewry's moral agenda.[88] The Board successfully integrated trade skills, homemaking and religion with English cultural norms.

The JBG's apprenticeship programme had goals that included, but extended beyond, economic self-sufficiency. They helped girls to 'become moral and industrious members of society' by building on the work of Jewish schools.[89] Leaders of Anglo-Jewry argued apprenticeships would prevent new workers from entering 'dead-end' trades and would 'revolutionize the occupations and circumstances of the Jewish poor'.[90] The loss of wages during training and the short-lived work experience of many women made this route seem impractical to most young people and their parents. The JGB felt parental apathy meant many young people failed to complete apprenticeships. They responded by creating a visitation system to educate parents about the benefits of training for less crowded trades.[91]

In addition to the workrooms, the JBG ran a dedicated apprenticeship programme for boys and girls. Apprenticeship options for boys far exceeded those for girls. Supervised by the Industrial Committee of the JBG, committee members assessed requests for loans to purchase tools for young workers and to cover their apprenticeship premiums. They offered transportation subsidies to promote placements beyond the East End. A typical apprenticeship arranged by the JBG set wages, hours and guaranteed the apprentice would not have to work on the Sabbath or Jewish festivals.[92] The committee tried to mediate when differences arose between apprentices and masters, though one committee member 'deplored the ignorance of the lads as to the nature of the trade when applying to the committee to be apprenticed'.[93] The high cancelation rate led to the appointment of a sub-committee in 1895 to look into the problem.[94]

In 1896, the committee met to discuss suggestions for decreasing the numbers of cancelled indentures, which included a new role for women. They proposed that the executive of the Industrial Committee create a subcommittee of ladies who would visit homes and meet with apprentices' parents. Drawing on women's natural maternal skills, the committee believed their influence on parents could 'obviate' problems such as 'insubordination and dishonesty of apprentices'.[95] Such a proposal points to the challenges of finding appropriate employment for fourteen-year-old boys and potential areas of tensions that might develop between well-intentioned philanthropists and parents who might experience visits from committee members as patronizing.

Hannah Hyam, a manager at two East End schools, enthusiastically supported apprenticeships. In 1902, she noted that large numbers of girls were entering the millinery business, and in a new tack, some girls now worked in electric lighting firms and a lead pencil factory.[96] Improvement in the conditions, wages and options of women's employment developed very slowly. Employers, and even the government, continued to view female wages as supplemental to the family, justifying the practice of paying women less than they required for self-support.[97]

The apprenticeship programme continued to grow in the first years of the twentieth century. In 1901, the Industrial Committee had 719 apprentices, forty-three of whom were girls, and a year later there were sixty-four girls among 724 apprentices.[98] The Board now placed apprentices in eighty trades and the *JC* contended that the Industrial Committee's success was so crucial to the Jewish working class, 'that no measure which can contribute to it dare be neglected'.[99] While the committee placed too few school-leavers to transform the Jewish occupational structure, it trained thousands of workers for expanded occupations, actively supporting young men and women as they transitioned to the workforce.

By 1903, the JBG consciously began the search for new apprenticeships for girls. During 1904, a subcommittee took responsibility for the growing types of training for which East End girls could apply. The Board strengthened supervision of apprenticeships by appointing a secretary and visitor to the subcommittee. Girls worked in thirteen different trades by 1904, among them, six new occupations. Training as florists, in wig-making, and as hairdressers became available. Finding new employers occupied an important part of the new secretary's time. Resistance to change, though, remained a problem. The Apprenticing Committee faced 'great difficulty' in persuading 'girls to go to new occupations, especially in the West End'.[100] Immigrants entered a crowded labour market and in 1904, the JAPGAW expressed concern over worsening conditions; appeals from unemployed workers 'in a state approaching starvation' had increased dramatically.[101] From the perspective of established Jewry, training was all the more important. Not only did it 'open up a steady career of productive labour', it contributed to a 'stable working-class element', which the Jewish community should welcome.[102]

As the apprenticeship programme developed, the committee made every effort to eliminate obstacles to its progress. Some girls who worked outside the East End did not like the fact that they had to bring an 'inadequate and dry' lunch to work. The chair, Nettie Adler encouraged women living in these areas to invite the young workers to have lunch at their homes several times per week. Adler's mother already aided one such girl, and the scheme seemed effective.[103] Other complications, of a religious nature, also arose. In 1904, the committee had to end apprenticeships in artificial flower-making because the industry no longer excused apprentices from work on the Sabbath and other holy days.[104] Three years later, the committee located a flower-maker who would meet their requirements, and added button-making to the list of apprenticeships.[105]

Poverty meant that many who appreciated the value of apprenticeships could not take advantage of them.[106] Writer Charles Poulsen left school shortly before turning fourteen; he knew an apprenticeship would prepare him for a skilled craft, but his father's unemployment meant Poulsen needed paying work.[107] Only a small percentage of East Enders entered apprenticeships; most took low waged jobs with little promise for the future.[108] Despite attempts to expand occupational options, as late as 1928, most of the members of the Stepney Jewish Girls' Club entered the needle trades.[109] In part, the Jewish community's efforts reflected the uneasiness they felt owing to criticism of Jewish workshops.

Placing young workers who lacked the support of families was particularly important to the committee. The Jews' Hospital and Orphan Asylum (JHOA) had difficulties finding apprenticeships and people to supervise new workers.[110] They also had trouble attracting men to work with orphans and serve as their guardians. Boys educated at the institution, stressed the annual report, needed 'friends whom they can consult in the difficulties of life, which their limited experience cannot help them solve'.[111] A special fund enabled Norwood to offer better training to particularly talented boys. The school kept a dossier on each child, recording 'their opinion of the pupil's capacity and conduct' and medical records.[112]

In the years before World War I, it became easier to place Jewish women in varied training and work options, evidence of increased parental acceptance of newer opportunities for their daughters. Language acquisition and acculturation meant Jewish girls regularly found employment in factories rather than sweatshops.[113] Nursing also began to attract more women. Formerly, many considered Jews 'foreigners' who 'would not fit easily into English ways and English comradeship'. Some Jewish women hesitated to enter nursing because of Sabbath observance and dietary restrictions.[114] Though largely a profession for higher class and better educated women, the Jewish community actively promoted nursing as a promising career.

Sabbath observance continued to affect the prospects of young women entering secretarial work. Many girls on the lists of the Sabbath Observance Bureau had little hope of finding a position that gave them time off for Sabbath and Jewish festivals.[115] As East Enders increased their skill levels, available jobs gradually drew them beyond the Jewish labour market. While employers had long expected employees to work on Sabbath, the more young people moved beyond the East End, the more difficult it was to find positions that allowed for Jewish observance.

The end of mass immigration did not eliminate Anglo-Jewry's concern over the working life of the East End's youth. In 1913, the *JC* estimated that nearly 3,000 fourteen-year-olds left school each year.[116] The Jewish community did not have the resources to assist thousands in finding suitable employment. Seen as a difficult time for young adults, Nettie Adler thought parents made matters worse because they often failed to 'consider the individual taste of a girl when choosing a trade for her'.[117] New workers rarely earned enough money to support themselves, causing conflict with their parents. Anglo-Jewish leaders continued to promote club membership to channel young workers, but the numbers of potential members surpassed available spaces, leaving many new workers unaffiliated.[118]

Initially, the war years proved difficult for many. By the start of January 1915, unemployment began to ease, and many women entered war industries. Numerous organizations established workshops, 'two of which deal[t] solely with Jewesses and alien and refugee women and girls'.[119] As the war continued, work at good wages became available for the 'capable able-bodied worker'. The sick, feeble, widowed and elderly suffered from inflation and scarcity. Between July 1914 and January 1918 the retail price of food rose over one hundred per cent.[120] Few school-leavers wanted apprenticeships and many took dead end jobs that would leave them unskilled after the war.

Like their male peers, girls took advantage of higher wages and increased freedoms that came in the wake of World War I. Leaders such as Ida Samuel, a member of the Chicksand School Care Committee and District Commissioner for Girl Guides, believed early entrance of working-class girls into the labour force led to a number of problems. In more affluent families, girls remained in school 'during the most important part of their education'.[121] Many East End girls fell prey to the temptations that extra money made possible, exacerbated by war-time darkened streets. It proved very hard to convince girls that high wages would not last and to get them to consider options beyond the Jewish trades of fur, tailoring and underclothing.[122]

In 1917, for the first time, the JBG received requests for assistance from 'respectable working men'.[123] The Board's workroom increased its capacity from twenty-four to thirty-three between December 1916 and 1917, but lost many working hours because of illness and anxiety caused by air raids.[124] The East End suffered a disproportionate amount of damage, forcing businesses to close and increasing the exodus of people to areas such as Stamford Hill and Golders Green. Many women left the labour market after the war, especially after demobilization.[125] Despite praise for their contributions to the war effort, trade unions, as well as the Labour Party favoured male workers and believed women should willingly leave the workforce.[126] Many women resisted a return to domestic service with its long hours, low pay and limits on freedom.[127]

The post-war years meant new economic challenges and many workers faced a period of unemployment. High inflation rates, for example, created difficulties for individuals and organizations, and the East End suffered physically.[128] In 1921, the JBG received 'unexampled demands for assistance', and decreased the amount of relief money they granted, made worse by rapid price increases until year's end.[129] That year the St George's Jewish Settlement described the area as a 'black spot'. 'It is ugly, dirty, and smelly ... the air from the river cannot often be recognised as sea breezes ... [and] many of the homes ought to be condemned'.[130] For several years after the end of the war, scarcity of materials led to increased building costs, and little new construction or rebuilding occurred.[131] By 1925, the JAPGAW reported that unemployment had abated and girls with training from a trade school could find work 'in good dressmaking establishments' and contribute towards their maintenance once again.[132]

The changes that emerged in the years after World War I led to greater occupational diversification. Schooling, new training and the prospect of a higher standard of living attracted women to new and growing sectors of the economy. The 1921 census illustrates these shifts. Among employed Russian-born women in London, nearly 18 per cent now entered the commercial and financial sectors and another 8 per cent worked as clerks, draughtsmen and typists; although, 54 per cent still found employment in some branch of the textile industry.[133] While some of these Russian women were likely non-Jewish émigrés who left after the Revolution, this shift undoubtedly reflected the changing work opportunities for Jewish women in the years following the First World War. During this same period, the segregation that had characterized the Jewish community began to diminish. Growing numbers of Jews and Christians attended school together and worked alongside each other.[134] By 1930, tailoring drew fewer Jewish men and women. Mechanization of the trade seemingly played a role. More men became furriers, engineers, hairdressers and barbers. Some commentators believed Jewish girls preferred workshops and the growth of factories led them to leave tailoring for dressmaking, clerical occupations or become shop assistants.[135]

Limited statistical data, as well as impressionistic evidence, support the view that during the interwar years, it was still rare for married Jewish women to work outside their homes. There were exceptions, however, such as the mother of Mark Fineman, who ran a stall near the Brunswick Buildings after her husband had died.[136] Ena Abrahams, who was born in 1924, recounted that her mother, who came to England at the turn of the century, worked her whole life. 'She was one of that rare generation of working women', noted Abrahams, acknowledging the significance of her mother's work experience. Even though adversity forced her mother to work, it widened her horizons: 'She actually became very much a woman of the world. And independent'.[137]

Norwood Orphanage's after-care committee continued placing girls in the workplace. Many remained in Jewish trades such as dressmaking and millinery. Others moved into the same employment as typical East End school leavers. Only one girl took advantage of an LCC scholarship to attend secondary school. In order to help their young women as they entered labour market – and out of the institution – Norwood offered ongoing guidance. Staff from the orphanage made over 600 visits to girls' homes and to workshops and businesses where they worked.[138]

According to historian David Fowler, teens, unlike young children, enjoyed a higher standard of living than the rest of their family, and even girls kept as much as 50 per cent of their income. Many used their wages for recreation and accessories.[139] Yet in London, although the vast majority of unmarried Jewish girls worked outside their homes, this did not lead to true autonomy. Occasionally a young single daughter demanded more control over the money she earned. However, in most instances, and in contrast to their brothers, young women turned over wages to their parents.[140] Brothers tended to be more independent. There were exceptions into the 1930s. Jack Stein, for example, left Deal Street School in 1931 at the age of fourteen at which point his father found him a job. He earned ten shillings a week, of which he gave eight to his mother.[141]

Conclusion

Jewish women generally spent less than ten years in the labour force and most lived at home, influenced by the Jewish traditions of immigrant home life. On the eve of World War I, growing numbers found employment beyond the East End and gained exposure to a much broader culture than their familiar immigrant neighbourhoods. While parents and club leaders exerted more significant control over the behaviour of young women than men, even an unsanitary workplace and minimal wages offered greater freedom than school or home, and introduced a generation of immigrants and children of immigrants to the developing consumer society and enabled them to sample new forms of leisure activity.

The shifting Jewish occupational structure demonstrates a pattern of acculturation, as well as the impact of gender, ethnicity and class on the working lives of immigrants. Jewish women faced competing influences. Often their families needed their income, but clearly the English environment and middle-class prodding discouraged married female employment outside the home. These occupational factors influenced home-life, child-rearing, the family economy and the ability of social reformers to reach out to women and into immigrant homes.

For women, the most significant effects of anglicization were felt during the years a girl worked outside her home, from the time she left school until she married – a much shorter working life than the average male. Yet, for women, work, like education, was clearly generational in its impact. Women who arrived as adults were less likely to enter the workforce, except out of necessity. Over time, young women were more likely to work; increased education, apprenticeships and changing attitudes, augmented their options. Nonetheless, in 1930, 'Auntie' expressed her displeasure in the *JC* that many Jewish boys and girls remained unskilled and did not take advantage of apprenticeship training, in part to avoid the cost of premiums. She argued that higher wages would offset expenses and the Jewish Industrial Committee had funds to support suitable candidates.[142]

With the passage of time, the working lives of East Enders more closely approximated those of other urban, working-class men and women. Young women increasingly participated in mainstream British currents of fashion and leisure. While many married women worked only part-time, out of necessity, and in their homes, nearly every Jewish woman entered the labour force. During those years, new ideas, people and places became part of Jewish women's everyday experience and greatly influenced their children, who eventually become a dominant force within British Jewry.

CONCLUSION

Historians often emphasize very rapid socio-economic mobility among Jewish immigrants. David Feldman challenges the notion that every Jew was 'a Rothschild bursting to get out', arguing that it is a 'teleological bias' to assume that the post-1945 Jewish socio-economic pattern is part of a continuous trend that began in the early days of migration.[1] Overall, from 1880 to the Second World War, the movement into the professional classes is striking, but census data and interviews suggest that this movement occurred during the interwar years and beyond. Thus, by 1935, *World Jewry* argued the time had come to replace images of the 'stunted, pallid Jew of the ghetto' with 'the reality of the young East-Ender of today ... whose love of sport and exercise is as ardent as that of the Englishman with generations of sporting tradition as a background'.[2]

Broadly speaking, that change occurred in three stages. Adults who arrived between 1880 and 1905 tended to cling to familiar Eastern European customs of language, food, work and, in many cases, religious and political beliefs. Established Jews reacted to their arrival with mixed feelings – a sense of solidarity and *tzedakah*, alongside fear of an anti-Semitic backlash. Hosts responded to the immigrants with a set of expectations that incorporated class, religious and gendered expectations. Among these were decorum, a certain submissiveness and gratitude, modernized Judaism, domesticity for women and girls, and self-reliance for men and boys.

At the outset of immigration, the community was largely reactive and developed sanitary, medical, educational and recreational programmes that discouraged alien, Eastern European habits, especially in areas most open to public view. As immigration slowed in the wake of the Alien's Act, fewer newcomers could reinforce Eastern European culture and the Jewish community could turn from reaction to a more coordinated programme of prevention.

After 1905, through to the end of World War I, the children of immigrants entered a more integrated network of communal services and absorbed the lessons of the host community through increased attendance at 'Jewish' board schools. Infant welfare programmes, clubs and religious education increased in size and sophistication, promoting British cultural patterns and advancing particular roles for women and men. A process that consciously focused on children, concerns about indifference to Jewish education and hints at growing gaps between parents and children emerge in the years before World War I.

During the final stage, the interwar years, patterns of the modern anglicized life took root. The war undermined many social structures. Military life exposed men to a wider range of people and places and had forced the Jewish community to convince others of their patriotism and to disavow charges of shirking and dual loyalties. Looking and acting British became all the more crucial, as did the experience of sharing a national crisis. While reinforcement of anglicization did not wholly disappear, Jewish organizations found themselves dealing with a third generation whose level of acculturation placed new demands on schools, clubs and religious leaders. Some explicitly concluded that anglicization had become a victim of its own success. Keeping young Jews English and Jewish, rather than eliminating foreignness, took on new urgency.

Measuring acculturation is difficult, but some obvious factors – acquisition of the English language, one's level of schooling and occupation, the location of one's home, the types of leisure activity in which one engaged – all suggest whether a woman or child moved into the mainstream of English society. Many first generation immigrants never learned English, travelled beyond the East End, or changed their dress or eating habits, but generally accepted government-sponsored education and allowed their children to participate in activities sponsored by native-born Jews.

The most thorough attempts at anglicization started with children. The curriculum and the vision of most headmasters, Moses Angel being the best example, consciously included the moulding of their charges. Next to schools, the clubs and charities of London had the most influence on women and children. Most Jewish societies investigated the validity of requests they received and focused on the deserving poor and ideals of self-help. Support came in many forms: food from the Bread, Meat and Coal charity, medical care and household help for new mothers, clothing and shelter for those at risk. Local government, missionary aid and private donations supplemented Jewish philanthropy. This safety net not only advanced anglicization, it moderated some of the worst effects of poverty.

Typical of the era, most assistance involved expectations. Some, like Helen Lucas, believed that poor women should wear bonnets when attending the JBG's workrooms. Philanthropists usually expected women to keep their homes and children clean and made charitable assistance limited enough to prevent beneficiaries from concluding that such charity was a reasonable substitute for self-reliance and independence. Cradle to grave, Jewish services were more comprehensive and far-reaching than those provided by other religious or ethnic groups, often anticipating the welfare state.

Tied together by heritage and a vulnerable status, established Jews and newcomers did not always share the same vision nor did East Enders always demonstrate the gratitude expected of them. These occasional hints of resistance challenge early views of Anglo-Jewish history that the transition from alien to Briton occurred in a linear pattern – a Jewish version of Whiggish history. In 1949, Joseph Leftwich reflected on his own experience: 'I belong to the East End generation which revolted against the old patronising arrogance of the "West End" towards us. I remember the condescension that put our back up'. Leftwich contended that charitable organizations lacked sensitivity towards 'our poor East End brethren'.[3]

In the years after World War I, Jews began moving out of the East End, Jewish schools were closing and increased income facilitated greater integration. On the eve of World War II, younger and more anglicized Jews rejected behaviours described as 'just old East End customs'. Young East Enders with an 'almost inordinate love of fashionable clothes and smart living', now sought 'to conform to the highest bourgeois standards'. On weekend evenings one found young men at hair salons 'being shaved, hot-towelled ... face-massaged, oiled and perfumed'. Young women indulged in 'mud-packs, "perms", hairwaving ... eyebrow plucking, shampooing, and manicuring'. Another sign of anglicization, Abies and Sollies became Alfs and Sids.[4] While few denied their Jewishness, many children and grandchildren of immigrants no longer practised traditional Judaism, which they saw as foreign. Regular synagogue worship declined. Even on Yom Kippur (the Day of Atonement), many attended for the sake of more observant parents.[5]

New priorities emerged in the Jewish community during the late 1930s, as Jews faced renewed anti-Semitism. Refugees, particularly from Germany, Austria and Czechoslovakia, fleeing from the threat of Nazism, sought asylum in England. These immigrants, better educated, more highly skilled and smaller in number than their predecessors, faced new problems. They entered England during years of economic depression. As they had done for the Eastern Europeans, Jewish communal leaders endeavoured to assist newcomers find work, learn English and spend their time in England as productively as possible. As a result of the war, many Jews relocated to neighbourhoods in the north and north-east. To a very great extent, they looked and acted as the English young adults they had been trained to become. Even the missionaries acknowledged these changes. Now that Jews spoke English and could take advantage of the new world before them, proselytizing became even more difficult.[6] Most Eastern European-style *chadarim* and Talmud Torahs closed; new synagogues appeared in London suburbs and the Jewish community of England looked almost as homogenized – as anglicized – as it had been before the wave of Eastern Europeans had arrived on England's shores.

NOTES

Introduction

1. D. Englander, 'Anglicized not Anglican: Jews and Judaism in Victorian Britain', in G. Parsons (ed.), *Religion in Victorian Britain*, 4 vols (Manchester: Manchester University Press, 1988), vol. 1, pp. 235–73, on pp. 238–9.

2. T. Endelman, 'Perspectives on Modern Anti-Semitism in the West', in D. Berger (ed.), *History and Hate: The Dimensions of Anti-Semitism* (Philadelphia, PA: Jewish Publication Society, 1986), pp. 108–9.

3. T. Endelman, *The Jews of Georgian England, 1714–1830: Tradition and Change in a Liberal Society* (Philadelphia, PA: Jewish Publication Society, 1979), p. 9.

4. A. M. Rose, *Sociology: The Study of Human Relations* (New York: Alfred A. Knopf, 1956), pp. 557–8, as cited by M. Gordon, *Assimilation in American Life: The Role of Race, Religion, and National Origin* (New York: Oxford University Press, 1964), pp. 65–6.

5. Rev. S. Levy, 'Problems of Anglicisation', paper delivered at Conference of Anglo-Jewish Ministers (1911), reprinted in the Jewish Annual, 6 (London, 1943), pp. 73–82, on p. 76.

6. King Edward I expelled England's Jews in 1290. L. Wolf, *Menasseh ben Israel's Mission to Oliver Cromwell* (London: Macmillan & Co., 1901).

7. Englander, 'Anglicized not Anglican', p. 240.

8. T. Endelman, *The Jews of Britain, 1656 to 2000* (Berkeley, CA: University of California Press, 2002), pp. 41–8.

9. On the 'Jew Bill', see G. A. Cranfield, 'The London Evening Post and the Jew Bill of 1753', *Historical Journal*, 8 (1965), pp. 16–30. T. Perry, *Public Opinion, Propaganda, and Politics in Eighteenth-Century England: A Study of the Jew Bill of 1753* (Cambridge, MA: Harvard University Press, 1962). M. Scult, *Millennial Expectations and Jewish Liberties* (Leiden: E. J. Brill, 1978).

10. C. Bermant, *The Cousinhood* (New York: Macmillan Co., 1971).

11. I. Finestein, 'The Anglo-Jewish Revolt of 1853', in *Jewish Society in Victorian England* (London: Vallentine Mitchell, 1993), p. 114.

12. A. Gilam, *The Emancipation of the Jews in England, 1830–1860* (New York: Garland, 1982), pp. 149–53 and T. Endelman, 'Communal Solidarity among the Jewish Elite of Victorian London', *Victorian Studies*, 28:3 (1985), pp. 491–526, fn 6, on p. 493. On the Continent, see D. Sorkin, *The Transformation of German Jewry, 1780–1840* (New York and Oxford: Oxford University Press, 1987). P. Albert, *The Modernization of French Jewry: Consistory and Community in the Nineteenth Century* (Hanover, NH: University Press of New England, 1977).

13. B. Harris, 'Anti-Alienism, Health and Social Reform in Late Victorian and Early Edwardian Britain', *Patterns of Prejudice*, 31:4 (1997), pp. 3–34, on pp. 6–7. Jews too accepted the notion of racial difference, see D. Stone, 'Of Peas, Potatoes, and Jews: Redcliffe N. Salaman and the British Debate over Jewish Racial Origins', *Jahrbuch des Simon-Dubnow Instituts – Simon Dubnow Institute Yearbook*, 3 (2004), pp. 221–40, on p. 224.

14. U. R. Q. Henriques, 'The Jewish Emancipation Controversy in Nineteenth-Century Britain', *Past and Present*, 40 (July 1968), pp. 126–46, on pp. 126–8.

15. R. Langham, *250 Years of Convention and Contention: A History of the Board of Deputies of British Jews, 1760–2010* (London: Vallentine Mitchell, 2010).

16. Finestein, 'The Anglo-Jewish Opinion during the Struggle for Emancipation, 1828–58', in *Jewish Society in Victorian England*, pp. 30–2.

17. Gilam, *The Emancipation of the Jews in England*, p. 151 and T. Endelman, 'English Jewish History', *Modern Judaism*, 11 (1991), pp. 91–109, on p. 101.

18. R. Bolchover, *British Jewry and the Holocaust* (Cambridge: Cambridge University Press, 1993), pp. 42–3, 77–82.

19. T. Endelman, 'The Englishness of Jewish Modernity in England', in J. Katz (ed.), *Toward Modernity: The European Jewish Model* (New Brunswick, NJ: Transaction Books, 1987), pp. 225–46, on p. 240.

20. Finestein, 'A Modern Examination of Macaulay's Case for the Civil Emancipation of the Jews', in *Jewish Society in Victorian England*, pp. 78–103, on p. 93.

21. Endelman, *The Jews of Britain, 1656 to 2000*, p. 107.

22. Tony Kushner's recent work not only looks at important provincial communities, but depictions of Jews in British history, suggesting the ways of remembering and forgetting Jews. T. Kushner, *Anglo-Jewry since 1066: Place, Locality and Memory* (Manchester: Manchester University Press, 2009).

23. C. Holmes, 'Immigrants and Refugees in Britain', in W. Mosse (ed.), *Second Chance: Two Centuries of German-speaking Jews in the United Kingdom* (Tubingen: J. C. B. Mohr, 1991), pp. 11–30, on p. 11.

24. T. Endelman, 'Writing English Jewish History', *Albion*, 27:4 (1995), pp. 623–36, on pp. 623–4.

25. Endelman, 'English Jewish History', p. 91.

26. M. Domnitz, *Immigration and Integration: Experiences of the Anglo-Jewish Community* (London: Council of Christians and Jews, [*c.* 1958]), p. 13.

27. A. M. Hyamson, 'The Ten Lost Tribes and the Return of the Jews to England', *Transactions of the Jewish Historical Society of England*, 5 (1902–5), pp. 115–47. N. Osterman, 'The Controversy over the Proposed Readmission of Jews to England (1655)', *Jewish Social Studies*, 3:3 (1941), pp. 301–28. D. Patinkin, 'Mercantilism and the Readmission of the Jews to England', *Jewish Social Studies*, 8:3 (1946), pp. 161–78. For more recent scholarly analysis, see D. Katz, *PhiloSemitism and the Readmission of the Jews to England 1603–1655* (Oxford: Clarendon Press, 1982) and D. Katz, 'English Redemption and Jewish Readmission in 1656', *Journal of Jewish Studies*, 34:1 (1983), pp. 73–91.

28. Works by Lucien Wolf and Cecil Roth indicate the tenor of early studies. By the 1950s, Anglo-Jewish historians demonstrated more interest in political and educational institutions.

29. Gertrude Himmelfarb challenges the notion that philanthropists aimed at social control and sought to undermine working-class culture to reinforce their own class interests. G. Himmelfarb, 'Victorian Philanthropy: The Case of Toynbee Hall', *American Scholar*, 59:3 (1990), pp. 373–84, on pp. 375–6.

30. V. D. Lipman, 'Mass Immigration and a Social Revolution', *CAJEX*, 5:2 (1965), pp. 92–100, on p. 100.
31. G. Alderman, *Modern British Jewry* (Oxford: Clarendon Press, 1992), p. viii.
32. K. Myers and I. Grosvenor, 'Birmingham Stories: Local Histories of Migration and Settlement and the Practice of History', *Midland History*, 36:2 (2011), pp. 149–62, on p. 149.
33. L. Gartner, *The Jewish Immigrant in England, 1870–1914* (London: George Allen and Unwin, 1960). V. D. Lipman, *Social History of the Jews in England, 1850–1950* (London: Watts & Co., 1954).
34. T. Endelman, 'Native Jews and Foreign Jews in London, 1870–1914', in D. Berger (ed.), *The Legacy of Jewish Migration: 1881 and its Impact* (New York: Social Science Monographs, Brooklyn College Press, 1983), pp. 109–25 and Endelman, *The Jews of Georgian England, 1714–1830*. Eugene Black's broad survey emphasizes communal management. E. Black, *The Social Politics of Anglo-Jewry, 1880–1920* (Oxford: Basil Blackwell, 1988).
35. Endelman emphasized these contributions in the preface to his 1999 paperback version. T. Endelman, *The Jews of Georgian England: 1714–1830 Tradition and Change in a Liberal Society* (Ann Arbor, MI: University of Michigan Press, 1999), pp. ix–xxiii, on pp. x, xi, xii, xii.
36. T. Kushner, *The Persistence of Prejudice: Antisemitism in British Society during the Second World War* (Manchester: Manchester University Press, 1989). For an assessment of historiographic analyses of anti-Semitism in Germany and England, see T. Weber, 'Anti-Semitism and Philo-Semitism among the British and German Elites: Oxford and Heidelberg before the First World War', *English Historical Review*, 118:475 (2003), pp. 86–119, especially pp. 89–90.
37. D. Cesarani, 'Anti-Alienism in England after 1914', *Immigrants and Minorities*, 6:1 (1987), pp. 5–29. D. Cesarani, *The Jewish Chronicle and Anglo-Jewry, 1841–1991* (Cambridge: Cambridge University Press, 1994).
38. D. Cesarani (ed.), *The Making of Modern Anglo-Jewry* (Oxford: Basil Blackwell, 1990).
39. B. Williams, *The Making of Manchester Jewry, 1740–1875* (Manchester: Manchester University Press, 1985).
40. J. Buckman, *Immigrants and the Class Struggle: The Jewish Immigrant in Leeds, 1880–1914* (Manchester: Manchester University Press, 1983).
41. D. Feldman, 'Jews in London, 1880–1914', in R. Samuel (ed.), *Patriotism: The Making and Unmaking of British National Identity*, 3 vols (London and New York: Routledge, 1989), vol. 2, pp. 207–29, on pp. 208, 219–20, 222–3.
42. D. Feldman, *Englishmen and Jews: Social Relations and Political Culture, 1840–1914* (New Haven, CT and London: Yale University Press, 1994), p. 382.
43. D. Englander, 'Booth's Jews: The Presentation of Jews and Judaism in Life and Labour of the People in London', *Victorian Studies*, 32 (1989), pp. 551–71, on p. 556. B. Cheyette, *Constructions of 'the Jew' in English Literature and Society: Racial Representations, 1875–1945* (New York: Cambridge University Press, 1993).
44. P. Hyman, 'Gender and the Shaping of Modern Jewish Identities', *Jewish Social Studies*, n.s., 8:2/3 (2002), pp. 153–61, on p. 154.
45. On New York, see P. Hyman, 'Culture and Gender: Women in the Immigrant Jewish Community', in D. Berger (ed.), *The Legacy of Jewish Migration: 1881 and its Impact* (New York: Social Science Monographs, Brooklyn College Press, 1983), pp. 157–68. On Paris, see N. Green, 'Gender and Jobs in the Jewish Community: Europe at the Turn of the Twentieth Century', *Jewish Social Studies*, n.s., 8:2/3 (2002), pp. 39–60.

46. R. Livshin, 'The Acculturation of the Children of Immigrant Jews in Manchester, 1890–1930', in Cesarani (ed.), *The Making of Modern Anglo-Jewry*, pp. 79–96.

47. G. Black, *J. F. S.: The History of the Jews' Free School, London since 1732* (London: Tymsder Publishing, 1998). See also: S. K. Greenberg, 'Compromise and Conflict: The Education of Jewish Immigrant Children in London in the Aftermath of Emancipation, 1881–1905' (PhD dissertation, Stanford University, 1985). For education of Jewish orphans, see L. Cohen, 'A Study in Institutionalism: the Jewish Children's Orphanage at Norwood' (PhD thesis, University of Southampton, 2010).

48. G. Short, 'Accounting For Success: The Education of Jewish Children in Late 19th Century England', *British Journal of Educational Studies*, 41:3 (1993), pp. 272–86.

49. S. Kadish, *'A Good Jew and a Good Englishman': The Jewish Lads' & Girls' Brigade, 1895–1995* (London: Vallentine Mitchell, 1995).

50. L. G. Kuzmack, *Woman's Cause: The Jewish Woman's Movement in England and the United States, 1881–1933* (Columbus, OH: Ohio State University Press, 1990).

51. E. Umansky, *Lily Montagu and the Advancement of Liberal Judaism: From Vision to Vocation* (New York: Edwin Mellen Press, 1983). E. Umansky, 'Lily Montagu', *Jewish Women: A Comprehensive Historical Encyclopedia* (20 March 2009), Jewish Women's Archive, online at http://jwa.org/encyclopedia/article/montagu-lily [accessed 28 June 2013].

52. R. Burman, 'The Jewish Woman as Breadwinner: The Changing Value of Women's Work in a Manchester Immigrant Community', *Oral History*, 10:2 (1982), pp. 27–39; R. Burman, 'Jewish Women and the Household Economy in Manchester, c. 1880–1920', in Cesarani (ed.), *The Making of Modern Anglo-Jewry*, pp. 55–75; and R. Burman, '"She Looketh Well to the Ways of her Household": The Changing Role of Jewish Women in Religious Life c. 1880–1930', in G. Malmgreen (ed.), *Religion in the Lives of English Women, 1760–1930* (Bloomington, IN: Indiana University Press, 1986), pp. 234–59, on pp. 237, 238, 252.

53. R. Adler, 'The Jew Who Wasn't There: Halakah and the Jewish Woman', in S. Heschel (ed.), *On Being a Jewish Feminist: A Reader* (New York: Schocken Books, 1983), pp. 12–18, on pp. 15–6.

54. Burman, '"She Looketh Well to the Ways of Her Household"', pp. 237, 249.

55. L. Marks, '"Dear Old Mother Levy's": The Jewish Maternity Home and Sick Room Helps Society, 1895–1939', *Journal of Social History of Medicine*, 3:1 (1990), pp. 61–88. L. Marks, 'The Experience of Jewish Prostitutes and Jewish Women in the East End of London at the Turn of the Century', *Jewish Quarterly*, 34:2 (1987), pp. 6–10. L. Marks, '"The Luckless Waifs and Strays of Humanity": Irish and Jewish Immigrant Unwed Mothers in London, 1870–1939', *Twentieth Century British History*, 3:2 (1992), pp. 113–37.

56. L. Marks, *Model Mothers: Jewish Mothers and Maternity Provision in East London, 1870–1939* (Oxford: Clarendon Press, 1994), pp. 8–9.

57. Americanization efforts also focused on children. See E. Rose, 'From Sponge Cake to Hamentashen: Jewish Identity in a Jewish Settlement House, 1885–1952', *Journal of American Ethnic History*, 13:3 (1994), pp. 3–23, on p. 7.

58. According to Dr E. W. Hope, the Liverpool Medical Officer of Health, Jewish families who earned as little as 10s. to 30s. per week, provided children with excellent care. *JC*, 3 April 1908.

59. C. Booth, *Life and Labour of the People in London*, 17 vols (London: Macmillan, 1902–3).

60. M. Brodie, *The Politics of the Poor: The East End of London, 1885–1914* (Oxford: Clarendon Press, 2004), pp. 2–3.

61. E. Ross, *Love and Toil: Motherhood in Outcast London, 1870–1918* (New York: Oxford University Press, 1993).

62. R. Finn, *Time Remembered* (London: Futura Publications, 1985), p. 13.
63. Ibid., pp. 177, 179.
64. On similar networks among Gentile women, see: E. Ross, 'Survival Networks: Women's Neighbourhood Sharing in London before World War I', *History Workshop*, 15 (1983), pp. 4–27.
65. J. White, *Rothschild Buildings: Life in an East End Tenement Block. 1887–1920* (London: Routledge and Kegan Paul, 1980), p. 111.
66. Jewish Museum, interview with K. R. Collins, tape 69, interviewed by J Schrnt Plotkin, 13 April 1986.
67. Ross, *Love and Toil*, pp. 27–55. M. P. Reeves, *Round about a Pound a Week* (London: Virago, 1979), pp. 94–112.
68. J. Burnett, *Plenty and Want: A Social History of Diet in England from 1815 to the Present Day* (London: Methuen and Co., 1983), pp. 177–212.
69. A. Davin, 'Loaves and Fishes: Food in Poor Households in Late Nineteenth-Century London', *History Workshop Journal*, 41 (1996), pp. 167–92, on p. 171.
70. Literary tradition, for example emphasizes the favoured position of sons. Rabbinic tradition characterizes women in lofty, but also in negative and patronizing terms. A. Lapidus Lerner, 'Lost Childhood in East European Hebrew Literature', in D. Kraemer (ed.), *The Jewish Family: Metaphor and Memory* (New York: Oxford University Press, 1989), pp. 95–108, on p. 99.
71. S. Gilley, 'English Attitudes to the Irish in England, 1789–1900', in C. Holmes (ed.), *Immigrants and Minorities in British Society* (London: Allen and Unwin, 1978), pp. 81–110. Z. Layton-Henry, *The Politics of Immigration* (Oxford: Blackwell Publishers, 1992). F. Neal, 'Immigration and Anti-Irish Feeling', in *Sectarian Violence: The Liverpool Experience, 1819–1914* (Manchester: Manchester University Press, 1988), pp. 105–24. J. Solomos, *Race and Racism in Britain*, 2nd edn (New York: St Martin's, 1993). L. Sponza, *Italian Immigrants in Nineteenth Century Britain: Realities and Images* (Leicester: Leicester University Press, 1988).
72. David Schloss claimed Jewish parents spoiled daughters, but did not give them 'any undue degree of freedom'. D. Schloss, 'The Jew as Workman', *Nineteenth Century*, 29 (1891), pp. 96–109, on p. 108.
73. The tradition continued in some form into the 1930s. Girls at the Norwood Orphanage received twenty-five pounds from the Isaac Davis Dowry Fund or Palmer Trust Fund upon their marriage. The Jewish Orphanage, Report for the Year 1935, p. 20.
74. Jewish Museum, interview with K. R. Collins.
75. Jewish Museum, interview with J. Stein, tape 112, interviewed by V. H. Seymour, 23 February 1988.
76. C. Hall, 'The Early Formation of Victorian Domestic Ideology', in S. Burman (ed.), *Fit Work for Women* (New York: St Martin's Press, 1979), pp. 15–32.
77. J. Harding and J. Kid Berg, *Jack Kid Berg: The Whitechapel Windmill* (London: Robson Books, 1987), p. 16. J. London, *People of the Abyss* (New York: Macmillan Co., 1903). J. Bush, 'East London Jews in the First World War', *London Journal*, 6:2 (1980), pp. 147–61, on p. 148.
78. Hartley Library, Special Collections, University of Southampton (hereafter, HL Southampton), MS132 AJ220/1/2, Diary of B. Henriques, 9 October 1913.
79. Few primary sources explain emigrants' personal motivations. Gur Alroey argues that letters to the Jewish Colonization Association and Jewish Territorial Organization provide important insights into women's experience of emigration. G. Alroey, '"And I Remained Alone in a Vast Land": Women in the Jewish Migration from Eastern Europe',

Jewish Social Studies: History, Culture, Society, n.s., 12:3 (Spring/Summer 2006), pp. 39–72, on pp. 40–1.

80. Three of London's Ashkenazi synagogues, the Great, the Hambro' and the New, established the Jewish Board of Guardians in 1859.

1 A Brief History of the Acculturation of a Jewish Community: London, 1880–1939

1. In 1889, 90 per cent of London's Jews lived in the East End, declining to about 60 per cent in 1931. N. Adler, 'Life and Labour in East London', in H. L. Smith (ed.), *The New Survey of London Life and Labour*, 9 vols (London: P. S. King & Son, Ltd, 1930–4), vol. 6, pp. 268–98, on pp. 270–1.
2. D. Englander, 'Policing the Ghetto: Jewish East London, 1880–1920', *Crime, Histoire & Societes/Crime, History & Societies*, 14:1 (2010), pp. 31–2.
3. Booth, *Life and Labour of the People in London*. Booth drew on detailed information gathered by school visitors. Englander, 'Booth's Jews', pp. 558–9.
4. White, *Rothschild Buildings*, p. 153.
5. The 1875 Artisans Dwelling Act, supported by reformers such as Octavia Hill and Samuel Barnett, gave government extensive powers to purchase slums. White, *Rothschild Buildings*, pp. 10–1.
6. C. Spector, *Volla Volla Jew Boy* (London: Centerprise Trust, Ltd, 1988), pp. 2, 3.
7. The *Forverts*, New York's Yiddish daily, received letters from immigrants and their children who found each other a source of embarrassment and frustration. See I. Metzger (ed.), *A Bintel Brief* (New York: Behrman House, 1971).
8. *JC*, 14 January 1910.
9. Kaplan argues women retained ties to Judaism – though not necessarily in terms of formal ritual – longer than men did. M. Kaplan, *The Making of the Jewish Middle Class: Women, Family, and Identity in Imperial Germany* (New York: Oxford University Press, 1991), pp. 64–84.
10. JBG, *Annual Report*, 1913, pp. 79–80.
11. *JC*, 27 February 1914.
12. S. Auerbach, 'Negotiating Nationalism: Jewish Conscription and Russian Repatriation in London's East End, 1916–1918', *Journal of British Studies*, 46:3 (2007), pp. 594–620, on pp. 598–99, 606–7. M. Levene, 'Going Against the Grain: Two Jewish Memoirs of War and Anti-War (1914–1918)', in M. Berkowitz, S. Tananbaum and S. Bloom (eds), *Forging Modern Jewish Identities, Identities: Public Faces and Private Struggles* (London: Vallentine Mitchell, 2003), pp. 81–114. A. Lloyd, 'Between Integration and Separation: Jews in Military Service in World War I Britain', *Jewish Culture and History*, 12:1–2 (2010), pp. 41–60, on pp. 41–2.
13. 'Anglo-Jewry under George V, 1910–1936', *The Jewish Yearbook* (London), 1937, pp. 356–75, on p. 366–7.
14. Bush, 'East London Jews in the First World War', pp. 149–50.
15. *JC*, 3 April 1914.
16. 'Anglo-Jewry under George V', p. 370.
17. *JC*, 3 July 1914.
18. Ibid., 2 January 1914.
19. Ibid., 20 March 1914.

20. J. Lewis, 'The Social History of Social Policy: Infant Welfare in Edwardian England', *Journal of Social Policy*, 9:4 (1980), pp. 463–86, on p. 464.
21. S. G. Jones, *Workers at Play: A Social and Economic History of Leisure, 1918–1939* (London: Routledge and Kegan Paul, 1986), pp. 34–7.
22. Harding and Berg, *Jack Kid Berg*, pp. 29, 28. By 1925, when Fineman began work as a JBG investigating officer, few people totally depended on Yiddish. Jewish Museum, interview with M. Fineman, tape 50, interviewed by C. Silvertown, January 27, 1986.
23. R. Graves and A. Hodge, *The Long Weekend: A Social History of Great Britain, 1918–1939* (New York: W.W. Norton, 1963), p. 42.
24. *World Jewry*, 27 September 1935.
25. Ibid., 3 January 1936.
26. D. Cesarani, 'A Funny Thing Happened on the Way to the Suburbs: Social Change in Anglo-Jewry between the Wars, 1914–1945', *Jewish Culture and History*, 1:1 (1998), pp. 5–26, on p. 6–8.
27. Harding and Berg, *Jack Kid Berg*, pp. 29, 33.
28. Jewish Museum, interview with K. R. Collins.
29. F.V., Oral History Interview, Jewish Women in London Group.
30. D. Glover, *Literature, Immigration, and Diaspora in Fin-de-Siècle England: A Cultural History of the 1905 Aliens Act* (Cambridge: Cambridge University Press, 2012), pp. 122–4.
31. E. Bristow, 'Causes of White Slavery', *Prostitution and Prejudice: The Jewish Fight against White Slavery, 1870–1939* (New York: Schocken Books, 1983), pp. 85–108. P. Nadell, 'The Journey to America by Steam: The Jews of Eastern Europe in Transition', *American Jewish History*, 71:2 (1981), pp. 269–84. Marks, 'The Experience of Jewish Prostitutes', pp. 6–10. L. Gartner, 'Anglo-Jewry and the Jewish International Traffic in Prostitution', *AJS Review*, 7/8 (1982–3), pp. 129–78, on pp. 130, 144. Alroey, '"And I Remained Alone in a Vast Land"', p. 55.
32. *JC*, 31 January 1902.
33. Board of Deputies of British Jews (hereafter, JBD), London Committee of Deputies of the British Jews, File B2/1/16, 'Grimsby: Schwartz Case', Letter from L. H. Woolfe (Senior) to Charles Emanuel, Solicitor and Secretary, 15 June 1910.
34. Harding and Berg, *Jack Kid Berg*, p. 32.
35. *JC*, 12 August 1881.
36. Ibid., 16 January 1880.
37. Ibid., 7 March 1880.
38. Ibid., 2 January 1880, 12 December 1879 and 19 December 1879.
39. Ibid., 9 January 1914.
40. Jewish Museum, Interview with Fineman.
41. Englander, 'Anglicized not Anglican', pp. 266–7.
42. *JC*, 19 June 1885. Cesarani, *The Jewish Chronicle and Anglo-Jewry*, pp. 70–82, 95–100.
43. S. Kaplan, 'The Anglicization of the East European Jewish Immigrant as seen by the London Jewish Chronicle', *YIVO Annual of Jewish Social Science*, 10 (1955), pp. 267–78, on p. 272.
44. This estimate is a conservative one since some German and Austrian Jews, escaped enumeration. On population issues, see Feldman, *Englishmen and Jews*, pp. 154–7. S. Joseph, 'Jewish Immigration to the United States', *Studies in History, Economics, and Public Law*, Table 8 (New York: Columbia University Press, 1914), p. 162. On the difficulties and efforts made to obtain accurate census data, see: Royal Commission on Alien Immigra-

tion (RCAI), *PP* 1903, IX, II. Minutes of Evidence, Cd. 1742, qq. 644–5, p. 33; q. 681, p. 35; q. 746–50, p. 37; q. 795–8, p. 38; q. 5666–72, p. 190.

45. M. A. G. O'Tuathaigh, 'The Irish in Nineteenth-Century Britain: Problems of Integration', *Transactions of the Royal Historical Society*, 5th series, 31 (1981), pp. 149–73, on p. 151.

46. M. Stanislawski, *Tsar Nicholas I and the Jews: The Transformation of Jewish Society in Russia, 1825–1855* (Philadelphia, PA: Jewish Publication, 1983). From 1825 to 1897, Russian Jewry increased from approximately 1.6 million to approximately five million. 'Population', *Encyclopedia Judaica* (Jerusalem: Keter Publishing House, 1972), Table 3, pp. 889–90.

47. L. P. Rastorgoueff, 'Disabilities of the Jews in Russia', *Jewish Review*, 3 (1912–13), pp. 106–29.

48. Small numbers of 'privileged Jews', could live outside the Pale (established in 1772). During the last twenty years of the nineteenth century, the Pale experienced mounting unemployment. L. Greenberg, *The Jews in Russia: The Struggle for Emancipation* (New York: Schocken Books, 1976) (vol. 1 first published 1944, vol. 2 first published 1951), vol. 2, pp. 32, 142, vol. 1, pp. 75, 9.

49. A. Weiner, 'Jewish Industrial Life in Russia', *Economic Journal*, 15:60 (1905), pp. 581–4, on pp. 582, 583, 584.

50. J. D. Klier, 'Russian Jewry on the Eve of the Pogroms', in J. D. Klier and S. Lambroza (eds), *Pogroms: Anti-Jewish Violence in Modern Russian History* (Cambridge: Cambridge University Press, 1992), pp. 3–12, on p. 3. Alroey, '"And I Remained Alone in a Vast Land"', pp. 42–3.

51. Sixty-one pogroms between 1903 and 1906 resulted in thousands of deaths and injuries to Jews and destruction of goods and property amounting to more than 5.21 million rubles. S. Lambroza, 'The Pogroms of 1903–1906', in Klier and Lambroza (eds), *Pogroms: Anti-Jewish Violence in Modern Russian History*, pp. 191–247, on pp. 218, 228. Emigration increased after the Kishinev pogrom. G. Alroey, 'Bureaucracy, Agents, and Swindlers: The Hardships of Jewish Emigration from the Pale of Settlement in the Early 20th Century', *Studies in Contemporary Jewry*, 19 (2003), pp. 214–31, on pp. 214–15. J. Klier, 'What Exactly Was the Shtetl'? in G. Estraikh and M. Krutikov (eds), *The Shtetl: Image and Reality* (Oxford: Legenda: published by the European Humanities Research Centre, 2000), pp. 23–35, on pp. 32–3.

52. Approximately 70 per cent of Jewish immigrants settled in America, particularly in New York. 2.5 million Jews went to the United States between 1880 and 1925, including a higher percentage of skilled workers than among English or German immigrants. N. Barou, *The Jews in Work and Trade*, 2nd edn (London: Trades Advisory Council of 1946), pp. 21–2. R. B. Helfgott, 'Trade Unionism among the Jewish Garment Workers of Britain and the United States', *Labor History*, 2:2 (1961), pp. 202–14, on p. 202.

53. S. Chotzinoff, *A Lost Paradise* (New York: Alfred A. Knopf, 1955).

54. C. Jones, 'Jewish immigration, c. 1870–1911', *Immigration and Social Policy in Britain* (London: Tavistock Publications, 1977), pp. 66–117, on p. 69.

55. J. Smith, 'The Jewish Immigrant', *Contemporary Review*, 76 (September 1899), pp. 425–36, on p. 426.

56. Ibid., p. 429.

57. 'The Alien Immigrant', *Blackwood's Magazine*, 173 (January 1903), pp. 132–41, on p. 135. For examples of typical criticisms, see The Earl of Dunraven, 'The Invasion of Des-

titute Aliens', *Nineteenth Century*, 31:184 (1892), pp. 985–1000; 'Foreign Undesirables', *Blackwood's Edinburgh Magazine*, 169:1024 (February, 1901), pp. 279–89.

58. Public Record Office (PRO), MEPOL 2/260/97779, 'Influx of Aliens', 6 December 1904.

59. 'The Outlook – The Growing Influx of Aliens', *Daily Mail*, 1 December 1904.

60. Glover, *Literature, Immigration, and Diaspora*, p. 49.

61. S. Koven, *Slumming: Sexual and Social Politics in Victorian London* (Princeton, NJ: Princeton University Press, 2004). N Roemer, 'London and the East End as Spectacles of Urban Tourism', *Jewish Quarterly Review*, 99:3 (2009), pp. 416–34.

62. JBG, *Annual Report*, 1884, p. 65. F. Prochaska, *The Voluntary Impulse: Philanthropy in Modern Britain* (London: Faber and Faber, 1988), p. 49.

63. *JC*, 1 October 1880.

64. Ibid.

65. White, *Rothschild Buildings*, p. 43.

66. A. Abrahams, 'End of an Era', *Jewish Monthly*, 4:9 (1950), pp. 572–7, on p. 573.

67. *JC*, 8 May 1891.

68. Ibid., 12 August 1881.

69. J. Dyche, 'The Jewish Immigrant', *Contemporary Review*, 75 (January/June, 1899), pp. 379–99. Arnold White, the well-known restrictionist, challenged Dyche. A. White, 'A Typical Alien Immigrant', *Contemporary Review*, 73 (February 1898), pp. 241–50.

70. *JC*, 12 August 1881.

71. Adler, 'Life and Labour in East London', p. 291.

72. To some extent, Jews created visiting committee to respond to missionizing. F. Prochaska, *Christianity and Social Service in Modern Britain* (Oxford: Oxford University Press, 2006), p. 64.

73. A similar pattern emerged in America. N. Sinkoff, 'Educating for "Proper" Jewish Womanhood: A Case Study in Domesticity and Vocational Training, 1897–1926', *American Jewish History*, 77:4 (1988), pp. 572–99, on pp. 573, 580.

74. Philadelphia's Neighborhood Center found many residents used their 'services selectively'. E. Rose, 'From Sponge Cake to Hamentashen', p. 15.

75. PRO, HO 45, 10303/117267/9779, 'Notes of Deputation from the Jewish Board of Deputies on the Aliens Bill', 19 May 1904. There was an increase of 88 foreigners and a decrease of 843 Britons, charged at the police stations in Whitechapel and Spitalfields when comparing 1881 to 1888. PRO, MEPOL 2/260/97779, Metropolitan Police, Division H, 18 June 1889.

76. *JC*, 3 January 1902.

77. Bernard Gainer contends that 'alien' clearly meant Jew. B. Gainer, *The Alien Invasion* (New York: Crane, Russak and Co., Inc., 1972), pp. 107–28. C. Kinloch Cooke, Secretary to Lord Dunraven, the Chairman of the House of Lord Select Committee on the Sweating System (1888), claimed that alienism was directed 'against the unrestricted admission of undesirable foreigners', not Jews. *JC*, 6 January 1905. J. Pellew, 'The Home Office and the Aliens Act, 1905', *Historical Journal*, 32:2 (1989), pp. 369–85.

78. *Tribune*, 18 October 1907.

79. D. L. Munby, *Industry and Planning in Stepney* (Oxford: Oxford University Press, 1951), pp. 44–5, 65. By the latter part of the nineteenth century, important industries in Stepney, including the docks and sugar refining, experienced severe decline.

80. Census of England and Wales 1901, *General Report*, Cd. 2174, p. 140.

81. The demographic profile of Jewish immigrants in America was similar to Britain. H. Gutman, *The Black Family in Slavery and Freedom, 1750–1925* (New York: Pantheon Books, 1976), p. 527.

82. 'European Immigration into the United States, its Nature and Effects', *PP* 1893–4, LXXI, C. 7113, p. 229. I. Howe, *The World of Our Fathers* (New York: Harcourt, Brace and Jovanovich, 1976), p. 80. See also, L. Gartner, 'Notes on the Statistics of Jewish Immigration to England, 1870–1914', *Jewish Social Studies*, 22:2 (1960), pp. 97–102.

83. S. Rosenbaum, 'A Contribution to the Study of the Vital and Other Statistics of the Jews in the United Kingdom', *Journal of the Royal Statistical Society*, 68 (1905), pp. 526–62, on pp. 526–7.

84. There were peaks in 1881–3, 1891, 1899–1902 and 1903–6. C. Jones, *Immigration and Social Policy in Britain*, pp. 68–9. Feldman, *Englishmen and Jews*, p. 148. K. Leech, 'The Role of Immigration in Recent East London History', *East London Papers*, 10:1 (1967), pp. 3–17, on p. 10.

85. House of Lords, Select Committee on the Sweating System, First Report, *PP* 1888, XX, Minutes of Evidence, q. 348, p. 29. The London Committee of Deputies of British Jews' 1904 estimate of 120,000 Jews in London was probably low. PRO, HO 45, 10303/117267/9779, 'Notes of Deputation from the Jewish Board of Deputies', 19 May 1904.

86. H. and S. Levin, 'Jubilee at Finchley' (London: Finchley Synagogue, 1976), p. 1. V. D. Lipman, 'The Rise of Jewish Suburbia', *Transactions of the Jewish Historical Society of England*, 21 (1968), pp. 78–103, on p. 91.

87. Census of England and Wales, as cited by Gartner, 'Notes on the Statistics of Jewish Immigration to England', p. 98.

88. Stepney averaged 169 persons per acre, the parish of St George's in the East, 201 and Mile End New Town, 308. London as a whole averaged sixty-one people per acre. Census of England and Wales, 1901, *General Report*, Cd. 2172, p. 141. Population density was far greater in New York's Lower East Side, reaching 700 residents per acre. Howe, *The World of Our Fathers*, p. 69.

89. In England, aliens constituted only .58 per cent of the population in 1891, and .69 per cent in 1901. American figures for 1891 were 13.71 per cent and 14.76 per cent in 1901, for France aliens amounted to 2.66 per cent in 1901 and 2.95 per cent in 1891. RCAI, *PP* 1903, IX, Report, Cd. 1741, I, p. 21.

90. Board of Trade (Alien Immigration), Reports on the Volume and Effects of the Recent Immigration from Eastern Europe into the United Kingdom, *PP* 1894, LXVIII, C. 7406, p. 36.

91. Reports on the Volume and Effects of Recent Immigration from Eastern Europe into the United Kingdom, Appendix I, pp. 138–9.

92. Lipman, 'The Rise of Jewish Suburbia', p. 89.

93. In America, immigrants known as 'birds of passage' crossed the Atlantic repeatedly. W. B. Bailey, 'The Bird of Passage', *American Journal of Sociology*, 18 (1912), pp. 391–7.

94. Census of England and Wales, 1881, as cited by Gartner, *The Jewish Immigrant in England*, appendix, p. 283.

95. Census of England and Wales, 1911, Birthplaces, IX, Cd. 7017, Table 1, p. 2.

96. Census of England and Wales, 1921, Vol. 7, *General Tables*, Table 46, p. 181. Non-Jewish immigration appears closer to the Jewish pattern than was actually the case. The Irish migration included a very high percentage of women, but far greater numbers of Irish

women remained single than Jewish women, suggesting that the Irish did not emigrate as families.

97. Compiled from Census of England and Wales, 1911, *Birthplaces*, IX, Cd. 7017, Table 4, 'Country of Birth, Condition as to Marriage and Ages of Males and Females of Foreign Nationality', pp. 176–7.

98. RCAI, II, Minutes of Evidence, Cd. 1742, q. 648–50, p. 33. Numbers of Alien Immigrants arriving at the Port of London by German and Dutch Steamers, RCAI, *PP* 1903, IX, III, Appendix to Minutes, Cd. 1741, Table LXII, p. 76. In New York as well, larger percentages of Jewish children crossed the ocean. Eleven per cent of Italian immigrants were under fourteen years of age, as compared to as many as 25 per cent of Jewish immigrants. T. Kessner, *The Golden Door: Italian and Jewish Immigrant Mobility in New York City, 1880–1915* (New York: Oxford University Press, 1977), pp. 31–2.

99. In 1902, the overall birth rate for London was 28.5 per 1000, but within St George's in the East (a parish with a large Jewish population), the birth rate was 44.1 per 1,000. Medical Officer of Health (MOH) for the Metropolitan Borough of Stepney, *Annual Report*, 1902, p. 7.

100. Ibid., 1907, p. 5.

101. Ibid., 1908, p. 5.

102. According to the 1949 Royal Commission on Population, 83 per cent of Jewish women who married in the 1920s practised birth control compared to a national average of 62 per cent. B. Kosmin, 'Nuptiality and Fertility Patterns of British Jewry 1850–1980', in D. A. Coleman (ed.), *Demography of Immigrants and Minority Groups in the United Kingdom* (London: Academic Press Inc., 1982), pp. 245–61, on p. 258.

103. Marks, *Model Mothers*, p. 82. In 1899, immigrant and native-born Jewish families had smaller families than other Americans, in principle, making it easier to provide for offspring. N. Goldberg, 'The Jewish Population in the United States', *The Jewish People, Past and Present*, 2 (New York: Central Yiddish Culture Organization, 1948), pp. 25–34, on pp. 26–7.

104. M. Sourasky, 'The Alleged High Fertility of Jews', *British Medical Journal*, 2 (1928), p. 469.

105. Rates fell from 199 per 1,000 to 145 per 1,000 in St George's in the East, and decreased from 147 per 1,000 to 104 per 1,000 in Whitechapel. MOH, *Annual Reports*, 1899–1909.

106. C. Dyhouse, 'Working-Class Mothers and Infant Mortality in England, 1895–1914', *Journal of Social History*, 12 (1978), pp. 248–67, on p. 248.

107. There was wide variation within the Borough, with a rate of 23.2 for Limehouse, 21.4 for St George's, 18.2 for Mile End and 17.4 for Whitechapel. MOH, *Annual Report*, 1904, pp. 6–7.

108. MOH, *Annual Report*, 1915, p. 7.

109. Interdepartmental Committee on Physical Deterioration, *PP* 1904, XXXII, Minutes of Evidence, Cd. 2210, q. 5575–7, p. 221. Horsfall, a germanophile and a social reformer believed recruiting statistics from the Boer War were evidence of degeneration. Vanessa Heggie questions the conclusion of contemporaries and historians who have reported that the military rejected more than 65 per cent of military volunteers. V. Heggie, 'Lies, Damn Lies, and Manchester's Recruiting Statistics: Degeneration as an 'Urban Legend' in Victorian and Edwardian Britain', *Journal of the History of Medicine and Allied Sciences*, 63:2 (2008), pp. 178–216, on pp. 181–2, 184–91.

110. Illiteracy among Polish immigrants averaged 35.4 per cent and among English immigrants 1 per cent. Joseph, 'Jewish Immigration to the United States from 1881–1910', p. 193. In comparison, Italian illiteracy rates for women reached over 74 per cent. Illiteracy rates of Eastern Europeans (living in the United States or arriving in the United States) were 38.4 per cent for 1899 and 36.6 per cent for 1900. *Reports of the United States Industrial Commission on Immigration*, 15 (New York: Arno Press, 1970), p. 431.

111. A. Kahan, 'The Impact of Industrialization in Tsarist Russia on the Socioeconomic Conditions of the Jewish Population', *Essays in Jewish Social and Economic History* (Chicago, IL: University of Chicago Press, 1986), pp. 45–6. Among Russians as a whole, literacy was approximately 21 per cent, compared to an average of 24.5 per cent among Jews, but ranged as high as 75.8 per cent in some communities. S. Zipperstein, 'Haskalah, Cultural Change, and Nineteenth-Century Russian Jewry: A Reassessment', *Journal of Jewish Studies*, 34:2 (1983), pp. 191–207, on pp. 197–8.

112. Jonathan Sarna argues somewhat unconvincingly that scholars have seriously underestimated the extent of return migration. J. Sarna, 'The Myth of No Return: Jewish Return Migration to Eastern Europe, 1881–1914', *American Jewish History*, 71 (1981), pp. 256–68.

113. 'Report of the Lancet Special Sanitary Commission on the Polish Colony of Jew Tailors', *Lancet* (3 May 1884), pp. 817–8, on p. 818. See also, PRO, MEPOL 2/260, Metropolitan Police Report, 16 June 1888; PRO, MEPOL 2/260, 'Immigration Foreigners', 26 July 1888, and, PRO, MEPOL 2/260, Metropolitan Police Report, 18 June 1889.

114. I am grateful to Pamela Walker for suggesting this formulation. According to David Feldman, new exclusive definitions of Englishness depicted Jews as unpatriotic, and inherently non-English. Feldman, 'Jews in London', p. 211. Jews and non-Jews referred to Jews as a race in the nineteenth and early twentieth centuries. Over time, the meaning of the term tended to change from one denoting ethnicity to an increasingly biological definition. See D. Cohen, 'Who Was Who? Race and Jews in Turn-of-the-Century Britain', *Journal of British Studies*, 41:4 (2002), pp. 460–83.

115. PRO, HO 45, 10303/117267/9779, 'Notes of the Deputation of the Jewish Board of Deputies', 19 May 1904.

116. *JC*, 1 October 1880.

117. Ibid., 17 January 1902.

118. B. Potter, 'East London Labour', *Nineteenth Century*, 24 (August 1888), pp. 161–83, on p. 177. Some early twentieth-century observers brought a 'warm and sympathetic' gaze to the working class, unlike Beatrice Potter (and Helen Dendy) whose appraisals were 'cool' and 'critical'. E. Ross, 'Good and Bad Mothers: Lady Philanthropists and London Housewives before the First World War', in K. McCarthy (ed.), *Lady Bountiful Revisited: Women, Philanthropy, and Power* (New Brunswick, NJ: Rutgers University Press, 1990), pp. 174–98, on p. 188. For a sympathetic assessment of the experiences of immigrants see: Mrs Brewer, 'Jews in London', *Sunday at Home* (29 August 1891), pp. 693–8.

119. Englander, 'Booth's Jews', pp. 552, 555, 556.

120. In comparison, nearly 40 per cent of Finsbury's population lived in overcrowded housing. In 1891, the Government established a standard for overcrowding. Using this standard, 11.2 per cent of the total population of England and Wales lived in overcrowded conditions in 1901. Census of England and Wales, 1901, *General Report*, Cd. 2174, pp. 40, 42, 141.

121. MOH, *Annual Report*, 1901, p. 66.

122. L. H. Montagu, 'The Girl in the Background', in E. J. Urwick (ed.), *Studies of Boy Life in Our Cities* (London, 1904, reprint New York: Garland Publishing, 1980), pp. 235–54, on pp. 236–7.

123. Census of England and Wales, 1921, Vol. 7, *General Tables*, Table 30, 'Private Families and Dwellings', p. 106. In 1921, there were 69,000 people, as opposed to 72,000 in 1911, 'living more than two persons to a room' in Stepney. MOH, *Annual Report*, 1922, p. 3.

124. Stepney Reconstruction Group, 'Living in Stepney, Past, Present and Future' (London: Pilot Press, 1945), p. 41.

125. Lipman, 'The Rise of Jewish Suburbia', p. 91.

126. Jewish Museum, interview with Fineman.

127. J. McGee, 'Social and Political Life of Jews in the East End, 1926–1939' (thesis submitted as an Entry for the Teachers' Certificate of Education, 1977), p. 9.

128. Bernhard Baron St George's Jewish Settlement (hereafter, BBSGJS), *Annual Report*, 1931–2, p. 6.

129. *JC*, 29 October 1938.

130. In 1900, there were approximately 25,000 Jewish school children in Stepney and Poplar, compared to 1951 when there were approximately 3000 Jewish children ages five to sixteen. 'The East End Problem', *Jewish Monthly*, 5:4 (1951), pp. 193–4, on p. 193.

2 Public Health in London's Jewish East End, 1880–1939

1. 'Tuberculosis among Jews', *British Medical Journal*, 25 (25 April 1908), pp. 1000–2, on pp. 1000–1. See also 'Some Diseases of the Jewish Race', *British Medical Journal*, 2:3575 (13 July 1929), pp. 51–2.

2. J. M. Efron, *Defenders of the Race: Jewish Doctors and Race Science in Fin-de-Siècle Europe* (New Haven, CT: Yale University Press, 1994). T. Endelman. 'Anglo-Jewish Scientists and the Science of Race', *Jewish Social Studies*, n.s., 11:1 (2004), pp. 52–92, on pp. 52–3; Stone, 'Of Peas, Potatoes, and Jews', pp. 221–40.

3. J. R. Walkowitz, *Prostitution and Victorian Society: Women, Class and the State* (Cambridge: Cambridge University Press, 1980), p. 71.

4. London Metropolitan Archives (hereafter, LMA) LCC/MIN/7343, Public Health Department, 'Report by the Medical Officer on the Sanitary Condition and Administration of Whitechapel', 15 October 1894.

5. Harris, 'Anti-Alienism, Health and Social Reform', pp. 4–5, 7.

6. A. White, 'The Invasion of Pauper Foreigners', *Nineteenth Century*, 23:133 (1888), pp. 414–22, on pp. 420–2.

7. 'Report by the Medical Officer on the Sanitary Condition and Administration of Whitechapel', 15 October 1894. 'Report of The Lancet Special Sanitary Commission on the Polish Colony of Jew Tailors', pp. 817–18.

8. In 1862, the Board established the Medical Committee. Three years later, N. S. Joseph proposed that the Committee appoint a sanitary inspector. In 1879 the cost of health care and the conclusion that illness was not denomination-specific, led the Committee to end medical services. In 1884, the Medical Committee and Sanitary Committee merged and became the Health Committee in 1911, emphasizing preventive care. Jewish Welfare Board Archives (hereafter, JWB), JBG, Minutes of the Sanitary Committee, 3 October 1911. On health policy, see Black, The Social Politics of Anglo-Jewry, pp. 158–67. Similar trends emerged in non-Jewish charities as well. G. Black, 'Health and

Medical Care of the Jewish Poor in the East End of London – 1880–1939' (PhD thesis, University of Leicester, 1987), pp. 56, 58.

9. *JC*, 9 July 1880.

10. A. Wohl, *Endangered Lives: Public Health in Victorian Britain* (Cambridge, MA: Harvard University Press, 1983), p. 6.

11. R. L. Henriques, *Fifty Years in Stepney*, Reproduction of Five talks on BBC, 17 to 21 January 1966, pp. 5–6.

12. Wohl, *Endangered Lives*, especially pp. 61–3, 110–2.

13. C. Poulsen, *Scenes from a Stepney Youth* (London: THAP Books, Ltd, 1988), pp. 25–31.

14. Stepney Reconstruction Group, 'Living in Stepney', p. 13.

15. J. S. Hurt, *Elementary Schooling and the Working Classes, 1860–1918* (London: Routledge and Kegan Paul, 1979), p. 103.

16. LMA, LCC/MIN/7381, Bundle 65, From Shirley Murphy, Medical Officer of Health to the Public Health & Housing Committee, 27 March 1901.

17. JBG, *Annual Report*, 1884, p. 27.

18. D. F. Schloss, 'Healthy Homes for the Working Classes', *Fortnightly Review*, 43:256 (1888), pp. 526–37, on p. 533.

19. JWB, Minutes of the Sanitary Committee, 27 July 1893, 6 December 1893. In 1904, when the Board's Sanitary Inspector resigned, they appointed two Lady Health Visitors. *JC*, 15 June 1906. The JBG's first sanitary inspectors were all male; by 1907, women filled most of the positions.

20. JWB Archives, The Board of Guardians for the Relief of the Jewish Poor, 'Report of the Special Committee on Consumption', May 1897.

21. JBG, *Annual Report*, 1900, p. 21.

22. JWB Archives, JBG, Minutes of the Sanitary Committee, February 1906.

23. Although a later example, Tammy Posner's mother placed her at Norwood after her husband's death, from approximately 1921–8. British Library Sound Archives, C525/16, Interview with T. Posner, interviewed by R. Krut, 13 July 1981.

24. MOH, *Annual Report*, 1907, p. 5.

25. JBG, *Annual Report*, 1913, p. 97. The Board's register had 1,795 cases at the end of 1912 and 969 at the end of 1911. JBG, *Annual Report*, 1912, p. 92.

26. Ibid., 1913, p. 97.

27. Ibid., 1912, p. 16.

28. Despite nearly 10,000 deaths in London during the 1870–3 smallpox epidemic, anti-vaccination forces increased during the final quarter of the century and likely reflected distaste for government intervention more than doubts about efficacy. Wohl, *Endangered Lives*, pp. 132–5. *PP* 1899, XXXVIII, Annual Report of the Medical Officer of Health for the Local Government Board, 1898, p. ix, cited in Wohl, *Endangered Lives*, pp. 135, 376.

29. MOH, *Annual Report*, 1901, pp. 31–3.

30. Ibid., 1902, p. 19.

31. HL Southampton, MS172 AJ250/6, Stepney Jewish Lads' Club (hereafter, SJLC), 'A Short History, 1901–26', p. 11.

32. G. R. Searle, *The Quest for National Efficiency: A Study in British Politics and Political Thought, 1899–1914* (Berkeley, CA: University of California Press, 1971), pp. 60–7. R. Soloway, 'Counting the Degenerates: The Statistics of Race Deterioration in Edwardian England', *Journal of Contemporary History*, 17:1 (1982), 137–64.

33. A. Davin, 'Imperialism and Motherhood', *History Workshop*, 5 (1978), pp. 9–65, on p. 11.
34. K. W. Jones, 'Sentiment and Science: The Late Nineteenth Century Pediatrician as Mother's Advisor', *Journal of Social History*, 17:1 (1983), pp. 79–96. In the United States, 'scientific' motherhood increasingly drew on experts in science and medicine. Apple, 'Constructing Mothers', p. 161.
35. Dyhouse, 'Working-Class Mothers and Infant Mortality in England', p. 250; F. B. Smith, *The People's Health, 1830–1910* (New York: Holmes and Meier Publishers, Inc., 1979), pp. 113–17; C. Dyhouse, 'Good Wives and Little Mothers: Social Anxieties and the School Girl's Curriculum', *Oxford Review of Education*, 3:1 (1977), pp. 21–35, on p. 30.
36. On changing perceptions of milk's value see P. Atkins, 'School Milk in Britain, 1900–1934', *Journal of Policy History*, 19:4 (2007), pp. 395–428, on pp. 395–9.
37. V. Fildes, 'Breast-feeding in London 1905–1919', *Journal of Biosocial Science*, 24:1 (1992), 53–70, on p. 64.
38. D. Dwork, *War is Good for Babies and Other Young Children: A History of the Infant and Child Welfare Movement in England, 1898–1918* (London: Tavistock Publications, 1987), pp. 88, 213.
39. MOH, *Annual Report*, 1912, p. 24.
40. Ibid., 1909, p. 31.
41. D. Dwork, *War is Good for Babies*, p. 30. Dyhouse, 'Good Wives and Little Mothers', p. 30.
42. MOH, *Annual Report*, 1910, p. 41.
43. H. Bosanquet, 'Physical Degeneration and the Poverty Line', *Contemporary Review*, 85 (1904), pp. 65–75, on pp. 65–6, 72–3. Bosanquet argued that Booth and Rowntree overstated the extent of poverty and underestimated the impact of ignorance and social policy.
44. Salaman, 'Anglo-Jewish Vital Statistics: A Survey and Consideration – II', *JC* Supplement, May 1921.
45. National Anti-Sweating League, 'Living Wages for Sweated Workers – Great National Demonstration' (London, 1908), p. 3.
46. MOH, *Annual Report*, 1908, p. 27.
47. 'Infantile Mortality and the Employment of Married Women in Factories', *Lancet* (22 September 1906), pp. 817–18, on p. 818.
48. MOH, *Annual Report*, 1909, p. 29.
49. Ibid., p. 30.
50. Dwork, *War is Good for Babies*, p. 26. See B. Harris, 'Public Health, Nutrition, and the Decline of Mortality: The McKeown Thesis Revisited', *Social History of Medicine*, 17:3 (2004), pp. 379–407, on pp. 397–99, 404–06.
51. The first English school for mothers opened in St Pancras in 1907. Dyhouse, 'Working-Class Mothers, and Infant Mortality in England', p. 249.
52. S. Tananbaum, 'Biology and Community: The Duality of Jewish Mothering in East London', in E. N. Glenn, G. Chang and L. Forcey (eds), *Mothering: Ideology Experience, and Agency* (New York: Routledge, 1994), pp. 311–32.
53. Statistics belie popular opinion that the workhouse attracted large numbers of foreigners. In 1891, the workhouse sheltered 13.5 per 1,000 of the general population and only 2.8 per 1,000 of the foreign population. In 1901, 15.1 per 1,000 of the general population and only 1.7 per 1,000 of the foreign population utilized the workhouse. In 1901 foreigners made up 18 per cent of the population of Stepney and 9 per cent of the East-

ern districts (Bethnal Green, Poplar, Shoreditch and Stepney). Census of England and Wales, 1901, *General Report*, Cd. 2174, p. 141.

54. Marks, *Model Mothers*, p. 188.
55. Gerson Papers, 'The Alice Model Nursery'. P. Gerson, 'Notes for Mr Gebert'.
56. Similarly, clubwomen in America redefined Jewish women's proper roles. See B. W. Wenger, 'Jewish Women and Voluntarism: Beyond the Myth of Enablers', *American Jewish History*, 79:1 (1989), pp. 16–36, and S. M. Chambré, 'Philanthropy in the United States', in *Jewish Women: A Comprehensive Historical Encyclopedia*. 20 March 2009, Jewish Women's Archive., at *http://jwa.org/encyclopedia/article/philanthropy-in-united-states* [accessed 13 June 2011].
57. According to the *JC*, the idea for the SRHS was Model's, but Bella Loewy spoke about it to Frederic Mocatta who helped Model and Loewy raise the money to help keep the society going for a year. *JC*, 9 May 1902.
58. C. Davies, 'The Health Visitor as Mother's Friends: A Woman's Place in Public Health, 1900–1914', *Social History of Medicine*, 1:1 (1988), pp. 39–59, on pp. 41–2.
59. *JC*, 9 May 1902.
60. JBG, *Annual Report*, 1896, p. 66.
61. Black, 'Health and Medical Care of the Jewish Poor', p. 109.
62. JBG, *Annual Report*, 1900, p. 21.
63. Ibid., 1901, p. 20.
64. Jewish Museum, Interview with P. Solomons, 8 December 1984.
65. *JC*, 7 April 1916. LMA, A/KE/520/7, Jewish Maternity Hospital (hereafter, *JMH*), Applications for Grants, 1921–34, 1934–7, p. 1. I am grateful to Lara Marks for this reference.
66. *JC*, 7 May 1915.
67. *JW*, 26 November 1913.
68. 'Conference of Jewish Women', Reprint, London: Jewish Chronicle Office, 1902, p. 41.
69. Many social commentators believed underfeeding was not merely a matter of economics, but of bad 'domestic practices'. Davin, 'Loaves and Fishes', pp. 180–1, 182.
70. *JC*, 28 November 1913.
71. Ibid., 2 January 1914.
72. BBSGJS, 'The First Step, Fiftieth Anniversary Review, 1914–64', p. 9.
73. Davin, 'Imperialism and Motherhood', p. 44.
74. *JC*, 15 October 1915.
75. *ELO*, 1 May 1926.
76. Ibid.
77. In 1922, the *JMH* applied for a grant to extend the hospital and in 1929 for a research laboratory. *JMH*, Applications for Grants, 1921–34.
78. Marcus Samuel (1853–1927) made his fortune in trade, banking and oil. He and his brother founded Shell Transport and Trade in 1897. V. D. Lipman, *A History of the Jews in Britain since 1858* (Leicester: Leicester University Press, 1990), p. 255. Lady Bearsted, who served as president of the Jewish Maternity District Nursing Society, died in 1927. *Jewish Graphic*, 21 January 1927 and 11 November 1927. Gerson Papers, 'Guide to Social Work in Great Britain' (London: Committee for Training Jewish Social Workers, n.d.), p. 8. *JC*, 2 June 1933.
79. Black, 'Health and Medical Care of the Jewish Poor', p. 109.
80. *Jewish Graphic*, 19 November 1926.
81. LMA, A/KE/520/7, *JMH*, approximately 1921.

82. *JC*, 2 June 1933.
83. *ELO*, 21 September 1935. JMH, 'Report for the Year', January 1 to December 31, 1936, p. 10. LMA, A/KE/520/7, JMH, Applications for Grants, 1921–34, 1934–7, JMH – Proposed New Site, Report by Mr Hugh Lett and Mr David Eccles (for Sir Ernest Pooley), February, 1937.
84. *ELO*, 17 September 1938.
85. JMH, Report for the Year January 1st to December 31st, 1936, p. 15.
86. *ELO*, 10 May 1930.
87. MOH, *Annual Report*, 1930, p. 85.
88. Ibid.
89. Jewish Mothers' Welcome and Infant Welfare Centre, *Annual Report*, 1932–3, pp. 5, 6.
90. Jewish Infant Welfare Centre (hereafter, JWIC), *Annual Report*, 1934–5, p. 5.
91. *ELO*, 14 January 1933.
92. JMH, Report for the year January 1st to December 31st, 1936, p. 22.
93. JWIC, *Annual Report*, 1934–5, p. 2.
94. Ibid., p. 3.
95. JMH, *Report of the Committee*, 1937, p. 13.
96. JWIC, *Annual Report*, 1938–9, pp. 4–5.
97. For example, in 1900 and 1901, the Jewish Ladies' Clothing Association distributed thousands of garments in East End schools. *JC*, 1 January 1902.
98. In Leeds, immigrant Jewish children also displayed signs of good nutrition. Interdepartmental Committee on Physical Deterioration, *PP* 1904, XXXII, Minutes of Evidence, Cd. 2210, Vol. II, q. 448, 450–2, p. 23.
99. *JW*, 3 December 1913.
100. Interdepartmental Committee on Physical Deterioration, *PP* 1904, XXXII, Minutes of Evidence, Vol. II, Cd. 2210, q. 8507–8, p. 320.
101. Interdepartmental Committee on Physical Deterioration, *PP* 1904, XXXII, Minutes of Evidence, Cd. 2210, q. 8524–27, p. 320.
102. RCAI, *PP* 1903, IX, Minutes of Evidence, Vol. II, Cd. 1742, q. 17877, p. 656.
103. S. Atkinson, 'Tuberculosis among Jews', *British Medical Journal*, 1 (1908), p. 1077.
104. E. Ross, '"Fierce Questions and Taunts": Married Life in Working-Class London, 1870–1914', *Feminist Studies*, 8:3 (1982), pp. 575–602.
105. 'Tuberculosis among Jews', p. 1001.
106. *JC*, 28 August 1914.
107. HL Southampton, MS132 AJ220/1/3, Diaries of B. Henriques, 23 March 1915.
108. *JW*, 3 December 1913.
109. The Oxford and St George's Jewish Settlement housed one of the first Infant Welfare Centres. Once it proved successful, they invited the local authority to take it over and fund its expansion. Henriques, 'Fifty Years in Stepney', pp. 7–8.
110. JBG, *Annual Report*, 1937, p. 17.
111. Ibid., 1912, pp. 17, 19–20.
112. Ibid., p. 16.
113. Board of Guardians for the Relief of the Jewish Poor. 'A Short Account of the Work of the Jewish Board of Guardians and Trustees for the Relief of the Jewish Poor', London, n.d., p. 15.
114. JBG, *Annual Report*, 1921, p. 14.
115. JBG, 'A Short Account', p. 15.
116. JHO, 'Appreciation in Medical Press', January 1930.

117. JHO, 'The East London Child Guidance Clinic Honorary Director's Report, 1927–1932', p. 5.
118. 'The Opening of the Brady Girls' Club and Settlement by H.R.H. The Duchess of York – Monday, June 24, 1935'.
119. A committed Social Darwinist, Pearson argued that 'the truly elevating struggle is not that between individuals but "the struggle of tribe against tribe, of race against race"'. To win the struggle, nations had to be a '"homogeneous whole", not "a mixture of superior and inferior races"'. K. Pearson, *National Life from the Standpoint of Science* (London, 1905), pp. 55, 50–1, as cited by B. Semmel, *Imperialism and Social Reform: English Social-Imperial Thought, 1895–1914* (Cambridge, MA: Harvard University Press, 1960), pp. 37–42. Pearson accepted that race predominance might make the subjection of women necessary. See Pearson, 'The Woman's Question' (1886) in *The Ethic of Free Thought* (London: A. & C. Black, 1900) as cited by Semmel, *Imperialism and Social Reform: English Social-Imperial Thought*, pp. 47, 48, 51.
120. K. Pearson and M. Moul, 'The Problem of Alien Immigration into Great Britain Illustrated by an examination of Russian and Polish Jewish Children', *Annals of Eugenics*, Part I, 1 (1925), pp. 5–127, on pp. 125–7, 16, 25–6.
121. They identified the same conditions in Leeds. Pearson and Moul, 'The Problem of Alien Immigration', I, pp. 25, 26.
122. While many scientists rejected Pearson and Moul's work, they did not necessarily deny 'racial' difference. G. Schaffer, '"Like a Baby with a Box of Matches": British Scientists and the Concept of "Race" in the Inter-war Period', *British Journal for the History of Science*, 38 (2005), pp. 307–24, on pp. 315–17.
123. Pearson and Moul, 'The Problem of Alien Immigration', I, pp. 31, 46.
124. JHO, *Annual Report*, 1928, p. 10. J. Rumyaneck, 'The Comparative Psychology of Jews and non-Jews – A Survey of the Literature', *British Journal of Psychology*, 21 (April 1931), pp. 404–26, on p. 409. See also M. Davies and A. G. Hughes, 'An Investigation into the Comparative Intelligence and Attainments of Jewish and Non-Jewish School Children', *British Journal of Psychology*, 18 (1927), pp. 134–46, on pp. 144–5.
125. JHO, *Annual Report*, 1925, p. 5.
126. See praise for JHO research in the *British Medical Journal* (28 December 1929). Quoted in: JHO, 'Appreciation in Medical Press', January 1930.
127. JHO, *Annual Report*, 1926, pp. 6–7.
128. Ibid., 1928, pp. 4–5.
129. Ibid., 1926, p. 6. Cumberland schools were so dark that doctors had inadequate light for vision tests. 'Annual Report of Chief Medical Officer of the Board of Education', *Lancet* (7 March 1914), p. 701, as cited by Smith, *The People's Health*, p. 182.
130. JHO, *Annual Report*, 1926, p. 6.
131. Ibid., 1925, p. 6.
132. Ibid., 1928, pp. 19–20.
133. JHO, 'What We Have Done and What We Are to Do', November 1930.
134. JHO, *Annual Report*, 1928, p. 20.
135. Ibid., 1929, p. 8.
136. Ibid., p. 9.
137. Ibid.
138. Ibid., p. 34.
139. JHO, *Annual Report*, 1930, p. 23.
140. Ibid., 1934, p. 10.

141. *JC*, 2 January 1880.
142. Poor Jews in Manchester, who also expressed concern over language barriers and ritual observance, demonstrated reluctance to utilize infirmaries. Discussion of a Jewish hospital in Manchester emerged in 1900; it opened in 1904. Some voiced uneasiness over the antisemitic potential of highlighting the unhealthiness of Jews. V. Heggie, 'Jewish Medical Charity in Manchester: Reforming Alien Bodies', *Bulletin of the John Rylands University Library of Manchester*, 87:1 (2005), pp. 111–32.
143. G. Black, *Lord Rothschild and the Barber: The Struggle to Establish the London Jewish Hospital* (London: Tymsder Publishing, 2000), pp. 52–8.
144. *JC*, 22 February 1907 and 14 May 1915.
145. HL Southampton, MS116/145 AJ363, London Jewish Hospital, 'Letter to the Editor from Rev. L. Geffen', *JC*, n.d. (21 November 1913).
146. Ibid. (5 December 1913).
147. Marks, *Model Mothers*, p. 107.
148. There was an active West End branch of the Jewish Hospital Movement. HL Southampton, MS116/145 AJ363, London Jewish Hospital, 'London Jewish Hospital', Letter from N. Jacobowicz, Honorary Secretary, London Jewish Hospital Association to A. Goodman Levy, Esq., M.D., 8 October 1908. *JC*, 9 January 1914. Similarly, large numbers of immigrant Jews in Manchester contributed to Manchester's Jewish hospital. Heggie, 'Jewish Medical Charity in Manchester', p. 127.
149. *ELO*, 6 March 1909.
150. *JC*, 21 May 1915.
151. *ELO*, 6 March 1909.
152. *Daily Telegraph*, 22 March 1913.
153. Most of the Mildmay Hospital's in-patients were Jews; they also had a convalescent home for Jewish patients. *JC*, 3 January 1913.
154. *ELO*, 1 November 1919.
155. *JC*, 28 May 1915.
156. LMA, A/KE/522/5, King Edward's Fund, London Jewish Hospital, Applications for Grants, 1920–37, 'Draft of Appeal', n.d., approx. January 1935.
157. Opponents to the Manchester Jewish hospital also argued it was possible to provide provision in existing hospitals and that Jews should support those institutions. Heggie, 'Jewish Medical Charity in Manchester', p. 119.
158. London Society for Promoting Christianity Amongst the Jews (hereafter, LSPC), *Annual Report*, 1883, p. 27.
159. The Mission Committee referenced the 1911–2 report of the British Society for the Propagation of the Gospel among the Jews, which claimed sixty-two conversions from numerous countries, including England. JBD, E3/28, Mission Committee, 'Report of the Executive Committee to the General Committee', appointed 24 November 1912, p. 5.
160. LSPC, *Annual Report*, 1900, p. 17.
161. *JC*, 16 January 1880.
162. University of Cambridge, MS 1871/88, Redcliffe Salaman, 'Boyhood and the Family Background', p. 32.
163. For similar issues in Soho, see E. Ross, 'Missionaries and Jews in Soho: "Strangers within Our Gates"', *Journal of Victorian Culture*, 15:2 (2010), pp. 226–38.
164. LMA, A/FWA/C/D12/1, 'Barbican Mission to the Jews, 1882–1943', reprinted from *The Record*, 29 December 1893.
165. LSPC, *Annual Report*, 1896, p. 15.

166. Ibid., 1895, p.20.
167. Ibid., 1897, p. 18.
168. *JC*, 25 April 1902.
169. East London Fund for the Jews. *Report for the Year 1927*, London.
170. JBD, Mission Committee, 'Report of the Executive Committee', p. 17.
171. Ibid., p. 21.
172. Ibid., p. 23.
173. Dr R. N. Salaman, 'Anglo-Jewish Vital Statistics: A Survey and Consideration, III', *JC Supplement*, June 1921.
174. LMA, A/FWA/C/D128/1, Barbican Mission to the Jews, *Immanuel's Witness*, 15:3 (1938).
175. *Immanuel's Witness*, 15:3 (1938), p. 38.
176. *Jewish Graphic*, 18 June 1926.
177. *Immanuel's Witness*, 15:3 (1938), p. 38.
178. Yiddish culture remained alive in the East End, sometimes serving as a bridge between the old country and the new. In 1915, Maurice Moscovitch returned to England determined to establish a permanent Yiddish playhouse. While entertaining, Yiddish theatre 'also counteracts the pernicious influences of assimilation, by preserving the Yiddish language and literature; it competes with the picture palaces, the music halls with their "beery associations", the missionary reading rooms and meeting places, and the gambling dens'. *JC*, 6 August 1915.
179. *World Jewry*, 11 October 1935.
180. In 1921, when the borough of Stepney opened three tuberculosis dispensaries, the JBG closed theirs.

3 Communal Networks: Taking Care of their Own and Efforts to Secure the Community's Reputation

1. JBG, *Annual Report*, 1893, p. 11.
2. For a listing by district of clubs, educational institutions, synagogues, chevrot, etc., see *JC*, 11 February 1910. The German Jewish community also created large numbers of institutions to aid poor Jews. Even when eligible for non-Jewish welfare, Jews drew on Jewish assistance. A. Bornstein, 'The Role of Social Institutions as Inhibitors of Assimilation: Jewish Poor Relief System in Germany, 1875–1925', *Jewish Social Studies*, 50:3/4 (Summer 1988–Autumn 1993), pp. 201–2, on pp. 201, 204–5.
3. A. Warren, '"Mothers for the Empire"? The Girl Guides Association in Britain, 1909–1939', in J. A. Mangan (ed.), *Making Imperial Mentalities: Socialisation and British Imperialism* (Manchester: Manchester University Press, 1990). pp. 96–109, on p. 98.
4. Like their non-Jewish peers, Jewish philanthropists lent their homes for charity bazaars. *JC*, 25 July 1902. F. K. Prochaska, *'Bazaars', Women and Philanthropy in 19th Century England* (Oxford: Clarendon Press, 1980), pp. 47–72.
5. Englander, 'Policing the Ghetto', p. 36.
6. A. Kershen, *Strangers, Aliens and Asians: Huguenots, Jews and Bangladeshis in Spitalfields, 1660–2000* (London: Routledge, 2005), pp. 114–22.
7. Endelman, 'Communal Solidarity among the Jewish Elite of Victorian', pp. 503–4.
8. Hyman, 'Gender and the Shaping of Modern Jewish Identities', p. 156.
9. Prochaska, *The Voluntary Impulse*, p. 43.

10. White, 'The Invasion of Pauper Foreigners', p. 419.
11. T. Brinkman, 'Managing Mass Migration: Jewish Philanthropic Organizations and Jewish Mass Migration from Easter Europe, 1868/1869–1914', *Leidschrift – Historisch Tijdschrift*, 22:1 (2007), pp. 71–89, on p. 75.
12. Lee Shai Weissbach notes that Jewish philanthropists in France wanted moral influence over the poor and to improve their situations to lessen the likelihood of communal disorder. L. S. Weissbach, 'The Nature of Philanthropy in Nineteenth-Century France and the Mentalité of the Jewish Elite', *Jewish History*, 8:1 (1994), pp. 191–204, on p. 193.
13. PRO, MH/19/237/97416, Papers Relating to Emigration and Immigration, Table VII, B, pp. 66–7 and Table IX, p. 70, 1904.
14. L. Magnus, *The Jewish Board of Guardians and the Men Who Made It* (London: The Jewish Board of Guardians, 1909). V. D. Lipman, *A Century of Social Service, 1859–1959: The History of the Jewish Board of Guardians* (London: Routledge and Kegan Paul, 1959). In the 1860s, the increase of Jewish immigrants, led German Jews to establish cradle to grave aid, in part to discourage begging. Bornstein, 'The Role of Social Institutions', p. 207.
15. Papers Relating to Emigration and Immigration, Appendix, pp. 67, 70, 1904.
16. *JW*, 18 May 1906.
17. JHO, *Annual Report*, 1931; JHO, 'The Difficult Child', reprinted from *The Medical Officer*, 30 May 1931; JHO, 'The East London Child Guidance Clinic', Honorary Director's Report, 1927–32. Weissbach emphasizes that French Jewish philanthropy drew on pre-existing French models, rather than any pioneering efforts. Weissbach, 'The Nature of Philanthropy in Nineteenth-Century France', p. 198.
18. *JC*, 17 June 1892.
19. JBG, *Annual Report*, 1900, p. 16.
20. The JBG and the Russo-Jewish Committee funded the return of 50,000 between 1880 and 1914. Lipman, *A Century of Social Service*, p. 96. Between 1882 and 1906, the Russo-Jewish Committee repatriated over 7,000 Jews and aided the emigration from England of approximately 7,500 additional refugees. Stettauer Papers, Anglo-Jewish Archives, AJ/22, as quoted by Black, *The Social Politics of Anglo-Jewry*, p. 255.
21. A. Hochberg, 'The Repatriation of Eastern European Jews from Great Britain: 1881–1914', *Jewish Social Studies*, 50:1/2 (1988–92), pp. 49–62, on pp. 50–1, 61.
22. JBG, *Annual Report*, 1885, p. 10.
23. *JC*, 15 May 1885.
24. PJTS, *Annual Report*, 1899–1900, p. 5.
25. *JC*, 3 January 1902.
26. Harding and Berg, *Jack Kid Berg*, p. 15.
27. *Jewish Graphic*, 8 April 1927.
28. Jews Temporary Shelter, *46th Annual Report*, for year ending October 1937, p. 6.
29. Ibid., *47th Annual Report*, for year ending October 1938, p. 4.
30. *JC*, 20 March 1914.
31. Ibid., 3 April 1914.
32. Ibid.
33. *JC*, 24 February 1905.
34. HL Southampton, Diary of Basil Henriques, 8 October 1913.
35. Lady (Ellen) Desart described philanthropy as an 'exact science'. Union of Jewish Women (hereafter, UJW), *Annual Report*, 1907, p. 27. C. S. Loch promoted this method for the COS (founded in 1869). See C. S. Loch, *Charity Organisation* (London: Swan Sonnen-

schein and Co., 1892). On the need to avoid duplication and improve communication, see T. Quid, 'Our Complex Uneconomical Charitable System. A Plea for Organization', Reprinted from the *Jewish Chronicle*. (London: Jewish Chronicle Office, 1905).

36. H. Bosanquet, *Social Work in London, 1869–1912, A History of the Charity Organisation Society* (London: J. Murray, 1914), p. 6.
37. Ibid., p. 43.
38. *JW*, 18 May 1906.
39. The COS also recognized that women visitors were becoming increasingly common; Loch dropped the masculine pronoun from the visitor's manual in 1882. Prochaska, *Women and Philanthropy*, p. 110. Prochaska, *The Voluntary Impulse*, p. 47.
40. By the last quarter of the nineteenth century, boroughs and cities began to hire women visitors, but typically had them deal with women and children, at work and home. C. Davies, 'The Health Visitor as Mother's Friends: A Woman's Place in Public Health, 1900–1914', *Social History of Medicine*, 1:1 (1988), pp. 39–59, on pp. 41, 47–51.
41. J. Lewis, *The Voluntary Sector, the State and Social Work in Britain: The Charity Organisation Society/Family Welfare Association since 1869* (Aldershot: Edward Elgar Publishing, Ltd, 1995), pp. 6–7.
42. *JC*, 21 February 1902.
43. Ibid., 23 May 1902.
44. *JW*, 31 January 1908.
45. *Queen*, 3 or 4 June 1913.
46. *JC*, 2 January 1914.
47. *Jewish Guardian*, 21 December 1921.
48. Unlike many historians, Susannah Taylor contends that philanthropy eased acculturation, and women's organizations did not intentionally promote anglicization. S. Taylor, 'The Role of Jewish Women in National, Jewish Philanthropic Organisations in Britain from c. 1880 to 1945' (PhD thesis, University of Southampton, February 1996), p. 22.
49. *ELO*, 6 May 1922. Miriam Moses was the daughter of Mark Moses, a Polish Jew, 'a prosperous clothing contractor and man of affairs in the East End'. Gartner, *The Jewish Immigrant in England*, p. 203. He was the spokesperson for the master tailors during the 1889 tailors' strike. W. Fishman, *East End Jewish Radicals* (London: G. Duckworth & Co., Ltd, 1975), note 6, p. 136.
50. Similar concerns also emerged in France and America after the turn of the century. R. Meckel, *'Save the Babies': American Public Health Reform and the Prevention of Infant Mortality, 1850–1929* (Baltimore, MD: Johns Hopkins University Press, 1990).
51. Educators responded by introducing housekeeping instruction in schools serving the working-class. Davin, 'Imperialism and Motherhood', pp. 26–7. See also, C. Dyhouse, *Girls Growing Up in Late Victorian and Edwardian England* (London: Routledge & K. Paul, 1981).
52. Gerson Papers, Gerson, 'Notes for Mr Gebert'. According to the *JC*, the new nursery opened in November 1900. It reported an increasing attendance and hoped to be able to accept up to fifty infants a day. *JC*, 7 February 1902.
53. *JC*, 28 February 1902.
54. Black, 'Health and Medical Care of the Jewish Poor', p. 104.
55. MOH, *Annual Report*, 1909, p. 32.
56. *JC*, 28 February 1902. On perceptions of irresponsible mothers, see Dyhouse, *Girls Growing Up*, pp. 257–9.
57. Day Nursery for Jewish Infants, *Second Annual Report*, 1898–9.

58. Black, 'Health and Medical Care of the Jewish Poor', p. 105.
59. *JC*, 10 February 1905.
60. Black, 'Health and Medical Care of the Jewish Poor', p. 105, and footnote 6, p. 105.
61. *JC*, 10 February 1905.
62. Ibid., 2 March 1906.
63. Ibid., 7 January 1910.
64. UJW, *Annual Report*, 1905, p. 9.
65. *JW*, 31 January 1908.
66. *Queen*, 10 February 1906.
67. 'Letter from Countess Desart', *JW*, 20 February 1911.
68. *JW*, 31 January 1908 and 22 May 1908; *JC*, 15 January 1904, 22 May 1908, 18 February 1910.
69. *JC*, 15 January 1904 and 12 February 1909. In January of 1901, Norwood brought women onto their Committee. *JC*, 25 January 1901.
70. Ibid., 12 February 1909.
71. Ibid., 22 January 1904.
72. UJW, *Annual Report*, 1903, p. 10.
73. *The Times*, 5 February 1906.
74. *Tribune*, 18 October 1907.
75. *JW*, 8 July 1904.
76. S. M., Jewish Women in London Group, Oral History Interview.
77. *JC*, 3 February 1905.
78. Ibid., 23 April 1915.
79. Ibid., 2 May 1902.
80. JBG, *Annual Report*, 1909, p. 80.
81. *JC*, 11 June 1915.
82. Ibid., 17 July 1931.
83. Ibid., 4 September 1914.
84. J. Spence, 'Working for Jewish Girls: Lily Montagu, Girls' Clubs and Industrial Reform 1890–1914', *Women's History Review*, 13:3 (2004), pp. 491–509, on p. 491. Obituary, 'Hon. Lilian Montagu', *The Times* (London), 24 January 1963, p. 15.
85. They served single unemployed women. *ELO*, 2 January 1915.
86. Lily Montagu used the columns of the *JC* to criticize the UJW for providing work to those she believed did not depend on it for survival. *JC*, 28 August 1914. The UJW's Julia Cohen responded that Montagu wrote in 'the stress and strain of the moment without communicating with the Union'. They too were helping to relieve unemployment; their clientele, though educated girls and women, were suffering as well. *JC*, 4 September 1914.
87. HL Southampton, MS129 AJ 26/A2, UJW, General Committee of the UJW, 15 December 1914, p. 1.
88. HL Southampton, MS AJ26/C4, UJW, 'Report of Meeting held at Mrs M. A. Spielman's house', 15 December 1914, p. 1.
89. *JW*, 19 January 1916.
90. *JC*, 6 November 1914.
91. UJW, 'Report of Meeting held at Mrs M. A. Spielman's house', 15 December 1914, p. 4.
92. UJW, General Committee of the UJW, 15 December 1914.
93. UJW, 'Report of Meeting held at Mrs M. A. Spielman's house', 15 December 1914, p. 3.
94. *JC*, 13 November 1914.

95. *Daily Telegraph*, 27 January 1915 and 1 February 1916.
96. Ibid., 1 February 1916.
97. *JC*, 2 July 1920.
98. Ibid., 6 August 1920. A bequest from Lady (Fanny E.) Bearsted, Samuel's mother, enabled the home to take in the full complement of boys beginning in 1922. Ibid., 26 May 1922.
99. Ibid., 22 November 1922.
100. HL Southampton, MS173/1/13/3, Jewish Board of Guardians, Minute Book of the Gerald Samuel and Denzil Myer Home, 8 May 1919.
101. Ibid., Letter from the Ladies' Committee, 22 November 1922.
102. Ibid., Meeting of the Committee, 9 April 1923; Warden's Report, 22 October 1923.
103. Ibid., Meeting at the Offices of the Board, 4 February 1925.
104. Ibid., Warden's Report, 31 January 1927.
105. Ibid., Warden's Report, 7 February 1933.
106. Ibid., Warden's Report, December 1933.
107. Ibid., Report of the Samuel and Myer Home for 1935.
108. Jewish Museum, interview with K. R. Collins. For more on this pattern among working-class women, see: Ross, 'Survival Networks: Women's Neighbourhood Sharing in London', pp. 4–27.
109. M. Beckman, *The Hackney Crucible* (London: Vallentine Mitchell, 1996), p. 85.
110. JAPGAW, *Annual Report*, 1926, p. 44.
111. JBG, *Annual Report*, 1931, p. 13.
112. Ibid., 1932, p. 13.

4 The Impact of Education: Anglicization of Jewish East Enders Begins with Schooling

1. During the mid-nineteenth century, prior to compulsory education, Jewish community sponsored schools served only 2,000 children. S. Singer, 'Jewish Education in the Mid-Nineteenth Century: A Study of the Early Victorian London Community', *Jewish Quarterly Review*, 78:2–3 (October 1986–January 1987), pp. 163–78, on p. 64. See also Greenberg, 'Compromise and Conflict', p. 63; Gartner, *The Jewish Immigrant in England*, pp. 220–40; Black, *The Social Politics of Anglo-Jewry*, pp. 104–32.
2. On educational priorities, see S. Heathorn, '"Let us Remember that We Too Are English": Constructions of Citizenship and National Identity in English Elementary Reading Books, 1880–1914', *Victorian Studies*, 38:3 (1995), pp. 395–427.
3. At the beginning of the century, classes in home economics and childcare became a critical component in girls' education in America as well. Apple, 'Constructing Mothers', pp. 169–71.
4. Officials also considered education as key to transforming Irish children. Irish loyalty required 'denationalising' them. Hickman suggests this was unique to the Irish, but arguably, many saw Jews in much the same light. See M. J. Hickman, 'Integration or Segregation? The Education of the Irish in Britain in Roman Catholic Voluntary-Aided Schools', *British Journal of Sociology of Education*, 14:3 (1993), pp. 285–300, on pp. 289, 297.
5. *JC*, 3 June 1898.
6. J. Carrier, 'Working Class Jews in Present-Day London: A Sociological Study' (MPhil thesis, University of London, 1969), p. 55.

7. Levy, 'Problems of Anglicisation', pp. 78, 77.
8. *JW*, 31 January 1908.
9. These figures indicate that the majority of Jewish children were born in England, suggesting that anti-alienists exaggerated the rates of immigration. *JC*, 3 January 1902 and *The Jewish Yearbook* (London), 1896–7, pp. 54–5.
10. *The Jewish Yearbook* (London), 1905–6, pp. 79–82.
11. Ibid., 1894–1924.
12. Hickman, 'Integration or Segregation', pp. 287, 288.
13. On the history of the Education Act of 1870, see J. Murphy, *The Education Act 1870 – Text and Commentary* (New York: Barnes and Noble, 1972) and Hurt, *Elementary Schooling and the Working Classes, 1860–1918*.
14. *JW*, 25 June 1909. Cohen attributed this to Harriet Martineau.
15. *The Jewish Yearbook* (London), 1896–1920.
16. Jews Free School (hereafter, JFS) Archives, H. M. Inspector's Report, November 1938, p. 1.
17. JFS Archives, J. Wagerman, 'The JFS in Days Gone By', unpublished Paper, n.d. See also: Black, *J. F. S: The History of the Jews' Free School*.
18. *JC*, 2 July 1982.
19. 'The Largest of our Elementary Schools', Supplement to the *Sphere*, 1 February 1908, p. i.
20. In June 1855, for example, Lord John Russell presided over the Festival Dinner that raised £2,000. The school, a 'model of order, comfort, and ventilation', served 1,600 boys and girls. *The Times*, 21 June 1855.
21. R. Cohen, 'The Influence of Jewish Radical Movements on Adult Education among Jewish Immigrants in the East End of London, 1881–1914' (MEd dissertation, University of Liverpool, 1977), p. 34; *The Jewish Yearbook* (London), 1896–7, p. 54.
22. 'The Largest of our Elementary Schools', 1 February 1908, p. i. By 1894, there were approximately 3,500 students enrolled.
23. *Jews' Free School Magazine*, 7:66 (1931), pp. 289–90.
24. Greenberg, 'Compromise and Conflict', p. 127.
25. JFS Archives, H. M. Inspector's Report, August 1913, pp. 1, 2. By 1913, JFS enrolments fell to approximately 1,100 girls and 1,600 boys. JFS Archives, JFS, Council District Inspection, May, 1913, p. 1.
26. *JC*, 2 January 1880; 21 March 1902.
27. JFS Archives, Exhibit on the History of the School, from section of the exhibit labelled '1880s', n.d.
28. Board of Trade (Alien Immigration), 'Reports on the Volume and Effects of Recent Immigration from Eastern Europe into the United Kingdom', p. 38.
29. *ELO*, 28 May 1904.
30. JFS, *Annual Report*, 1884, p. 13. Attendance among Jewish children was even higher in Leeds, ranging from 91 to 94 per cent in 1901. *JC*, 17 January 1902. The Chapman Street School in London had a lower percentage of attendance, averaging in the mid- to high seventies in 1880, 1882 and 1894. LMA, EO/PS/12/C29/3, 'Inspector's Report', Lower Chapman Street School, 15, 16, 17 June 1880. LMA, EO/PS/12/C29/5, 'Inspector's Report', Lower Chapman Street School, 2, 3, 4 May 1882. LMA, EO/PS/12/C29/17, 'Managers' Yearly School Report', Lower Chapman Street, October, 1894. The percentage of Jewish students at Lower Chapman Street School is unclear and the school operated during the Jewish holidays. In 1896 nine girls won attendance awards, and twenty more would have, 'but being Jewesses their enforced holidays prevented' it.

LMA, EO/PS/12/C29/23, 'Managers' Yearly School Report', Lower Chapman Street, October, 1896.

31. A. Eichholz, 'The Jewish School-Child', *Jewish Literary Annual* (1903), pp. 66–78, on p. 69.

32. JFS Archives, JFS, H. M. Inspector's Report, February 1907, p. 3.

33. S. Auerbach, '"Some Punishment Should Be Devised": Parents, Children, and the State in Victorian London', *Historian*, 71:4 (2009), pp. 757–79, on pp. 759–60. Critics pointed to the physical and moral dangers of child labour. N. Adler, 'Children as Wage-Earners', *Fortnightly Review*, 73:437 (1903), pp. 918–27.

34. Auerbach notes that critiques of parents' moral failings diminished somewhat with the development of the child welfare movement in the 1880s. Auerbach, '"Some Punishment Should Be Devised"', p. 765.

35. JFS had thirty-five boys and twenty-four girls per teacher. P. L. S. Quinn, 'The Jewish Schooling Systems of London, 1656–1956' (PhD thesis, University of London, 1958), p. 550.

36. 'The Largest of Our Elementary Schools', 1 February 1908, pp. i, iv. Miscellaneous photographs, labelled 1900–14, show girls in the scullery, gymnasium, swimming, starching clothing, ironing a bonnet, cutting a pattern and of an English class for foreign girls.

37. Quinn, 'The Jewish Schooling Systems', p. 562.

38. JFS Archives, Wagerman, 'The JFS in Days Gone By', p. 2.

39. Cheder met in the late afternoon or evening; immigrants usually called melamedim, served as the teachers. Often, classes met in the melamid's home and escaped sanitary inspection.

40. Quinn, 'The Jewish Schooling Systems', p. 561.

41. Cohen, 'The Influence of Jewish Radical Movements', p. 34.

42. *JC*, 2 April 1880.

43. JFS, *Annual Report*, 1884, pp. 13–14.

44. *ELO*, 20 May 1882 and *ELO*, 5 January 1889. The Stepney Jewish Schools reported that 90 per cent of the boys and 91 per cent of the girls passed the February exams. In 1888, 95 per cent of Old Castle Street students, many of whom entered speaking only Yiddish, passed their exams. *ELO*, 2 April 1888.

45. JFS, *Annual Report*, 1884, Speech by the Right Honourable A. J. Mundella at the Festival Dinner, 1884, 15. J. Spain, 'Mundella, Anthony John (1825–1897)', *ODNB*.

46. JFS, *Annual Report*, 1884, p. 7.

47. The Tower Hamlets area had ninety elementary schools. I. Osborne, 'Achievers of the Ghetto', Tower Hamlets Library, London, n.d.

48. Greenberg, 'Compromise and Conflict', p. 67.

49. Ibid., pp. 77–8.

50. Quinn, 'The Jewish Schooling Systems', pp. 514–16.

51. Approximately one-half to two-thirds of the students attended Jewish Schools and the remainder 'Jewish' board schools. Quinn, 'The Jewish Schooling Systems', p. 517. See also N. Bentwich, 'Jewish Educational Disorganisation in London', *Jewish Review*, 3 (1912–13), pp. 355–66, on pp. 356–7.

52. Quinn, 'The Jewish Schooling Systems', p. 583. Estimates from 1900 indicate that some 2000 Jewish children attended schools where they participated in Christian prayer. *JC*, 7 December 1900.

53. Chicksand Street School taught 600, Berner Street, 3,000, and Hanbury Street Board School, about 400 Jewish children. LMA, Acc. 2893/1, Federation of Synagogues

Records, Report of the Federation of Synagogues on Chedorim, Meeting of the Board on Hebrew Education and Religious Training, adopted 7 April 1891.

54. The founders, mostly middle-class Jews, had ties to the anglicized orthodox United Synagogue.
55. JADRK, *Annual Report*, 1887, p. 12.
56. Jews' Infant Schools, with approximately 1,000 children, earned 614 pounds and fifteen shillings, twenty-two pounds more than the previous year. *JC*, 9 July 1880. The Old Castle Street Board School with 1400 students, of whom 95 per cent were Jewish, earned an additional one hundred and twenty pounds. *JC*, 30 July 1880.
57. On average, schools in England and Wales earned 15*s*. 8*d*. per head and Jewish schools, 17*s*. 5*d*. per head. 'Annual Report of the Lords of the Committee of Privy Council on Education for 1880', quoted in the *JC*, 1 October 1880.
58. LMA, EO/PS/12/C88/1, 'Managers' Yearly School Report', Commercial Street, January, 1896. LMA, EO/PS/12/C88/6, 'Managers' Yearly School Report', Commercial Street, February 1899.
59. LMA, EO/PS/12/C88/8, 'Managers' Yearly School Report', Commercial Street, February 1900.
60. LMA, EO/PS/12/C29/36, 'Managers' Yearly School Report', Lower Chapman Street, October 1902.
61. *JC*, 12 December 1902.
62. At the Lower Chapman School, 104 girls missed four to six weeks owing to 'hopping' and Jewish holidays. LMA, EO/PS/12/C29/29, 'Managers' Yearly School Report', Lower Chapman Street, October 1899.
63. 'Festival of Britain', Anglo-Jewish Exhibition at University College, London, 1951, p. 7.
64. G. Alderman, *London Jewry and London Politics, 1889–1986* (London: Routledge, 1989), pp. 45–6.
65. PRO, ED109/4014/150501, Davenant Foundation School, H. M. Inspector's Report, 1910, pp. 8, 5.
66. JFS Archives, H. M. Inspector's Report, February 1907, p. 1.
67. JFS, Council District Inspection, May 1913, p. 1.
68. JFS Archives, H. M. Inspector's Report, August 1913, p. 2.
69. PRO, ED109/4005/100501, Stepney Central Foundation Girls' School, H. M. Inspector's Report, 1915, pp. 12, 13.
70. Stepney Central Foundation Girl's School, H. M. Inspector's Report, 1915, p. 4.
71. H. Gaffen, Jewish Women in London Group, Oral History Interview.
72. E. Abrahams, Jewish Women in London Group, Oral History Interview.
73. Dyhouse, 'Good Wives and Little Mothers', pp. 31–2.
74. Apple, 'Constructing Mothers', pp. 169–71.
75. PRO, ED/109/4020/100501, Raine's School, H. M. Inspector's Report, 1910, p. 15.
76. Ibid., pp. 14, 6.
77. Ibid., pp. 18, 17.
78. Ibid., p. 18.
79. *JC*, 10 July 1914. According to Allen Warren, educational emphasis on motherhood declined after World War One and schools focused more on 'girls as future citizens' and less on domestic preparation. Warren, '"Mothers for the Empire"?', pp. 98–9.
80. *JC*, 12 March 1915.
81. C. Lewis, A Soho Address 1965, p. 1, as cited by White, *Rothschild Buildings*, p. 153.

82. Stepney Central Foundation Girls' School, H. M. Inspector's Report, 1915, p. 4. PRO, ED109/4007, Stepney Central Foundation Girls' School, H. M. Inspector's Report, 1926, p. 4.
83. 'Festival of Britain', p. 7; Greenberg argues that in fact, East End schools did not encourage scholars to enter academic secondary schools or university. Greenberg, 'Compromise and Conflict', p. 128.
84. W. H. Winch, 'Christian and Jewish Children in East End Elementary Schools – Some Comparative Characteristics in Relation to Race and Social Class', *British Journal of Psychology*, 20:3 (1930), pp. 261–73, on p. 264.
85. Stepney Central Foundation Girls' School, H. M. Inspector's Report, 1926, p. 12.
86. PRO, ED109/4016, Davenant Foundation School, H. M. Inspector's Report, 1927, pp. 12–13.
87. PRO, ED109/4022, Raine's School for Boys, H. M. Inspector's Report, 1935, pp. 9–10.
88. PRO, ED109/4023, Raine's School for Girls, H. M. Inspector's Report, November 1935, pp. 6–9.
89. Ibid., p. 11.
90. JFS Archives, H. M. Inspector's Report, November 1938, p. 2; *ELO*, 12 December 1936.
91. Ibid., January 1939, pp. 2–3.
92. Ibid., November 1938, p. 1.
93. Abrahams, Oral History Interview.
94. Jews' Hospital and Orphan Asylum (hereafter, JHOA), *Annual Report*, 1909, p. 15
95. Ibid., p. 16.
96. N. Roberts, 'Character in the Mind: Citizenship, Education and Psychology in Britain, 1880–1914', *History of Education*, 33:2 (2004), pp. 177–97, on pp. 177–80.
97. HL Southampton, MS127 AJ19/C5, Norwood Archive, 'Sulking and Punishment Book', 12 and 13 July 1914, 21 August 1914.
98. *JC*, 16 July 1915.
99. Ibid.
100. *ELO*, 5 January 1889.
101. Atkins, 'School Milk in Britain, 1900–1934', p. 395.
102. Ibid., pp. 415–16. Atkins challenges the consensus that school meals played a small but crucial role in the development of the welfare state. He contends that school milk programs changed perceptions of 'social welfare provision', but in a largely symbolic fashion. Atkins, 'School Milk in Britain', p. 417.
103. JFS Archives, Wagerman, 'The JFS in Days Gone By', p. 2.
104. LMA, EO/PS/12/C29/36, Managers' Yearly School Report, Lower Chapman Street, October, 1902. EO/PS/12/C29/39, Managers' Yearly School Report, Tower Hamlets, Lower Chapman Street, St George's in the East, School Year Ended October, 1903.
105. Managers' Yearly School Report, Lower Chapman Street, October 1903.
106. LMA, EO/PS/12/C29/32, Managers' Yearly School Repor', Lower Chapman Street, October 1900.
107. LMA, EO/PS/12/C88/17, 'Managers' Yearly School Report', Commercial Street, February 1904.
108. *JC*, 4 December 1914.
109. *JW*, 17 May 1907.
110. *JC*, 25 June 1909.
111. Ibid., 13 February 1914.
112. UJW, *Annual Report*, 1912, p. 17.

113. LMA, EO/PS/12/C88/6, Managers' Yearly School Report, Commercial Street, February 1899.

114. Managers' Yearly School Report, Commercial Street, February 1900.

115. LMA, EO/PS/12/C88/10, Managers' Yearly School Report, Commercial Street, February 1901.

116. 'Managers' Yearly School Report', Commercial Street, February 1901.

117. For analysis of intervention by LCC, see S. Pennybacker, *A Vision for London 1889–1914: Labour, Everyday Life and the LCC Experiment* (London: Routledge, 1995), esp. pp. 202–10.

118. PRO, ED/77/9/97779, Mr W. K. Spencer, Whitechapel Buckle Street Jews' Infants School, H. M. Inspector's Report, 28 and 30 May 1912, pp. 1, 2.

119. *JC*, 4 December 1914. The open-air school movement, part of the early twentieth century campaign against tuberculosis, while progressive and preventive, also had a moral agenda and sometimes remained blind to scientific evidence. See L. Bryder, '"Wonderlands of Buttercup, Clover and Daisies": Tuberculosis and the Open-Air School Movement in Britain, 1907–39', in R. Cooter (ed.), *In the Name of the Child: Health and Welfare, 1880–1940* (London: Routledge, 1992), pp. 72–95.

120. JFS Archives, JFS, H. M. Inspector's Report, April 1912, p. 1.

121. Dyhouse, *Girls Growing Up*, pp. 123–4.

122. JFS, *Annual Report*, 1933–4, p. 17.

123. LMA, EO/PS/12/C88/25, Report of an Inspection of Commercial Street LCC Combined School, 14 October 1936.

124. Education Aid Committee (hereafter, EAC), *Report to Subscribers*, 1904–5, pp. 4–5. For example, they helped the daughter of a cap-maker take violin lessons. At her debut, a famous violinist offered to take her on as his student and the EAC helped raise funds for her living expenses. EAC, *Report to Subscribers*, 1904–5, p. 7.

125. EAC, *Report to Subscribers*, 1904–5, p. 9.

126. Ibid., 1906–7, p. 7 and Education Aid Society (hereafter, EAS), *Annual Report*, 1907–8, p. 11. The Education Aid Committee changed its name to Society in its 1907–8 report. UJW, *Annual Report*, 1907, pp. 11–12.

127. EAS, *Annual Report*, 1913–14, p. 6.

128. Ibid., 1917–18.

129. *JC*, 5 May 1916.

130. JBD, File E3/42, LCC Scholarships, Notes of interview between Sir Stuart M. Samuel, Bart accompanied by Charles H. L. Emanuel, and Mr Cyril Cobb, and Sir Robert Blair, 14 November 1917.

131. Ibid.

132. Alderman, *London Jewry and London Politics*, p. 66.

133. JBD, File E3/42, LCC Scholarships, Letters from students born abroad to the Board of Deputies, n.d.

134. JBD, File E3/42 2/2, Education Committee, extract from the Report presented to the Education Committee of the LCC, Letter from J. H. Gater, Education Officer, LCC to Secretary Board of Deputies of British Jews, 20 July 1928.

135. Pearson and Moul, 'The Problem of Alien Immigration into Great Britain', I, p. 10

136. Pearson and Moul claimed that approximately one-third of the parents were unable to read any language. Ibid., I, pp. 10, 11.

137. 'London Jewish School Children', 'The Report of the London Elementary Education Sub-Committee', *Jewish Guardian*, 3 April 1925.

138. Quinn, 'The Jewish Schooling Systems', p. 583.

139. *JC*, 1 January 1897.

140. Ibid., 21 March 1902.

141. S. Abrams, YIVO Oral History Collection, #92, p. 3.

142. S. M., Oral History Interview.

143. M. Zborowski and E. Herzog, *Life is with People: The Culture of the Shtetl* (New York: Schocken Books, 1962), p. 132.

144. *JC*, 1 January 1897.

145. Russo-Jewish Committee, *Annual Report*, 1897, p. 34 as cited by Cohen, 'The Influence of Jewish Radical Movements', p. 123.

146. During 1894–5, there were 48,000 attendances at English classes, a slight decline from the previous year. Russo-Jewish Committee, *Annual Report*, 1894–5, p. 11.

147. Russo-Jewish Committee, *Annual Report*, 1897, p. 34, as cited by Cohen, 'The Influence of Jewish Radical Movements', p. 123.

148. *JC*, 1 January 1897.

149. Quinn, 'The Jewish Schooling Systems', p. 583 ff.

150. *World Jewry*, 1 November 1935.

151. Morris Winchevsky and Eliyahu Wolf Rabbinowitz launched the *Poilishe Yidel* on 25 July 1884, which became the *Die Tsukunft* in November. Rabbinowitz and Winchevsky split and in 1885, Winchevsky started *Arbeter Fraint*. Winchevsky left England for America in 1894 and in 1898, Rudolph Rocker took over the *Arbeter Fraint*. Cohen, 'The Influence of Jewish Radical Movements', p. 81.

152. Cohen, 'The Influence of Jewish Radical Movements', p. 80.

153. *Die Tsait*, 7 April 1918.

154. *ELO*, 10 September 1938. HL Southampton, MS132 AJ195, Henriques Papers, 2 June 1932.

155. JFS, H. M. Inspector's Report, November, 1938, p. 2.

156. Julia Cohen received praise from the *JC* for her efforts in setting up a domestic science course. *JC*, 7 March 1902. The Manchester Jewish Ladies' Visiting Association favoured having girls spend their last year at school 'learning Household Management'. 'Report of the Conference of Jewish Women', pp. 63–4.

157. Some 700 students of all ages attended Settles Street Evening Classes. The advanced class read Sherlock Holmes, whose mysteries 'should appeal to the 'Yeshiba' spirit of the students'. *JC*, 27 February 1914.

158. Salaman, 'Anglo-Jewish Vital Statistics: A Survey and Consideration – I', *JC Supplement*, 29 April 1921.

159. Winch, 'Christian and Jewish Children', p. 267.

160. JFS, *Annual Report*, 1933–4, pp. 4, 13.

161. JFS, H. M. Inspector's Report, November 1938, p. 2.

162. Ibid.; January 1939, p. 2.

5 Religious Education: Conflicting Educational Views within the Jewish Community

1. In 1906, approximately 24,000 children received a Jewish education from all the institutions. Somewhat inflated, this figure included children attending more than one type of class. *The Jewish Yearbook* (London), 1906–7, p. 88. For an overview of options, see

Rev. S. Polack, 'The Need for a Central Organizing Authority', *Jewish Literary Annual* (1906), pp. 57–66.
2. L. G. Bowman, 'The Code of Instruction', *Jewish Literary Annual* (1906), pp. 24–33.
3. Alderman, *Modern British Jewry*, pp. 85–6.
4. Gartner, *The Jewish Immigrant in England*, p. 203. Montagu chaired a meeting of members of minor Synagogues and Chevras in October 1887. In November, the representatives established 'The Federation of Minor Synagogues'. At the first Board meeting in December, they chose Lord Rothschild as President and Samuel Montagu as Vice President. LMA, Acc. 2893/1, Federation of Synagogues Records, 6 November 1887, 4 December 1887.
5. The United Synagogue's fees for membership and burial exceeded most immigrants' budgets. Furthermore, immigrants questioned the rabbinical competency and authority of Chief Rabbi Adler. Alderman, *Modern British Jewry*, p. 154.
6. S. Sharot, 'Reform and Liberal Judaism in London, 1840–1940', *Jewish Social Studies*, 41:3/4 (1979), pp. 211–28, on p. 215.
7. United Synagogue, 'East End Scheme', Report of the Special Committee, 28 June 1898, pp. 1, 2.
8. Quinn, 'The Jewish Schooling Systems', p. 559.
9. *JC*, 23 January 1880.
10. Ibid., 30 January 1880.
11. Ibid., 23 January 1880.
12. JFS Archives, Letter from Rothschild to Revd. Dr Adler, 17 April 1891 in response to Adler's request of 12 April 1891.
13. *JC*, 30 January 1880.
14. JADRK, *Annual Report*, 1888, p. 13.
15. *JC*, 2 February 1902.
16. Ibid., 21 February 1902.
17. Ibid.
18. Ibid., 30 January 1880. In approximately, 1889, the Melamedim formed a union. Their president noted how poorly English Jews understood East End Jews. Ibid., 21 October 1904.
19. Ibid., 30 January 1880.
20. LMA, Acc. 2893/1, Report of the Federation of Synagogues on Chedorim, 7 April 1891.
21. H. M. Wiener, 'The Problem of the Talmud Torahs', *Jewish Literary Annual* (1906), pp. 67–74, on p. 67.
22. *JC*, 23 January 1880.
23. JREB, *Annual Report*, 1902, p. 23. Levy retired as honorary superintendent of JREB classes in 1902, after twenty-six years of service.
24. JADRK, *Annual Report*, 1881, p. 6.
25. Ibid., 1890, p. 15.
26. Ibid., 1882, pp. 3–4.
27. *JC*, 9 July 1880.
28. JADRK, *Annual Report*, 1887, p. 12.
29. Ibid., 1891, p. 7.
30. LMA, Acc. 2893/1, Report of the Federation of Synagogues on Chedorim, 7 April 1891.
31. Ibid.
32. Ibid. On 9 October 1891, the Federation set up an Educational Committee to deal with the suggestions.

33. Wiener, 'The Problem of the Talmud Torahs', p. 73.
34. Talmud Torah Trust, *Report of the Executive Committee*, January 1927–December 1931, p. 16.
35. *JC*, 28 February 1902.
36. In 1921, the JREB dissolved its Teacher Training Committee and the Jewish War Memorial took over its work. JREB, *Annual Report*, 1921, p. 15.
37. JREB, *Annual Report*, 1907, p. 14.
38. Ibid., 1908, p. 16; 1910, p. 18; and 1911, p. 19.
39. Ibid., 1902, 1912. According to Arthur Franklin, the JREB taught 10,000 students in 1907. *ELO*, 15 June 1907.
40. *JC*, 6 January 1905.
41. Ibid., 13 January 1905.
42. Bentwich, 'Jewish Educational Disorganisation in London', p. 360.
43. *JW*, 31 January 1908.
44. Bentwich, 'Jewish Educational Disorganisation', p. 361.
45. Ibid., p. 362. Inadequate Jewish education characterized much of the modern world. The journalist, Zionist and author, Israel Cohen blamed communal authorities, but also cited parental attitude as major factor. I. Cohen, *Jewish Life in Modern Times* (New York: Dodd, Mead and Co., 1914), p. 289.
46. *JC*, 3 July 1914.
47. 'Talmud Torah for Girls', *ELO*, 11 March 1916.
48. *JC*, 3 September 1915.
49. Ibid.
50. Ibid., 21 May 1915.
51. Bentwich, 'Jewish Educational Disorganisation', p. 357.
52. LMA, EO/PS/8/17, JREB, Attendance Committee, Minute Book, 5 December 1916.
53. Ibid., 9 November 1921; 9 November 1925; 1 November 1927; 28 March 1927.
54. *JC*, 11 February 1910.
55. Ibid.
56. Ibid., 26 June 1914.
57. JREB, *Annual Report*, 1912, pp. 27–8.
58. Ibid., 1911, pp. 26–7 and 1912, p. 27.
59. Ibid., 1913, p. 28.
60. *JC*, 15 May 1914.
61. LSPC, *Annual Report*, 1914, p. 20
62. *JC*, 7 May 1915.
63. Ibid.
64. Ibid., 22 May 1914.
65. Ibid., 2 January 1914.
66. JREB, *Annual Report*, 1913, p. 19
67. Ibid., 1917, p. 13.
68. Ibid., 1913, p. 20.
69. Ibid., 1908, p. 22 and 1915, p. 18.
70. Ibid., 1915, pp. 17–8.
71. Ibid., 1916, p. 13.
72. Ibid., 1918, p. 13.

73. Graves and Hodge, *The Long Weekend*, pp. 113–17. For a discussion of secularization in the period leading up to the war, see J. Harris, *Private Lives, Public Spirit: Britain, 1870–1914* (London: Penguin Books, 1994), pp. 150–79.

74. HL Southampton, MS116/87, Jewish War Memorial, Letter to Major Lionel de Roth-schild, M.P., O.B.E. from R(obert) Waley-Cohen, F. C. Stern and Swaythling, 5 May 1919.

75. Letter to Major Lionel de Rothschild, M.P, 5 May 1919.

76. JREB, *Annual Report*, 1919, p. 12.

77. Ibid., 1922, p. 12; 1925, p. 19; 1926, p. 11; 1927, p.13; 1928, p. 15; 1929, pp. 11, 22.

78. Ibid., 1929, p. 11.

79. Dr A. Sourasky, 'Race, Sex and Environment in the Development of Myopia', *British Journal of Ophthalmology* (April 1928), pp. 197–21, on p. 197.

80. JHO, 'Appreciation in the Medical Press', January 1930.

81. JHO, *Annual Report*, 1928, p. 5.

82. JREB, *Annual Report*, 1921, p. 14.

83. *Jewish Graphic*, 2 April 1926.

84. JREB, *Annual Report*, 1929, p. 12.

85. Ibid., 1930, p. 11.

86. H. Adler, 'Consecration Classes for Girls', in *Some Defects in Teaching and their Remedy, Educational Publication*, no. 6 (London: Council of the Jewish War Memorial, 1924–5), p. 10. The Committee for Jewish Education of the Jewish War Memorial named Herbert Adler Director of Jewish Education by in 1922. JREB, *Annual Report*, 1922, p. 12.

87. Adler, 'Consecration Classes for Girls', p. 10.

88. *JC*, 7 November 1924 and 6 February 1925.

89. *JFS School Magazine*, 7:61 (April 1930), p. 158.

90. Central Committee for Jewish Education, *Annual Report*, 1930–1, p. 11.

91. *ELO*, 11 June 1938.

92. JHO, *Annual Report*, 1929–30, pp. 23–4; 1934, p. 7.

93. JREB, *Annual Report*, 1930, p. 11.

94. The JREB reported that between 1920 and 1931, the school population in LCC areas declined by 20 per cent and the JREB classes by a little over 20 per cent. Ibid., 1931, p. 13.

95. JREB, Attendance Committee, Minute Book, 28 January 1931.

96. P. Osen, Jewish Women in London Group, Oral History Interview.

97. Talmud Torah Trust, *Report of the Executive Committee*, January 1927–December 1931, p. 16.

98. LMA, File EO/PS/2/20, Letter from Nathan Morris, Education Officer and Secretary of the JREB to Major White, 12 October 1936.

99. LMA, File EO/PS/2/20, Letter from Major White to LCC Education Officer's Department, 15 October 1936.

100. LMA, File EO/PS/2/20, Letter from LCC Education Officer's Department (probably Mr Rich) to Mr Bennett, 5 February 1937.

101. LMA, EO/PS/2/20, Letter from Bowman of the JREB to E. M. Rich, Education Officer of LCC, 10 June 1937.

102. LMA, File EO/PS/2/20, Letter from Mrs D. D. Barnett, Headmistress, Christian Street School, to E. M. Rich, 10 June 1937.

103. Rev. W. T. Gidney, *The History of the London Society for Promoting Christianity Amongst the Jews, from 1809 to 1908* (London: London Society for Promoting Christianity Amongst the Jews, 1908), pp. 591–2.

104. LSPC, *Annual Report*, 1910, p. 24.

105. Typically, the annual report listed between two and twenty baptisms per year. LSPC, *Annual Report*, 1893, p. 11; 1903, p. 11.

106. Mid-nineteenth century missionaries underestimated the opposition they would generate, and used questionable techniques to 'bribe' children to the mission. R. H. Martin, 'United Conversionist Activities among the Jews in Great Britain 1795–1815: Pan-Evangelicalism and the London Society for Promoting Christianity amongst the Jews', *Church History*, 46:4 (1977), pp. 437–52, on pp. 457, 450–1.

107. 'Bread Cast upon the Water', London Society for Promoting Christianity among the Jews, 1925, pp. 23, 24.

108. In 1911, the Borough of Stepney had slightly fewer than 44,000 Russians and Russian-Poles. Census of England and Wales, 1911, *Birthplaces*, Vol. IX, Cd. 7017, p. xix.

109. Ross, 'Missionaries and Jews in Soho' pp. 237–8.

110. On other occasions, the Society claimed not to accept children in their classes without parental permission. Their own annual report suggests otherwise. LSPC, *Annual Report*, 1914, p. 20.

111. Jewish Free Reading Room (hereafter, JFRR), 'A Brief Sketch of How the Society for the Distribution of Jewish Literature and the Jewish Free Reading Room came into Being' (London: Jewish Free Reading Room, 1928), pp. 1–2.

112. Ibid., pp. 4, 6.

113. *ELO*, 22 January 1927.

114. JFRR, 'A Brief Sketch', p. 5.

115. Ibid., p. 7.

116. JHO, *Annual Report*, 1926, p. 2.

117. The JHO encouraged benefactors to stipulate that schools had to use donations for hygienic purposes, as well as instruction. Ibid., 1929, pp. 7–9.

118. Bentwich, 'Jewish Educational Disorganisation', p. 355.

119. *ELO*, 20 May 1882.

120. *World Jewry*, 7 February 1936.

6 Jewish Clubs and Settlement Houses: The Impact of Recreational Programmes on the Anglicization of East Enders

1.   The Jewish Lads' Brigade, and especially its militarism, had detractors. Kadish, 'A Good Jew and a Good Englishman', see esp. ch. 4, pp. 95–136. Baden Powell's Scouts generated a similar reaction. T. M. Proctor, *On My Honour: Guides and Scouts in Interwar Britain* (Philadelphia, PA: American Philosophical Society, 2002), pp. 13, 14.

2.   On the founding and goals of settlements and missions, see N. Scotland, *Squires in the Slums: Settlements and Missions in Late-Victorian London* (London: IB Tauris, 2007).

3.   HL Southampton, MS172 AJ250/4, SJLC, *Stepney Jewish Club Chronicle* (hereafter, SJCC), 1:11 (December 1903), p. 4.

4.   BBSGJS, *Annual Report*, 1927–8, p. 6.

5.   *JC*, 12 December 1902.

6.   Scotland, *Squires in the Slums*, pp. xii–xiii.

7.   E. K. Abel, 'Canon Barnett and the First Thirty Years of Toynbee Hall' (PhD thesis, Queen Mary College, University of London, 1969), p. 19.

8. Ultimately, Barnett's views were somewhat authoritarian and paternalistic. After 1900, Barnett increased his emphasis on social research, which widened the gap between Toynbee residents and neighbours. S. Meacham, *Toynbee Hall and Social Reform, 1880–1914: The Search for Community* (New Haven, CT: Yale University Press, 1987), pp. 123, 126, 128–9.

9. Meacham, *Toynbee Hall*, p. 2.

10. Toynbee Hall, *Sixth Annual Report of the Universities' Settlement in East London*, 1890, p. 8.

11. BBSGJS, *Annual Report*, 1927–8, p. 6.

12. 'Guide to Jewish Social Work in Great Britain', p. 5.

13. S. Tananbaum, '"Ironing out the Ghetto Bend": Sports, Character and Acculturation among Jewish Immigrants in Britain', *Journal of Sport History*, 31:1 (2004), pp. 53–75. Kadish, 'A Good Jew and a Good Englishman', pp. 38, 42. R. A. Voeltz, '"… A Good Jew and a Good Englishman": The Jewish Lads' Brigade, 1894–1922', *Journal of Contemporary History*, 23:1 (1988), pp. 119–27, on p. 120. H. Hendrick, *Images of Youth: Age, Class, and the Male Youth Problem, 1880–1920* (Oxford: Clarendon Press, 1990), pp. 157–80.

14. *JC*, 19 April 1907; J. Springhall, *Coming of Age: Adolescence in Britain, 1860–1960* (Dublin: Gill and Macmillan, Ltd, 1986), pp. 120–1.

15. P. Bailey, *Leisure and Class in Victorian England: Rational Recreation and the Contest for Control, 1830–1885* (London: Routledge and Kegan Paul, 1978), p. 124.

16. D. G. Dee, 'Jews and British Sport: Integration, Ethnicity and Anti-Semitism, c1880–c1960' (PhD thesis, De Montfort University, Leicester, 2011), p. 43.

17. T. S. Presner, 'Muscle Jews and Airplanes: Modernist Mythologies, the Great War, and the Politics of Regeneration', *Modernism/modernity*, 13:4 (2006), pp. 701–28, on pp. 701, 704, 711.

18. Many associate 'muscular Judaism' with its Christian form and proponent Charles Kingsley. See N. Vance, *The Sinews of the Spirit: The Ideal of Christian Manliness in Victorian Literature and Religious Thought* (Cambridge: Cambridge University Press, 1985) and J. Springhall, 'Building Character in the British Boy: The Attempt to Extend Christian Manliness to Working-Class Adolescents, 1880–1914', in Mangan and Walvin (eds), *Manliness and Morality* (New York: St Martins, 1987), pp. 52–74. S. Tananbaum, '"To their Credit as Jews and Englishmen": Services for Youth and the Shaping of Jewish Masculinity in Britain, 1890s–1930s', in L. Delap and S. Morgan (eds), *Men, Masculinities and Religious Change* (Basingstoke: Palgrave Macmillan, 2013), pp. 90–118.

19. British Library of Political and Economic Science, London School of Economics, Passfield Papers, VII, I, pp. 53–54 as cited by R. O'Day and D. Englander, *Mr Charles Booth's Inquiry: Life and Labour of the People in London Reconsidered* (London: Hambledon Press, 1993), pp. 77–8. Another racial stereotype, many connected the vice of gambling to Jewish intellect. Englander, 'Booth's Jews', p. 557.

20. Proctor, *On My Honour*, pp. 67–8.

21. Black, *The Social Politics of Anglo-Jewry*, pp. 24–5, 137–8, 225–6.

22. *JC*, 14 March 1902. Robert Pyke thought those interested in helping immigrants should promote the opening of a Jewish section of the Polytechnic. *JC*, 8 December 1905.

23. Ibid., 12 April 1901.

24. Ibid., 12 December 1902.

25. Ibid., 19 April 1901.

26. Ibid., 12 December 1902.

27. 'Conference of Jewish Women', 1902, p. 66. The 1934 New Survey of London claimed that boys' clubs, first established in 1896, predated girls' clubs. The Jewish Working Girls' Club (Lady Magnus' Club), opened in 1886. British Library of Political and Economic Science, LSE, New Survey of London, London School of Economics, File 3/9, 'Jewish Lads' Brigade'. Sidney Bunt dated the opening of Leman Street to 1883. S. Bunt, *Jewish Youth Work in Britain – Past, Present and Future* (London: National Council of Social Service, 1975). The Club moved to a new facility above the Soup Kitchen in Leman Street late in 1902 or early 1903. Cohen, 'The Influence of Jewish Radical Movements on Adult Education', p. 120.

28. Mass Observation carried out a survey in 1966. The Boys' Brigade, founded in the 1880s, was inter-denominational. By the 1890s, a rival Anglican movement emerged. Baden-Powell's Boy Scouts (founded 1908), combined militaristic, imperial and nature lore. They supported religion generally, but eschewed denominational ties. P. Wilkinson, 'English Youth Movements, 1908–30', *Journal of Contemporary History*, 4:2 (1969), pp. 3–23, on pp. 3, 4, 6, 7, 10, 11, 14.

29. For Montagu's views on young people's attitudes toward Judaism, see L. Montagu, 'Religious Education in Clubs', *Jewish Literary Annual* (1906), pp. 51–6.

30. Spence, 'Working for Jewish Girls', p. 493.

31. Ibid., pp. 506–7.

32. HL Southampton, MS172 AJ250/4, SJLC, 'PMV', 'My Ideal of a Boy's Club', *SJCC*, 1:1 (February 1903), p. 3.

33. Ibid., SJLC, 'The Sections of the Club', *SJCC*, 1:2 (March 1903), p. 2.

34. Ibid., 1:3 (April 1903), p. 4.

35. HL Southampton, MS116/138 AJ348, Brady Street Club for Working Lads, Folder 4, *Tenth Annual Report*, 1905–6, pp. 7–8.

36. HL Southampton, MS152 AJ136, West Central Jewish Lads' Club, Scrapbook (from *JC*, 31 March 1905).

37. *JC*, 31 March 1905.

38. HL Southampton, MS116/138 AJ348, Brady Street Club for Working Boys, Folder 4, *First Annual Report*, 1896–7, p. 5. Lady Rothschild convinced Lord Rothschild to use the site of the Old Vicarage of St Mary's to create a social cub for residents of Brady Street Buildings, part of the Four Per Cent Industrial Dwellings Company. Brady Street Club for Working Boys, Folder 4, *The Bradian, Diamond Jubilee*, 1896–1956.

39. Brady Street Club for Working Boys, *First Annual Report*, 1896–7, pp. 5–6.

40. HL Southampton, MS172 AJ250/4, SJLC, *SJCC*, 1:7 (August 1903), p. 1.

41. 'Form of Pledge
    I, ..., as a Jew and an Englishman, and as a straightforward and honest lad, do hereby solemnly pledge my word of honour that I will not enter into, engage in any horse-racing, betting or gambling in any shape or form whatever while I remain a member of this Club, and further, I will use my best endeavours to prevent and dissuade any other members of the Club, or any other of my associates from so doing. I make this solemn declaration of my own free will, and do solemnly undertake to faithfully keep this, my determination'.
    Signed................
    Date........... ....Witness'
    HL Southampton, MS172 AJ250/4, SJLC, 'Stepney Jewish Lads' Club Anti-Gambling Association', *SJCC*, 1:7 (August 1903), p. 3.

42. HL Southampton, MS172 AJ250/4, SJLC, *SJCC*, 1:8 (September 1903), p. 3.

43. Brady Street Club for Working Boys, *First Annual Report*, 1896–7, p. 7.
44. Ibid., pp. 6–9.
45. *JW*, 7 December 1900.
46. *JC*, 15 July 1938.
47. HL Southampton, MS244, JLB, *First Annual Report*, February 1897–31 March 1898, pp. 10–11.
48. Ibid.
49. Ibid., pp. 10–11, 18.
50. HL Southampton, MS244, JLB, *Annual Report*, 1 April 1902–30 April 1903, p. 11.
51. While founded with religious motivations, the Boys' Brigade's drill, uniforms and camping appealed to some working class youth. Wilkinson, 'English Youth Movements', p. 5.
52. *JC*, 13 January 1905. Butler Street Girls' Club, *First Annual Report for the Butler Street Girls' Club*, Butler Street, Spitalfields, year ending November 1903.
53. *JC*, 12 December 1902.
54. HL Southampton, MS172 AJ250/4, SJLC, *SJCC*, 1:5 (June 1903), p. 7.
55. JBG, 'A Short Account of the Jewish Board of Guardians', p. 12.
56. HL Southampton, MS172 AJ250/4, SJLC, *SJCC*, 1:10 (November 1903), p. 1.
57. Ibid., SJLC, *SJCC*, 1:11 (December 1903), p. 4.
58. *JC*, 9 February 1900.
59. *JW*, 7 December 1900. For an extensive discussion of clubs and sport, see Dee, 'Jews and British Sport', especially pp. 45–79.
60. West Central Jewish Lads' Club, Scrapbook (from *JW*, 12 October 1900).
61. HL Southampton, MS172 AJ250/4, SJLC, *SJCC*, 1:1 (1 February 1903), pp. 1–2.
62. Ibid., 'PMV', 'My Ideal of a Boy's Club', *SJCC*, 1:1 (1 February 1903), p. 2.
63. Ibid., *SJCC*, 1:8 (September 1903), p. 2.
64. Ibid., *SJCC*, 1:11 (December 1903), p. 2.
65. *JC*, 28 January 1910.
66. Moses Davis founded the Beatrice Club for Jewish Working Girls in 1901 in memory of his daughter, Beatrice. *JC*, 27 July 1906. Beatrice Club for Jewish Working Girls, *Annual Report*, January 1911, pp. 7, 6.
67. Beatrice Club, *Annual Report*, 1911, p. 5.
68. Ibid., p. 6.
69. UJW, *Annual Report*, 1907, pp. 30–1.
70. Nearly half of boys from ages fourteen to eighteen were members of boys' clubs in 1914. HL Southampton, AJY220/3/6/5, 'Schedules of attendance at Jewish institutions', as cited by Dee, 'Jews and British Sport', p. 53.
71. BBSGJS, 'The First Step', p. 5.
72. Ibid.
73. Jewish Museum, interview with M. Fineman.
74. BBSGJS, *Annual Report*, 1928–9, pp. 5, 7.
75. Henriques diary entry, as cited in BBSGJS, 'The First Step', p. 8. Maude Stanley, active in English clubs, had concerns about race deterioration and hoped clubs would discourage early marriages. M. Stanley, *Clubs for Working Girls* (1904), pp. 216–7 and C. E. B. Russell, *Social Problems of the North* (1913), p. 72, as cited by Hendrick, Images of Youth, p. 174.
76. BBSGJS, 'The First Step', p. 9.
77. Jewish Museum, interview with M. Fineman.
78. *JC*, 6 August 1915.

79. Ibid., 2 January 1914.
80. Ibid.
81. Mid-Victorian term applied to professionally-trained Jewish religious leaders.
82. *JC*, 16 January 1914.
83. Ibid., 9 January 1914.
84. Ibid.
85. Ibid., 16 January 1914.
86. Ibid.
87. Ibid., 2 January 1914.
88. Ibid., 9 January 1914.
89. Ibid.
90. JWB Archives, JAPGAW, Minutes of the General Purposes Committee, 17 April 1917 and JAPGAW, *Annual Report*, 1925, p. 28.
91. *JC*, 31 March 1916.
92. Ibid., 25 June 1916.
93. SJLC, 'A Short History 1901–1926', p. 21. See also the description of enlistment and military honours: 'Anglo-Jewry under George V, 1910–1936', *The Jewish Yearbook* (London, 1937), pp. 356–75, on pp. 359–61.
94. St George's Jewish Settlement, *Annual Report*, 1919–20, pp. 9–10.
95. *Jewish Graphic*, 25 February 1927.
96. St George's Jewish Settlement, *Fifth Annual Report*, 1923–4, p. 3.
97. Henriques believed one way to stem irreligion was to promote a more modern type of Judaism and encouraged the development of Progressive or Liberal Judaism and a synagogue at the Settlement. BBSGJS, *Sixth Annual Report of the St George's Jewish Settlement*, 1924–5, p. 7.
98. Henriques, *Fifty Years in Stepney*, p. 12.
99. HL Southampton, MS172 AJ/250/1, SJLC, Box 1, Managers' Meeting, 28 January 1926.
100. Proctor, *On My Honour*, pp. 2, 3.
101. St George's Jewish Settlement, *Annual Report*, 1919–20, pp. 9–10.
102. Ibid., 1923, p. 3.
103. Henriques, *Fifty Years in Stepney*, p. 13.
104. SJLC, 'A Short History, 1901–1926', p. 23.
105. The West London and Liberal Jewish Synagogues established St George's Jewish Settlement as a War Memorial. BBSGJS, *Annual Report*, 1929–30, p. 11.
106. *First Report of the St George's Jewish Settlement*, 1919–20, p. 10.
107. St George's Jewish Settlement, *Annual Report*, 1925–6, p. 9.
108. Ibid., 1923–4, p. 3.
109. Ibid., 1924–5, p. 3; *Jewish Guardian*, 26 December 1924.
110. The founding of Girl Guides in 1910 had an important impact on scouting. Initially a middle class movement, the addition of girls, and programs for young people of different ages, meant that by the 1920s and 1930s, scouting 'attract[ed] youth from a variety of class, religious, and regional backgrounds'. Proctor, *On My Honour*, pp. 1, 2.
111. BBSGJS, 'The First Step', p. 23.
112. Jones, *Workers at Play*, pp. 34–7.
113. Jewish Museum, interview with K. R. Collins.
114. Ibid.
115. *Jewish Graphic*, 13 April 1928.

116. Ibid.
117. *JC*, 2 January 1914.
118. *Jewish Graphic*, 13 April, 1928.
119. BBSGJS, 'The First Step', p. 16.
120. *JC*, 29 September 1922. The Settlement, which planned to include a synagogue in its new Berner Street site, would not be large enough to accommodate the 1,200–1,500 who attended the Progressive Rosh Hashanah and Yom Kippur services at the Settlement. St George's Jewish Settlement, *Annual Report*, 1927–8, p. 9.
121. *Jewish Graphic*, 14 January 1926.
122. Ibid., 11 February 1927.
123. Ibid., 17 December 1926.
124. SJLC, 'A Short History, 1901–1926', pp. 27–8.
125. Ibid., p. 28.
126. M. Berkowitz and R. Ungar, *Fighting Back? Jewish and Black Boxers in Britain* (London: Jewish Museum and University College London, 2007). Cabinet maker Sam Clarke noted in 1918, that a number of Jewish boxing champions hailed from the East End. He described the period as 'the hungry years' – and that never again would there be so many Jewish boxers. S. Clarke, *Sam an East End Cabinet Maker The Pocket book Memoir of Sam Clarke, 1907 1979* (London: Inner London Education Authority, 1982). A similar pattern emerged in the United States. S. Riess, 'A Fighting Chance: The Jewish American Boxing Experience, 1890–1940', *American Jewish History*, 74:3 (1985), pp. 223–54.
127. Interview with Lady Janner, Interviewed by S. Tananbaum, 13 May 1986. In 1924, Janner became the first woman on the Brady Street Council.
128. St George's Jewish Settlement, *Annual Report*, 1924–5, p. 5.
129. HL Southampton, MS132 AJ/195, Henriques Papers, 2 August 1929.
130. BBSGJS, *Annual Report*, 1928–9, p. 9.
131. BBSGJS, 'The First Step', p. 28.
132. Adler, 'Life and Labour in East London', p. 289.
133. BBSGJS, *Annual Report*, 1929–30, p. 9.
134. Ibid., 1932–3, p. 4.
135. Ibid., 1931–2, p. 6.
136. Ibid., p. 14.
137. Ibid., 1934–5, p. 7.
138. Ibid., p. 9.
139. Ibid., 1932–3, p. 5.
140. Ibid.
141. JAPGAW, *Annual Report*, 1930, p. 47.
142. BBSGJS, *Annual Report*, 1934–5, p. 3.
143. Ibid., 1935–6, p. 11.
144. Ibid., p. 3.
145. BBSGJS, 'The First Step', p. 37.
146. B. Henriques, *Club Leadership*, 3rd edn (London: Oxford University Press, 1948), p. 215.
147. Ibid.
148. Ibid., p. 247.
149. Within Zionist, socialist, and communist youth movements, sexual experimentation was, apparently, more common than within other Jewish clubs. S. Smith, 'Sex, Leisure

and Jewish Youth Clubs in Inter-War London', *Jewish Culture and History*, 1:9 2007, p. 14.

150. Beckman, *The Hackney Crucible*, pp. 152–3.
151. Montagu, 'The Girl in the Background', pp. 238–9.
152. Ibid., p. 253.
153. L. Montagu, *My Club and I: The Story of the West Central Girl's Club*, 2nd edn (London: Neville Spearman, Ltd/Herbert Joseph, Ltd, 1954), p. 81.
154. Ibid. p. 55.
155. Ibid., p. 57.
156. Montagu, 'The Girl in the Background', p. 234.
157. Montagu, *My Club and I*, p. 80.
158. Montagu, 'The Girl in the Background', p. 252.
159. Ibid., pp. 252–3.
160. Brady Associated Clubs, *Annual Report*, 1933.
161. Ibid.
162. Jewish Museum Archives, Programme, 'The Opening of the Brady Girls' Club and Settlement by H. R. H. The Dcuhess of York – Monday 24 June 1935'.
163. *ELO*, 2 April 1938.
164. After the war only thirty boys and girls attended regularly. Gerson Papers, 'Synopsis', Author unknown, n.d. (after 1969), p. 16.
165. Jewish Museum Archives, 'Silver Jubilee, 1928–1952', Stepney Jewish Girls' Club, 1952, p. 3. Gerson worked at Stepney Jewish Clubs and Settlement from 1928 to 1973. Between 1944 and 1946 she took a leave of absence to lead the first Jewish Relief Unit to Egypt, Italy, and Albania. Gerson Papers, Announcement for the London Borough of Tower Hamlets Libraries Department, Annual Lecture, 21 November 1974.
166. P. Gerson, 'Social Service in the Jewish Community', *Tower Hamlets*, 1974.
167. Ibid., p. 19.
168. Jewish Working Girls' Club, *Annual Report*, 1932, pp. 8, 9.
169. Beatrice Club, *Annual Report*, 1938, p. 8.
170. British Library of Political and Economic Science, LSE, NSOL, File 3/10, 'Social Organisations of Girls'.
171. Beckman, *The Hackney Crucible*, p. xxiv.
172. BBSGJS, *Annual Report*, 1936–7, pp. 4, 5.
173. Beatrice Club, *37th Annual Report*, January 1938, p. 3.
174. Beatrice Club, *Annual Report*, 1938, p. 3.
175. Jewish Museum Archives, 'First Steps of Saleswomanship', *Stepney Jewish Girls' Club Magazine*, May 1938, pp. 9–11.
176. Jewish Museum Archives, 'Looking Back – 1927–1937', Stepney Jewish Girls' Club.
177. BBSGJS, *Annual Report*, 1937–8, p. 5.
178. AJY, *Annual Report*, 1938, p. 8.
179. BBSGJS, 'The First Step', p. 41.
180. St George's Jewish Settlement, *Annual Report*, 1926–7, p. 8.
181. See for example the *East London Observer*, 20 June 1936 and 2 April 1938.

7 Women's and Children's Moral Health in London's East End, 1880–1939: The Making and Unmaking of Jews and 'Jewesses'

1. Gartner, 'Anglo-Jewry and the Jewish International Traffic in Prostitution', pp. 129–31.
2. P. Hyman, 'The Jewish Body Politic: Gendered Politics in the Early Twentieth Century', *Nashim: A Journal of Jewish Women's Studies & Gender Issues*, 2 (1999), pp. 37–51, on p. 38.
3. L. Bland, '"Purifying" the Public World: Feminist Vigilantes in Late Victorian England', *Women's History Review*, 1:3 (1992), pp. 397–412. J. Daggers and D. Neal (eds), *Sex, Gender and Religion: Josephine Butler Revisited* (New York: Peter Lang, 2006), pp. 13–16.
4. Bristow, *Prostitution and Prejudice*, p. 242.
5. P. Knepper, '"Jewish Trafficking" and London Jews in the Age of Migration', *Journal of Modern Jewish Studies*, 6:3 (2007), pp. 239–56, on p. 245.
6. JWB Archives, 'Jewish Ladies Society for Prevention and Rescue Work', First Minute Book, 23 March 1885. Gartner, 'Anglo-Jewry and the Jewish International Traffic in Prostitution', p. 150. According to Paul Knepper, the visitor (Mrs Herbert) was the wife of a missionary. Knepper, '"Jewish Trafficking"', p. 240.
7. JWB Archives, 'Jewish Ladies Society', First Minute Book, 23 March 1885.
8. JAPGAW, *Annual Report*, 1898, p. 15.
9. Claude Montefiore, Sir Moses Montefiore's great nephew, was, for a short time in 1888, the first Jew to serve on the London School Board and would become a founder of Liberal Judaism. Alderman, *London Jewry and London Politics*, p. 18. According to the archival guide to the collections at the University of Southampton, the Jewish Ladies' Society changed its name on 26 March 1897, after noting the increasing role of the Gentleman's Committee. Archival List of MS173, Archives of Jewish Care, 1757–1989. The organization added Children to its name in 1932.
10. M. A. Kaplan, *The Jewish Feminist Movement in Germany: The Campaigns of the Jüdischer Frauenbund, 1904–1938* (New York: Greenwood Press, 1979), pp. 4, 11.
11. JAPGAW, *Annual Report*, 1899, pp. 10, 11.
12. 'Transactions of the International Congress on the White Slave Traffic', p. 147. JAPGAW, 'Report of the Gentlemen's Committee', *Annual Report*, 1898, p. 15.
13. A man who had worked at the Russian Consulate in Buenos Aires claimed that there were 3,000 European women 'enslaved' in '"tolerated houses" in Buenos Aires', at least half were Russians, many of whom were Jews. Mrs Henry Fawcett, LL.D., 'Transactions of the International Congress on the White Slave Traffic', held in London on the 21, 22 and 23 of June 1899, at the invitation of the National Vigilance Association London: NVA, 1899, p. 140. S. M. Deutsch, *Crossing Borders, Claiming a Nation: A History of Argentine Jewish Women, 1880–1955* (Durham, NC and London: Duke University Press, 2010), pp. 106–7.
14. Alroey, 'Bureaucracy, Agents, and Swindlers', pp. 223–4.
15. Prochaska, *Women and Philanthropy*, pp. 182–221. Certainly, Jewish feminists shared concerns about marriage and family life, but these specific issues appear only rarely in the JAPGAW sources.
16. According to Ena Abrahams, she and her friends knew little about sex and the community considered pregnancy before marriage dreadful. E. Abrahams, 'I Had This Other Life ... ', in Jewish Women in London Group (eds), *Generations of Memories* (London: Women's Press, Ltd, 1989), pp. 93–4.

17. Knepper, '"Jewish Trafficking"', p. 244.
18. Similarly, members of the Argentinean Jewish community created the Sociedad Israelita de Protección a Niñas y Mujeres 'Ezras Noschim' to prevent and eliminate prostitution and to maintain the respectability of poor Jews. Deutsch, *Crossing Borders*, pp. 107, 124.
19. S. Tananbaum, '"Morally Depraved and Abnormally Criminal": Jews and Crime in London and New York, 1880–1940', in Berkowitz et al. (eds), *Forging Modern Jewish Identities: Public Faces and Private Struggles* (London: Vallentine Mitchell, 2003), pp. 115–39, on p. 115.
20. Jewish Ladies Society, First Minute Book, 24 April 1885.
21. Ibid., 12 June 1885.
22. JAPGAW, *Annual Report*, 1898, p. 27.
23. Gartner, 'Anglo-Jewry and the Jewish International Traffic in Prostitution', p. 136.
24. JAPGAW, *Annual Report*, 1898, p. 28.
25. Ibid., 1904, p. 13.
26. Ibid., p. 16.
27. Ibid., p. 7.
28. Ibid., 1898, pp. 15–16
29. Ibid.
30. S. Mumm, 'Josephine Butler and the International Traffic in Women', in Daggers and Neal (eds), *Sex, Gender and Religion* (New York: Peter Lang, 2006), pp. 55–71, on p. 58.
31. 'Official Report of the Jewish International Conference on the Suppression of the Traffic in Women and Girls', held on 5, 6, 7 April 1910 in London, convened by the Jewish Association for the Protection of Girls and Women (London: Central Bureau, Jewish Association for the Protection of Girls and Women, 1910), p. 25.
32. Ibid., p. 30.
33. JAPGAW, *Annual Report*, 1898, p. 12; *Annual Report*, 1904, pp. 14, 16.
34. On irregular marriages, see D. Englander, 'Stille Huppah (Quiet Marriage) among Jewish Immigrants in Britain', *Jewish Journal of Sociology*, 34:2 (1992), pp. 85–109.
35. There were eight cases in 1896. The forty-four cases from 1898 were just a fraction of the total, as others had escaped detection. JAPGAW, 'Report of the Gentlemen's Committee', *Annual Report*, 1898, p. 15.
36. JAPGAW, *Annual Report*, 1898, p. 20.
37. Ibid., pp. 16–17.
38. Ibid., 1904, p. 18.
39. *JC*, 19 March 1909.
40. Miss Denhoff (Sara Pyke House) and Mrs Harrison (JAPGAW) attended the meeting. Henriques expressed admiration for the women and remarked that Harrison 'knows 14 dialects of Yiddish!' HL Southampton, Diary of Basil Henriques, 19 October 1913.
41. JAPGAW, *Annual Report*, 1925, p. 37
42. Ibid., p. 34.
43. Ibid., p. 33.
44. Ibid., p. 34.
45. Ibid., 1926, p. 17.
46. Ibid., 1898, p. 49.
47. In 1904, 1246 (of those ninety-four were Christian) young women passed through the SPH, 415 of whom remained at least one night. Ibid., 1904, p. 46.
48. Ibid., p. 51.
49. Ibid., pp. 53.

50. Ibid., p. 54.
51. Ibid., p. 54.
52. Ibid., p. 55.
53. JAPGAW, Minutes of the General Purposes Committee, 30 June 1919.
54. Ibid., 23 November 1919.
55. JAPGAW, *Annual Report*, 1919, p. 63.
56. Ibid., p. 64.
57. *JC*, 26 September 1919.
58. JAPGAW, *Annual Report*, 1919, p. 67.
59. Ibid., p.72.
60. Ibid., pp. 72–3
61. Ibid., p. 74.
62. Ibid., 1927, p. 31.
63. Ibid., 1898, p. 39.
64. Ibid., 1899, p. 32.
65. Ibid., pp. 30–1.
66. Ibid., 1898, p. 35.
67. Ibid., p. 34.
68. Ibid., 1899, p. 30.
69. Ibid., 1904, p. 39.
70. Ibid.
71. Ibid., pp. 33–4.
72. Ibid., p, 54.
73. Ibid., p. 53.
74. Ibid., 1904, p. 8.
75. P. Levine, 'The White Slave Trade and the British Empire', in L. Knafla (ed.), *Crime, Gender and, Sexuality in Criminal Prosecutions* (Westport, CT: Greenwood, 2002), pp. 132–46, on p. 134.
76. JAPGAW, *Annual Report*, 1904, p. 23.
77. Ibid., p. 35,
78. Ibid., pp. 38–9.
79. Prochaska, *Women and Philanthropy*, p. 182.
80. JAPGAW, *Annual Report*, 1904, p. 44.
81. *JC*, 8 January 1915.
82. Ibid.
83. *JC*, 28 May 1915.
84. Ibid., 8 January 1915.
85. JAPGAW, *Annual Report*, 1919, p. 12.
86. Ibid., p. 13.
87. Ibid., p. 53.
88. Ibid., p. 50
89. Ibid., p. 55.
90. Ibid., 1926, p. 54.
91. Ibid., p. 55.
92. Ibid., pp. 55, 62.
93. Ibid., 1930, p. 45.
94. Ibid., 1919, p. 91.
95. Ibid., 1925, p. 61.

96. Ibid., 1919, pp. 92–3.
97. Ibid., 1910, pp. 91–2.
98. Ibid., p. 91.
99. JC, 2 May 1902.
100. JAPGAW, *Annual Report*, 1904, p. 36.
101. Ibid., 1925, p. 28. 1927, p. 25.
102. HL Southampton, Diary of Basil Henriques, 13 October 1913.
103. JBG, *Annual Report*, 1919, p. 23.
104. JAPGAW, *Annual Report*, 1919, p. 27.
105. Ibid., p. 26.
106. Ibid.
107. According to statistics on crime, annual arrests for prostitution declined from approximately 11,000 women in England and Wales between 1900 and 1904 to about 3,000 in the late 1920s, although some believed there was a large increase in the numbers of "'amateurs'", not accounted for by the statistics. J. Bourke, *Working-Class Cultures in Britain, 1890–1960* (London: Routledge, 1994), pp. 37–8.
108. St George's Jewish Settlement, *Annual Report*, 1934–5, p. 11.
109. JBG, *Annual Report*, 1919, p. 25.
110. Ibid., p. 9.
111. JAPGAW, *Annual Report*, 1919, p. 11.
112. Ibid., 1925, p. 13. Sir William Clarke Hall, recruited Basil Henriques to serve as a magistrate. K. Bradley, 'Juvenile Delinquency, the Juvenile Courts and the Settlement Movement 1908–1950: Basil Henriques and Toynbee Hall', *Twentieth Century British History*, 19:2 (2008), pp. 133–55, on p. 141.
113. JAPGAW, *Annual Report*, 1919, p. 15.
114. Ibid., 1925, p. 13.
115. *Jewish Graphic*, 18 May 1928.
116. JAPGAW, Minutes of the General Purposes Committee, 27 April 1917, p. 4.
117. Ibid., September 1917.
118. Salaman, 'Anglo-Jewish Vital Statistics', IV, July 1921, p. 2.
119. JAPGAW, *Annual Report*, 1925, p. 31.
120. Ibid., 1926, pp. 43–4.
121. Ibid., 1927, p. 24.
122. Ibid., p. 25.
123. JAPGAW, Minutes of the General Purposes Committee, 17 April 1917.
124. Ibid., 13 June 1917, pp. 1–2.
125. JAPGAW, *Annual Report*, 1925, p. 28.
126. Black, *The Social Politics of Anglo-Jewry*, pp. 238–42.
127. *JC*, 24 September 1880.
128. PRO, HO45 9673, Letter from Louis Davidson, United Synagogue, to Sir Richard Asheton Cross, Bart., M.P., H. M. Secretary of State for the Home Departments, 12 January 1886.
129. *JC*, 24 September 1880.
130. Letter from Davidson to Asheton Cross, 12 January 1886.
131. PRO, HO45 9673, Letter from Arthur Cohen, President, London Committee of Deputies of the British Jews, to The Honourable Henry Matthews, Q.C., M.P., Secretary of State for the Home Department, 6 July 1888.
132. Letter from Davidson to Asheton Cross, 12 January 1886.

133. Ibid.
134. PRO, HO45 9673, Letter R. R. Redmayne, Secretary of Reformatory, Infirmary, New-castle on Tyne, to Rev. S. Friedberg, 5 June 1888.
135. *JC*, 21 May 1915.
136. Ibid.
137. HL Southampton, MS173/1/61, Archives of Jewish Care, Letter from Mr Ornstein, Secretary of the Visiting Committee of the United Synagogue, Minute Book, Industrial Committee, 1894–1963, 31 October 1894.
138. JAPGAW, *Annual Report*, 1919, pp. 13–14.
139. *Jewish Graphic*, 18 May 1928.
140. JAPGAW, *Annual Report*, 1919, pp. 82–3.
141. HL Southampton, MS173 2/8/11, Archives of Jewish Care, Montefiore House School, Montefiore House School Admissions Register, 1919–35.
142. JAPGAW, *Annual Report*, 1925, pp. 31–2.
143. Ibid., 1904, p. 36.

8 Becoming English in the Workplace

1. L. D. Smith, 'Greeners and Sweaters: Jewish Immigration and the Cabinet-Making Trade in East London, 1880–1914', *Jewish Historical Studies*, 39 (2004), pp. 103–20, on p. 106. B. Kosmin, 'Traditions of Work Amongst British Jews', in S. Wallman (ed.), *Ethnicity at Work* (London: Macmillan Press, Ltd, 1979), pp. 37–68, on p. 44. I. M. Rubinow, 'Economic Conditions of the Jews in Russia', Bulletin of the Bureau of Labor', 15 (1907), pp. 487–583, on p. 500.
2. Zborowski and Herzog, *Life is with People*, pp. 128–31.
3. A. Ruppin, *The Jews in the Modern World* (London: Macmillan and Co., Ltd, 1934), p. 277.
4. C. Baum, P. Hyman and S. Michel, *The Jewish Woman in America* (New York: New American Library, 1975), p. 55.
5. I. Etkes, 'Marriage and Torah Study among Lomdim in Lithuania in the Nineteenth Century', in Kraemer (ed.), *The Jewish Family*, pp. 153–78.
6. Simon Kuznets estimated that 64 per cent of Jewish immigrants in American were skilled workers, only 21 per cent were labourers or servants, and 5.5 per cent worked in commerce. S. Kuznets, 'Immigration of Russian Jews to the United States –Background and Structure', *Perspectives in American History*, 9 (1975), pp. 35–124, on pp. 104–5.
7. C. Baum, 'What Made Yetta Work? The Economic Role of Eastern European Jewish Women in the Family', *Response*, 18 (1973), pp. 32–8, on p. 32.
8. Burman, 'The Jewish Woman as Breadwinner', pp. 28, 30.
9. S. Glenn, *Daughters of the Shtetl: Life and Labor in the Immigrant Generation* (Ithaca, NY: Cornell University Press, 1990), pp. 69–70, 85, 239–40.
10. M. Barrett and M. McIntosh, 'The "Family Wage": Some Problems for Socialists and Feminists', *Capital and Class*, 11 (1980), pp. 51–72, on p. 57.
11. House of Lords, Select Committee on the Sweating System. First Report, *PP* 1888, XX, q. 3261–3, 3267, pp. 320–1. Late nineteenth-century feminist Ada Heather-Biggs argued that not only were a working-class woman's wages part of maintaining herself and not 'helping' her husband or father, but that women's employment was hardly a new phenomenon. A. Heather-Bigg, 'The Wife's Contribution to the Family Income', *Economic Journal*, 4:13 (1894), pp. 51–8, on pp. 53–4.

12. *JC*, 13 June 1890.

13. J. Dyche, 'The Jewish Workman', *Contemporary Review*, 73 (January, 1898), pp. 35–50, on p. 38.

14. Interdepartmental Committee on Physical Deterioration, *PP* 1904, XXXII, Minutes of Evidence, Cd. 2210, qq. 1165–9, 1173, p. 54.

15. F. M. Foster, 'Women as Social Reformers', *National Review*, 13:74 (1889), pp. 220–5, on pp. 223–4.

16. For an extended discussion on occupations and economic status, see Feldman, *Englishmen and Jews*, pp. 155, 159–65.

17. Definitions of sweated labour vary, and generally include excessive hours of labour, extremely low wages and unsanitary work conditions. J. J. Mallon, 'Sweating and Wages Boards', *Reformers Yearbook 1901*, pp. 124–8. L. Gartner, 'The History of a Sweater', *East London Papers*, 4:2 (1961), pp. 53–61, on p. 53.

18. J. Schmiechen, *Sweated Industries and Sweated Labor: The London Clothing Trades, 1860–1914* (Urbana, IL: University of Illinois Press, 1984), p. 26.

19. JHOA, *Annual Reports*, 1882, p. 6.

20. 'The Lancet Special Sanitary Commission on "Sweating" among Tailors at Liverpool and Manchester', *Lancet*, 131:3372 (14 April 1888), pp. 740–2, on p. 740.

21. While doing research in the East End, Beatrice Potter (Webb) described the work conditions and atmosphere of a typical workshop. B. Potter, 'Pages from a Work-Girl's Diary', *Nineteenth Century*, 24:139 (September 1888), pp. 301–14. Trade unionist Lewis Lyons exposed Potter's greatly exaggerated claims of workshop experience. Englander, 'Booth's Jews', fn 21, p. 560.

22. C. Black, 'Women and Work', New Review, 5 (1891), pp. 213–21, on pp. 215, 218.

23. Board of Trade (Alien Immigration), Reports on the Volume and Effects of the Recent Immigration from Eastern Europe into the United Kingdom, p. 108.

24. For a description of home and work conditions of eight East End women, see C. Black, 'Some East-End Workwomen', *National Review*, 13:78 (1889), pp. 788–98.

25. C. Black, 'London Tailoresses', *Economic Journal*, 14:56 (1904), pp. 555–67, on p. 555.

26. *Anti-Sweater*, August 1886, p. 3.

27. S. Dobbs, *The Clothing Workers of Great Britain* (London: George Routledge and Sons, Ltd, 1928), p. 178.

28. Board of Trade (Alien Immigration), Reports on the Volume and Effects of Recent Immigration from Eastern Europe into the United Kingdom, p. 120.

29. Gartner, *The Jewish Immigrant in England*, pp. 95–6.

30. B. McLaren, 'The Sweating System', Women's Liberal Federation (London: Women's Printing Society, Ltd, 1890), p. 15.

31. UJW, *Annual Report*, 1909, pp. 17–18. During the Victorian period, many women received advice to prepare for employment in the colonies. See A. J. Hammerton, *Emigrant Gentlewomen: Genteel Poverty and Female Emigration, 1830–1914* (London: Croom Helm, 1979), especially pp. 148–94.

32. Compiled from Board of Trade (Alien Immigration), Reports on the Volume and Effects of Recent Immigration from Eastern Europe into the United Kingdom and Census of England and Wales, 1911, *Birthplaces*, IX, Cd. 7017, Table 5, 'Country of Birth and Occupation of Foreigners, London Administrative County', pp. 220–8.

33. JAPGAW, *Annual Report*, 1898, p. 56.

34. Board of Trade (Alien Immigration), Reports on the Volume and Effects of Recent Immigration from Eastern Europe into the United Kingdom, 'Summary Table showing

occupations of Russians and Russian Poles in East London and Hackney, according to the Census of 1891', Appendix IV, p. 154.

35. Census of England and Wales, 1901, *General Report*, Cd. 2174, p. 144.

36. In the 1930s, however, refugees from Nazi Europe accepted positions as domestics in order to emigrate from Germany. Many found the work degrading, having themselves employed domestic help prior to their emigration. T. Kushner, 'An Alien Occupation – Jewish Refugees and Domestic Service in Britain, 1933–1948', in Mosse, et al. (eds), *Second Chance: Two Centuries of German-speaking Jews in the United Kingdom*, pp. 555–78.

37. H. Diner, *Erin's Daughters in America: Irish Immigrant Women in the Nineteenth Century* (Baltimore, MD: Johns Hopkins University Press, 1983), pp. 82–3, 117.

38. Rudimentary calculations suggest that even with significant 'slack' periods, garment workers earned more than domestics during the late nineteenth century. See E. Higgs, 'Domestic Service and Household Production', in A. John (ed.), *Unequal Opportunities – Women's Employment in England 1800–1918* (Oxford: Basil Blackwell, 1986), pp. 125–50, on pp. 138, 148. House of Lords, Select Committee on the Sweating System, XXI, Second Report, *PP* 1888, pp. 584–8. I am grateful to Deborah Dash Moore for suggesting this comparison.

39. *JC*, 1 August 1902.

40. Ibid., 3 January 1885.

41. Ibid., 9 May 1902.

42. Census of England and Wales, 1901, *General Report* Cd. 2174, 'Principal Occupations', p. 144.

43. While often credited with the creation of this 'task system', Anne Kershen contests this. See A. J. Kershen, *Uniting the Tailors: Trade: Unionism amongst the Tailors of London and Leeds, 1870–1939* (Ilford: Frank Cass & Co., 1995), pp. 10–1 and A. Kershen, 'Yiddish as a Vehicle for Anglicization', in A. Newman and S. Massil (eds) *Patterns of Migration, 1850–1914* (London: JHSE, 1996), pp. 59–67, on p. 61.

44. *Anti-Sweater*, January 1887, p. 1.

45. Dobbs, *The Clothing Workers*, pp. 73, 75.

46. 'Report of the Lancet Special Sanitary Commission of the Polish Colony of Jew Tailors', p. 817.

47. Labour organizers took advantage of the larger textile factories in Leeds and boasted better organized textiles trades. The Leeds Tailors' and Garment Workers Trade Union had a separate Jewish section. According to Dobbs, the Union attracted most Jewish men and women, but owing to poor organization, few Christian women joined the Union. Dobbs, *The Clothing Workers*, pp. 45–6.

48. *ELO*, 11 December 1880.

49. *JC*, 25 April 1884.

50. Ibid.

51. Ibid., 2 May 1884.

52. *People's Press*, 23 August 1890.

53. *JC*, 19 July 1895.

54. Ibid., 21 January 1910.

55. Umansky, 'Lily Montagu'.

56. Spence, 'Working for Jewish Girls', p. 495.

57. L. H. Montagu, *My Club and I: The Story of the West Central Jewish Club*, 2nd edn (1944; London: Neville Spearman & Herbert Joseph, 1954), p. 64, as cited by Spence, 'Working for Jewish Girls', p. 495.

58. Spence, 'Working for Jewish Girls', p. 506.
59. Montagu, 'The Girl in the Background', p. 235.
60. Ibid., pp. 235–6.
61. Ibid., p. 238.
62. Ibid., pp. 235, 239.
63. A. Kershen, 'Trade Unionism amongst the Jewish Tailoring Workers of London and Leeds, 1872–1915', in *The Making of Modern Anglo-Jewry*, pp. 34–52, on p. 36.
64. Kershen, *Uniting the Tailor*, p. 48.
65. Although some argue that the Jewish labour movement in London remained weak, unionism in general, did make inroads in England. The English branch of the Women's Trade Union League, founded in 1874, sought to raise women's economic status through increased wages and the organization of trade unions. See G. Boone, *The Women's Trade Union League in Great Britain and the United States* (New York: Columbia University Press, 1942).
66. LMA, LCC/MIN/7331, Bundle, E32, 'Inquiries made into the Sanitary Condition of the Workshops on D. F. Schloss' List', LCC Public Health Department, 22 December 1892.
67. 'Report of the Lancet Special Sanitary Commission of the Polish Colony of Jew Tailors', pp. 817–18.
68. '*The Lancet* Special Sanitary Commission on "Sweating" among Tailors at Liverpool and Manchester', p. 740.
69. L. Selitrenny, 'The Jewish Working Women in the East End', *Social Democrat*, 2 (1898), pp. 271–5, on pp. 274, 275.
70. East London Observer, 16 June 1888 as cited by Kershen, *Uniting the Tailors*, p. 14.
71. *Anti-Sweater*, September 1886, p. 3.
72. Eisenberger came to London from Hungary with her aunt, but the aunt moved onto America. House of Lords, Select Committee on the Sweating System, *First Report*, PP 1888, XX, qq. 2843–53, p. 276.
73. 'Report of the Lancet Special Sanitary Commissions of the Polish Colony of Jew Tailors', p. 818.
74. Report to the Board of Trade on the Sweating System at the East End of London, by the Labour Correspondent of the Board [John Burnett], *PP* 1887, LXXXIX and House of Lords, Select Committee on the Sweating System, *First Report*, PP 1888, XX. Second Report, *PP* 1888, XXI.
75. Glover, *Literature, Immigration, and Diaspora*, p. 74. On deliberations of the 1888 House of Lords, Select Committee on the Sweating System, see N. N. Feltes, 'Misery or the Production of Misery: Defining Sweated Labour in1890', *Social History*, 17:3 (1992), pp. 441–52, Ltd Stable URL: http://www.jstor.org/stable/4286051 [accessed 17 June 3013].
76. House of Lords, Select Committee on the Sweating System, *First Report*, PP 1888, XX, Minutes of Evidence, q. 3267, p. 321.
77. Gertrude Himmelfarb argues that Webb was a philo-semite and appreciated the qualities of East End Jews. While certainly one must place Webb's language and ideas in the context of the time, her descriptions of Jews indicate discomfort and distaste and certainly a sense of otherness. See G. Himmelfarb, 'The Jew as Victorian', in *The De-Moralization of Society: From Victorian Virtues to Modern Values* (New York: Alfred A. Knopf, 1995), pp. 170–87. For a view of Webb that differs from Himmelfarb's, see Y. Gorni, 'Beatrice Webb's Views on Judaism and Zionism', *Jewish Social Studies*, 40:2 (1978), pp. 95–114.

78. LMA, 'Inquiries made into the Sanitary Condition of Workshops on D. F. Schloss's List', 22 December 1892.
79. '*The Lancet* Special Sanitary Commission "Sweating" among Tailors at Liverpool and Manchester', p. 740.
80. JBG, *Annual Report*, 1885, p. 23.
81. R. H. Tawney, 'The Establishment of Minimum Rates in the Tailoring Industry under the Trade Boards Act of 1909', Studies in the Minimum Wage, No. 11, Ratan Tata Foundation, University of London (London: G. Bell and Sons, Ltd, 1915), p. 125.
82. JBG, *Annual Report*, 1880, p. 11.
83. *JC*, 11 June 1880.
84. JBG, *Annual Reports*, 1881, p. 48; 1883, p. 27; 1885, p. 38; 1901, p. 74; 1902, p. 74.
85. *JC*, 11 June 1880.
86. JBG, *Annual Report*, 1881, p. 15.
87. Ibid., p. 48.
88. *JC*, 25 June 1880.
89. JBG, *Annual Report*, 1881, p. 48.
90. Ibid., 1882, p. 22.
91. Ibid., 1886, p. 23.
92. Clarke, *Sam an East End Cabinet Maker*, p. 15.
93. HL Southampton, MS1731/6/1, Archives of Jewish Care, Industrial Committee, Minutes of the Industrial Committee, 26 July 1894.
94. Ibid., 25 July 1895.
95. Ibid., 26 February 1896.
96. *JC*, 2 May 1902.
97. W. Seccombe, 'Patriarchy Stabilized: The Construction of the Male Breadwinner Wage Norm in Nineteenth-Century Britain', *Social History*, 11:1 (1986), pp. 53–76, on pp. 53–4.
98. JBG, *Annual Report*, 1902, p. 61.
99. *JC*, 14 March 1902.
100. JBG, *Annual Report*, 1904, p. 67.
101. JAPGAW, *Annual Report*, 1904, p. 63.
102. *JC*, 9 September 1904.
103. JBG, *Annual Report*, 1905, p. 73.
104. Ibid. p. 74.
105. JBG, *Annual Report*, 1908, p. 80.
106. *JC*, 25 December 1908.
107. Poulsen, a self-taught man, worked in the garment trades and as a cabbie. He joined the Young Communist League in 1930, began writing in 1946. In the 1960s, he taught popular courses and led tours focusing on London. Charles Poulsen, 'Obituary', *Guardian,* Thursday, 13 December 2001.
108. E. J. Yeo, '"The Boy is the Father of the Man": Moral Panic over Working-Class Youth, 1850 to the Present', *Labour History Review*, 69:2 (2004), pp. 185–99, on p. 191.
109. P. Gerson, *Gerson Papers*, 'East London Jews', p. 4.
110. JHOA, *Annual Report*, 1909, p. 9.
111. Ibid.
112. Ibid., p. 12.
113. Kershen, *Uniting the Tailors*, pp. 46–7.
114. *JW*, 18 February 1910.

115. *JC*, 2 January 1914.
116. Ibid., 31 January 1913.
117. UJW, 'Conference of Jewish Women', 1902, p. 67.
118. *JC*, 31 January 1913.
119. *ELO*, 2 January 1915.
120. JBG, *Annual Report*, 1917, p. 22.
121. *JC*, 1 November 1918.
122. Ibid.
123. JBG, *Annual Report*, 1917, p. 21.
124. Ibid. p. 72.
125. JAPGAW, *Annual Report*, 1919, p. 11.
126. Braybon, *Women Workers in the First World War*, pp. 175–7, on p. 177.
127. Ibid., pp. 175–7 and Graves and Hodge, *The Long Weekend*, pp. 44–5.
128. While the immediate post-war disruptions led to high unemployment, Graves and Hodge argue that overall, demobilization went well and by November 1920, unemployment stood at about 500,000. See Graves and Hodge, *The Long Weekend*, p. 30. Bourke offers evidence that contradicts this optimistic assessment, noting that unemployment stood at 1.5 million during the winter of 1920 and fluctuated between 1.2 and 2 million during the 1920s and reached 3 million during the early 1930s. Approximately one-third of wholesale tailors experienced unemployment during the 1920s. J. Bourke, *Working Class Cultures in Britain*, pp. 108–9.
129. JBG, *Annual Report*, 1921, p. 10.
130. St George's Jewish Settlement, *Annual Report*, 1921–2, p. 3.
131. Increased building and its related benefits to the economy, jobs and the expanding availability of decent homes for workers began around 1923. The homes contributed to improved health and raised workers to the ranks of the lower-middle class. Graves and Hodge, *The Long Weekend*, pp. 33, 171.
132. JAPGAW, *Annual Report*, 1925, p. 49.
133. Census of England and Wales, 1921, Vol. 4, 'Foreign Born Population of Alien and Unstated Nationality, by Country of Birth and Occupation', p. 134.
134. H. Pollins, *Economic History of the Jews in England* (Rutherford, NJ, 1982): 188–9 as cited by B. Lammers, 'The Birth of the East Ender: Neighborhood and Local Identity in Interwar East London', *Journal of Social History*, 39:2 (2005), pp. 331–4, on p. 338.
135. Adler, 'London Life and Labour', pp. 284–6.
136. Jewish Museum, interview with Fineman.
137. Abrahams, Oral History Interview.
138. JHOA, *Annual Report*, 1927, pp. 21, 22.
139. D. Fowler, *The First Teenagers: The Lifestyle of Young Wage-Earners in Interwar Britain* (London: Woburn Press, 1995), pp. 95–7.
140. This pattern also characterized the experience of Italian women in America. Italian men rarely relinquished their wages. L. Odencrantz, *Italian Women in Industry: A Study of Conditions in New York City* (New York: Russell Sage Foundation, 1911), p. 32. Data from the United States indicates that Jewish daughters contributed 89 per cent, and Jewish sons 70 per cent, of their wages to the family fund. See Glenn, *Daughters of the Shtetl*, ft 122, p. 265.
141. Jewish Museum, interview with Stein.
142. *JC*, 1 August 1930.

Conclusion

1. Feldman, *Englishmen and Jews*, pp. 143–4.
2. *World Jewry*, 14 November 1935.
3. J. Leftwich, 'East End Story', *Jewish Monthly*, 3:4 (1949), p. 223.
4. *World Jewry*, 6 December 1935.
5. Ibid., 3 January 1936.
6. LSPC, *Annual Report*, 1930–1.

WORKS CITED

Manuscript and Archival Sources

Board of Deputies of British Jews (JBD), Woburn House, London

File B2/1/16, 'Grimsby: Schwartz Case', Letter from L. Woolfe (Senior) to Charles Emanuel, Solicitor and Secretary, 15 June 1910.

File E3/28, Mission Committee, 'Report of the Executive Committee to the General Committee', appointed 24 November 1912.

File E3/42, LCC Scholarships, Notes of Interview between Sir Stuart M. Samuel, Bart accompanied by Mr Charles H. L. Emanuel, Mr Cyril Cobb, and Sir Robert Blair, 14 November 1917. Letters from students born abroad to the Board of Deputies, n.d.

File E3/42 2/2, Education Committee, extract from the Report presented to the Education Committee of the LCC, 'Eligibility of Alien Children for the Council's Scholarships and Exhibitions', 11 July 1928. Letter from J. H. Gater, Education Officer, LCC, to Secy. of the Board of Deputies of British Jews, 20 July 1928.

File E3/11/2, Letter from S. Cohen, General Secy. of JAPGAW, to organizations involved in combatting White Slavery, 30 May 1927.

British Library of Political and Economic Science, London School of Economics, London

File 3/9, Charles Booth Collection; New Survey of London, 'Jewish Lads' Brigade'.

File 3/10, 'Social Organisations of Girls'.

Gerson Papers, Phyllis Gerson, London

'The Alice Model Nursery'

'Building Fund Appeal', Stepney Jewish (B'nai B'rith) Girls' Club, n.d. (c. 1936).

Notes for Mr Gebert.

'Guide to Jewish Social Work in Great Britain' (London: Committee for Training Jewish Social Workers, n.d.).

Hartley Library, Special Collections, University of Southampton (HL, Southampton)

MS116/87, Jewish War Memorial, Letter to Major Lionel de Rothschild, M.P., O.B.E. from R(obert) Waley-Cohen, F. C. Stern and Swaythling, 5 May 1919.

MS116/138 AJ348, Folder 4, Brady Street Club for Working Lads, *First Annual Report*, 1896–7, *Tenth Annual Report*, 1905–6, *The Bradian, Diamond Jubilee, 1896–1956*.

MS116/145 AJ363, London Jewish Hospital, 'Letter to the Editor from Rev. L. Geffen', *JC*, n.d. (21 November 1913), 'The London Jewish Hospital', Letter to the Editor from Mr F. S. Franklin, JC, n.d. (5 December 1913).

MS127 AJ19/C5, Norwood Archive, Sulking and Punishment Book, 12 and 13 July 1914, 21 August 1914.

MS129 AJ26/A2, Union of Jewish Women (UJW), General Committee of the Union of Jewish Women, 15 December 1914.

MS129 AJ26/C4, UJW, Report of Meeting held at Mrs M. A. Spielman's house, 15 December 1914.

MS132 AJ195, Henriques Papers.

MS132 AJ220/1/2, Diary of Basil Henriques.

MS132 AJ2201/3, Diary of Basil Henriques.

MS172 AJ250/1, Stepney Jewish Lads' Club, Minute Book No. 4, Commenced January 1924–September 1935.

MS172 AJ250/4, Stepney Jewish Lads' Club, *Stepney Jewish Club Chronicle* (February 1903–January 1904).

MS172 AJ250/6, Stepney Jewish Lads' Club, 'A Short History, 1901–1926'.

MS173/1/13/3, Jewish Board of Guardians, Minute Book of the Gerald Samuel and Denzil Myer Home.

MS173/1/6/1, Archives of Jewish Care, Minute Book, Industrial Committee, 1894–1963.

MS173/2/8/11, Archives of Jewish Care, Montefiore House School Admissions Register, 1919–35.

MS244, Jewish Lads' Brigade, Annual Reports, *First Annual Report*, February 1897–31 March 1898, *Annual Report*, April 1902–30 April 1903.

Jewish Welfare Board Archives (JWB), London

'Jewish Ladies Society for Prevention and Rescue Work', First Minute Book.

Jewish Association for the Protection of Girls and Women (JAPGAW), Minutes of the General Purposes Committee.

Minutes of the Sanitary Committee, 1893–1911.

Report of the Special Committee on Consumption, May 1897.

Jews' Free School (JFS) Archives, London

Exhibit on the History of the School, J. Wagerman, 'The JFS in Days Gone By', unpublished paper, n.d.

Letter from Rothschild to Revd Dr Adler, 17 April 1891 in response to Adler's request of 13 April 1891.

H. M. Inspector's Report, February 1907.

H. M. Inspector's Report, April 1912.

H. M. Inspector's Report, August 1913.

H. M. Inspector's Report, November 1938.

H. M. Inspector's Report, January 1939.

Jewish Museum Archives, London

Programme, 'The Opening of the Brady Girls' Club and Settlement by H. R. H. The Duchess of York – Monday 24 June 1935'.

'First Steps of Saleswomanship', *Stepney Jewish Girls' Magazine* (May 1938).

'Looking Back – 1927–1937', Stepney Jewish Girls' Club.

'Silver Jubilee, 1928–1952', Stepney Jewish Girls' Club.

London Metropolitan Archives (LMA), London

A/FWA/C/D12/1, Barbican Mission to the Jews.

A/FWA/C/D128/1, 'Immanuel's Witness', 16 (June 1938).

Acc 2893/1, Federation of Synagogues Records.

A/KE/522/5, King Edward's Fund, London Jewish Hospital, Applications for Grants, 1920–37.

EO/PS/2/20, LCC Education Officer's Department.

EO/PS/8/17, Jewish Religious Education Board, Attendance Committee Minute Book.

EO/PS/12/C29/3, Inspector's Report, Tower Hamlets Division, Lower Chapman Street School, Inspection 15, 16, 17 June 1880.

EO/PS/12/C29/5, School Board for London, Inspector's Report, Tower Hamlets Division, Lower Chapman Street School, Inspection 2, 3, 4 May 1882.

EO/PS/12/C29/17, Managers' Yearly School Report', Tower Hamlets, Lower Chapman Street, St George's in the East, School Year Ended October, 1894.

EO/PS/12/C29/22, Managers' Yearly School Report, Tower Hamlets, Lower Chapman Street, St George's in the East, School Year Ended October, 1895.

EO/PS/12/C29/23, Managers' Yearly School Report, Tower Hamlets, Lower Chapman Street, St George's in the East, School Year Ended October, 1896.

EO/PS/12/C29/29, 'Managers' Yearly School Report, Tower Hamlets, Lower Chapman Street, St George's in the East, School Year Ended October, 1899.

EO/PS/12/C29/32, Managers' Yearly School Report, Tower Hamlets, Lower Chapman Street, St George's in the East, School Year Ended October, 1900.

EO/PS/12/C29/36, Managers' Yearly School Report, Tower Hamlets, Lower Chapman Street, St George's in the East, School Year Ended October, 1902.

EO/PS/12/C29/39, Managers' Yearly School Report, Tower Hamlets, Lower Chapman Street, St George's-in-the-East, School Year Ended October, 1903.

EO/PS/12/C88, Managers' Yearly School Report, Tower Hamlets, Commercial Street, Whitechapel Board School, School Year Ended February, 1900.

EO/PS/12/C88/1, Managers' Yearly School Report, Tower Hamlets, Commercial Street, Whitechapel, Transferred Temporary, Board School, School Year ended January, 1896.

EO/PS/12/C88/6, Managers' Yearly School Report, Tower Hamlets, Commercial Street, Whitechapel Board School, School Year Ended February, 1899.

EO/PS/12/C88/8, Managers' Yearly School Report, Tower Hamlets, Commercial Street, Whitechapel Board School, School Year Ended February, 1900.

EO/PS/12/C88/10, 'Managers' Yearly School Report', Tower Hamlets, Commercial Street, Whitechapel Board School, School Year Ended February, 1901.

EO/PS/12/C88/15, Managers' Yearly School Report, Tower Hamlets, Commercial Street, Whitechapel Board School, School Year Ended February, 1903.

EO/PS/12/C88/17, Managers' Yearly School Report, Tower Hamlets, Commercial Street, Whitechapel Board School, School Year Ended February, 1904.

EO/PS/12/C88/22, H. M. Inspector's Report, Whitechapel Commercial Street LCC School, 16 April 1907.

EO/PS/12/C88/25, Report of an Inspection of Commercial Street LCC Combined School, 14 October 1936.

LCC/MIN/7331, LCC Public Health Department.

LCC/MIN/7343, LCC Public Health Department.

LCC/MIN/7381, LCC Public Health Department.

Mocatta Library, University College London

Jews' Free School Magazine.

Public Record Office (PRO), London

Home Office, HO 45, Alien Restriction.

Ministry of Health, MH 19.

Ministry of Education, ED/77, ED/109.

Ministry of Police, MEPOL 2/260.

Tower Hamlets Library

Gerson, P., 'Social Service in the Jewish Community', London, Tower Hamlets, 1974.

Interviews

Jewish Museum, London

K. R. Collins, tape 69, interviewed by Judith Schrnt Plotkin, 13 April 1986.

M. Fineman, tape 50, interviewed by Cyril Silvertown, 27 January 27 1986.

P. Solomons, 8 December 1984.

J. Stein, tape 112, interviewed by V. H. Seymour, 23 February 1988.

Jewish Women in London Group, Oral History Interviews, E. Abrahams, H. Gaffen, S. M., P. Osen, F. V.

Lady Janner, interviewed by S. Tananbaum, 13 May 1986.

YIVO Archives, New York

Oral History Collection, S. Abrams, no. 92.

Government Documents

Census of England and Wales, 1891, 1901, 1911, 1921.

Report to the Board of Trade on the Sweating System at the East End of London, by the Labour Correspondent of the Board (John Burnett), *PP* 1887, LXXXIX.

House of Lords, Select Committee on the Sweating System, First Report, *PP* 1888, XX, Second Report, *PP*, 1888, XXI.

European Immigration into the United States, Its Nature and Effects, *PP* 1893–4, LXXI, C. 7113.

Board of Trade (Alien Immigration), Reports on the Volume and Effects of the Recent Immigration from Eastern Europe into the United Kingdom, *PP* 1894, LXVIII, C. 7406.

Royal Commission on Alien Immigration, *PP* 1903, IX, Report, Cd. 1741, Vol. I, Minutes of Evidence, Cd. 1742, Vol. II, Appendix, Cd. 1741–I, Vol. III.

Interdepartmental Committee on Physical Deterioration, *PP* 1904, XXXIII, Report and appendix, Cd. 2175, II, List of Witnesses and Minutes of Evidence, Cd. 2210, III, Appendix and General Index, Cd. 2186.

Reports of the United States Industrial Commission on Immigration, 15, Reprint (New York: Arno Press, 1970).

Annual Reports

Association for Jewish Youth, *Annual Report*, 1938.

The Beatrice Club for Jewish Working Girls, *Annual Report*, 1911, 1938.

The Bernhard Baron St George's Jewish Settlement, *Annual Report*, 1927–38.

The Bernhard Baron St George's Jewish Settlement, 'The First Step – Fiftieth Anniversary Review, 1914–1964'.

Board of Guardians for the Relief of the Jewish Poor, *Annual Reports*, 1880–1939.

Brady Associated Clubs, *Annual Report*, 1931, 1933, 1935.

Butler Street Girls' Club, *First Annual Report for the Butler Street Girls' Club*, Butler Street, Spitalfields, year ending November 1903.

Central Committee for Jewish Education, *Annual Report*, 1923–4, 1930–1.

Day Nursery for Jewish Infants, *Second Annual Report*, 1898–9.

East London Fund for the Jews, *Report for the Year*, 1927.

Education Aid Committee, *Report to Subscribers*, 1904–7.

Education Aid Society, *Annual Report*, 1907–29.

Jewish Association for the Diffusion of Religious Knowledge (JADRK), *Annual Report*, 1882, 1885, 1886, 1887, 1888, 1890, 1891, 1892, 1893.

Jewish Association for the Protection of Girls and Women, *Annual Report*, 1894–1936.

Jewish Health Organisation, *Annual Report*, 1924–38.

Jewish Health Organisation of Great Britain, 'The East London Child Guidance Clinic', *Honorary Director's Report*, 1927–32.

Jewish Infant Welfare Centre, *Annual Report*, 1934–5, 1938–9.

Jewish Maternity Hospital, Report for the Year, January 1st to December 31st, 1936.

Jewish Maternity Hospital, *Report of the Committee*, 1937.

Jewish Mothers' Welcome and Infant Welfare Centre, *Annual Report*, 1932–3.

Jewish Infant Welfare Centre, *18th Annual Report*, 1934–5.

Jewish Orphanage, *Report for the Year 1933, 1934, 1935*.

Jewish Religious Education Board, *Annual Report*, 1896–1938.

Jewish Working Girls' Club, *Annual Report*, 1931, 1932.

The Jewish Yearbook (London), 1894–1929.

Jews' Free School, *Annual Report*, 1884, 1933–4.

Jews' Hospital and Orphan Asylum, *Annual Report*, 1909.

Jews' Temporary Shelter, *Annual Report*, 1937, 1938.

Leman Street Girls' Club, *Fifty-second Annual Report*, 1937–8.

London Society for Promoting Christianity among the Jews, *Annual Report*, 1883–1916.

Medical Officer of Health for the Metropolitan Borough of Stepney, *Annual Report*, 1899–1933.

Poor Jews' Temporary Shelter, *Annual Report*, 1899–1900.

Russo-Jewish Committee, *Annual Report*, 1894–5.

St George's Jewish Settlement, *Annual Report*, 1919–27.

Talmud Torah Trust, *Report of the Executive Committee*, January 1927–December 1931.

Toynbee Hall, Fifth and Sixth *Annual Report Universities' Settlement in East London*, London, 1889, 1890.

Union of Jewish Women, *Annual Report*, 1903–38.

Primary Sources

Adler, H., 'Consecration Classes for Girls', in *Some Defects in Teaching and their Remedy*, Educational Publication, no. 6 (London: Council of the Jewish War Memorial, 1924–5).

Adler, N., 'Children as Wage Earners', *Fortnightly Review*, 73:437 (1903), pp. 918–27.

—, 'Life and Labour in East London', in H. L. Smith (ed.), *The New Survey of London Life and Labour*, 9 vols (London: P. S. King & Son, 1930–5), vol. 6, pp. 268–98.

'The Alien Immigrant', *Blackwood's Magazine*, 173 (1903), pp. 132–41.

'Anglo-Jewry under George V, 1910–1936', *The Jewish Yearbook* (London, 1937), pp. 356–75.

Atkinson, S., 'Tuberculosis among Jews', *British Medical Journal* (2 May 1908), p. 1077.

Bailey, W. B., 'The Bird of Passage', *American Journal of Sociology*, 18 (1912), pp. 391–7.

Bentwich, N., 'Jewish Educational Disorganisation in London', *Jewish Review*, 3 (1912–13), pp. 355–66.

Black, C., 'Some East End Workwomen', *National Review*, 13:78 (1889), pp. 788–98.

—, 'Women and Work', *New Review*, 5 (1891), pp. 213–21.

—, 'London Tailoresses', *Economic Journal*, 14:56 (1904), pp. 555–67.

Blair, R., 'The Outlook of the Rising Generation', *Edinburgh Review*, 238:486 (1923), pp. 379–97.

Board of Guardians for the Relief of the Jewish Poor, 'A Short Account of the Work of the Jewish Board of Guardians and Trustees for the Relief of the Jewish Poor' (London, n.d.).

Boone, G., *The Women's Trade Union League in Great Britain and the United States* (New York: Columbia University Press, 1942).

Booth, C., *Life and Labour of the People in London*, first series, rev. edn, reprints of economic classics (1902; New York: A. M. Kelly Publishers, 1969).

—, *Life and Labour of the People in London*, 17 vols (London: Macmillan, 1902–3).

Bosanquet, H., 'Physical Degeneration and the Poverty Line', *Contemporary Review*, 85 (1904), pp. 65–75.

—, *Social Work in London, 1869–1912: A History of the Charity Organization Society* (London: J. Murray, 1914).

Bowman, L. G., 'The Code of Instruction', *Jewish Literary Annual* (London, 1906), pp. 24–33.

'Bread Cast upon the Water', London Society for Promoting Christianity among the Jews, 1925.

Brewer, Mrs, 'Jews in London', *Sunday at Home, 1948* (29 August 1891), pp. 693–8.

Clarke, S., *Sam an East End Cabinet Maker – The Pocket-book Memoir of Sam Clarke, 1907–1979* (London: Inner London Education Authority, 1982).

Davies, M., and A. G. Hughes, 'An Investigation into the Comparative Intelligence and Attainments of Jewish and Non-Jewish School Children', *British Journal of Psychology*, general section, 18, part 2 (1927), pp. 134–46.

Dobbs, S. P., *The Clothing Workers of Great Britain* (London: George Routledge and Sons, 1928).

Domnitz, M., *Immigration and Integration – Experiences of the Anglo-Jewish Community* (London: Council of Christians and Jews, [*c*. 1958]).

Dunraven, The Earl of, 'The Invasion of Destitute Aliens', *Nineteenth Century*, 31:184 (1892), pp. 985–1000.

Dyche, J., 'The Jewish Workman', *Contemporary Review*, 73 (1898), pp. 35–50.

—, 'The Jewish Immigrant', *Contemporary Review*, 75 (1899), pp. 379–99.

Eichholz, A., 'The Jewish School-Child', *Jewish Literary Annual* (London, 1903), pp. 66–78.

Fairfield, L., 'The Alleged High Fertility of Jews', *British Medical Journal*, 2:3532 (15 September 1928), p. 510.

—, 'Section of Medical Sociology', *British Medical Journal*, 2:3528 (18 August 1928), p. 310.

'Foreign Undesirables', *Blackwood's Edinburgh Magazine*, 169:1024 (1901), pp. 279–89.

Foster, F. M., 'Women as Social Reformers', *National Review*, 13:74 (1889), pp. 220–5.

Fox, S., 'The Invasion of Pauper Foreigners', *Contemporary Review*, 53 (1888), pp. 855–67.

Gidney, Rev W. T., *The History of the London Society for Promoting Christianity Amongst the Jews, from 1809 to 1908* (London: London Society for Promoting Christianity Amongst the Jews, 1908).

Heather-Biggs, A., 'The Wife's Contribution to the Family Income', *Economic Journal*, 4:13 (1894), pp. 51–8.

Hyamson, A. M., 'The Ten Lost Tribes and the Return of the Jews to England', *Transactions of the Jewish Historical Society of England*, 5 (1902–5), pp. 115–47.

'Infantile Mortality and the Employment of Married Women in Factories', *Lancet*, 22 (September 1906), pp. 817–18.

'The Jewish Board of Guardians and "The *Lancet* Report"', *Lancet* (24 May 1884), pp. 948–9.

Jewish Health Organisation, 'Appreciation in the Medical Press' (London, January 1930).

—, 'What We Have Done and What We Are to Do' (November, 1930).

—, 'The Difficult Child', reprinted from *Medical Officer* (30 May 1931).

Joseph, S., 'Jewish Immigration to the United States from 1881–1910', *Studies in History, Economics, and Public Law* (New York: Columbia University Press, 1914).

Levy, Reverend S., 'Problems of Anglicisation', paper delivered at Conference of Anglo-Jewish Ministers (1911), reprinted in the *Jewish Annual*, 6 (London, 1943), pp. 73–82.

Loch, C. S., *Charity Organisation* (London: Swan Sonnenschein and Co., 1892).

Mallon, J. J., 'Sweating and Wages Boards', *Reformers Yearbook* (1901), pp. 124–8.

McLaren, B., 'The Sweating System', The Women's Liberal Federation (London: Women's Printing Society, Ltd, 1890).

A Member of the Committee, 'A Brief Sketch of How the Society for the Distribution of Jewish Free Reading Room Came into Being, with an Outline of its Work during the First Years of its Existence' (London: Jewish Free Reading Room, 1928).

Montagu, L. H., 'The Girl in the Background' (1904), in E. J. Urwick (ed.), *Studies of Boy Life in Our Cities*, reprint (New York: Garland Publishing, 1980), pp. 235–54.

—, 'Religious Education in Clubs', *Jewish Literary Annual* (London, 1906), pp. 51–6.

—, *My Club and I: The Story of the West Central Girl's Club*, 2nd edn (London: Neville Spearman, Ltd and Herbert Joseph, Ltd, 1954).

National Anti-Sweating League, 'Living Wages for Sweated Workers', National Demonstration, London, 1908.

Odencrantz, L., *Italian Women in Industry: A Study of Conditions in New York City* (New York: Russell Sage Foundation, 1911).

'Official Report of the Jewish International Conference on the Suppression of the Traffic in Girls and Women held on April 5th, 6th and 7th, 1910, in London, Convened by the Jewish Association for the Protection of Girls and Women' (London: Association for the Protection of Girls and Women, 1910).

Pearson, K., and M. Moul, 'The Problem of Alien Immigration into Great Britain, Illustrated by an Examination of Russian and Polish Jewish Children', *Annals of Eugenics*, 1:1–2 (1925), pp. 5–127; 3:1–2 (1928), pp. 1–76 and 3–4 (1928), pp. 201–64.

Polack, Rev. S., 'The Need for a Central Organizing Authority', *Jewish Literary Annual* (London, 1906), pp. 57–66.

Potter, B., 'East London Labour', *Nineteenth Century*, 24 (1888), pp. 161–83.

—, 'Pages from a Work-Girl's Diary', *Nineteenth Century*, 24:139 (1888), pp. 301–14.

Quid, T., 'Our Complex Uneconomical Charitable System. A Plea for Organization', reprinted from the *Jewish Chronicle* (London: Jewish Chronicle Office, 1905).

Rastorgoueff, L. P., 'Disabilities of the Jews in Russia', *Jewish Review*, 3 (1912–13), pp. 106–29.

'Report of the Conference of Jewish Women', reprint (London: Jewish Chronicle Office, 1902).

'Report of the *Lancet* Special Commission on the Polish Colony of Jew Tailors', *Lancet* (3 May 1884), pp. 817–18.

Reeves, M. P., *Round about a Pound a Week* (London: Virago, 1979).

Rosenbaum, S., 'A Contribution to the Study of the Vital and Other Statistics of the Jews in the United Kingdom', *Journal of the Royal Statistical Society*, 68:3 (1905), pp. 526–62.

Rubinow, I. M., 'Economic Conditions of the Jews in Russia', *Bulletin of the Bureau of Labor* 15 (1907), pp. 487–583.

Rumyaneck, J., 'The Comparative Psychology of Jews and Non-Jews – A Survey of the Literature', *British Journal of Psychology*, general section 21, part 4 (April 1931), pp. 404–26.

Salaman, Dr R. N., 'Anglo-Jewish Vital Statistics: A Survey and Consideration', reprinted from the *Jewish Chronicle*, April, May, June, July, August 1921.

Schloss, D. F., 'Healthy Homes for the Working Classes', *Fortnightly Review*, 43:256 (1888), pp. 526–37.

—, 'The Jew as Workman', *Nineteenth Century*, 29 (1891), pp. 96–109.

Selitrenny, L., 'The Jewish Working Women in the East End', *Social Democrat*, 2 (1898), pp. 271–5.

Smith, L. D., 'Greeners and Sweaters: Jewish Immigration and the Cabinet-Making Trade in East London, 1880–1914', *Jewish Historical Studies*, 39 (2004), pp. 103–20.

Smith, J., 'The Jewish Immigrant', *Contemporary Review*, 76 (1899), pp. 425–36.

'Some Diseases of the Jewish Race', *British Medical Journal*, 2:3575 (13 July 1929), pp. 51–2.

Sourasky, Dr A., 'Race, Sex and Environment in the Development of Myopia', *British Journal of Ophthalmology* (1928), pp. 197–121.

Sourasky, M., 'The Alleged High Fertility of Jews', *British Medical Journal*, 2:3531 (1928), p. 469.

'The Lancet Special Sanitary Commission on "Sweating" among Tailors at Liverpool and Manchester', *Lancet*, 131:3372 (14 April 1888), pp. 740–2.

Tawney, R. H., 'The Establishment of Minimum Rates in the Tailoring Industry under the Trade Boards Act of 1909', *Studies in the Minimum Wage*, 11, Ratan Tata Foundation, University of London (London: G. Bell and Sons, Ltd, 1915).

'Transactions of the International Congress on the White Slave Traffic', held in London on the 21st, 22nd, and 23rd of June, 1899, at the Invitation of the National Vigilance Association London: NVA, 1899.

'Tuberculosis among Jews', *British Medical Journal* (25 April 1908), pp. 1000–2.

United Synagogue, 'East End Scheme', Report of the Special Committee (28 June 1898).

Weiner, A., 'Jewish Industrial Life in Russia', *Economic Journal*, 15:60 (1905), pp. 581–4.

White, A., 'The Invasion of Pauper Foreigners', *Nineteenth Century*, 23:133 (1888), pp. 414–22.

—, 'A Typical Alien Immigrant', *Contemporary Review*, 73 (1898), pp. 241–50.

Wiener, H. M., 'The Problem of the Talmud Torahs', *Jewish Literary Annual* (London, 1906), pp. 67–74.

Winch, W. H., 'Christian and Jewish Children in East End Elementary Schools – Some Comparative Characteristics in Relation to Race and Social Class', *British Journal of Psychology*, 20 (1930), pp. 261–73.

Wolf, L., *Menasseh ben Israel's Mission to Oliver Cromwell* (London: Macmillan & Co., 1901).

Secondary Sources

Abel, E., 'Canon Barnett and the First Thirty Years of Toynbee Hall' (PhD thesis, Queen Mary College, University of London, 1969).

Abrahams, A., 'End of an Era', *Jewish Monthly*, 4:9 (1950), pp. 572–7.

Adler, R., 'The Jew Who Wasn't There: *Halakah* and the Jewish Woman', in S. Heschel (ed.), *On Being a Jewish Feminist: A Reader* (New York: Schocken Books, 1983), pp. 12–18.

Albert, P., *The Modernization of French Jewry: Consistory and Community in the Nineteenth Century* (Hanover, NH: University Press of New England, 1977).

Alderman, G., *London Jewry and London Politics, 1889–1986* (London: Routledge, 1989).

—, *Modern British Jewry* (Oxford: Clarendon Press, 1992).

Alroey, G., 'Bureaucracy, Agents, and Swindlers: The Hardships of Jewish Emigration from the Pale of Settlement in the Early 20th Century', *Studies in Contemporary Jewry*, 19 (2003), pp. 214–31.

—, '"And I Remained Alone in a Vast Land": Women in the Jewish Migration from Eastern Europe', *Jewish Social Studies: History, Culture, Society*, n.s., 12:3 (2006), pp. 39–72.

Apple, R. D., 'Constructing Mothers: Scientific Motherhood in the Nineteenth and Twentieth Centuries', *Social History of Medicine*, 8:2 (1995), pp. 161–78.

Atkins, P., 'School Milk in Britain, 1900–1934', *Journal of Policy History*, 19:4 (2007), pp. 395–428.

Auerbach, S., 'Negotiating Nationalism: Jewish Conscription and Russian Repatriation in London's East End, 1916–1918', *Journal of British Studies*, 46:3 (2007), pp. 594–620.

—, '"Some Punishment Should Be Devised": Parents, Children, and the State in Victorian London', *Historian*, 71:4 (2009), pp. 757–79.

Bailey, P., *Leisure and Class in Victorian England: Rational Recreation and the Contest for Control, 1830–1885* (London: Routledge and Kegan Paul, 1978).

Barou, N., *The Jews in Work and Trade*, 2nd edn (London: Trades Advisory Council, 1946).

Barrett, M., and M. McIntosh, 'The "Family Wage": Some Problems for Socialists and Feminists', *Capital and Class*, 11 (1980), pp. 51–72.

Baum, C., 'What Made Yetta Work? The Economic Role of Eastern European Jewish Women in the Family', *Response*, 18 (1973), pp. 32–8.

Baum, C., P. Hyman and S. Michel, *The Jewish Woman in America* (New York: New American Library, 1975).

Beck, A., 'Issues in the Anti-Vaccination Movement in England', *Medical History*, 4:4 (1960), pp. 310–21.

Berkowitz, M., and R. Ungar, *Fighting Back? Jewish and Black Boxers in Britain* (London: Jewish Museum, London, and University College London, 2007).

Bermant, C., *The Cousinhood* (New York: Macmillan Co., 1971).

Black, E., *The Social Politics of Anglo-Jewry, 1880–1920* (Oxford: Basil Blackwell, 1988).

Black, G., 'Health and Medical Care of the Jewish Poor in the East End of London – 1880–1939' (PhD thesis, University of Leicester, 1987).

—, *J. F. S.: The History of the Jews' Free School, London since 1732* (London: Tymsder Publishing, 1998).

—, *Lord Rothschild and the Barber: The Struggle to Establish the London Jewish Hospital* (London: Tymsder Publishing, 2000).

Bland, L., '"Purifying" the Public World: Feminist Vigilantes in Late Victorian England', *Women's History Review*, 1:3 (1992), pp. 397–412.

Bolchover, R., *British Jewry and the Holocaust* (Cambridge: Cambridge University Press, 1993).

Bornstein, A., 'The Role of Social Institutions as Inhibitors of Assimilation: Jewish Poor Relief System in Germany, 1875–1925', *Jewish Social Studies*, 50:3–4 (1988–93), pp. 201–22.

Bourke, J., *Working-Class Cultures in Britain, 1890–1960* (London: Routledge, 1994).

Bradley, K., 'Juvenile Delinquency, the Juvenile Courts and the Settlement Movement 1908–1950: Basil Henriques and Toynbee Hall', *Twentieth Century British History*, 19:2 (2008), pp. 133–55.

Braybon, G., *Women Workers in the First World War* (London: Routledge, 1989).

Brinkman, T., 'Managing Mass Migration: Jewish Philanthropic Organizations and Jewish Mass Migration from Easter Europe, 1868/1869–1914', *Leidschrift; Historisch Tijdschrift*, 22:1 (2007), pp. 71–89.

Bristow, E., *Prostitution and Prejudice: The Jewish Fight against White Slavery, 1870–1939* (New York: Schocken Books, 1983).

Bryder, L., '"Wonderlands of Buttercup, Clover and Daisies": Tuberculosis and the Open-Air School Movement in Britain, 1907–39', in R. Cooter (ed.), *In the Name of the Child: Health and Welfare, 1880–1940* (London: Routledge, 1992), pp. 72–95.

Buckman, J., *Immigrants and the Class Struggle: The Jewish Immigrant in Leeds, 1880–1914* (Manchester: University of Manchester Press, 1983).

Bunt, S., *Jewish Youth Work in Britain, Past, Present and Future* (London: National Council of Social Service, 1975).

Burman, R., 'The Jewish Woman as Breadwinner: The Changing Value of Women's Work in a Manchester Immigrant Community', *Oral History*, 10:2 (1982), pp. 27–39.

—, '"She Looketh Well to the Ways of Her Household": The Changing Role of Jewish Women in Religious Life, c. 1880–1939', in G. Malmgreen (ed.), *Religion in the Lives of English Women, 1760–1930* (Bloomington, IN: Indiana University Press, 1986), pp. 234–59.

—, 'Jewish Women and the Household Economy in Manchester, c. 1880–1920', in D. Cesarani (ed.), *The Making of Modern Anglo-Jewry* (Oxford: Basil Blackwell, 1990), pp. 55–75.

—, 'Middle-Class Anglo-Jewish Lady Philanthropists and Eastern European Jewish Women: The First National Conference of Jewish Women, 1902', in J. Grant (ed.), *Migration and Empire Women* (Stoke-on-Trent: Trentham Books, 1996), pp. 123–49.

Burnett, J., *Plenty and Want: A Social History of Diet in England from 1815 to the Present Day* (London: Methuen and Co., 1983).

Bush, J., 'East London Jews in the First World War', *London Journal*, 6:2 (1980), pp. 147–61.

Carrier, J., 'Working Class Jews in Present-Day London: A Sociological Study' (MPhil thesis, University of London, 1969).

Cesarani, D., 'Anti-Alienism in England after 1914', *Immigrants and Minorities*, 6:1 (1987), pp. 5–29.

— (ed.), *The Making of Modern Anglo-Jewry* (Oxford: Basil Blackwell, 1990).

—, 'The Transformation of Authority in Anglo-Jewry, 1914–1940', in D. Cesarani (ed.), *The Making of Modern Anglo-Jewry* (Oxford: Basil Blackwell, 1990), pp. 115–40.

—, *The Jewish Chronicle and Anglo-Jewry, 1841–1991* (Cambridge: Cambridge University Press, 1994).

—, 'A Funny Thing Happened on the Way to the Suburbs: Social Change in Anglo-Jewry between the Wars, 1914–1945', *Jewish Culture and History*, 1:1 (1998), pp. 5–26.

Chambré, S. M., 'Philanthropy in the United States', *Jewish Women: A Comprehensive Historical Encyclopedia* (20 March 2009), Jewish Women's Archive, online at http://jwa.org/encyclopedia/article/philanthropy-in-united-states [accessed 13 June 2011].

Cheyette, B., *Constructions of 'the Jew' in English Literature and Society: Racial Representations, 1875–1945* (New York: Cambridge University Press, 1993).

Cohen, D., 'Who was Who? Race and Jews in Turn-of-the-Century Britain', *Journal of British Studies*, 41:4 (2002), pp. 460–83.

Cohen, L., 'A Study in Institutionalism – the Jewish Children's Orphanage at Norwood' (PhD thesis, University of Southampton, 2010).

Cohen, R., 'The Influence of Jewish Radical Movements on Adult Education among Jewish Immigrants in the East End of London, 1881–1914' (MEd dissertation, University of Liverpool, 1977).

Cranfield, G. A., 'The London Evening Post and the Jew Bill of 1753', *Historical Journal*, 8 (1965), pp. 16–30.

Daggers, J., and D. Neal (eds), *Sex, Gender and Religion* (New York: Peter Lang, 2006).

Davies, C., 'The Health Visitor as Mother's Friends: A Woman's Place in Public Health, 1900–1914', *Social History of Medicine*, 1:1 (1988), pp. 39–59.

Davin, A., 'Imperialism and Motherhood', *History Workshop*, 5 (1978), pp. 9–65.

—, 'Loaves and Fishes: Food in Poor Households in Late Nineteenth-Century London', *History Workshop Journal*, 41 (1996), pp. 167–92.

Dee, D. G., 'Jews and British Sport: Integration, Ethnicity and Anti-Semitism, c1880–c1960' (PhD thesis, De Montfort University, 2011).

Deutsch, S., *Crossing Borders, Claiming a Nation: A History of Argentine Jewish Women, 1880–1955* (Durham, NC and London: Duke University Press, 2010).

Diner, H., *Erin's Daughters in America: Irish Immigrant Women in the Nineteenth Century* (Baltimore, MD: Johns Hopkins University Press, 1983).

Dwork, D., *War is Good for Babies and other Young Children: A History of the Infant and Child Welfare Movement in England, 1898–1918* (London: Tavistock Publications, 1987).

Dyhouse, C., 'Good Wives and Little Mothers: Social Anxieties and the School Girl's Curriculum', *Oxford Review of Education*, 3:1 (1977), pp. 21–35.

—, 'Working-Class Mothers and Infant Mortality in England, 1895–1914', *Journal of Social History*, 12:2 (1978), pp. 248–67.

—, *Girls Growing Up in Late Victorian and Edwardian England* (London: Routledge and Kegan Paul, 1981).

'East End Problem', *Jewish Monthly*, 5:4 (1951), pp. 193–4.

Efron, J., *Defenders of the Race: Jewish Doctors and Race Science in Fin-de-Siecle Europe* (New Haven, CT: Yale University Press, 1994).

Endelman, T., *The Jews of Georgian England: 1714–1830 Tradition and Change in a Liberal Society* (Philadelphia, PA: Jewish Publication Society, 1979).

—, 'Native Jews and Foreign Jews in London, 1870–1914', in D. Berger (ed.), *The Legacy of Jewish Migration: 1881 and its Impact* (New York: Social Science Monographs, Brooklyn College Press, 1983), pp. 109–25.

—, 'Communal Solidarity among the Jewish Elite of Victorian London', *Victorian Studies*, 28:3 (1985), pp. 491–526.

—, 'Perspectives on Modern Anti-Semitism in the West', in D. Berger (ed.), *History and Hate: The Dimensions of Anti-Semitism* (Philadelphia, PA: Jewish Publication Society, 1986), pp. 95–114.

—, 'The Englishness of Jewish Modernity in England', in J. Katz (ed.), *Toward Modernity: The European Jewish Model* (New Brunswick, NJ: Transaction Books, 1987), pp. 225–46.

—, 'English Jewish History', *Modern Judaism*, 11 (1991), pp. 91–109.

—, 'Writing English Jewish History', *Albion*, 27:4 (1995), pp. 623–36.

—, *The Jews of Georgian England: 1714–1830 Tradition and Change in a Liberal Society* (Ann Arbor, MI: University of Michigan Press, 1999).

—, *The Jews of Britain, 1656 to 2000* (Berkeley, CA: University of California Press, 2002).

—, 'Anglo-Jewish Scientists and the Science of Race', *Jewish Social Studies*, n.s., 11:1 (2004), pp. 52–92.

Englander, D., 'Anglicized not Anglican: Jews and Judaism in Victorian Britain', in G. Parson (ed.), *Religion in Victorian Britain*, 4 vols (Manchester: Manchester University Press, 1988), vol. 1, pp. 235–73.

—, 'Booth's Jews: The Presentation of Jews and Judaism in *Life and Labour of the People in London*', *Victorian Studies*, 32 (1989), pp. 551–71.

—, 'Policing the Ghetto: Jewish East London, 1880–1920', *Crime, Histoire & Societes/Crime, History & Societies*, 14:1 (2010), pp. 29–50.

—, '*Stille Huppah* (Quiet Marriage) among Jewish Immigrants in Britain', *Jewish Journal of Sociology*, 34:2 (1992), pp. 85–109.

Etkes, I., 'Marriage and Torah Study among *Lomdim* in Lithuania in the Nineteenth Century', in D. Kraemer (ed.), *The Jewish Family: Metaphor and Memory* (New York: Oxford University Press, 1989), pp. 153–78.

Feldman, D., *Englishmen and Jews: Social Relations and Political Culture, 1840–1914* (New Haven, CT and London: Yale University Press, 1994).

—, 'Jews in London, 1880–1914', in R. Samuel (ed.), *Patriotism: The Making and Unmaking of British National Identity*, 3 vols (London and New York: Routledge, 1989), vol. 2, pp. 207–29.

Feltes, N., 'Misery or the Production of Misery: Defining Sweated Labour in 1890', *Social History*, 17:3 (1992), pp. 441–52.

'Festival of Britain', Anglo-Jewish Exhibition at University College, London, 1951.

Fildes, V., 'Breast-Feeding in London 1905–1919', *Journal of Biosocial Science*, 24:1 (1992), pp. 53–70.

Finestein, I., *Jewish Society in Victorian England* (London: Vallentine Mitchell, 1993).

Fishman, W., *East End Jewish Radicals* (London: G. Duckworth & Co., 1975).

Fowler, D., *The First Teenagers: The Lifestyle of Young Wage-Earners in Interwar Britain* (London: Woburn Press, 1995).

Gainer, B., *The Alien Invasion* (New York: Crane, Russak, and Co., Inc., 1972).

Gartner, L., *The Jewish Immigrant in England, 1870–1914* (London: George Allen & Unwin, 1960).

—, 'Notes on the Statistics of Jewish Immigration to England, 1870–1914', *Jewish Social Studies*, 22:2 (1960), pp. 97–102.

—, 'The History of a Sweater', *East London Papers*, 4:2 (1961), pp. 53–61.

—, 'Anglo-Jewry and the Jewish International Traffic in Prostitution', *AJS Review*, 7/8 (1982–3), pp. 129–78.

Gilam, A., *The Emancipation of the Jews in England, 1830–1860* (New York: Garland, 1982).

Gilley, S., 'English Attitudes to the Irish in England, 1789–1900', in C. Holmes (ed.), *Immigrants and Minorities in British Society* (New York: Allen and Unwin, 1978), pp. 81–110.

Glenn, S., *Daughters of the Shtetl: Life and Labor in the Immigrant Generation* (Ithaca, NY: Cornell University Press, 1990).

Glover, D., *Literature, Immigration, and Diaspora in Fin-de-Siècle England: A Cultural History of the 1905 Aliens Act* (Cambridge: Cambridge University Press, 2012).

Goldberg, N., 'The Jewish Population in the United States', in *The Jewish People, Past and Present*, 4 vols (New York: Central Yiddish Culture Organization, 1948), vol. 2, pp. 25–34.

Gordon, M., *Assimilation in American Life: The Role of Race, Religion, and National Origins* (New York: Oxford University Press, 1964).

Gorni, Y., 'Beatrice Webb's Views on Judaism and Zionism', *Jewish Social Studies*, 40:2 (1978), pp. 95–114.

Graves, R., and A. Hodge, *The Long Weekend: A Social History of Great Britain, 1918–1939* (New York: W. W. Norton, 1963).

Green, N., 'Gender and Jobs in the Jewish Community: Europe at the Turn of the Twentieth Century', *Jewish Social Studies*, n.s., 8:2/3 (2002), pp. 39–60.

Greenberg, L., *The Jews in Russia: The Struggle for Emancipation*, 2 vols (New York: Schocken Books, 1976), vol. 1 (1944); vol. 2 (1951).

Greenberg, S. K., 'Compromise and Conflict: The Education of Jewish Immigrant Children in London in the Aftermath of Emancipation, 1881–1905' (PhD dissertation, Stanford University, 1985).

Gutman, H., *The Black Family in Slavery and Freedom, 1750–1925* (New York: Pantheon Books, 1976).

Hall, C., 'The Early Formation of Victorian Domestic Ideology', in S. Burman (ed.), *Fit Work for Women* (New York: St Martin's Press, 1979), pp. 15–32.

Hammerton, A., *Emigrant Gentlewomen: Genteel Poverty and Female Emigration, 1830–1914* (London: Croom Helm, 1979).

Harris, B., 'Anti-Alienism, Health and Social Reform in Late Victorian and Early Edwardian Britain', *Patterns of Prejudice*, 31:4 (1997), pp. 3–34.

—, 'Public Health, Nutrition, and the Decline of Mortality: The McKeown Thesis Revisited', *Social History of Medicine*, 17:3 (2004), pp. 379–407.

Harris, J., *Private Lives, Public Spirit: Britain, 1870–1914* (London: Penguin Books, 1994).

Heathorn, S., '"Let us Remember that We Too are English": Constructions of Citizenship and National Identity in English Elementary Reading Books, 1880–1914', *Victorian Studies*, 38:3 (1995), pp. 395–427.

Heggie, V., 'Jewish Medical Charity in Manchester: Reforming Alien Bodies', Bulletin of the John Rylands University Library of Manchester 87:1 (2005), pp. 111–32.

—, 'Lies, Damn Lies, and Manchester's Recruiting Statistics: Degeneration as an "Urban Legend" in Victorian and Edwardian Britain', *Journal of the History of Medicine and Allied Sciences*, 63:2 (2008), pp. 178–216.

Hendrick, H., *Images of Youth: Age, Class, and the Male Youth Problem, 1880–1920* (Oxford: Clarendon Press, 1990).

Henriques, B., *Club Leadership*, 3rd edn (London: Oxford University Press, 1948).

Henriques, R. L., 'Fifty Years in Stepney', Reproduction of Five talks on BBC, 17th–21st January, 1966.

Henriques, U. R. Q., 'The Jewish Emancipation Controversy in Nineteenth-Century Britain', *Past and Present*, 40 (1968), pp. 126–46.

Hickman, M. J., 'Integration or Segregation? The Education of the Irish in Britain in Roman Catholic Voluntary-Aided Schools', *British Journal of Sociology of Education*, 14:3 (1993), pp. 285–300.

Higgs, E., 'Domestic Service and Household Production', in A. John (ed.), *Unequal Opportunities – Women's Employment in England 1800–1918* (Oxford: Basil Blackwell, 1986), pp. 125–50.

Himmelfarb, G., 'Victorian Philanthropy: The Case of Toynbee Hall', *American Scholar*, 59:3 (1990), pp. 373–84.

—, 'The Jew as Victorian', in *The De-Moralization of Society: From Victorian Virtues to Modern Values* (New York: Alfred A. Knopf, 1995), pp. 170–87.

Hochberg, S., 'The Repatriation of Eastern European Jews from Great Britain: 1881–1914', *Jewish Social Studies*, 50 (1988–92), pp. 49–62.

Holmes, C., 'Immigrants and Refugees in Britain', in W. Mosse (ed.), *Second Chance: Two Centuries of German-speaking Jews in the United Kingdom* (Tubingen: J. C. B. Mohr, 1991), pp. 11–30.

Howe, I., *The World of Our Father* (New York: Harcourt, Brace Jovanovich, 1976).

Hurt, J. S., *Elementary Schooling and the Working Classes, 1860–1918* (London: Routledge and Kegan Paul, 1979).

Hyman, P., 'Culture and Gender: Women in the Immigrant Jewish Community', in D. Berger (ed.), *The Legacy of Jewish Migration: 1881 and its Impact* (New York: Social Science Monographs, Brooklyn College Press, 1983), pp. 157–68.

—, 'The Jewish Body Politic: Gendered Politics in the Early Twentieth Century', *Nashim: A Journal of Jewish Women's Studies & Gender Issues*, 2 (1999), pp. 37–51.

—, 'Gender and the Shaping of Modern Jewish Identities', *Jewish Social Studies*, n.s., 8:2/3 (2002), pp. 153–61.

Jewish Women in London Group, *Generations of Memories* (London: Women's Press, 1989).

Jones, K., 'Sentiment and Science: The Late Nineteenth Century Pediatrician as Mother's Advisor', *Journal of Social History*, 17:1 (1983), pp. 79–96.

Jones, S. G., *Workers at Play: A Social and Economic History of Leisure, 1918–1939* (London: Routledge and Kegan Paul, 1986).

Kadish, S., *'A Good Jew and a Good Englishman': The Jewish Lads' and Girls' Brigade, 1895–1995* (London: Vallentine Mitchell, 1995).

Kaplan, M., *The Jewish Feminist Movement in Germany: The Campaigns of the Judischer Frauenbund, 1904–1938* (Westport, CT: Greenwood Press, 1979).

—, *The Making of the Jewish Middle Class: Women, Family, and Identity in Imperial Germany* (New York: Oxford University Press, 1991).

Kaplan, S., 'The Anglicization of the East European Jewish Immigrant as Seen by the London Jewish Chronicle', *YIVO Annual of Jewish Social Science*, 10 (1955), pp. 267–78.

Katz, D., *Philo-Semitism and the Readmission of the Jews to England, 1603–1655* (Oxford: Clarendon Press, 1982).

—, 'English Redemption and Jewish Readmission in 1656', *Journal of Jewish Studies*, 34:1 (1983), pp. 73–91.

Kershen, A., 'Trade Unionism amongst the Jewish Tailoring Workers of London and Leeds, 1872–1915', in D. Cesarani (ed.), *The Making of Modern Anglo-Jewry* (Oxford: Basil Blackwell, 1990), pp. 34–52.

—, *Uniting the Tailors: Trade Unionism amongst the Tailors of London and Leeds, 1870–1939* (Ilford: Frank Cass & Co., 1995).

—, 'Yiddish as a Vehicle for Anglicization', in A. Newman and S. Massil (eds), *Patterns of Migration, 1850–1914* (London: JHSE, 1996), pp. 59–67.

—, *Strangers, Aliens and Asians: Huguenots, Jews and Bangladeshis in Spitalfields, 1660–2000* (London: Routledge, 2005).

Kessner, T., *The Golden Door: Italian and Jewish Immigrant Mobility in New York City, 1880–1915* (New York: Oxford University Press, 1977).

Klier, J., 'Russian Jewry on the Eve of the Pogroms', in J. Klier and S. Lambroza (eds), *Pogroms: Anti-Jewish Violence in Modern Russian History* (Cambridge: Cambridge University Press, 1992), pp. 3–12.

—, 'What Exactly Was the Shtetl?', in G. Estraikh and M. Krutikov (eds), *The Shtetl: Image and Reality* (Oxford: Legenda, published by the European Humanities Research Centre, 2000), pp. 23–35.

Knepper, P., '"Jewish Trafficking" and London Jews in the Age of Migration', *Journal of Modern Jewish Studies*, 6:3 (2007), pp. 239–56.

Kosmin, B., 'Traditions of Work Amongst British Jews', in S. Wallman (ed.), *Ethnicity at Work* (London: Macmillan Press, 1979), pp. 37–68.

—, 'Nuptiality and Fertility Patterns of British Jewry 1850–1980', in D. A. Coleman (ed.), *Demography of Immigrants and Minority Groups in the United Kingdom* (London: Academic Press, 1982), pp. 245–61.

Koven, S., *Slumming: Sexual and Social Politics in Victorian London* (Princeton, NJ: Princeton University Press, 2004).

Kushner, T., *The Persistence of Prejudice: Antisemitism in British Society during the Second World War* (Manchester: Manchester University Press, 1989).

—, 'An Alien Occupation – Jewish Refugees and Domestic Service in Britain, 1933–1948', in W. E. Mosse et al. (eds), *Second Chance: Two Centuries of German-speaking Jews in the United Kingdom* (Tubingen: LBI with J. C. B. Mohr [Paul Siebeck] Publishers, 1991), pp. 555–78.

—, *Anglo-Jewry since 1066: Place, Locality and Memory* (Manchester: Manchester University Press, 2009).

Kuzmack, L. G., *Woman's Cause: The Jewish Woman's Movement in England and the United States, 1881–1933* (Columbus, OH: Ohio State University Press, 1990).

Kuznets, S., 'Immigrations of Russian Jews to the United States – Background and Structure', *Perspectives in American History*, 9 (1975), pp. 35–124.

Lambroza, S., 'The Pogroms of 1903–1906', in J. D. Klier and S. Lambroza (eds), *Pogroms: Anti-Jewish Violence in Modern Russian History* (Cambridge: Cambridge University Press, 1992), pp. 191–247.

Lammers, B., 'The Birth of the East Ender: Neighborhood and Local Identity in Interwar East London', *Journal of Social History*, 39:2 (2005), pp. 331–44.

Langham, R., *250 Years of Convention and Contention: A History of the Board of Deputies of British Jews, 1760–2010* (London: Vallentine Mitchell, 2010).

Layton-Henry, Z., *The Politics of Immigration* (Oxford: Blackwell Publishers, 1992).

Lazarus, M., *A Club Called Brady* (London: New Cavendish Books, 1996).

Leech, K., 'The Role of Immigration in Recent East London History', *East London Papers*, 10:1 (1967), pp. 3–17.

Lerner, A. L., 'Lost Childhood in East European Hebrew Literature', in D. Kraemer (ed.), *The Jewish Family: Metaphor and Memory* (New York: Oxford University Press, 1989), pp. 95–108.

Levin, H., and S. Levin, *Jubilee at Finchley: 1926–1976 Story of a Congregation* (London: Finchley Synagogue, 1976).

Levine, P., 'The White Slave Trade and the British Empire', in L. Knafla (ed.), *Crime, Gender and, Sexuality in Criminal Prosecutions* (Westport, CT: Greenwood, 2002), pp. 132–46.

Levene, M., 'Going Against the Grain: Two Jewish Memoirs of War and Anti-War (1914–1918)', in M. Berkowitz, S. Tananbaum and S. Bloom (eds), *Forging Modern Jewish Identities, Identities: Public Faces and Private Struggles* (London: Vallentine Mitchell, 2003), pp. 81–114.

Lewis, J., 'The Social History of Social Policy: Infant Welfare in Edwardian England', *Journal of Social Policy*, 9:4 (1980), pp. 463–86.

—, *The Voluntary Sector, the State and Social Work in Britain: The Charity Organisation Society/Family Welfare Association since 1869* (Aldershot: Edward Elgar Publishing Ltd, 1995).

Lipman, V. D., *Social History of the Jews in England, 1850–1950* (London: Watts & Co., 1954).

—, *A Century of Social Service, 1859–1959: The History of the Jewish Board of Guardians* (London: Routledge and Kegan Paul, 1959).

—, 'Mass Immigration and a Social Revolution', *CAJEX*, 5:2 (1965), pp. 92–100.

—, 'The Rise of Jewish Suburbia', *Transactions of the Jewish Historical Society of England*, 21 (1968), pp. 78–103.

—, *A History of the Jews in Britain since 1858* (New York: Holmes and Meier, 1990).

Livshin, R., 'The Acculturation of Children of Immigrant Jews in Manchester, 1890–1930', in D. Cesarani (ed.), *The Making of Modern Anglo-Jewry* (Oxford: Basil Blackwell, 1990), pp. 79–96.

Lloyd, A., 'Between Integration and Separation: Jews in Military Service in World War I Britain', *Jewish Culture and History*, 12:1–2 (2010), pp. 41–60.

McGee, J., 'The Social and Political Life of the Jews in the East End of London: 1926–1939' (thesis submitted for the Teachers' Certificate of Education, 1977).is this considered mac?? Or should it be after Martin?

Magnus, L., *The Jewish Board of Guardians and the Men Who Made It* (London: Jewish Board of Guardians, 1909).

Marks, L., 'The Experience of Jewish Prostitutes and Jewish Women in the East End of London at the Turn of the Century', *Jewish Quarterly*, 34:2 (1987), pp. 6–10.

—, '"Dear Old Mother Levy's": The Jewish Maternity Home and Sick Room Helps Society, 1895–1939', *Journal of Social History of Medicine*, 3:1 (1990), pp. 61–88.

—, '"The Luckless Waifs and Strays of Humanity": Irish and Jewish Immigrant Unwed Mothers in London, 1870–1939', *Twentieth Century British History*, 3:2 (1992), pp. 113–37.

—, *Model Mothers: Jewish Mothers and Maternity Provision in East London, 1870–1939* (Oxford: Clarendon Press, 1994).

Martin, R. H. 'United Conversionist Activities among the Jews in Great Britain 1795-1815: Pan-Evangelicalism and the London Society for Promoting Christianity amongst the Jews', Church History 46:4 (1977), pp. 437–452.

Meacham, S., *Toynbee Hall and Social Reform, 1880–1914: The Search for Community* (New Haven, CT: Yale University Press, 1987).

Meckel, R., *'Save the Babies': American Public Health Reform and the Prevention of Infant Mortality, 1850–1929* (Baltimore, MD: Johns Hopkins University Press, 1990).

Metzger, I., *A Bintel Brief* (New York: Behrman House, 1971).

Mumm, S., 'Josephine Butler and the International Traffic in Women', in J. Daggers and D. Neal (eds), *Sex, Gender and Religion* (New York: Peter Lang, 2006), pp. 55–71.

Munby, D., *Industry and Planning in Stepney* (Oxford: Oxford University Press, 1951).

Murphy, J., *The Education Act 1870 – Text and Commentary* (New York: Barnes and Noble, 1972).

Myers, K., and I. Grosvenor, 'Birmingham Stories: Local Histories of Migration and Settlement and the Practice of History', *Midland History*, 36:2 (2011), pp. 149–62.

Nadell, P., 'The Journey to America by Steam: The Jews of Eastern Europe in Transition', *American Jewish History*, 71:2 (1981), pp. 269–84.

Neal, F., 'Immigration and anti-Irish feeling', *Sectarian Violence: The Liverpool Experience, 1819–1914* (Manchester: Manchester University Press, 1988), pp. 105–24.

O'Day, R., and D. Englander, *Mr Charles Booth's Inquiry: The Life and Labour of the People in London Reconsidered* (London: Hambledon Press, 1993).

Osborne, I., 'Achievers of the Ghetto', Tower Hamlets Library, London, n.d.

Osterman, N., 'The Controversy over the Proposed Readmission of Jews to England (1655)', *Jewish Social Studies*, 3:3 (1941), pp. 301–28.

O'Tuathaigh, M. A. G., 'The Irish in Nineteenth-Century Britain: Problems of Integration', *Transactions of the Royal Historical Society*, 5th series, 31 (1981), pp. 149–73.

Patinkin, D., 'Mercantilism and the Readmission of the Jews to England', *Jewish Social Studies*, 8:3 (1946), pp. 161–78.

Pellew, J., 'The Home Office and the Aliens Act, 1905', *Historical Journal*, 32:2 (1989), pp. 369–85.

Pennybacker, S., *A Vision for London, 1889–1914: Labour, Everyday Life and the LCC Experiment* (London: Routledge, 1995).

Perry, T., *Public Opinion, Propaganda, and Politics in Eighteenth-Century England: A Study of the Jew Bill of 1753* (Cambridge, MA: Harvard University Press, 1962).

'Population', *Encyclopedia Judaica* (Jerusalem: Keter Publishing House, 1972), table 3.

Presner, T., 'Muscle Jews and Airplanes: Modernist Mythologies, the Great War, and the Politics of Regeneration', *Modernism/Modernity*, 13:4 (2006), pp. 701–28.

Prochaska, F. K., *Women and Philanthropy in 19th Century England* (Oxford: Clarendon Press, 1980).

—, *The Voluntary Impulse: Philanthropy in Modern Britain* (London: Faber & Faber, 1988).

—, *Christianity and Social Service in Modern Britain* (Oxford: Oxford University Press, 2006).

Proctor, T., *On My Honour: Guides and Scouts in Interwar Britain* (Philadelphia, PA: American Philosophical Society, 2002).

Quinn, P. L. S., 'The Jewish Schooling Systems of London, 1656–1956' (PhD thesis, University of London, 1958).

Riess, S., 'A Fighting Chance: The Jewish American Boxing Experience, 1890–1940', *American Jewish History*, 74:3 (1985), pp. 223–54.

Roberts, N., 'Character in the Mind: Citizenship, Education and Psychology in Britain, 1880–1914', *History of Education*, 33:2 (2004), pp. 177–97.

Roemer, N., 'London and the East End as Spectacles of Urban Tourism', *Jewish Quarterly Review*, 99:3 (2009), pp. 416–34.

Rose, E., 'From Sponge Cake to *Hamentashen*: Jewish Identity in a Jewish Settlement House, 1885–1952', *Journal of American Ethnic History*, 13:3 (1994), pp. 3–23.

Ross, E., '"Fierce Questions and Taunts": Married Life in Working-Class London, 1870–1914', *Feminist Studies*, 8:3 (1982), pp. 575–602.

—, 'Survival Networks: Women's Neighbourhood Sharing in London before World War I', *History Workshop*, 15 (1983), pp. 4–27.

—, 'Good and Bad Mothers: Lady Philanthropists and London Housewives before the First World War', in K. McCarthy (ed.), *Lady Bountiful Revisited: Women, Philanthropy, and Power* (New Brunswick, NJ: Rutgers University Press, 1990), pp. 174–98.

—, *Love and Toil: Motherhood in Outcast London, 1870–1918* (New York: Oxford University Press, 1993).

—, 'Missionaries and Jews in Soho: "Strangers within Our Gates"', *Journal of Victorian Culture*, 15:2 (2010), pp. 226–38.

Ruppin, A., *The Jews in the Modern World* (London: Macmillan & Co., 1934).

Sarna, J., 'The Myth of No Return: Jewish Return Migration to Eastern Europe, 1881–1914', *American Jewish History*, 71:2 (1981), pp. 256–68.

Schaffer, G., '"Like a Baby with a Box of Matches": British Scientists and the Concept of "Race" in the Inter-war Period', *British Journal for the History of Science*, 38 (2005), pp. 307–24.

Schmiechen, J., *Sweated Industries and Sweated Labor: The London Clothing Trades, 1860– 1914* (Urbana, IL: University of Illinois Press, 1984).

Scult, M., *Millennial Expectations and Jewish Liberties* (Leiden: E. J. Brill, 1978).

Searle, G. R., *The Quest for National Efficiency: A Study in British Politics and Political Thought, 1899–1914* (Berkeley, CA: University of California Press, 1971).

Seccombe, W., 'Patriarchy Stabilized: The Construction of the Male Breadwinner Wage Norm in Nineteenth-Century Britain', *Social History*, 11:1 (1986), pp. 53–76.

Semmel, B., *Imperialism and Social Reform: English Social-Imperial Thought, 1895–1914* (Cambridge, MA: Harvard University Press, 1960).

Sharot, S., 'Native Jewry and the Religious Anglicization of Immigrant Jews in London, 1870–1905', *Jewish Journal of Sociology*, 16:1 (1974), pp. 39–56.

—, 'Reform and Liberal Judaism', *Jewish Social Studies*, 41:3–4 (1979), pp. 211–28.

Short, G., 'Accounting For Success: The Education of Jewish Children in Late 19th Century England', *British Journal of Educational Studies*, 41:3 (1993), pp. 272–86.

Singer, S., 'Jewish Education in the Mid-Nineteenth Century: A Study of the Early Victorian London Community', *Jewish Quarterly Review*, n.s., 77:2–3 (October 1986 – January 1987), pp. 163–78.

Sinkoff, N., 'Educating for "Proper" Jewish Womanhood: A Case Study in Domesticity and Vocational Training, 1897–1926', *American Jewish History*, 77:4 (1988), pp. 572–99.

Smith, F., *The People's Health, 1830–1910* (New York: Holmes and Meier Publishers, 1979).

Smith S., 'Sex, Leisure and Jewish Youth Clubs in Inter-War London', *Jewish Culture and History*, 1:9 (2007), pp. 1–26.

Solomos, J., *Race and Racism in Britain*, 2nd edn (New York: St Martin's, 1993).

Soloway, R., 'Counting the Degenerates: The Statistics of Race Deterioration in Edwardian England', *Journal of Contemporary History*, 17:1 (1982), pp. 137–64.

Sorkin, D., *The Transformation of German Jewry, 1780–1840* (New York and Oxford: Oxford University Press, 1987).

Spence, J., 'Working for Jewish Girls: Lily Montagu, Girls' Clubs and Industrial Reform 1890–1914', *Women's History Review*, 13:3 (2004), pp. 491–509.

Sponza, L., *Italian Immigrants in Nineteenth Century Britain: Realities and Image* (Leicester: Leicester University Press, 1988).

Springhall, J., *Coming of Age: Adolescence in Britain, 1860–1960* (Dublin: Gill and Macmillan, 1986).

—, 'Building Character in the British Boy: The Attempt to Extend Christian Manliness to Working-Class Adolescents, 1880–1914', in J. A. Mangan and J. Walvin (eds), *Manliness and Morality: Middle-Class Masculinity in Britain and America, 1800–1940* (New York: St Martin's Press, 1987), pp. 52–74.

Stanislawski, M., *Tsar Nicholas I and the Jews: The Transformation of Jewish Society in Russia, 1825–1855* (Philadelphia, PA: Jewish Publication Society, 1983).

Stepney Reconstruction Group, 'Living in Stepney, Past, Present and Future' (London: Pilot Press, 1945).

Stone, D., 'Of Peas, Potatoes, and Jews: Redcliffe N. Salaman and the British Debate over Jewish Racial Origins', *Jahrbuch des Simon-Dubnow Instituts – Simon Dubnow Institute Yearbook*, 3 (2004), pp. 221–40.

Tananbaum, S., 'Making Good Little English Children: Infant Welfare and Anglicisation in London, 1880–1939', *Immigrants and Minorities*, 12:2 (1993), pp. 176–99.

—, 'Biology and Community: The Duality of Jewish Mothering in East London', in G. Chang and L. Forcey (eds), *Mothering: Ideology Experience, and Agency* (New York: Routledge, 1994), pp. 311–32.

—, '"Morally Depraved and Abnormally Criminal": Jews and Crime in London and New York, 1880–1940', in Berkowitz et al. (eds), *Forging Modern Jewish Identities: Public Faces and Private Struggles* (London: Vallentine Mitchell, 2003), pp. 115–39.

—, '"Ironing out the Ghetto Bend": Sports, Character and Acculturation among Jewish Immigrants in Britain', *Journal of Sport History*, 31:1 (2004), pp. 53–75.

—, '"To their Credit as Jews and Englishmen": Services for Youth and the Shaping of Jewish Masculinity in Britain, 1890s–1930s', in L. Delap and S. Morgan (eds), *Men, Masculinities and Religious Change* (Basingstoke: Palgrave Macmillan, 2013), pp. 90–118.

Taylor, S., 'The Role of Jewish Women in National, Jewish Philanthropic Organisations in Britain from c. 1880 to 1945' (PhD thesis, University of Southampton, 1996).

Umansky, E., *Lily Montagu and the Advancement of Liberal Judaism: From Vision to Vocation* (New York: Edwin Mellen Press, 1983).

—, 'Lily Montagu', *Jewish Women: A Comprehensive Historical Encyclopedia* (20 March 2009), Jewish Women's Archive, online at http://jwa.org/encyclopedia/article/montagu-lily [accessed 30 September 2011].

Vance, N., *The Sinews of the Spirit: The ideal of Christian Manliness in Victorian Literature and Religious Thought* (Cambridge: Cambridge University Press, 1985).

Voeltz, R., '"... A Good Jew and a Good Englishman": The Jewish Lads' Brigade, 1894–1922', *Journal of Contemporary History*, 23:1 (1988), pp. 119–27.

Walkowitz, J., *Prostitution and Victorian Society: Women, Class and the State* (Cambridge: Cambridge University Press, 1980).

Warren, A., '"Mothers for the Empire"? The Girl Guides Association in Britain, 1909–1939', in J. A. Mangan (ed.), *Making Imperial Mentalities: Socialisation and British Imperialism* (Manchester: Manchester University Press, 1990). pp. 96–109.

Weber, T., 'Anti-Semitism and Philo-Semitism among the British and German Elites: Oxford and Heidelberg before the First World War', *English Historical Review*, 118:475 (2003), pp. 86–119.

Wenger, B., 'Jewish Women and Voluntarism: Beyond the Myth of Enablers', *American Jewish History*, 79:1 (1989), pp. 16–36.

Weissbach, L., 'The Nature of Philanthropy in Nineteenth-Century France and the Mentalité of the Jewish Elite', *Jewish History*, 8:1 (1994), pp. 191–204.

White, J., *Rothschild Buildings: Life in an East End Tenement Block. 1887–1920* (London: Routledge and Kegan Paul, 1980).

Wilkinson, P., 'English Youth Movements, 1908–30', *Journal of Contemporary History*, 4:2 (1969), pp. 3–23.

Williams, B., *The Making of Manchester Jewry, 1740–1875* (Manchester: Manchester University Press, 1985).

Wohl, A., *Endangered Lives: Public Health in Victorian Britain* (Cambridge, MA: Harvard University Press, 1983).

Zborowski, M., and E. Herzog, *Life is with People: The Culture of the Shtetl* (New York: Schocken Books, 1962).

Zipperstein, S., 'Haskalah, Cultural Change, and Nineteenth-Century Russian Jewry: A Reassessment', *Journal of Jewish Studies*, 34:2 (1983), pp. 191–207.

Newspapers

Anti-Sweater.

Daily Mail.

Daily Telegraph.

Die Tsait.

East London Observer.

Jewish Chronicle.

Jewish Graphic.

Jewish Guardian.

Jewish World.

Leader.

Queen.

Sphere.

The Times.

Tribune.

World Jewry.

Literature

Beckman, M., *The Hackney Crucible* (London: Vallentine Mitchell, 1996).

Chotzinoff, S., *A Lost Paradise* (New York: Alfred A. Knopf, 1955).

Finn, R., *Time Remembered* (London: Futura Publications, 1985), first published in 1963 as *No Tears in Aldgate*.

Harding, J., and J. Berg, *Jack Kid Berg: The Whitechapel Windmill* (London: Robson Books, 1987).

London, J., *People of the Abyss* (New York: Macmillan Co., 1903).

Poulsen, C., *Scenes from a Stepney Youth* (London: THAP Books Ltd, 1988).

Spector, C., *Volla Volla Jew Boy* (London: Centerprise Trust, Ltd, 1988).

INDEX